Intercultural Competence Higher Education

Intercultural Competence in Higher Education features the work of scholars and international education practitioners in understanding the learning outcomes of internationalization, moving beyond rhetoric to concrete practice around the world.

Devoted exclusively to exploring the central learning outcomes of internationalization efforts, this edited volume contains a refreshing combination of chapters and case studies from interdisciplinary and cross-cultural contributors, including:

- cutting-edge issues within intercultural competence development, such as intersectionality, mapping intercultural competence, and assessment;
- the role of higher education in developing intercultural competence for peacebuilding in the aftermath of violent conflict;
- facilitating intercultural competence through international student internships;
- interdisciplinary and cross-cultural contributions from over 19 countries including Japan, Russia, Serbia, South Africa, and Vietnam;
- the latest research and thinking on global, intercultural, and international learning outcomes, with a unique emphasis on newer voices.

Intercultural competence has become an essential element in international as well as domestic education. This text provides the latest thinking and research within the context of internationalization, presents practical case studies on how to integrate this into the preparation of global-ready students and will be of interest to postgraduate students, international education administrators, and practitioners, as well as scholars and researchers in a variety of disciplines who have an interest in intercultural and global competence.

Darla K. Deardorff is Executive Director of the Association of International Education Administrators, an international leadership organisation based at Duke University, North Carolina, USA.

Lily A. Arasaratnam-Smith is Director of Research at Alphacrucis College, Australia. She is an Associate Professor of Communication with primary expertise in intercultural communication competence.

Internationalization in Higher Education

Series Editor: Elspeth Jones

This series addresses key themes in the development of internationalization within Higher Education. Up-to-the-minute and international in both appeal and scope, books in the series focus on delivering contributions from a wide range of contexts and provide both theoretical perspectives and practical examples. Written by some of the leading experts in the field, they are vital guides that discuss and build upon evidence-based practice and provide a clear evaluation of outcomes.

Titles in the series

Governing Cross-Border Higher Education
Christopher Ziguras and Grant McBurnie

Tools for Teaching in an Educationally Mobile World
Jude Carroll

Developing the Global Student
Higher Education in an Era of Globalization
David Killick

Comprehensive Internationalization
Institutional Pathways to Success
John Hudzik

Internationalizing the Curriculum
Betty Leask

The Globalization of Internationalization
Emerging Voice and Perspectives
Hans de Wit, Jocelyne Gacel-Ávila, Elspeth Jones, and Nico Jooste

Intercultural Competence in Higher Education
International Approaches, Assessment and Application
Darla K. Deardorff and Lily A. Arasaratnam-Smith

Intercultural Competence in Higher Education

International Approaches, Assessment and Application

Edited by Darla K. Deardorff and
Lily A. Arasaratnam-Smith

LONDON AND NEW YORK

First published 2017
by Routledge
2 Park Square, Milton Park, Abingdon, Oxon OX14 4RN

and by Routledge
711 Third Avenue, New York, NY 10017

Routledge is an imprint of the Taylor & Francis Group, an informa business

British Library Cataloguing in Publication Data
A catalogue record for this book is available from the British Library

Library of Congress Cataloguing in Publication Data
Names: Deardorff, Darla K., editor | Arasaratnam-Smith, Lily A., editor.
Title: Intercultural competence in higher education : international approaches, assessment and application / edited by Darla K. Deardorff and Lily A. Arasaratnam-Smith.
Description: First edition. | New York : Routledge, 2017.
Identifiers: LCCN 2016046382 (print) | LCCN 2017018798 (ebook) |
ISBN 9781315529257 (ebk) | ISBN 9781138693845 (hardback : alk. paper) |
ISBN 9781138693852 (paperback : alk. paper) | ISBN 9781315529257 (ebook)
Subjects: LCSH: International education. | Internationalism–Study and teaching (Higher) | Intercultural communication–Study and teaching. | Cultural competence.
Classification: LCC LC1090 (ebook) | LCC LC1090 .I5419 2017 (print) |
DDC 378/.0162–dc23
LC record available at https://lccn.loc.gov/2016046382

ISBN: 978-1-138-69384-5 (hbk)
ISBN: 978-1-138-69385-2 (pbk)
ISBN: 978-1-315-52925-7 (ebk)

Typeset in Galliard
by Out of House Publishing

Printed and bound in Great Britain by
TJ International Ltd, Padstow, Cornwall

Darla: *To my incredibly supportive family and to colleagues around the world for their inspirational work.*

Lily: *To my husband Clive who always brings out the best in me.*

Contents

About the contributors *xii*
Series foreword *xxi*
Acknowledgements *xxiii*

Introduction 1
DARLA K. DEARDORFF AND LILY A. ARASARATNAM-SMITH

PART I
Introduction to intercultural competence **5**

1 Intercultural competence: An overview 7
LILY A. ARASARATNAM-SMITH

2 Rethinking intercultural competence: Cultural humility in internationalising higher education 19
JANN MURRAY-GARCÍA AND MELANIE TERVALON

3 The role of empathy in fostering intercultural competence 32
CAROLYN CALLOWAY-THOMAS, LILY A. ARASARATNAM-SMITH, AND DARLA K. DEARDORFF

4 Towards transformative reciprocity: Mapping the intersectionality of interdisciplinary intercultural competence 43
DANIEL J. PARACKA AND TOM PYNN

5 The role of higher education institutions in developing intercultural competence in peace-building in the aftermath of violent conflict 53
SAVO HELETA AND DARLA K. DEARDORFF

PART II
Development and assessment of intercultural competence 65

6 Intercultural competence development in higher education 67
JEANINE GREGERSEN-HERMANS

7 New competencies for intercultural communication: Power, privilege, and the decolonisation of higher education in South Africa 83
MELISSA STEYN AND FINN REYGAN

8 Chinese perspectives on intercultural competence in international higher education 95
YI'AN WANG, DARLA K. DEARDORFF, AND STEVE J. KULICH

9 Mapping intercultural competence: Aligning goals, outcomes, evidence, rubrics, and assessment 110
SCOTT G. BLAIR

10 The big picture of intercultural competence assessment 124
DARLA K. DEARDORFF

PART III
Application of intercultural competence 135

11 Introduction to case studies in developing and assessing intercultural competence: Twenty-nine case studies from around the world 137
DARLA K. DEARDORFF AND LILY A. ARASARATNAM-SMITH

CS1 Intercultural seminars: An educational intervention with sojourners at a Portuguese university 144
JOANA ALMEIDA

CS2 Intercultural competence in practice: A peer-learning and reflection-based university course to develop intercultural competence 151
NADINE BINDER

CS3 Intercultural competence through global citizenship 156
HUBA BOSHOFF AND ALECIA ERASMUS

CS4 The Virginia Commonwealth University Global Bridge: Closing academic and cultural spans in first-year courses 160
HILARY J. CASSIL, TERRY FRANSON, AMBER BENNETT HILL, AND BETH KREYDATUS

CS5 English for specific purposes course for Russian medical students: Focus on intercultural competence 164
NADEZDA CHERNYAK

CS6 An online learning journey of diversity and bias 169
LIZA LAI SHAN CHOI AND SONYA L. JAKUBEC

CS7 Intercultural competence for classes of mixed-discipline students in New Zealand 174
DEBORAH CORDER

CS8 Weill Cornell Medicine-Qatar strives to instil cultural competence training in the medical education curriculum 180
MAHA ELNASHAR, HUDA ABDELRAHIM, AND STELLA C. MAJOR

CS9 Intercultural communication for international mobility 186
IRINA GOLUBEVA

CS10 Intercultural competence at Texas Christian University 192
CHRISTOPHER T. HIGHTOWER

CS11 Intercultural communication and engagement abroad 197
JANE JACKSON

CS12 GQ + CQ + SQ + EQ = Global Synergy 202
ANNETTE KARSERAS

CS13 Intercultural development programme 209
CARRIE KARSGAARD AND LEAH SANFORD

CS14 Development of intercultural communicative competence: A course for pre-service EFL (English as a foreign language) teachers 214
NINA LAZAREVIĆ

CS15 Making cultural diversity work 219
KATRIEN MERTENS AND JAN VAN MAELE

CS16 Facilitating intercultural competencies through international student internships: Making links to future professional selves after internships 224
SUSAN OGURO

CS17 Teaching intercultural competence to undergraduate international students in Vietnam 229
CATHERINE PECK, MELANIE BROWN, AND FREDERIQUE BOUILHERES

CS18 Comprehensive and integrated intercultural development: A model for institutional change 234
PAULA J. PEDERSEN

CS19 Global learning at Agnes Scott College 239
JANELLE S. PEIFER AND ELAINE MEYER-LEE

CS20 From intercultural adaptation experience to intercultural competence in a multicultural classroom 244
AN RAN

CS21 Issues in global displacement: Exploring community-based language learning 249
DEBORAH S. REISINGER

CS22 'Intercultureality' at work 254
CLAUDIA BULNES SÁNCHEZ AND EVEKE DE LOUW

CS23 Introducing intercultural awareness in a lifelong learning process: Reflections on a formal setting course 260
ROSA SANTIBÁÑEZ-GRUBER, CONCEPCIÓN MAIZTEGUI-OÑATE, AND MARIA YAROSH

CS24 Integrating diversity in academic teaching: Theology and Religious Studies 265
PETER-BEN SMIT, HESTER RADSTAKE, GERDIEN BERTRAM-TROOST, AND SIEMA RAMDAS

CS25 Developing intercultural competence through international travel experience at Spelman College 269
DIMEJI R. TOGUNDE AND ROKHAYA FALL

CS26 A collaborative volunteer project in Vietnam 275
EIKO UJITANI

CS27 Inclusion through changing the conversation: A case study on the NorQuest community dialogue on inclusion 280
CHERYL WHITELAW, SARAH APEDAILE, AND TODD ODGERS

CS28 The Businet international weeks 285
JASON WILLIAMS AND JOËLLE HIETBRINK

CS29 (Dis)connecting Mayan and Mexican *interculturidad* with social justice in a US graduate preparation programme 289
TAMARA YAKABOSKI AND MATT BIRNBAUM

12 Intercultural competence in international higher education: Emerging themes, issues, implications, and future directions 294
DARLA K. DEARDORFF AND LILY A. ARASARATNAM-SMITH

Index *303*

About the contributors

Co-editors

Darla K. Deardorff is the current executive director of the Association of International Education Administrators, a national leadership organisation based at Duke University (United States), where she holds affiliated faculty appointments in education and international comparative studies. In addition, she holds faculty appointments at several other universities around the world including in China, Japan, and South Africa, as well as serving on the faculty of a Harvard University institute and the prestigious Summer Institute of Intercultural Communication in Portland, Oregon. Author of six published books and numerous book chapters and articles, she is widely published in international education, intercultural competence/learning and assessment, and global leadership. Regularly invited to speak and consult around the world, she holds a doctorate from North Carolina State University in the United States. She can be reached at d.deardorff@duke.edu.

Lily A. Arasaratnam-Smith is the Director of Research and an Associate Professor of Communication at Alphacrucis College, Australia. Her primary expertise is in intercultural communication competence; other research interests include intercultural contact-seeking behaviour, attitudes toward diversity, and sojourner identity. She is a member of the International Academy for Intercultural Research and Associate Editor of the International Journal of Intercultural Relations. Lily is bilingual and her research is influenced by her personal intercultural experiences, which include living in four countries and nine cities. Lily holds a doctorate in communication from Rutgers, State University of New Jersey in the United States.

Contributors

Huda Abdelrahim is a Senior Specialist in Cultural Competence in Healthcare, at the Institute for Population Health, Weill Cornell

Medicine-Qatar. She holds a Bachelor of Science and Post Graduate Diploma in Education. Ms Abdelrahim's research interest is in Education & Intercultural Communication and its impact in health care.

Joana Almeida is a Research Associate at Newcastle University, UK. She holds a PhD in Education from the University of Aveiro, Portugal, and was a visiting scholar at SIT Graduate Institute, United States. She develops research in international education, internationalisation of higher education, student mobility, intercultural competence facilitation, and assessment.

Ran An is Professor in the School of International Education at South China University of Technology. She holds her PhD degree at the University of Reading. She is the principal investigator of the Key Project of National Social Science Foundation, China. She has published more than 70 papers and (co)authored/(co)edited 15 books.

Sarah Apedaile is an Intercultural Specialist and Faculty Development Advisor at NorQuest College in Edmonton, Alberta, Canada. She brings a commitment to reflective practice, self-compassion, and dialogue to her work supporting inclusive engagement and reconciliation through applied research, curriculum development, and workshop facilitation.

Amber Bennett Hill is Director of International Student and Scholar Programs and the English Language Program at Virginia Commonwealth University in the United States. She holds a PhD in American Civilization from the University of Pennsylvania.

Gerdien Bertram-Troost is Assistant Professor in Religious Education at the Faculty of Theology and Assistant Professor in Educational Foundations at the Faculty of Behavioural and Movement Sciences at Vrije Universiteit Amsterdam, the Netherlands. She holds a master's degree in Educational Psychology from Leiden University, the Netherlands.

Nadine Binder is a doctoral candidate in Psychology at the Bremen International Graduate School of Social Sciences in Germany. She holds an MA in Management of Cultural Diversity from Tilburg University in the Netherlands. She also works as a freelance trainer and coach, specialising in intercultural competence and personal leadership.

Matt Birnbaum is Associate Professor of Higher Education and Student Affairs Leadership at the University of Northern Colorado, United States. He holds a PhD in Higher Education from the University of Arizona. Matt serves as a program coordinator and chairs the Department of Leadership, Policy, and Development.

Scott G. Blair is Director of Assessment and Sustainability at The Education Abroad Network. Trained as a historian, he holds his MA from Georgetown and a doctorate from the University of Paris Panthéon-Sorbonne. From his base in Paris, he advocates for behavioural-based learning outcomes assessment and sustainability literacy in international higher education.

Huba Boshoff is the Manager of Partnerships and Internationalisation. She holds a master's degree in Higher Education.

Frederique Bouilheres is a Senior Academic Developer at RMIT University Vietnam. She has a master's in Accounting from Montpellier, France and an MBA in Education from Keele University, UK. She has recently submitted her PhD thesis to Curtin University, Australia.

Melanie Brown is Senior Academic Developer at RMIT in Vietnam. She holds a master's degree in International Communication from Macquarie University in Australia. Melanie has worked in Vietnam for the past 10 years and is currently undertaking a doctoral degree in Education focusing on the use of communities of practice.

Claudia Bulnes Sánchez is International Policy Advisor at The Hague University of Applied Sciences. She holds a degree in Teaching English and Spanish as a foreign language from the University of Oviedo and University Antonio de Nebrija in Spain. She provides staff training on internationalisation of the curriculum at The Hague University of Applied Sciences.

Carolyn Calloway-Thomas, immediate Past President of the World Communication Association, is Chair and Professor of African American and African Diaspora at Indiana University, United States. She holds a PhD in Communication and Culture from Indiana University. She is author of *Empathy in the Global World: An Intercultural Perspective* and co-author of *Intercultural Communication: A Text with Readings and Intercultural Communication.*

Hilary J. Cassil is a mathematics instructor at Virginia Commonwealth University (VCU) in the United States. She holds a master's degree in Theoretical Mathematics from the VCU. Her teaching is application-based and she strives to make it accessible to all students.

Nadezda Chernyak is a PhD candidate at Lomonosov Moscow State University in Russia. She holds an MA degree in Linguistics and Intercultural Communication from Lomonosov Moscow State University in Russia and an MA degree in Bioethics/Medical Ethics from Case Western Reserve University in the United States.

Liza Lai Shan Choi holds a Master of Nursing degree from the University of Calgary. Originally from Hong Kong, Liza is based at the Mount Royal University, Canada, where she researches the underlying processes leading to acquiring language and nursing competencies. She is also interested in the impact of an online course on bias on nursing student learning.

Deborah (Debbie) Corder is Associate Head at the School of Language and Culture, Auckland University of Technology, New Zealand. She holds an MA from Massey University, New Zealand. Having taught Japanese at secondary and tertiary levels, she now mainly teaches intercultural competence, which, along with study abroad, is her main research interest.

Eveke de Louw is International Policy Advisor at The Hague University of Applied Sciences (THUAS). She holds a master's degree in English Language and Literature. Her main role in THUAS is to develop staff training on internationalisation of the curriculum and co-curriculum.

Maha Elnashar is Director at the Center for Cultural Competence in the Institute of Population Health at Weill Cornell Medicine-Qatar. She holds a graduate degree and BA in Translation/Interpretation. She is a licensed trainer by the CCHCP, United States. Her research interest focuses on cultural influence in health care. She has published various articles in peer-reviewed journals.

Alecia Erasmus is Coordinator: Information Management and Erasmus+ at Stellenbosch University International, Stellenbosch University, South Africa. She holds a master's degree in Ancient Languages from Stellenbosch University. She coordinates and facilitates the short course in Global Citizenship that forms part of the co-curricular offering at Stellenbosch University.

Rokhaya Fall is the Coordinator of Study Abroad and International Student Services at Spelman College, United States. She holds an MS in Social Work from Clark Atlanta University. Ms Fall is responsible for the advisement and recruitment of students planning to study abroad as well as the collection and analysis of data on global initiatives.

Teresa (Terry) Franson is an adjunct instructor at Virginia Commonwealth University in Richmond, Virginia, United States. She holds a master's degree in English from Wake Forest University, Winston-Salem, North Carolina, United States.

Irina Golubeva is Head of the International Mobility Office at the University of Pannonia, Hungary, where she also lectures in Intercultural Communication and Translation Studies. She holds a PhD degree in Language Studies from the University of Pécs in Hungary, and her main research interests concern intercultural communication and internationalisation of higher education.

Jeanine Gregersen-Hermans is Pro Vice Chancellor International at Glasgow Caledonian University, Scotland. She holds a PhD in Internationalisation of Higher Education from Universita Cattolica del Sacro Cuore, Italy.

Jeanine focuses on internationalisation, organisational change, and intercultural competence development in higher education and has been teaching and working at universities across Europe.

Savo Heleta works as the Manager of Internationalization at Home and Research at Nelson Mandela Metropolitan University's Office for International Education in Port Elizabeth, South Africa. Savo's research interests range from higher education internationalisation, higher education in post-war settings, conflict analysis, and post-war reconstruction and development.

Joëlle Hietbrink is Lecturer in Intercultural Communication and Spanish, and Internationalisation Coordinator at Stenden University of Applied Sciences in the Netherlands. She holds a master's degree in Romance Languages and Cultures, specialising in Spanish, from Groningen University. Currently, she is carrying out a PhD on Assessing Intercultural Competence.

Christopher T. Hightower is the Assistant Director for Institutional Effectiveness at Texas Christian University in the United States. He holds a doctorate in Education from Texas Christian University. He serves on the executive committee and performs assessment for the comprehensive internationalisation effort on his campus.

Jane Jackson is Professor in the English Department at the Chinese University of Hong Kong. She holds a PhD from the University of Toronto, Canada. A recipient of numerous external research grants and awards, she has published widely on study abroad, intercultural communication/education, language and identity, internationalisation, and eLearning.

Sonya L. Jakubec is an Associate Professor at Mount Royal University in Calgary, Canada. She holds a PhD in Nursing from the University of Calgary. Her research concentrates on applied, community health strategies, as well as creative pedagogy, and teaching/learning for research literacy.

Annette Karseras is adjunct faculty at Japanese Universities – Keio 慶應義塾大学, Temple テンプル大学ジャパン, Tokyo Metropolitan 首都大学東, Tsuda 津田塾大学, & TUFS 東京外国語大学 where she promotes win-win 'partnering between worlds'. She has a master's degree from the School of Cultural Studies, University of Leicester.

Carrie Karsgaard is an International Student Advisor at the University of British Columbia. She holds an MA in Cultural Studies and Education from UBC and is currently working on her PhD in Educational Policy Studies at the University of Alberta.

Beth Kreydatus is Associate Professor at Virginia Commonwealth University. She holds a degree in American History from the College of William and

Mary, in the United States. She presently teaches first-year seminars in the Department of Focused Inquiry.

Steve J. Kulich is Founder/Director of the SISU Intercultural Institute (SII) and Distinguished Professor at Shanghai International Studies University, PR China. He holds a PhD in Intercultural Communication/Education from Humboldt University in Berlin, Germany. Awarded for his contributions to the IC field in China, he is President-elect of the International Association of Intercultural Relations.

Nina Lazarević is an Assistant Professor at the University of Niš, Serbia. She holds a PhD in Applied Linguistics/Intercultural Competence from the University of Novi Sad, Serbia. She is a researcher, teacher-trainer, president of the local English language teachers' association, and a Fulbright Visiting Scholar program alumna.

Concepción Maiztegui-Oñate is a tenured lecturer at the Faculty of Psychology and Education at the Universidad de Deusto, Spain, and she is a researcher at the Pedro Arrupe Human Rights Institute. Her current research project focuses on citizenship, participation, and community development in contexts of diversity.

Stella C. Major is Associate Professor of Family Medicine at Weill Cornell Medicine in Qatar. She holds an MBBS from the University of London, and is a Fellow of the Royal College of General Practitioner in UK. She is a practising clinician, international educator, and researcher.

Katrien Mertens is Plurality & Diversity Coordinator, and Opportunity Coach for disadvantaged students at UC Leuven Limburg, Belgium. She holds an MSc in Adult Education from VUB, Belgium. She has conducted research on perceptions of success among minority groups, and teaches courses on cultural diversity, appreciative inquiry, and personal growth.

Elaine Meyer-Lee, Associate Vice President for Global Learning and Leadership Development at Agnes Scott College, United States, holds a doctorate in Human Development and Psychology from Harvard University, United States. She has led, assessed, published, and presented widely on intercultural higher education for 15 years, and is currently President of NAFSA.

Jann Murray-García, MD, MPH (University of California (UC) San Francisco; UC Berkeley, United States) is an Assistant Adjunct Professor and Founding Faculty Member of UC Davis's Betty Irene Moore School of Nursing. Her publications on race, health care, and child development have appeared in *The New England Journal of Medicine, Academic Medicine,* and *Journal of Health Care for the Poor and Underserved.*

Todd Odgers is the Principal of the NorQuest College Centre for Intercultural Education (CIE) in Edmonton, Canada. He holds an MA in Intercultural Relations from Antioch University in the United States. The CIE is unique in Canada, building intercultural competence for educators, business, government, and non-governmental organisations, nationally and internationally.

Susan Oguro is Associate Professor and Director, Internationalisation for the Faculty of Arts and Social Sciences at the University of Technology Sydney, Australia. She holds a PhD in Education from the University of Sydney. Her research interests include Intercultural Education and Human Rights Education.

Daniel J. Paracka, Jr, is Director of Campus Internationalization at Kennesaw State University. He holds a PhD in International Education Policy from Georgia State University. With more than 25 years of international education leadership experience, Dr Paracka's scholarship focuses on intercultural learning and global engagement.

Catherine Peck is the Manager, Learning and Teaching at RMIT University Vietnam. She is a PhD Candidate in Linguistics at Macquarie University, Australia. Her research interests include intercultural competence development and discourse analysis.

Paula J. Pedersen is Assistant Professor of Psychology and Faculty Fellow for Equity and Inclusion Education and Training at the University of Minnesota Duluth, United States. Dr Pedersen has published in the areas of human sexuality, study abroad, equity and diversity, and civic engagement and teaching and learning.

Janelle S. Peifer is an Assistant Professor of Psychology at Agnes Scott College in the United States. She holds a PhD in Clinical Psychology from the University of Virginia in the United States. Her research examines intra- and inter-cultural processes of college students' intercultural competence development.

Thomas (Tom) Pynn is Senior Lecturer of Interdisciplinary Studies at Kennesaw State University in the United States. He holds an MA in Literature and an MA in Philosophy from the University of Mississippi in the United States. His interests span religion, poetry, and religious philosophy, both western and non-western.

Hester Radstake is an independent researcher and teacher trainer in the Netherlands and Portugal. She holds a PhD in Educational Sciences from the University of Amsterdam in the Netherlands. Her focus is on diversity sensitive teaching and citizenship education.

Siema Ramdas is a researcher and lecturer at the Vrije Universiteit Amsterdam in the Netherlands. She coaches teachers in higher education in subjects related to diversity and the international classroom.

Deborah S. Reisinger is Director of the Cultures and Languages Across the Curriculum initiative at Duke University, where she is an Assistant Professor of the Practice in Romance Studies and an affiliate faculty member in the Duke Global Health Institute. Reisinger's work examines the impact of language and culture on identity, inclusion, and community.

Finn Reygan is Senior Researcher at the University of the Witwatersrand in South Africa. He holds a PhD in Psychology from University College Dublin. His work focuses on issues of diversity in education.

Leah Sanford is Manager, International Programs and Services at University of British Columbia in Canada. She holds degrees in Linguistics, Education (BA), and Intercultural Communication (MA) from Royal Roads and Simon Fraser Universities in British Columbia, Canada. Her research and interests lie in diversity, equity, intercultural, identity, and anti-racist ideologies, theories, and pedagogies.

Rosa Santibáñez-Gruber holds a PhD in Pedagogy from the University of Deusto, Spain, and a Diploma in Criminology from the University of the Basque Country. She is currently Professor at the University of Deusto. She is Chief Researcher of the Intervention: Quality of Life and Social Inclusion research team.

Peter-Ben Smit is Professor of Contextual Biblical Interpretation at Vrije Universiteit Amsterdam, the Netherlands. He holds a doctorate in New Testament studies, Anglican Studies and the degree of 'Habilitation' in Church History. Currently, he specialises in masculinity and religion.

Melissa Steyn holds the South African National Research Chair in Critical Diversity Studies and is Director of the Centre for Diversity Studies at the University of the Witwatersrand, Johannesburg. She holds a PhD from the University of Cape Town, South Africa. She is best known for her work on whiteness in post-apartheid South Africa.

Melanie Tervalon is a Health Policy Consultant in the United States. She holds a medical degree from the University of California, San Francisco, and a master's degree in Public Health and a Bachelor of Science degree, both from the University of California, Berkeley, United States. With Jann Murray-Garcia, she coined and developed the concept of 'Cultural Humility'.

Dimeji R. Togunde is the Associate Provost for Global Education & Professor of International Studies at Spelman College, United States. He holds a PhD degree in Development Sociology from Cornell University, United States, and leads the campus internationalisation and its assessment. He is also responsible for building and sustaining strategic international partnerships to enhance Spelman's international initiatives.

Eiko Ujitani is an Associate Professor of English and Intercultural Communication in the Department of British and American Studies at Nagoya University of Foreign Studies in Japan. She holds an EdD from Murdoch University in Australia. Her research interests are intercultural communicative competence, service-learning, and second language acquisition.

Jan Van Maele teaches communication at KU Leuven, Belgium. He holds a PhD in Applied Linguistics from UCL, Belgium. His main research interests are language assessment and intercultural communication, with a focus on intercultural learning in educational and engineering settings, in collaboration with partners in Europe, China, Cuba, and Japan.

Yi'an Wang is Professor at Hangzhou Dianzi University in PR China. He holds a PhD in Intercultural Communication from Shanghai International Studies University in PR China. His research interest focuses on intercultural competence development and assessment and its application in different contexts, intercultural adjustment, and intercultural training.

Cheryl Whitelaw is Applied Research Manager at NorQuest College in Canada. She holds a Master of Education from the University of Lethbridge in Canada. She holds intercultural communication as a peacemaking practice to create social cohesion within a diverse society.

Jason Williams is Head of the Department for Computing at Cardiff Metropolitan University in the UK. He holds a PhD in the Performance Analysis of Sport from the University of Wales. His research areas cover the use of technology in sport for performance analysis and internationalisation in higher education.

Tamara Yakaboski, PhD, is Associate Professor of Higher Education and Student Affairs Leadership at the University of Northern Colorado, United States. She holds both her MA and PhD in Higher Education from the University of Arizona, United States. She teaches and researches higher education organisation and administration, international higher education, and women's issues.

Maria Yarosh works at the Tuning Academy, University of Deusto, Spain. She holds an MA in Lifelong Learning from the Institute of Education, London, and a PhD in Education (Translator Intercultural Competence Development) from the University of Deusto. She is currently focusing on staff-development activities for university teachers.

Series foreword

This series addresses the rapidly changing and highly topical field of internationalisation in higher education. Increasingly visible in institutional strategies as well as national and international agendas since the latter part of the twentieth century, internationalisation has been informed by diverse disciplines including anthropology, languages and communication, business and marketing, pedagogy, and environmental studies. In part, its rise can be seen as a response to globalisation and growing competition among higher education institutions. However, it also responds to the recognition that students must be prepared for changing local and global environments in both personal and professional life.

The diverse and complex dimensions of contemporary internationalisation require institutions to adjust and define the concept for their own purposes, adding to the richness of our understanding. Insights from countries where institutional and curricular internationalisation is a more recent development will enhance our awareness of the benefits and challenges of internationalisation practice over the coming years.

There are compelling drivers for university leaders to adopt an integrated rather than a uni-dimensional approach to internationalisation. Intensifying competition for talent, changes in global student flows, international branch campuses, and growing complexity in cross-border activity, along with the rising influence of institutional rankings, all provide economic impetus and reputational consequences of success or failure. Meanwhile, added incentive is provided by the awareness that the intercultural competence required for global contexts is equally important for living and working in today's increasingly diverse multicultural societies. Rising employer and student demand reflects growing interest in international and intercultural experiences and competencies. Internationalisation thus has both global and more local intercultural interests at its heart.

Internationalisation as a powerful force for change is an underlying theme of this series, in contrast to economic or brand-enhancing aspects of international engagement. It seeks to address these complex topics as internationalisation matures into its next phase. It aims to reflect contemporary concerns, with volumes geared to the major questions of our time. Written or edited by leading thinkers and authors from around the world, while giving a voice to emerging researchers, the series offers theoretical perspectives with practical applications, focusing on some of the critical issues in this developing field for higher education leaders and practitioners alike.

The current volume focuses on the crucial topic of intercultural competence. With a wide range of contributors from around the world, it addresses the development and assessment of intercultural competence both from theoretical and practical points of view. Through the extensive case studies, readers will gain insight into how concepts have been applied in different countries and types of institutions.

At the time of writing, the world is facing troubling times with a rise in nationalism, populism, and anti-globalism in many countries. A better understanding of living and working with cultural 'others' may be one way of countering such worrying isolationist tendencies. This volume appears at a timely moment therefore, emphasising for higher education institutions the importance of including intercultural competence as part of their broader internationalisation strategies.

Elspeth Jones, Emerita Professor of the Internationalization of Higher Education Series Editor

Acknowledgements

Darla: We would like to express deep appreciation to all of our contributors for working with us on this book project, to Elspeth Jones, series editor, for making this opportunity possible, and to the Routledge team for working with us over the course of this book project. And a special thank you goes to my co-editor Lily A. Arasaratnam-Smith for giving so much to this project and for our cross-cultural collaboration and friendship which span two continents.

Lily: I would like to acknowledge my parents for the opportunities they gave me to see the world, which in turn sparked my interest in intercultural communication. In regards to this particular project, I acknowledge my co-editor Darla K. Deardorff not only for her scholarly contributions and leadership in this project but especially for her friendship and collegiality.

Introduction

Darla K. Deardorff (Duke University) and
Lily A. Arasaratnam-Smith (Alphacrucis College)

One of the main drivers of internationalisation of higher education is that of global, intercultural, and international learning outcomes (Nelson Mandela Bay Declaration on the Future of International Higher Education). It is thus very timely to have a book in this series that is devoted exclusively to exploring this central outcome of internationalisation efforts. Featuring newer voices and diverse perspectives, both disciplinarily and geographically, this edited volume highlights the latest thinking and practice on intercultural competence as one of the key dimensions with global and international learning outcomes. The chapters in this volume will help propel scholars and international educators further in understanding what these intercultural outcomes entail, moving beyond rhetoric and past work in this area. This book builds on the seminal work of the 2009 *Sage Handbook of Intercultural Competence* as well as the 2009 *Handbook of Research in Education Abroad*. A unique feature of this volume is the exclusive focus on intercultural learning within the academy – approaches, perspectives, and practical strategies, based on research – in addressing intercultural learning for students, administrators, and academics. Specifically, the twenty-nine case studies from around the world provide concrete examples of how intercultural competence is being addressed and assessed within higher education institutions globally.

Part I provides an introduction to intercultural competence as a learning outcome of internationalisation and includes chapters on cutting-edge topics within current intercultural competence research, with an emphasis on bringing theory and research to practice through discussion of practical implications within the higher education context. Specifically, Chapter 1 by Arasaratnam-Smith lays a foundation for the text by outlining a brief history of the scholarship around intercultural competence as well as highlighting several models and definitions of intercultural competence that are references in the subsequent case studies. Murray-García and Tervalon, in Chapter 2, provide an interdisciplinary lens through their discussion of cultural humility from a healthcare perspective since cultural humility is emerging as a key element when researching intercultural competence. In Chapter 3, Calloway-Thomas, a professor in African-American and African Diaspora Studies, along with co-contributors Arasaratnam-Smith and Deardorff, delves into the crucial role of empathy within intercultural competence.

Paracka and Pynn, in Chapter 4, discuss the bigger picture of intercultural competence and social change, presenting a transformational model of interdisciplinary intercultural competence. And in Chapter 5, Heleta and Deardorff examine the role of higher education institutions in developing intercultural competence in post-conflict societies, which is a currently under-studied yet critical topic that deserves further attention in its application to a real-world issue such as post-conflict reconstruction.

Part II delves further into developing and assessing intercultural competence within a higher education context starting with Chapter 6 by Gregersen-Hermans who clearly outlines research-based steps that higher education institutions can take in developing students' intercultural competence. Chapters 7 and 8 explore intercultural competence from perspectives outside of the Global North with Steyn and Reygan presenting South African perspectives on this concept and Wang, Deardorff, and Kulich highlighting recent research from China on intercultural competence with implications for higher education institutions. The last two chapters in this section address the key area of measuring intercultural competence with Blair, in Chapter 9, providing a mapping approach to assessing intercultural competence with a focus on evidence and Deardorff, in Chapter 10, drawing lessons from the case studies in Part III, along with her own work in intercultural competence assessment.

Part III provides concrete case studies on how intercultural competence is addressed and assessed within specific contexts around the world including from such countries as Canada, Japan, Mexico, Qatar, and South Africa, as well as from a variety of disciplinary contexts including business, medicine, and theology and religious studies, in addition to the more traditional education abroad programmes. There was an overwhelming response to the global call for case-study proposals, and those selected reflect different approaches from universities around the world. While not all parts of the world could be represented, there is rich diversity in the twenty-nine case studies selected. (See Table 11.1 for an at-a-glance table of the case studies.) The concluding chapter draws all three sections together in highlighting common themes as well as future trends and directions in regard to intercultural competence within the internationalisation of higher education.

This volume can be used as both a textbook (for use in intercultural communication courses and higher education courses), especially the case studies, as well as a reference work for university administrators engaged in internationalising their institutions, including within and beyond the curriculum. University administrators may find the case studies useful as training material for workshops. In addition, scholars and academics in a variety of disciplines will find this text helpful in the chapters highlighting newer research topics as well as in providing concrete examples, tied to theory and research, of how to develop and assess intercultural competence in higher education. Readers are encouraged to continue the conversation.

Intercultural competence is a topic that is relevant to multiple disciplines, and our current understanding of it has been developed by contributions in research from multiple disciplines. Its practical application and relevance cannot be overstated. Hence it is a topic that has and will generate conversations across disciplinary, vocational, and regional boundaries. Just as our personal development of intercultural competence is an ongoing process, so is our collective understanding of it. Hence conversation about intercultural competence must continue and evolve as the world and its cultures evolve. Our book is one contribution to this conversation.

Part I

Introduction to intercultural competence

Chapter 1

Intercultural competence

An overview

Lily A. Arasaratnam-Smith (Alphacrucis College)

Our present understanding of intercultural competence today has been shaped by decades of research in multiple disciplines such as sociology, anthropology, psychology, education, and communication, to name a few. I must preface this chapter by acknowledging that this chapter is influenced by my particular familiarity with communication and informed by published works in English in communication and other disciplines. The section on early works in intercultural competence is particularly focused on known works arising from the United States. Hence, while this is a broadly representative account of research in intercultural competence, it is by no means a comprehensive account of the body of literature on intercultural competence.

A brief history

Much of the literature in intercultural competence can be traced back to works in the 1960s and some even in the 1930s in the United States. For example, Rachel D. DuBois (1982–93) is known to have planted seeds of understanding between culturally diverse groups through her contribution to curriculum in intercultural education and the founding of several groups devoted to intercultural programmes. In the 1960s, research of American service personnel travelling and living overseas produced understanding of some components of effective intercultural communication, which included flexibility, stability, curiosity, sensitivity, etc. (e.g., see Ezekiel 1968; Gardner, 1962; Smith, 1966). It is interesting to note that during the same period of time psychologist Robert W. White (1959) proposed that competence is 'an organism's capacity to interact effectively with its environment' (p. 297). Hence the concept of competence was also present during this time. Anthropologist Edward T. Hall (1914–2009) is another noteworthy contributor to early works in intercultural studies, with classic publications such as *The Silent Language* (1959) that have shaped much of later thinking.

In the 1970s, there were some deliberate attempts to conceptualise and study what was called cross-cultural effectiveness (Ruben, Askling, & Kealey, 1977). Using quantitative techniques, researchers developed measures to assess cross-cultural competence; also labelled intercultural competence, or intercultural adaptation (Hammer, Gudykunst, & Wiseman, 1978; Ruben & Kealey, 1979).

Variables such as flexibility, openness, curiosity, etc., were identified as key contributors to communicating effectively across cultures or rather adapting effectively to another culture. Publishing outlets such as the *International Journal of Intercultural Relations* (*IJIR*) were started in the late 1970s, signalling the increased interest in the study of intercultural relations.

In the 1980s, researchers continued to develop and refine instruments to assess intercultural *communication* competence (such as Bennett, 1986; Dinges, 1983; Hammer, 1987); the interest in the topic highlighted by a special issue of *IJIR* in 1989 dedicated to intercultural communication competence. Intercultural communication was being studied from the perspective of individuals from two distinct (national) cultures interacting with each other (i.e. interpersonal communication between individuals from different cultures). In fact, Spitzberg and Cupach's (1984) definition of (interpersonal) communication competence as effective and appropriate communication has been foundational in influencing later definitions of intercultural competence.

In the 1990s, the study of intercultural competence continued to mature, with the publication of several theories of intercultural competence, many of which have stood the test of time until this day (see Arasaratnam, 2016, for more). The momentum in research in intercultural competence has continued into the 2000s, with contributions to this research by multiple scholars from diverse disciplines. For a comprehensive review of intercultural competence research up to 2009, see Spitzberg and Changnon (2009). *IJIR* published another special issue of intercultural competence in 2015, some twenty-five years since the seminal 1989 special issue. In addition to commentaries from issue editors Lily A. Arasaratnam and Darla K. Deardorff, both of whom have contributed to research in intercultural competence (Arasaratnam & Doerfel, 2005; Arasaratnam, 2006; Deardorff, 2006, 2009) in the 2000s onwards, the special issue included reflections from some of the contributors in the 1989 issue as well as new research in intercultural competence from a variety of disciplines. This is one illustration of the fact that research in intercultural competence has endured the test of time and matured and grown into a rich interdisciplinary pursuit.

Labels and definitions

Because of the wide interest in intercultural competence in multiple disciplines, nuanced and varied labels of this concept are prolific. This has caused a measure of confusion, exacerbated by little cross-referencing between disciplines that research intercultural competence (Arasaratnam, 2014). Bradford, Allen, & Beisser (2000) recognised this in their attempt to synthesise existing definitions and labels of intercultural competence and concluded that intercultural communication competence and intercultural effectiveness have been used interchangeably in literature. In medicine and related disciplines, cultural competence is the known label. While some have used the label 'intercultural sensitivity' to describe intercultural competence, others have argued that sensitivity, while a necessary component of intercultural competence, is not equivalent to competence

(Chen & Starosta, 2000). Possibly due to its origins in cultural acculturation studies, intercultural competence has also been sometimes used interchangeably with acculturation, adaptation, and even multiculturalism. Arasaratnam (2016) observes that these labels too are conceptually distinct from intercultural competence. What then, is intercultural competence?

Effectiveness (the ability to achieve one's goals in a particular exchange) and appropriateness (the ability to do so in a manner that is acceptable to the other person) are two components of intercultural competence prevalent in literature. Scholars also generally agree that intercultural competence has cognitive, affective, and behavioural dimensions. Spitzberg and Changnon (2009) offer the following definition: '*intercultural competence* is the appropriate and effective management of interaction between people who … represent different or divergent affective, cognitive, and behavioral orientations to the world' (p. 7). It is imperative to observe that, in defining intercultural competence, one must consider the concept holistically, seeing that there are multiple elements at play here not just an individual's own abilities. That is, interpersonal communication inherently involves the perception and abilities of more than one person, which in turn are influenced by the individuals' cultural worldview as well as the parameters of the context in which this communication takes place. There are critics among scholars who observe that study of intercultural competence and indeed intercultural relations has a distinct individualistic flavour that does not adequately take into account wider perspectives (for a detailed dialogue, see Alexander et al., 2014).

Models and frameworks

The variables that influence or contribute to intercultural competence have been of great interest to researchers since the 1960s. Relatedly, the way in which these variables interact with one another has also been of interest, resulting in various compositional, casual, developmental, and other models of intercultural competence. An overarching grand theory of intercultural competence is yet to be developed, though there are several widely used and tested theories.

As it is not within the scope of this chapter to provide a comprehensive account of models and frameworks of intercultural competence, this chapter will focus on the models proposed by the editors of this book and other known models of intercultural competence with which the case studies in this book engage, with the exception of one other well-known model from the field of intercultural communication. As such, these models are as follows: the Process Model of Intercultural Competence (Deardorff, 2006), the Integrated Model of Intercultural Communication Competence (Arasaratnam, 2006), the Intercultural Competencies Dimensions Model (Fantini, 2009), the Intercultural Competence Model by Byram (1997), and the Developmental Model of Intercultural Sensitivity (Bennett, 1986). Additionally, the Anxiety/Uncertainty Management (AUM) Model (Gudykunst, 1993, 1995) is also presented. This is not a comprehensive list of the models and frameworks to which the case studies refer; it is instead an overview of some of the more widely referenced models.

The Process Model of Intercultural Competence

Based on a study of twenty-three intercultural experts using Delphi methodology, Deardorff (2006) proposed a compositional model in which she identified the components of intercultural competence which in turn informed the Process Model of Intercultural Competence, which outlines relationships between attitudes, knowledge, and internal and external desired outcomes (see Figure 1.1). Deardorff advocates progressive assessment of intercultural competence, using multiple techniques. Qualitative and quantitative assessments are suggested,

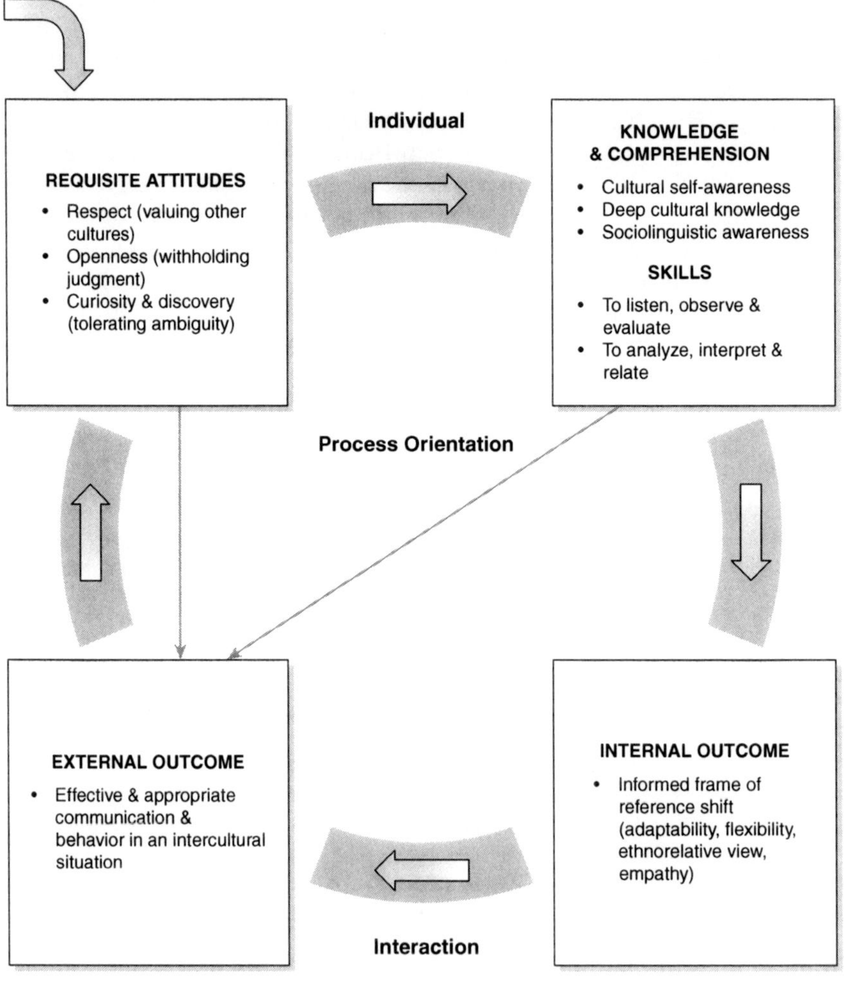

Figure 1.1 Deardorff Process Model of Intercultural Competence (2006).

noting that it is important to not only consider the types of assessment used but also the purpose of the assessment. Deardorff's model has been widely influential in international higher education, as illustrated by the fact that it is a key theoretical framework in several of the case studies in this volume.

The Integrated Model of Intercultural Communication Competence

The Integrated Model of Intercultural Communication Competence (IMICC) was based on findings from a study in which thirty-seven participants from fifteen countries were asked to describe a competent intercultural communicator; from these descriptions, Arasaratnam and Doerfel (2005) used semantic network analysis to identify five key variables that were common among all responses, namely empathy, experience, motivation, listening, and positive attitude towards other cultures. The IMICC (see Figure 1.2) was designed and empirically tested, showing a causal relationship between these variables (Arasaratnam, 2006; Arasaratnam, Banerjee, & Dembek, 2010a). A variation of the model was further developed to include sensation-seeking and ethnocentrism as variables that influence intercultural competence (Arasaratnam & Banerjee, 2011). The inclusion of

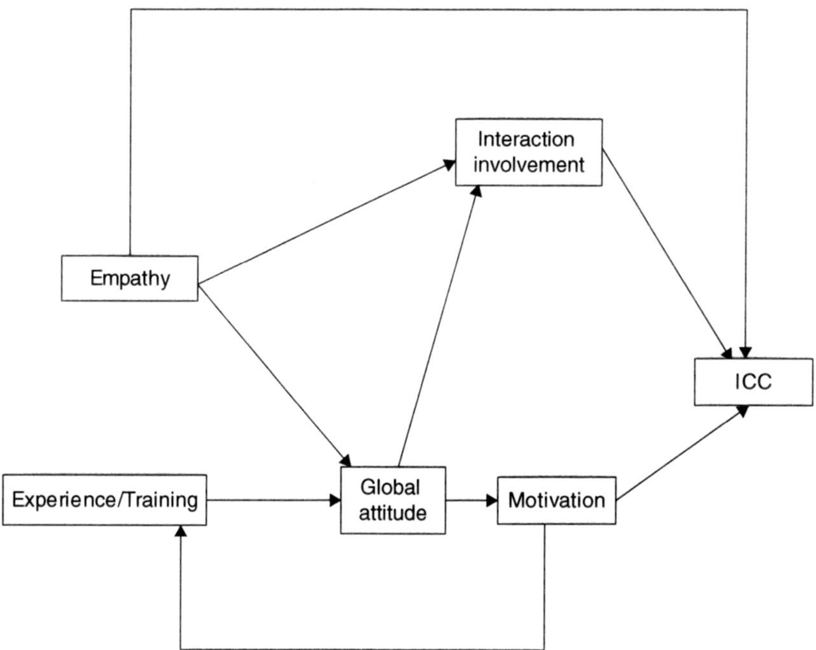

Figure 1.2 The Integrated Model of Intercultural Communication Competence by Arasaratnam (2006).

sensation-seeking is particularly interesting from an international higher education perspective because there is evidence to suggest that high sensation-seekers are predisposed to engage in intercultural contact-seeking behaviour such as study-abroad programmes, for example (Arasaratnam, 2006; Arasaratnam, Banerjee, & Dembek, 2010b).

Intercultural competencies dimensions

Based on a wide review of literature which informed the conceptualisation of intercultural competence and on empirical testing (Fantini, 2006), the intercultural competencies dimensions provide a framework for assessing intercultural competence (see Figure 1.3). It identifies eight attributes (empathy, openness, patience, curiosity, flexibility, suspended judgement, tolerance for ambiguity, and humour), three interrelated areas (formation and maintenance of relationships, communication without disorientation, cooperation for mutual benefit), and four dimensions (knowledge, skills, attitudes, awareness). Fantini (2009) proposes that introspection and self-reflection promote enhanced awareness. Fantini's framework is widely used, as illustrated by case studies by Almeida and Oguro in this book.

Intercultural Competence Model

Byram's Intercultural Competence Model (1997) allows for a distinction between those whose identities are conflicted due to exposure to two cultures (bicultural) and those whose identities seamlessly negotiate between cultures (intercultural). Unlike many other models of intercultural competence, this model places

Figure 1.3 Intercultural competencies dimensionsions (Fantini, 2009).

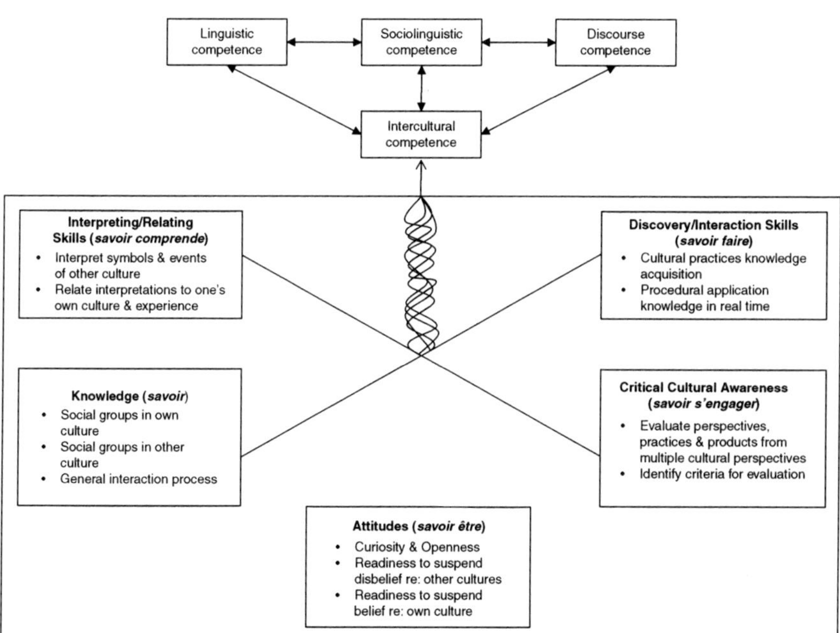

Figure 1.4 Intercultural Competence Model (Byram, 1997).

a heavy emphasis on language (see also Byram, 2014). The use of Byram's model (Figure. 1.4) is illustrated in the case studies by Corder, Lazarevic, and Peck et al., for example.

Developmental Model of Intercultural Sensitivity

The Developmental Model of Intercultural Sensitivity (DMIS) (Bennett, 1986) is a process model that outlines one's linear progression from ethnocentrism to ethnorelativity through six distinct stages (Figure. 1.5). The ethnocentric stages begin with denial (the conviction that one's own cultural view is the real one), progressing to defence (a binary view of one's culture versus others' cultures), and minimisation (seeing others' cultures with the frameworks that pre-exist in one's own culture). From minimisation, one progresses to the ethnorelative stages, which, in sequence, are acceptance (the recognition of one's own culture as one of many equally valid cultures), adaptation (modifying one's behaviour in order to accommodate others' cultural expectations), and integration (internalising aspects of others' worldviews into one's own sense of identity). The DMIS is widely studied in its contribution to assessment (Hammer, Bennett, & Wiseman, 2003) and widely used in training, as illustrated in the case studies by (such as Hightower, Jackson, and Pedersen, among others) in this book.

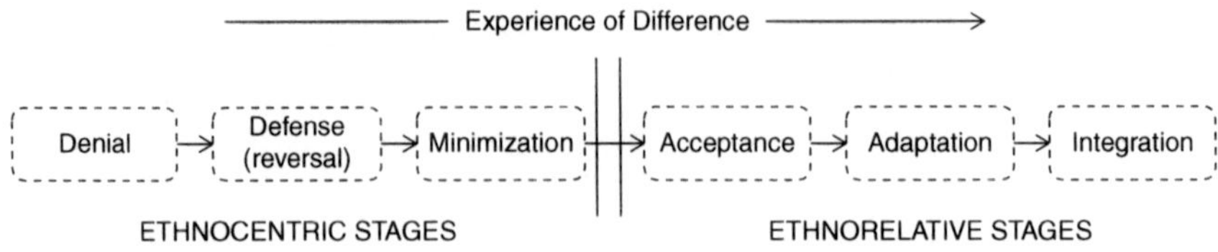

Figure 1.5 Developmental Model of Intercultural Sensitivity (Bennett, 1986).

Anxiety/Uncertainty Management (AUM)

Defining effective communication (i.e. intercultural competence) as communication where there are least number of misunderstandings, Gudykunst (1993, 1995) proposes that when we encounter culturally different others, we face a certain measure of uncertainty which in turn causes anxiety. The effective management of this anxiety is necessary for effective (intercultural) communication. The AUM Model (Figure. 1.6) proposes that mindfulness acts as a mediating variable in the anxiety/uncertainty management process. A mindful person is deliberately cognisant of cultural differences and constantly adjusting accordingly, instead of operating on autopilot.

Intercultural competence: the big picture

The attractiveness of intercultural competence as an area of study is its immediate practical relevance. From university-level study-abroad programmes to national-level diversity programmes, the prospect of facilitating the development of intercultural competence is inviting to those who understand the vital role that intercultural competence plays in human interactions across society. Research in intercultural competence spans over several academic disciplines as well as in applied fields. The importance of having some frameworks through which to understand intercultural competence is becoming increasingly recognised, as illustrated for example by the UNESCO (2013) publication on conceptual and operational framework of intercultural competence. There are, of course, some challenges to pervasive and effective development of intercultural competence across multiple levels of society.

First, research in intercultural competence, while receiving increasing input from multiple cultural perspectives, still remains heavily influenced by the developed world whose worldview and access to certain technologies inevitably shape how intercultural competence is studied. One of the challenges of this is that the training methods and tools developed through such research often assume access to certain facilities in order to implement these methods. That may not always be the case in developing countries where resources (including time/means for personal education) are limited.

Second, 'competence' remains a challenging word for many who see it as a Westernised concept that is closely associated with skills and performance. While the word itself may be nuanced appropriately when it comes to intercultural

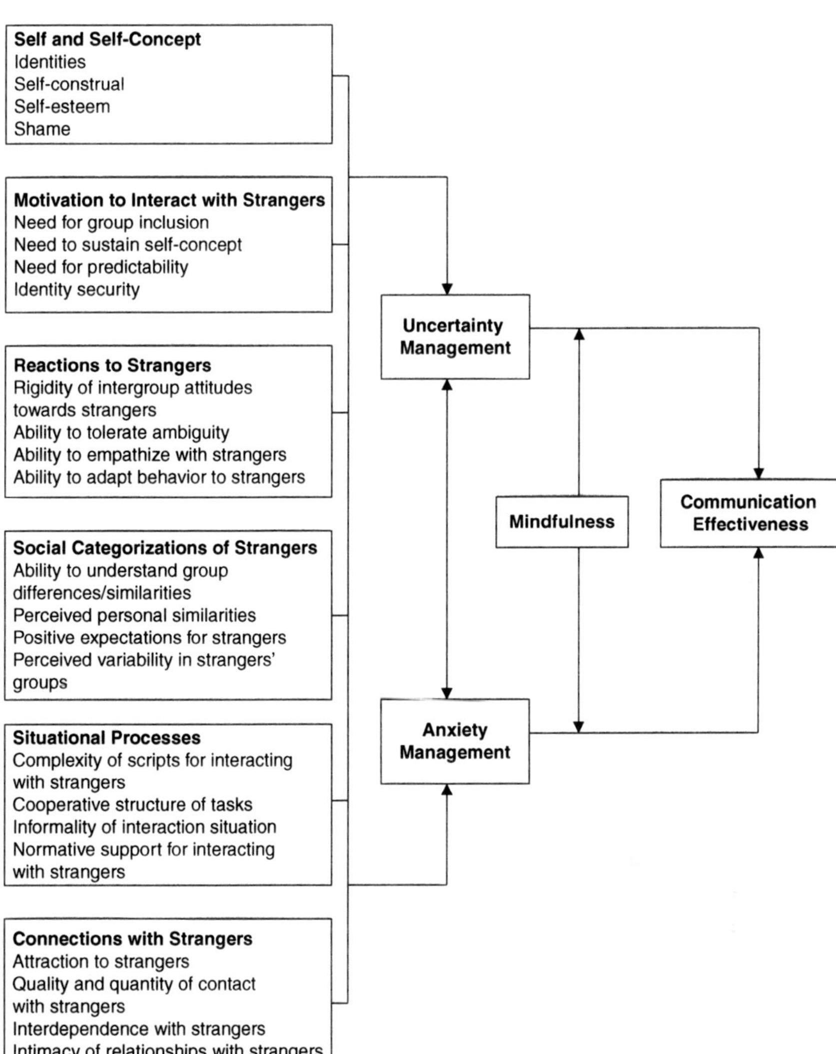

Figure 1.6 Adapted from Gudykunst (2002).

communication, it nevertheless carries a certain bias. It may also be indicative of the bias of the English language in which most known research in intercultural competence is currently available. Until there is room for intercultural dialogue that includes multiple cultural and linguistic perspectives on this subject, we may continue to face this particular challenge.

Third, it is undeniable that intercultural competence has a relational element to it; as such it involves time and patient persistence. Intercultural competence is not something that can be guaranteed, like learning a computer software or learning the lyrics of a new song. In other words, just because you do a short course in intercultural competence does not guarantee that you're going to come out of it 'competent'. It is a learning process, and the learning happens over time. This reality is not compatible with a results-oriented world that wants quick results for the shortest time investment. Some trainers may be tempted to promise just that, to assure a company, for example, that their employees will be 'interculturally competent' if they do their two-hour training course. We as researchers of intercultural competence need to be responsible and cautious when it comes to communicating expectations of a particular intercultural-competence training course or exercise. It is not exciting to advertise that, while short courses do help move us along in our understanding of intercultural competence, developing intercultural competence is a lifelong commitment. Nevertheless, it is the reality that must be communicated.

Fourth, and related to my first point, those of us who are English-speaking researchers from developed countries must be particularly cognisant of the fact that we do not represent the entirety of the world. It is easy to assume that our views are normative. For example, in the preparation of this volume, I was interested to note a curious phenomenon in the case studies. All authors were asked to provide their affiliation – those who were not from the United States provided the name of the institution and the country. Most of those from the United States simply provided the name of the institution, not the country. I am not sure whether this is because they assumed everyone knew where that institution was or because the 'default' country was the United States. Perhaps this was just a fluke. Nevertheless, I think a global mindset demands us to position ourselves in the globe as a representative of a particular cultural perspective, contributing to the larger conversation.

While this is not an exhaustive list, it identifies some of the concerns that we as students, educators, practitioners, and researchers must bear in mind. The more we can draw from multiple disciplinary, cultural, and linguistic perspectives, the richer our understanding of intercultural competence.

References

Alexander, B. K., Arasaratnam, L. A., Avant-Mier, R., Durham, A., Flores, L., Leeds-Hurwitz, W., Mendoza, S. L., Oetzel, J., Osland, J., Tsuda, Y., Yin, J., & Halualani, R. (2014). Identifying key intercultural urgencies, issues, and challenges in today's world: Connecting our scholarship to dynamic contexts and historical moments. *Journal of International and Intercultural Communication*, *7*(1), 38–67.

Arasaratnam, L. A. (2005). Sensation seeking and international students' satisfaction of experiences in the United States. *Journal of Intercultural Communication Research*, *34*, 184–94.

—— (2006). Further testing of a new model of intercultural communication competence. *Communication Research Reports*, *23*(2), 93–9.

—— (2014). Ten years of research in intercultural communication competence: A retrospective. *Journal of Intercultural Communication*, *35*. Retrieved from www.immi.se/intercultural/nr35/arasaratnam.html

—— (2016). Intercultural competence. *Oxford research encyclopedia of communication*. Retrieved from http://communication.oxfordre.com/view/10.1093/acrefore/9780190228613.001.0001/acrefore-9780190228613-e-68?rskey=xHW2UU&result=1

Arasaratnam, L. A., & Banerjee, S. C. (2011). Sensation seeking and intercultural communication competence: A model test. *International Journal of Intercultural Relations*, *35*(2), 226–33.

Arasaratnam, L. A., Banerjee, S. C., & Dembek, K. (2010a). The Integrated Model of Intercultural Communication Competence (IMICC): Model test. *Australian Journal of Communication*, *37*(3), 103–16.

—— (2010b). Sensation seeking and the Integrated Model of Intercultural Communication Competence. *Journal of Intercultural Communication Research*, *39*(2), 69–79.

Arasaratnam, L. A., & Doerfel, M. L. (2005). Intercultural communication competence: Identifying key components from multicultural perspectives. *International Journal of Intercultural Relations*, *29*(2), 137–63.

Bennett, M. J. (1986). A developmental approach to training for intercultural sensitivity. *International Journal of Intercultural Relations*, *10*(2), 179–96.

Bradford, L., Allen, M., & Beisser, K. R. (2000). An evaluation and meta-analysis of intercultural communication competence research. *World Communication*, *29*(1), 28–51.

Byram, M. (1997). *Teaching and assessing intercultural communication competence*. New York, NY: Multilingual Matters.

—— (2014). Twenty-five years on: From cultural studies to intercultural citizenship. *Language, Culture & Curriculum*, *27*(3), 209–25.

Chen, G. M., & Starosta, W. J. (2000). The development and validation of the intercultural communication sensitivity scale. *Human Communication*, *3*, 1–15.

Deardorff, D. K. (2006). The identification and assessment of intercultural competence as a student outcome of internationalization at institutions of higher education in the United States. *Journal of Studies in International Education*, *10*(3), 241–66.

—— (2009). *The Sage handbook of intercultural competence*. Thousand Oaks, CA: Sage.

Dinges, N. (1983). Intercultural competence. In D. Landis & R. W. Brislin (Eds.), *Handbook of intercultural training*, vol. I: *Issues in theory and design* (pp. 176–202). New York, NY: Pergamon.

Ezekiel, R. S. (1968). The personal future and Peace Corps competence. *Journal of Personality and Social Psychology*, *8*(Monograph Supplement, 2, Pt. 2), 1–26.

Fantini, A. E. (2006). *Exploring and assessing intercultural competence*. Brattleboro, VT: Federation of the Experiment in International Living.

—— (2009). Assessing intercultural competence: Issues and tools. In D. K. Deardorff (Ed.), *The Sage handbook of intercultural competence* (pp. 456–76). Thousand Oaks, CA: Sage.

Gardner, G. H. (1962). Cross-cultural communication. *Journal of Social Psychology*, *58*(2), 241–56.

Gudykunst, W. B. (1993). Toward a theory of effective interpersonal and intergroup communication: An anxiety/uncertainty management (AUM) perspective. In R. L. Wiseman & J. Koester (Eds.), *Intercultural communication competence* (pp. 33–71). Newbury Park, CA: Sage.

—— (1995). Anxiety/uncertainty management (AUM) theory. In R. L. Wiseman (Ed.), *Intercultural communication theory* (pp. 8–58). Thousand Oaks, CA: Sage.

Hall, E. T. (1959). *The silent language*. New York, NY: Anchor Books.

Hammer, M. R. (1987). Behavioral dimensions of intercultural effectiveness: A replication and extension. *International Journal of Intercultural Relations, 11*(1), 65–88.

Hammer, M. R., Bennett, M. J., & Wiseman, R. L. (2003). Measuring intercultural sensitivity: The intercultural development inventory. *International Journal of Intercultural Relations, 27*(4), 421–43.

Hammer, M. R., Gudykunst, W. B., & Wiseman, R. L. (1978). Dimensions of intercultural effectiveness: An exploratory study. *International Journal of Intercultural Relations, 2*(4), 382–93.

Ruben, B. D., Askling, L. R., & Kealey, D. J. (1977). Cross-cultural effectiveness. In D. S. Hoopes, P. B. Pedersen, & G. Renwick (Eds.), *Overview of intercultural education, training, and research*, vol. I: *Theory* (pp. 92–105). Washington, DC: Society for Intercultural Education, Training, and Research.

Ruben, B. D., & Kealey, D. J. (1979). Behavioral assessment of communication competency and the prediction of cross-cultural adaptation. *International Journal of Intercultural Relations, 3*(1), 15–47.

Smith, M. B. (1966). Explorations in competence: A study of Peace Corps teachers in Ghana. *American Psychologist, 21*, 555–66.

Spitzberg, B. H., & Changnon, G. (2009). Conceptualizing intercultural competence. In D. K. Deardorff (Ed.), *The Sage handbook of intercultural competence* (pp. 2–52). Thousand Oaks, CA: Sage.

Spitzberg, B. H., & Cupach, W. R. (1984). *Interpersonal communication competence*. Thousand Oaks, CA: Sage.

White, R. W. (1959). Motivation reconsidered: The concept of competence. *Psychological Review, 66*(5), 297–333.

Chapter 2

Rethinking intercultural competence

Cultural humility in internationalising higher education

Jann Murray-García (University of California, Davis) and Melanie Tervalon (Melanie Tervalon Consulting)

The health and well-being of the world's nations and its diverse peoples depend on all nations recognising our collective interdependence and shared destinies. Post-secondary educators occupy an important resource to prepare this and subsequent generations of the world's people to highly value and pursue respectful, mutually beneficial global citizenship.

Intercultural competence is one term used by post-secondary educators worldwide to describe the set of skills and desirable educational outcomes for their students in working towards an optimally healthy world community (Dimitrov, Dawson, Olson, & Meadows, 2014). In this chapter, we use Deardorff's definition of intercultural competence, summarised as 'The effective and appropriate behavior and communication in intercultural situations' (2006, p. 1).

'Cultural competence' is conceptually similar to 'intercultural competence' and is perhaps the most common term used in the United States to refer to optimal training outcomes of health professionals and trainees. 'Cultural competence' is defined as 'A set of congruent behaviors, attitudes, and policies that come together in a system, agency, or among professionals that enables effective work in cross-cultural situations' (Cross, 1989). In the United States, especially in physician training, 'competence' traditionally implies a static endpoint, a sense of mastery, or an ability to exert control towards a predetermined outcome. The notion of 'competence' in our interactions with diverse peoples is therefore unsettling to some, especially to members of and allies to politically disenfranchised groups whose histories in the United States include enslavement, genocide, internment, and economic exploitation (Danieli, 1998; Takaki, 2008). To alert medical educators to the potential pitfalls inherent in the term 'competence' when involved in cross-cultural interactions, the term 'cultural humility' was proposed as an alternative to cultural competence (Tervalon & Murray-García, 1998). Cultural humility is defined as 'a commitment and active engagement in a lifelong process that individuals enter into on an ongoing basis with patients, communities, colleagues, and with themselves' (Tervalon & Murray-García, 1998, p. 118).

Highlighting the distinction between cultural competence and cultural humility exposes important nuances of the cultural frameworks and socio-historical worldviews with which service providers and clinicians approach their patients and administer institutions. For health-profession educators, the distinction often brings into critical perspective the following: what we *think* we are teaching; what we *actually* teach; *how* we teach; *who* is doing the teaching; how we *name* what we teach, and the implications of that naming; and how our students experience our best pedagogical, ideological, and moral intentions across a wide range of trainee cultural backgrounds and developmental levels (Murray-García & García, 2008; Murray-García, Harrell, García, Gizzi, & Simms-Mackey, 2014).

Shared charges and challenges

A substantial proportion of healthcare encounters in the United States are cross-cultural encounters. The United States is a racially, ethnically, linguistically, religiously diverse nation, and that diversity continues to increase (Frey, 2015). Approximately 15 per cent of the US population lives in poverty, but this is highly variable by race/ethnicity and age (Henry J. Kaiser Foundation, 2013). For instance, in 2014, 22 per cent of US children lived in poverty, including 36 per cent of Native American children, 39 per cent of black children, and 32 per cent of Hispanic children (Kids Count Data Center).

In contrast, the relative *lack* of diversity among US physicians intensifies the likelihood that healthcare encounters in the United States will be cross-cultural. The combined percentages of black, Native American, or Hispanic US physicians and medical school faculty are 9 per cent and 5 per cent, respectively (Association of American Medical Colleges [AAMC], 2014, 2016). Over half of US medical students are from families with incomes in the highest quintile of all US families (AAMC, 2008). The resultant demographic mismatch between US physicians and patients coexists with persistent racial, ethnic, and income-based inequalities in health status, healthcare quality, and the allocation of healthcare services (Nelson, Smedley, & Stith, 2002).

Finally, the United States has been a racially segregated nation from its inception, though much less so today. Populations that were geographically displaced and subjected to genocide (Native Americans), captured, exported, and enslaved from Africa to build the wealth of the early United States (African Americans), or whose land underwent forced incorporation into the new nation (Mexican Americans) are still socio-politically and substantially geographically marginalised, on Native American reservations and in 'inner cities'. Many of the nation's poorest new immigrants reside in highly segregated neighbourhoods as well. As it did during the time of the Revd Dr Martin Luther King, Jr., Sunday morning church remains 'the most segregated hour' in the United States, as 86 per cent of those US residents who identify as Christian (75 per cent of the US population) attend churches that are racially homogenous (Newport, 2015; Stetzer, 2015). Because of this high level of racial segregation, and the loss of jobs from central cities to the suburbs, many institutions that train medical students and physicians serve mostly non-white, poor populations. An overwhelmingly white and relatively financially privileged cadre of physicians delivers this clinical service.

Thus, US medicine is learned and practised across a number of racial, cultural, economic, and linguistic borders. We suspect that these contrasts in social status, wealth, and opportunity between US physicians and patients mirror some of the contrasts in social power, resources, and sense of entitlement possessed by some (but not all) of the students who have the opportunity and financial privilege to study abroad, compared with those students and other people they may meet while studying in developed, developing, or otherwise less privileged host nations.

Cultural humility versus cultural competence

Cultural competence initiatives in healthcare and health professions training in the United States began over twenty years ago (Cross, 1989). Today, intercultural competence mandates are a part of curricula and accreditation standards for nearly all US medical schools (LCME, 2013; AAGME, 2013). And yet, even after two decades of instructing, training, and writing in this area of health and human-service professions education, *we remain cautious.*

In the face of intense professional socialisation not to show weakness, along with the intense, 'American' apprehension of being labelled as 'racist', we feared and saw medical students and physicians attempt mastery of cross-cultural interactions as mechanistically as if they were learning and performing the use of a stethoscope, or the reading of an X-ray. In the context of this complex mix of anxieties, motivations, and time pressures of clinical medicine, there exists a dangerous recipe for the ethnocentric stereotyping of socio-culturally, historically, and sometimes linguistically vulnerable patients, transformed into 'the Other', to be successfully manipulated towards a prescribed, satisfactory cultural outcome.

For us, a more forgiving, attainable, and respectful goal for trainees and seasoned clinicians was *humility* rather than competence. We describe

> a process that requires humility as individuals continually engage in self-reflection and self-critique as lifelong learners and reflective practitioners; … A process that requires humility in how physicians bring into check power imbalances that exist in the dynamics of physician-patient communication … and it is a process that requires humility to develop and maintain mutually respectful and dynamic partnerships with communities.
>
> (Tervalon & Murray-García, 1998, p. 188)

It was quite revolutionary twenty years ago for physician education in particular to identify an ongoing developmental process as outcome. The explicit highlighting of this distinction should be embraced by international educators as well.

Lifelong learning and critical self-reflection

As Deardorff (n.d., 2006) and others assert, it seems incumbent upon the international educator to emphasise for students a developmental trajectory in intercultural learning that is lifelong. Students' learning does not begin when they step on the plane or train to their host country, nor does it end when they step foot again on their home soil.

Students deserve the reminder that they arrive in host countries with the shared, and rarely examined, human tendency towards cultural, racial, and religious bias and discrimination. What does that bias towards international students look like in the domestic country, outside of the protective walls of the university community? Chow (2013) describes incredibly hurtful statements and discriminatory experiences international students have experienced on US campuses. In a more extreme example, students of African descent attending one Russian university describe harrowing experiences of fear for their physical safety at the hands of White Supremacist skinheads and others (Mydans, 2003).

Students may not be aware of the histories of colonisation, of conquest, of cultural invasion, and of ongoing marginalisation some host residents may face daily. And yet, these marginalised people and their activities may be some of the most 'exotic' and 'entertaining' of attractions students are encouraged to see while touring their host country. Perhaps they were told to avoid black Americans in the United States (Chow, 2013) but to make sure they attended a hip-hop concert; or not to worry about the relatively poor, low-performing schools of the Zainichi ethnics in Japan (Moon, n.d.); or to pay attention to something other than the lower life expectancies and other health problems of the Maori of New Zealand, except to make sure they attended a Maori cultural festival.

Paltridge, Mayson, and Schapper (2014) report on public discourse in the Australian media that portrays foreign students from China and India as commodities and economic units and as exploiters of the immigration system. Do these media portrayals follow students and play out in the international classroom? If so, how are domestic students in host countries urged to recognise this discrimination against international students and act on their behalf?

We have found that the deliberate cultivation of awareness comes from stimulating self-critique and reflection about biases we often hold for 'the Other'. Self-reflection is taught not as an ethereal activity but as a serious skill and necessary discipline, in what Freire (1970) describes as a lifelong, ongoing cycle of reflection and action in our relationship-building and constructive, humanising service to 'the Other', recognising that 'the Other' is not just someone across a national border but those who are different from us within our own communities.

Multiple pedagogical approaches have been useful in introducing critical self-reflection for medical students who have had little exposure to diversity as well as medical students who have had disenfranchising experiences common to those that many patients face. For example, presenting and exploring compelling data that establish discrimination as fact and present, local reality, and not simply the 'perceptions' of disenfranchised students and peoples, or as only part of the past; the creative use of media, most often provocative cinema, but also poetry, literature, and selections from newspapers and popular trade journals such as *Time* or *Newsweek*; facilitated dialogue across cultures in small groups; directed journaling, with a controversial or provocative prompt; and access to an ongoing, non-judgemental, skilfully facilitated 'community of dialogue' in which to practise our verbal awkwardness in talking about these issues (Murray-García et al., 2005, 2014).

Perhaps what requires the most sustained energy is attention to our own biases as educators. These unrecognised and unscrutinised biases breed power imbalances that can go unchecked and can make for isolating, silencing, and demoralising experiences for international and domestic students from marginalised communities. Sometimes, explicitly or by default, patterns of our nation's historical colonialism get reproduced and uncritiqued within our instructional arenas. This is certainly true of physician educators in Western universities. In the United States, students of colour and students underrepresented in medical school are more likely to report experiencing racial harassment and less supportive social and classroom environments than white students (Orom, Semalulu, & Underwood, 2013). A European Canadian medical student described the denigrating example her clinical teacher set: 'We had a Native man come in and told us he wasn't feeling well or whatever. And we went into the other room and the doctor said, "So do you think this is a dumb Indian or a smart Indian?" And I went, "What?! ... This is a person I'm supposed to be learning from"' (Beagan, 2003, p. 852).

Apparently, the parallel phenomenon of colonialist traditions and values are creeping into the international classroom (Zeleza, 2012; Rennick, 2015). In interviews with Australian academics, Joseph (2012) picked up this sentiment:

> It's high time for university lecturers to become culturally sensitive ... those former colonized nations have been humiliated for more than a century, and many, many lecturers here they don't realize ... but in many Asian eyes they are quite arrogant, Western cultures can be very arrogant ... So I think our lecturers need to have that kind of respect and treat our students decently.
>
> (p. 243)

There is no more powerful lesson than our actions as educators.

As educators, our inability or lack of discipline to do the lifelong, ongoing work of self-reflection and self-critique will limit and undermine our effectiveness in transmitting knowledge and our ability to participate in the transformational promise of international education for a global community.

Mitigating power imbalances

Beyond medical knowledge and clinical skill, US physicians' social standing in society, life opportunities, formal education, parental and current income, and institutional legitimacy *privileges* their knowledge and cultural interpretation of illness episodes and the physician–patient encounter over that of their patients (Joseph, 2012; Tervalon & Murray-García, 1998; Waitzkin, 1993; Wear, 2003). Our socially ascribed mantle of 'privileged knowledge' thus requires an active and repeated laying aside of our assumed expertise and in humility becoming the *students* of our patients (Tervalon & Murray-García, 1998).

Apparently, there is a parallel of this kind of 'privileged knowledge' in the context of 'the politics of knowledge production' in international education as well (Clifford & Montgomery, 2014; Joseph, 2012; Stier, 2004). Joseph (2012) writes, 'There are many cultures, and some through webs of power come to dominate, be it within the classroom or other social spaces. The work of education is, then, to understand power and culture as played out through identity strategies and pedagogical practices within educational spaces' (p. 246). Students, especially those from Western nations and nations with rigid economic or social caste systems, must understand positions of power they may possess, perhaps unknowingly, in host countries (Freire, 1970; Gupta, 2006; Jon, 2012; Roberts, 2014; Stier, 2004). For instance, students must be reminded of the privilege international travel and study is, relative to the opportunities available to the vast majority of peoples worldwide, perhaps even in the host country. Indeed, there are students, too, for whom studying abroad requires great personal and family sacrifice.

We find that many white medical students and physicians in the United States have not experienced their whiteness and their racial reality as a topic of inquiry like other racial minorities have, at least in the United States. Because of the ubiquity of US white cultural symbols in the West and beyond, getting white students to see their privilege in the world is like getting fish to see the water in which they swim (DiAngelo, 2012; Murray-García, 1999).

International educators, too, will likely need to specifically alert white students to how their white skin will often be an incredible source of social power in foreign countries. Educators must name for our students these current patterns and tenacious remnants of white superiority that have survived the demise of colonies decades and even centuries ago to become something like 'White is right. White is smartest. White is best.'

One example with health implications radically reinforces this message: the skin-lightening industry worldwide, despite the danger of mercury and other chemical toxicity, will generate revenue near $20 billion by 2018 (Oaklander, 2014; WHO, 2011). Sixty per cent of the skin products in India are for skin-whitening. In China, Togo, and Nigeria, 40 per cent, over 50 per cent, and over 75 per cent of women respectively, use skin lighteners on a regular basis (WHO, 2011).

Students must be taught to understand that this phenomenon does not require intentionality on the parts of white or Western students to be harmful. In another example, a white male colleague of ours described his intense discomfort and guilt when his host guide told him not to worry about gaining the trust or respect of the students he would be teaching English to in one Asian country. 'After all,' he was told, 'you're a white American male. You will be seen as somewhat of a god over here.'

It can be a painful process to begin this recognition and acknowledgement in the host country. Students will need our guidance, to see and mitigate these power imbalances and *to desire to do so* for the sake of our global community.

We assume that the last thing international educators and students want is for local citizens in a host country to be subjected to imperialistic behaviours of students who have not been taught to 'see' and question their privilege and positionality in the world. For example, Korean students in one study were described by Jon (2012) as being 'grateful for international [Western] students coming to Korea' but expressed unpleasant feelings towards those who came to Korea solely to entertain themselves without experiencing Korean culture or interacting with Korean students.

Ironically, Jon (2012) noted within the same study that domestic (Korean) students at this university 'felt themselves as having lower status than ... and tended to empower those from Western European countries and [those] who spoke English, but discriminate against those from less economically developed and less powerful countries in Asia' (p. 450).

Unexamined power imbalances can mean that higher-status students don't have to embrace and walk through challenges that test them to their core, where transformation takes place.

Our students can miss these opportunities if we don't explicitly teach the value of cultural humility, surrendering an immediate need to 'fix' things or to narrowly see their hosts as responsible for fixing every little thing. Unrecognised or exploitative power imbalances can thus work against transformative learning by feeding a false sense of mastery and 'competence', keeping both students and professors from being open to new ways of negotiating the world (Tervalon & Murray-García, 1998). Thus, cultural humility can be seen as a prerequisite to intercultural competence.

This challenging and important work for physician educators in the United States is to get members of the dominant race and economic class to see their privilege in not having to notice their race and the power one possesses to delegitimise, ignore, or cognitively cast aside the experiences of non-white or poorer peers and patients (DiAngelo, 2012; Murray-García et al., 2005, 2014). This is especially true for students who hold a notion of themselves as wanting to 'help' people, as is true too of international students. Among this group of students, the notion of self-critique and interrogating their privilege can be received as unnecessarily burdensome and as a questioning of their purest of motivations.

Because of US educators' typical avoidance or under-appreciation of the need to openly make visible and critique their nation's racial hierarchy, it is common for us, as African-American female physicians in the United States, to have our clinical judgements or administrative strategies questioned by our more socially privileged students and even colleagues. In writing this, we wonder if host professors are forced to deal with the arrogance of some international students or even professors from sending countries. Would your professor-colleagues be able to tell you about such a phenomenon without you becoming defensive or incredulous? (We have experienced such defensiveness and denial as a challenge and threat to our relationships with physician peers.)

The task of teaching students how to mitigate power imbalances inherent in intercultural encounters thus begins with explicitly identifying and carefully documenting these imbalances for ***and*** with students. Few will see this often painful and awkward process of increasing self-awareness and giving up power as valuable without personally knowing role models who are actively engaged in this lifelong learning and ongoing self-critique and reflection. *We* as professors are some of the most influential role models of cultural humility, often doing our learning publicly, as our mistakes and cultural missteps are on display in the classroom.

Students are relieved to know we as professors are not immune from being misinformed or from possessing subconscious biases that leak out into our behaviour or speech. Students need to see us resist the temptation to become defensive, to anxiously need to explain ourselves in the face of our own ignorance or of having wounded someone. We suspect this 'public learning as role modelling' will look differently in different cultures, but for us, this set of moment-by-moment decisions has to be public and visible to our students. No amount of reading about cultural humility, in our view, can produce the kind of attractive, compelling role models that make the considerable emotional work of this kind of learning worth the present effort or lifelong commitment.

Non-paternalistic mutually beneficial relationships

'I went into the inner city to help/tutor/mentor/work in a health clinic': this is a sentiment we frequently read on medical-school applications when students describe their cross-cultural encounters in the United States. Such cross-class and cross-cultural community service is often an unwritten requirement to get into medical schools in the United States. A critical, societal-level perspective on why the United States has a perpetual population of 'disadvantaged' or 'minority' peoples is not a requirement of such experiences. Young people can be largely unaware of long-standing structural issues that daily further entrench US inequality. There is a void of instructional leadership present to connect the dots and explore the socio-historical and political factors that create this inequality, not only across nations but often across neighbourhoods within the same US city (Coates, 2015; Hernandez, 2009; Metzl & Hansen, 2014).

Thus, such volunteer work, often performed with missionary zeal, has the potential to be both laudable ***and*** exploitative of the disenfranchised whom we need in our autobiographical scripts of heroic service (Freire, 1970). This uninterrogated community service risks a toxic, paternalistic approach that can lead to students feeling great about themselves, that they 'helped' those who 'need' them, and secured an experience that will look good on medical-school applications.

However, they often emerge from these experiences untrained to see the generations of adaptive strengths within disenfranchised communities. Furthermore, it can lead disenfranchised communities that to some degree depend on this assistance nonetheless feeling used.

As with US medical students, international students stand to lose a deep appreciation and insistence on the expertise and essential contribution of the least powerful and the most likely historically and presently silenced. Can you imagine a problem-solving curriculum featuring cross-national purpose building and commitment to the healthiest of global communities and citizenry, without students knowing how to listen and create the emotional, relational, and physical spaces for the disenfranchised to share their gifts and unique insight into how we create the best possible and most sustainable world community?

This is as true in the classroom as it is within the institutions in which our students learn both an official as well as an unwritten or hidden curriculum (Murray-García & García, 2008). The witnessed institutional 'curriculum' and climate often speaks 'louder' than anything we could teach or model as individuals. Individual and institutional actions can contradict and undermine the most noble of platitudes and goals.

Conclusion

As US health-professions educators and international educators, our tasks in preparing our students for respectful, effective cross-cultural interactions are in some ways strikingly similar. The distinction between cultural competence and cultural humility is one that we have found helpful as educators in both identifying outcomes and honouring our educational tasks to inspire and nurture an active, ongoing, lifelong developmental process. Cultural humility is a process that continually asks us to leverage the life skills of self-reflection and courageous self-critique. Cultural humility asks us to interrupt and mitigate power imbalances that we create or have otherwise inherited and sometimes subconsciously or intentionally perpetuate or worsen. And cultural humility asks us to honour, search out, and highlight the expertise that resides in nations and communities that are often on the short end of the power dynamic because of past and ongoing geographic, economic, cultural, and intellectual exploitation and colonialism.

International educators are at the precarious intersection of economic motivation, professional advancement, devotion to a sustainable global community, and inspiring student connections for cross-cultural learning and understanding. The ideal student connections result from international education that will nurture respect and interdependence rather than the economic plunder of an increasingly lucrative global export commodity (post-secondary education) and the reproduction of hierarchies that harm us all.

We believe we share this daily challenge with international educators. Our desire is to go far beyond equipping our students with the professional privilege and technical ability to exploit new geographic, financial, and social territory. Rather, we aim to inculcate students and trainees with an undeniable and irresistible sense of our shared humanity. The full expression of this shared humanity depends on us eliminating the risk of reproducing patterns of devaluing, dehumanisation, inequality, and exploitation that have defined much of our cross-cultural training, international dialogue, and educational pedagogy.

References

Association of American Medical Colleges (AAMC). (2008a). Diversity of US families by parental income. Retrieved from www.aamc.org/download/102338/data/aibvol8no1.pdf

—— (2008b). Diversity of US medical students by parental income. Retrieved from www.aamc.org/download/102338/data/aibvol8no1.pdf

—— (2014). Physicians by race, ethnicity, and sex, 2013. Retrieved from http://aamcdiversityfactsandfigures.org/section-ii-current-status-of-us-physician-workforce/#fig1

—— (2016). US medical school faculty, 2015. Retrieved from www.aamc.org/data/facultyroster/reports/453490/usmsf15.html

Accreditation Council for Graduate Medical Education (ACGME). (2013). ACGME common program requirements. Retrieved from www.acgme.org/acgmeweb/Portals/0/PFAssets/ProgramRequirements/CPRs2013.pdf

Beagan, B. L. (2003). 'Is this worth getting into a big fuss over?' Everyday racism in medical school. *Medical Education*, *37*(10), 852–60.

Chow, Y. (2013) Race, racism, and international students in the United States. Retrieved from www.nacada.ksu.edu/Resources/Academic-Advising-Today/View-Articles/Race--Racism--and-International-Students-in-the-United-States.aspx

Clifford, V., & Montgomery, C. (2014). Challenging conceptions of western higher education and promoting graduates as global citizens. *Higher Education Quarterly*, *68*(1), 28–45.

Coates, T. (2014). The case for reparations. *The Atlantic*. June. Retrieved from www.theatlantic.com/magazine/archive/2014/06/the-case-for-reparations/361631/

Coates, T. (2015). *Between the world and me*. New York, NY: Random House.

Cross, T. L. (1989). Towards a culturally competent system of care: A monograph on effective services for minority children who are severely emotionally disturbed. Retrieved from http://files.eric.ed.gov/fulltext/ED330171.pdf

Danieli, Y. (Ed.) (1998). *International handbook of multigenerational legacies of trauma*. New York, NY: Plenum.

Deardorff, D. K. (n.d). Theory reflections: Intercultural competence framework/model. Retrieved from www.nafsa.org/_/file/_/theory_connections_intercultural_competence.pdf

—— (2006). Identification and assessment of intercultural competence as a student outcome of internationalization. *Journal of Studies in International Education*. *10*(3), 241–66.

DiAngelo, R. (2012). *What Does It Mean to Be White? Developing White Racial Literacy*. New York, NY: Peter Lang.

Dimitrov, N., Dawson, D., Meadows, K., & Olsen, K. (2014). Developing the intercultural competence of graduate students. *Canadian Journal of Higher Education*, *43*(3), 86–103.

Freier, P. (1970). *Pedagogy of the oppressed*. New York, NY: Herder and Herder.

Freire, P. (2007). *Pedagogy of the oppressed* (M. B. Ramos, Trans.). New York, NY: Continuum. First published 1970.

Frey, W. (2015). In the US, diversity is the new majority. *Los Angeles Times*. 6 March. Retrieved from www.latimes.com/opinion/op-ed/la-oe-0310-frey-no-racial-majority-america-20150310-story.html

Gupta, A. (2006). Affirmative action in higher education in India and the US: A study in contrasts. University of California, Berkeley, Center for Studies in Higher Education.

Henry J. Kaiser Family Foundation. (2013) Distribution of US population by race/ethnicity, 2010–50. 18 March. Retrieved from http://kff.org/disparities-policy/slide/distribution-of-u-s-population-by-raceethnicity-2010-and-2050/

—— (2016) Poverty rate by race and ethnicity. Retrieved from http://kff.org/other/state-indicator/poverty-rate-by-raceethnicity/

Hernandez, J. (2009). Redlining revisited: mortgage lending patterns in Sacramento 1930–2004. *International Journal of Urban and Regional Research*, *33*(2), 291–313.

Herriot, P., & Pemberton, C. (1995). *Competitive advantage through diversity: Organizational learning from difference*. Thousand Oaks, CA: Sage.

Jon, J. (2012). Power dynamics with international students: From the perspective of domestic students in Korean higher education. *Higher Education*, *64*(4), 441–54.

Joseph, C. (2012). Internationalizing the curriculum: Pedagogy for social justice. *Current Sociology*, *60*(2), 239–57.

Kids Count Data Center. (2017). Kids in poverty by race and ethnicity. Retrieved from http://datacenter.kidscount.org/data/tables/44-children-in-poverty-by-race-and-ethnicity#detailed/1/any/false/869,36,868,867,133/10,11,9,12,1,185,13/324,323

Krieger, N. (1996). Inequality, diversity and health: Thoughts on 'race/ethnicity' and 'gender'. *Journal of the American Medical Women's Association*, *51*(4), 133–6.

Liaison Committee on Medical Education (LCME). (2013). Function and structure of a medical school. Retrieved from www.lcme.org/publications/functions2013june.pdf

Metzl, J. M., & Hansen, H. (2014). Structural competency: Theorizing a new medical engagement with stigma and inequality. *Social Science & Medicine*, *103*, 126–33.

Moon, R. (n.d.) Koreans in Japan. Stanford Program on International and Cross-Cultural Education. Retrieved from http://spice.fsi.stanford.edu/docs/koreans_in_japan

Murray-García, J. (1999). The public's health, its national identity, and the continuing dilemma of minority status. *Journal of Health Care for the Poor and Underserved*, *10*(4), 397–408.

Murray-García, J., & García, J. A. (2008). The institutional context of multicultural education: What is your institutional curriculum? *Academic Medicine*, *83*(7), 646–52.

Murray-García, J. L., Harrell, S., García, J. A., Gizzi, E., & Simms-Mackey, P. (2005). Self-reflection in multicultural training: Be careful what you ask for. *Academic Medicine*, *80*(7), 694–701.

—— (2014). Dialogue as skill: Training a US physician workforce that can talk about race. *American Journal of Orthopsychiatry*, *84*(5), 590–6.

Mydans, S. (2003). African students' harsh lesson: Racism is astir in Russia. *New York Times*. 18 December. Retrieved from www.nytimes.com/2003/12/18/world/moscow-journal-african-students-harsh-lesson-racism-is-astir-in-russia.html

Nelson, A., Smedley, B., & Stith, A. (Eds.) (2002). *Unequal treatment: Confronting racial and ethnic disparities in health care*. Washington, DC: National Academies Press.

Newport, F. (2015). Percentage of Christians in US drifting down, but still high. *US Gallop Daily*. Retrieved from www.gallup.com/poll/187955/percentage-christians-drifting-down-high.aspx

Oaklander, M. (2014). Skin whitening candy is coming. *Time Magazine*. 26 August. Retrieved from http://time.com/3181942/skin-whitening-candy/

Orom, H., Semalulu, T., & Underwood III, W. (2013). The social and learning environments experienced by underrepresented minority medical students: A narrative review. *Academic Medicine*, *88*(11), 1765–77.

Paltridge, T., Mayson, S., & Schapper, J. (2014). Welcome and exclusion: An analysis of *The Australian* newspaper's coverage of international students. *Higher Education*, *68*(1), 103–16.

Pew Research Center. (2013). The most (and least) culturally diverse countries in the world. 18 July. Retrieved from www.pewresearch.org/fact-tank/2013/07/18/the-most-and-least-culturally-diverse-countries-in-the-world/

Redden, E. (2012). 'I'm not racist but'. *Inside Higher Education*. 16 October. Retrieved from www.insidehighered.com/news/2012/10/16/tensions-simmer-between-american-and-international-students

Rennick, J. (2015). Learning that makes a difference: Pedagogy and practice for learning abroad. *Teaching and Learning Inquiry*, *3*(2), 71–88.

Roberts, A. (2014). Why caste still matters in India. *The Economist*. 24 February. Retrieved from www.economist.com/blogs/economist-explains/2014/02/economist-explains-9

Spring, J. (2008). Research on globalization and education. *Review of Educational Research*, *78*(2), 330–63.

Stetzer, E. (2015). The most segregated hour of the week? Reflections on church diversity on Martin Luther King, Jr. Retrieved from www.christianitytoday.com/edstetzer/2015/january/most-segregated-hour-of-week.html

Stier, J. (2004). Taking a critical stance toward internationalization ideologies in higher education: Idealism, instrumentalism and educationalism. *Globalisation, Societies and Education*, *2*(1), 1–28.

Takaki, R. (2008). *A different mirror. A history of multicultural America* (rev. edn). New York, NY: Little Brown & Company.

Tervalon, M. (2003). Components of culture in health for medical students' education. *Academic Medicine*, *78*(6), 570–6.

Tervalon, M., & Murray-Garcia, J. (1998). Cultural humility versus cultural competence: A critical distinction in defining physician training outcomes in multicultural education. *Journal of Health Care for the Poor and Underserved*, *9*(2), 117–25.

Waitzkin, H. (1993). *The politics of medical encounters: How patients and doctors deal with social problems.* New Haven, CT: Yale University Press.

Wear, D. (2003). Insurgent multiculturalism: Rethinking how and why we teach culture in medical education. *Academic Medicine, 78*(6), 549–54.

What is cultural competence? (Office of Minority Health) HRSA. Retrieved from www.hrsa.gov/culturalcompetence/index.html

World Health Organisation (WHO). (2011). Mercury in skin lightening products. Retrieved from www.who.int/ipcs/assessment/public_health/mercury_flyer.pdf

Zeleza, P. T. (2012). Internationalization in higher education: Opportunities and challenges for the Knowledge Project in the Global South. *Internationalisation of Higher Education: Perspectives from the South. SARUA Leadership Dialogue Series, 2*(2), 6–18.

Chapter 3

The role of empathy in fostering intercultural competence

Carolyn Calloway-Thomas (Indiana University), Lily A. Arasaratnam-Smith (Alphacrucis College), and Darla K. Deardorff (Duke University)

Given the turmoil of the present age, one could argue that intercultural competence is desperately needed. Much of the literature on intercultural competence includes references to empathy (Calloway-Thomas, 2010; Arasaratnam, 2014; Spitzberg & Changnon, 2009). Yet what is empathy, what is the context of empathy, and how can this essential element of intercultural competence be addressed specifically within international higher education? In other words, what are the empathetic literacies that need further attention within the development of intercultural competence? This chapter briefly traces the stages of development of empathy, examines its role in intercultural competence, explores three principles of empathetic literacies that are essential to developing comprehensive intercultural competence, and engages with empathy in the context of international higher education.

Empathy

Of all the sentiments that have the potential to alter what we do interculturally and especially in higher education, none is more important than empathy.

Empathy is the moral glue that holds civil society together; unless humans have robust habits of mind and reciprocal behaviour that lead to empathy, society as we know it will crumble. In his book, *Concern for Others*, Kitwood (1990) gives one of the clearest and most concise reasons why empathy matters: 'our countless small and unreflective actions toward each other, and the patterns of living and relating which each human being gradually creates. It is here that we are systematically respected or discounted, accepted or rejected, enhanced or diminished in our personal being' (p. 149; qtd. in Vetlesen, 1994, p. 9).

And what is the meaning of this complex term, *empathy*? Empathy is a difficult concept to grasp. That is the great historical and philosophical fact that we must face at the outset. The term we call *empathy* was first coined in the mid-nineteenth century by Vischer (1994), who aligned it with the psychological theory of art. Vischer and others attributed it not to its present usage of feeling for and with others but more aesthetically, to art. Their observations revealed that a strong empathy must obtain between performer and listener/reader in order for the latter to understand, 'feel', or 'experience' the aesthetic object, whether a poem, a play, an opera, a jazz composition, or a novel.

In nineteenth-century Germany, Kant and Hegel saw *Einfuhlung* (empathy) as a vehicle for the 'expression of feelings and emotions' (Weiner, 1974, p. 2). By the mid-1900s, empathy was no longer thought of as merely a feeling for an aesthetic object but rather had evolved into the rubric of *empathy*, a term coined by American psychologist Tichener (1909) as a translation of the German *Einfuhlung*.

Part of the difficulty in defining empathy lies in the complex nature of the concept. Another difficulty is that there is 'no complete agreement on the purpose of empathy ... in the literature', as Ridley and Lingle (1996, p. 23) observe. Within intercultural competence literature, research in empathy has often relied on an early definition by Ruben (1976) who characterises empathy as, 'the capacity to clearly project an interest in others as well as to obtain and reflect a reasonably complete and accurate sense of another's thoughts, feelings, and/or experiences' (p. 340). In one sense, empathy means other-regarding and the 'generation of concern for the well-being of recipients' (Ridley & Lingle, 1996, p. 23). In another sense, empathy is not necessarily other-regarding and may serve unkind as well as kind purposes, as Fontaine (2001) observes. The term *empathy*, as it will be employed here, is the ability 'imaginatively' to enter into and participate in the world of the cultural 'Other' cognitively, affectively, and behaviourally. This is consistent with the conceptualisation of empathy in intercultural competence literature.

Having posited this working definition, it is also important to recognise the capaciousness of the term because, as Holzwarth (2004) points out, 'If we can enter imaginatively into the mind of one who suffers, why can we not do the same with one who causes suffering?' (p. 2). Holzwarth's notion is significant for what it reveals about the very nature and uses of empathy: 'When we discover in ourselves the emotional capacity to engage the experiences of another, we realize that this capacity can apply almost anywhere' (2004, p. 2). And it can certainly apply to international higher education, where opportunities pose new challenges and opportunities for awareness of cultural differences as students interact with culturally different others.

Empathy as an explanatory concept for understanding why people behave as they do with certain consequences can be pursued only so far. However, as Italian philosopher Giambattista Vico (1968) and German poet and critic Johann Gottfried Herder observe, although cultures differ in historical context, customs, traditions, attitudes, beliefs, and practices, humans are endowed with faculties that make them capable of understanding others across time and space. The notion of 'imaginative placement' or 'feeling one's way into' another constitutes the essence of the term *empathy*.

Vital to understanding the idea of imaginative placement and its implications for crafting intercultural competence on campuses is the reciprocal relationship between two interacting individuals, whether a professor or an administrator, even if one is not physically present. This process, in a practical and tender way, also includes the notion of feelings. 'To feel yourself into everything' implies emotional participation in another person's experience. The connection between empathy and feeling is seen as a 'bridge to civility', to use Berman's term (1998). Some scholars also argue that empathy can be divided into stages. Thus, it becomes important to focus on this aspect next to demonstrate the vitality of the concept for understanding global human affairs and for fostering intercultural competence.

Barriers to developing (intercultural) empathy

In developing intercultural empathy, it is important for educators to be aware of the barriers that may hinder this development. According to Zhu (2011, p. 117), there are several barriers to developing intercultural empathy including the following:

1. stereotypes and prejudices that may lead to negative inferences towards others;
2. overreliance on human universals without paying attention to cultural differences;
3. lack of awareness of cultural differences, especially in underlying values patterns of thinking;
4. 'indiscriminate application' of one's own cultural practices.

Higher education institutions, as well as educators themselves, need to examine their curriculum and programmes to ensure that such barriers are addressed and that adequate measures are put in place to overcome such barriers as much as possible.

Stages of empathy

How is empathy developed? Drawing on Husserlian intersubjectivity, Depraz (2001, p. 172) argues that 'lived empathy' has 'four different and complementary states':

1. a passive association of my lived body with your body;
2. an imaginative self-transposal in your psychic states;
3. an interpretive understanding of yourself as being an alien to me;
4. an ethical responsibility towards yourself as a person (enjoying and suffering).

The first type of empathy is passive and serves to recognise the Other as a moving, breathing, and living human being. Although this stage is primal, it is significant in promoting human consciousness because it allows us to identify the Other as belonging to the human species. Thompson (2001) believes that this sort of empathy is manifest in an 'immediate pairing or coupling of the bodies of self and other in action' (p. 17).

The second level of empathy, according to Depraz (2001), occurs when one moves from perceiving 'global resemblance of our body-style' to being able spontaneously to transpose oneself into the self of the other. This stage clearly relates to Vico's notion of exploring different ways of living (Berlin, 1991). *True* empathy relies heavily on being able to understand mental states that the other might not have experienced at first hand. What is critical for the development of intercultural competence, however, is the notion that humans have the capacity to 'transpose' others' feelings into their own.

The third step involves understanding and communication. At this stage, one expresses (verbal or not) and interprets others' views, which lead to understanding (and also misunderstanding). This stage involves a human's ability to explain, predict, and describe the sentiments of others.

The final stage of empathy that Depraz (2001) offers is ethical responsibility. And although she does not offer a fully developed elaboration of what is meant by ethics in all of its permutations, Depraz does suggest that ethics involves 'affection and considering the other as having emotions: suffering, enjoying' (2001, p. 173). In this respect, Depraz's fourth stage is in line with other accounts of empathy that privileges emotions.

Empathy and intercultural competence

The relationship between empathy and intercultural competence is well established. In an early study, Ruben and Kealey (1979) identified empathy as one of seven variables instrumental for effective cross-cultural adaptation. They characterise empathy as the 'capacity to "put oneself in another's shoes" – or to behave as if one could' (Ruben and Kealey, 1979, p. 17). Similar findings were replicated in later studies; for example, in a study in which lay persons representing fifteen countries were asked to describe the qualities of a competent intercultural communicator, empathy was one of the five qualities that were common in all responses (Arasaratnam & Doerfel, 2005). Research in intercultural competence is in fact replete with evidence of the positive relationship between empathy and intercultural competence. (Cultural) empathy has been associated with cooperation and problem-solving (Euwema & Van Emmerik, 2007), intercultural effectiveness (Herfst, Van Oudenhoden, & Timmerman, 2008; Nesdale 2012) and with intercultural competence itself (Gibson & Zhong, 2005). In terms of assessment, there are a number of quantitative instruments, one of which is the Cultural Empathy Subscale of the Multicultural Personality Questionnaire (Van der Zee & Van Oudenhoven, 2000), which is influenced by Ruben and Kealey's early works.

The role of empathy in intercultural competence cannot be overstated. Arasaratnam, Banerjee, & Dembek (2010), for example, found that there is a direct causal relationship between empathy and intercultural competence as well as between empathy and positive attitudes towards people of other cultures and active listening, both of which are also variables associated with intercultural competence in wider research. There is even evidence to suggest that empathy compensates for instances when one has no prior experiences in intercultural communication (Arasaratnam, 2006). Empathy thus must be a key component of any programme designed to facilitate the development of intercultural competence.

Towards empathetic literacy

Being human means that a person is attuned properly to the wishes and concerns of others in civil society. 'Accustom yourself not to be inattentive to what another person says', notes Aurelius, and 'as far as possible, enter into his mind' (1983, 6.53). But not all human beings are attentive enough, respectful, and caring towards others, despite intercultural training in colleges and universities; this is where a programme of empathetic literacy can gain resonance.

Empathetic literacy matters because it is necessary to focus on skills and competencies that will make us better world citizens, oiling the cultural machinery of goodwill. Empathetic literacy is defined as knowledge and information-based skills that help global citizens respond to and manage intercultural encounters caringly and competently. Empathetic citizens should have the ability to understand, analyse, interpret, and communicate ideas, feelings, and behaviour across a range of intercultural settings within and beyond one's own society.

Although the principles and basic curriculum of pedagogy of empathy might vary cognitively and geographically, the following set of conceptual principles is essential.

Global respect

The notion of the 'dignity of humanity in every other man' or woman, then, plays a key role in understanding a real value of empathetic literacy. In fact, this element of empathy can be found in the Universal Declaration of Human Rights. Given the centrality of respect, how do we show we value the other as a human being? We should be inclined to show this respect both verbally and non-verbally, especially when we disagree with others' beliefs, values, and opinions. In communicating with a person from another culture, we should actively search for ways to elevate humanity and not denigrate it. Above all, we should resist any move towards dehumanisation of the other, which would include the use of destructive stereotypes. We should routinise and add huge doses of kindness to our repertoire of quotidian, everyday behaviour and seek out individual connections with others and in particular those who are 'not like us'. In this crucial way, empathy can perform a lubricating function, making a difference on college campuses by using methods and skills that stress respect for the dignity of all.

Mutuality

Mutuality is the notion of trying to find common understanding within an intercultural encounter. Although there are fascinating variations in human culture – from campus to campus, from region to region, and from society to society – if we are to succeed in communicating interculturally, we must also search for significant or deeper points of similarity within cultures. Some scholars assume that there are many things that unite us. Murdock (1945) reminds us that all people have a concept of beauty, follow rules of etiquette, tell jokes, dance, make music, feel anger, participate in sports, gather food, and use systems of economic exchange, ranging from the euro to the nira. And while these similarities are indeed true at the universal level, there are certainly differences at the cultural and individual levels, which become core to navigating the complexities of human relationships.

In our efforts at seeking mutuality, we should keep the similarities that bind us to others in the foreground as we explore the differences, be they cultural, religious, socio-economic, gender, and so on. In communicating with a person from a different background, we should actively search for some mutual ground that allows for an authentic exchange of ideas and feelings. This search for common ground requires curiosity and openness, meaning that we must be willing to entertain ideas and beliefs that might not be consistent with our own worldview.

Trust

Trust is the bond that holds societies together, and it urgently demands attention, especially in post-conflict societies. Fukuyama (1995) maintains that the drive for social capital is deep and meaningful. Trust undergirds most aspects of society, including ethical habits, common purposes, norms, and values. Most crucially, the communitarian principle of trust tells another human being how much faith one has in his or her ideas and values, and whether the person should be taken seriously. Trust is the essential element in building relationships with others, both within and beyond one's 'moral circle', which is considered to be a key goal of intercultural competence (Hofstede, Pedersen, & Hofstede, 2002).

Implications for higher education institutions

In developing intercultural competence within courses and programmes at higher education institutions, the aspect of empathy becomes critical to address. Specifically, how are institutions prepared to address empathetic literacy of global respect, mutuality, and trust? Let's take a closer look at the contexts of international higher education and healthcare education.

Healthcare education

Quite a few higher education institutions have programmes related to health care, given its critical place within any society. Empathy – and specifically cultural empathy – is already playing a role within healthcare courses, in particular because empathy is the primary element in cultural competence as described by healthcare scholars (Gibson & Zhang, 2005). Empathy is challenging, though, for healthcare providers since 'Understanding the needs of the patient is often complicated by differences in beliefs, values, health behaviour and communication style preferences between cultural groups' (Logan, Steel, & Hunt, 2014, p. 10). Nonetheless, there has been quite a bit research around empathy in healthcare contexts that advocates for a multidimensional model of empathy that encompasses both cognitive and non-cognitive processes, along with emotional and behavioural dimensions (Davis, 1996; Larson & Yao, 2005). In the healthcare context, there is evidence to suggest that patients do not perceive practitioners as genuinely empathetic unless there is some emotional engagement (Morse et al., 1992; Stepien & Baernstein, 2006). This points to the importance of the patient perspective in developing healthcare professionals' empathy. A key implication then, for higher education institutions, is not to address empathy in the abstract but to understand the role of empathy in specific contexts including how crucial perceived *authentic* empathy is from the perspective of the interactants. This means that partnerships between interactants become increasingly important; according to Anand and Lahiri (2009), 'Together, providers and patients co-create interculturally competent health care that is respectful and effective. Only through these partnerships can we ensure optimal patient outcomes' (p. 401). In addition, advances have been made in assessing this multidimensional element of empathy within healthcare contexts through such measures as the classic questionnaires from Hogan (1969) and Mehrabian & Epstein (1972) which remain in use today along with Davis's Interpersonal Reactivity Index developed in 1983, the Empathy Construct Rating Scale (La Monica, 1981), the Empathic Understanding Subscale of the Barrett–Lennard Relation Inventory (BLRI; 1962, 1969), the Jefferson Scale of Physician Empathy (Hojat et al., 2002), the Reynolds Empathy Scale (Reynolds, 2000), and the Consultation And Relational Empathy (CARE) Measure (Mercer, Maxwell, Heaney, & Watt, 2004). Higher education in general could benefit and build on the work done within healthcare education around the development and measurement of empathy within culturally competent care.

International higher education

There are several levels at which empathy can be addressed within international higher education, from courses to partnerships.

At the course level, curricula in any discipline can be reviewed and mapped as to what extent do curricula foster respect and mutuality, as well as trust. For example, the principles undergirding empathy can manifest in the following questions which educators can explore about their own courses:

- How are different viewpoints represented? By whom?
- Who is telling whose story?

- What are the significant deeper points of human connection around a particular issue or topic?
- What more needs to be learned about this topic or issue?
- What are the common goals and purposes within this topic?
- What are the underlying assumptions, ideas, and values? How might these be similar and/or different from those holding a different set of assumptions, ideas, and values?

At the programme level, such as a study-abroad or service-learning programme, such programmes can be reviewed as to what extent the stages of empathy are addressed in orientation programmes and to what extent authentic human interactions are integrated into the programme. In particular, the mutuality of the interaction becomes incredibly important. Too often, the power dynamic between the interactants may be such that the sojourner is motivated by a desire 'to help' the other when in regard to true mutuality it becomes more about an attitude of 'what can I learn?' and 'how can we work together toward a common goal?' What common goals are being addressed *together*? Institutions need to take a careful look at how all impacted communities benefit from the presence of international and exchange students and examine the nature of reciprocity that is occurring, being mindful of Freire's observation that

> In this phenomenon, the invaders penetrate the cultural context of another group, in disrespect of the latter's potentialities; they impose their own view of the world upon those they invade and inhibit the creativity of the invaded by curbing their expression. All domination involves invasion – at times physical and overt, at times camouflaged, with the invader assuming the role of a helping friend.
>
> (2000, p. 150)

At the institutional level, partnerships and agreements can be reviewed in terms of the extent of mutuality found within such agreements. How is each institution benefiting the other? What is each institution gaining and learning from the other? How are the behaviours/responses of one institution perceived and received by the other? Does the partnership exist so that both can benefit or is one institution privileged over the other? What is the degree of trust between the institutions? How do the institutions/partners demonstrate respect? Partnerships and agreements need to model the three empathetic literacies discussed in this chapter: global respect, mutuality, and trust.

Conclusion

As the moral glue that holds civil society together, as well as a core component of intercultural competence, empathy is increasingly important to address within higher education institutions, from the curriculum to programmes to institutional matters such as partnerships. Embracing the three principles of empathetic literacies – that of global respect, mutuality, and trust – is essential at all levels of an institution, regardless of the institutional and geographic context. Moreover, empathy cannot be addressed in the abstract but rather needs to be considered within specific contexts from the perspectives of all interactants and as multidimensional beyond cognitive processes to also include non-cognitive, emotional, and behavioural dimensions. In the end it becomes more about our responsibility to others – both individually and institutionally – than about loyalty to oneself. Empathy in the big picture is about what makes us human for, as Seneca (1995) stated, 'while we still remain among human beings, let us cultivate humanity'.

References

Anand, R., & Lahiri, I. (2009). Developing skills for interculturally competent care. In D. K. Deardorff (Ed.), *The Sage handbook of intercultural competence* (pp. 387–402). Thousand Oaks, CA: Sage.

Arasaratnam, L. A. (2006). Further testing of a new model of intercultural communication competence. *Communication Research Reports, 23*(4), 93–9.

—— (2014). Ten years of research in intercultural communication competence: A retrospective. *Journal of Intercultural Communication, 35.* Retrieved from www.immi.se/intercultural/nr35/arasaratnam.html

Arasaratnam, L. A., Banerjee, S. C., & Dembek, K. (2010). The integrated model of intercultural communication competence (IMICC): Model test. *Australian Journal of Communication, 37*(3), 103–16.

Arasaratnam, L. A., & Doerfel, M. L. (2005). Intercultural communication competence: Identifying key components from multicultural perspectives. *International Journal of Intercultural Relations, 29*(2), 137–63.

Aurelius, M. (1983). *Meditations* (G. M. A. Grube, Trans.). Indianapolis, IN: Hackett.

Barrett-Lennard, G. T. (1962). Dimensions of therapist response as causal factors in therapeutic change. *Psychological Monographs*: General and Applied, 76(43), 1.

Barrett-Lennard, G. T. (1969). *Technical note on the 64-item revision of the Relationship Inventory.* University of Waterloo.

Berlin, I. (1991). *The crooked timber of humanity: Chapters in the history of ideas.* New York, NY: Knopf.

Berman, S. H. (1998). The bridge to civility: Empathy, ethics, and service. *School Administrator, 55*(5), 27–32.

Calloway-Thomas, C. (2010). *Empathy in the global world: An intercultural perspective.* Thousand Oaks, CA: Sage.

Davis, M. H. (1983). Measuring individual differences in empathy: Evidence for a multidimensional approach. *Journal of Personality and Social Psychology, 44*(1), 113–26.

—— (1996). *Empathy: A social-psychological approach.* Oxford: Westview Press.

Depraz, N. (2001). The Husserlian theory of intersubjectivity as alterology: Emergent theories and wisdom traditions in the light of genetic phenomenology. *Journal of Consciousness Studies, 8*(5–6), 169–78.

Euwema, M. C., & Van Emmerik, I. J. H. (2007). Intercultural competencies and conglomerated conflict behaviors in intercultural conflicts. *International Journal of Intercultural Relations*, *31*(4), 427–41.

Fontaine, P. (2001). The changing place of empathy in welfare economics. *History of Political Economy*, *33*(3), 387–409.

Freire, P. (2000). *Pedagogy of the oppressed*. New York, NY: Continuum.

Fukuyama, F. (1995). *Trust: Social Virtues and the Creation of Prosperity*. New York, NY: Free Press.

Gibson, D. W., & Zhong, M. (2005). Intercultural communication competence in the healthcare context. *International Journal of Intercultural Relations*, *29*(5), 621–34.

Herfst, S. L., Van Oudenhoven, J. P., & Timmerman, M. E. (2008). Intercultural effectiveness training in three Western immigrant countries: A cross-cultural evaluation of critical incidents. *International Journal of Intercultural Relations*, *32*(1), 67–80.

Hofstede, G. J., Pedersen, P. B., & Hofstede, G. (2002). *Exploring culture: Exercises, stories and synthetic cultures*. Yarmouth, ME: Intercultural Press.

Hogan, R. (1969). Development of an empathy scale. *Journal of Consulting and Clinical Psychology*, *33*(3), 307–16.

Hojat, M., Gonnella, J. S., Nasca, T. J., Mangione, S., Vergare, M., & Magee, M. (2002). Physician empathy: definition, components, measurement, and relationship to gender and specialty. *American Journal of Psychiatry*, *159*, 1563–9.

Holzwarth, J. (2004). Liberty's horizons: Politics and the value of cultural attachment. Unpublished doctoral dissertation, Department of Politics, Princeton University.

Kant, I. (1991). *The metaphysics of morals* (M. Gregory, Trans.). Cambridge: Cambridge University Press.

Kitwood, T. (1990). *Concern for others*. London and New York, NY: Routledge.

Larson, E. B., & Yao, X. (2005). Clinical empathy as emotional labor in the patient–physician relationship. *Journal of the American Medical Association*, *293*(9), 1100–6.

Logan, S., Steel, Z., & Hunt, C. (2014) A systematic review of effective intercultural communication in mental health. *Cross-Cultural Communication*, *10*(5), 1–11.

Mehrabian, A., & Epstein, N. (1972). A measure of emotional empathy. *Journal of Personality*, *40*(4), 525–43.

Mercer, S. W., Maxwell, M., Heaney, D., & Watt, G. (2004). The consultation and relational empathy (CARE) measure: development and preliminary validation and reliability of an empathy-based consultation process measure. *Family Practice*, *21*(6), 699–705.

La Monica, E. L. (1981). Construct validity of an empathy instrument. *Research in Nursing & Health, 4(4)*, 389–400.

Morse, J. M., Anderson, G., Bottorff, J. L., Yonge, O., O'Brien, B., Solberg, S. M., et al. (1992). Exploring empathy: A conceptual fit for nursing practice? *Journal of Nursing Scholarship*, *24*(4), 273–80.

Murdock, G. (1945) Common denominator of cultures. In R. Linton (Ed.), *Science of Man in the World Crises*. New York, NY: Columbia University Press.

Nesdale, D., De Vries Robbe, M., & Van Oudenhoven, J. P. (2012). Intercultural effectiveness, authoritarianism, and ethnic prejudice. *Journal of Applied Social Psychology*, *42*(5), 1173–91.

Reynolds, W. (2000). *The measurement and development of empathy in nursing.* Aldershot: Ashgate.

Ridley, C. R., & Lingle, D. W. (1996). Cultural empathy in multicultural counseling: A multidimensional process model. In P. Pedersen, J. Drugans, W. Lonner, & J. Trimble (Eds.), *Counseling across cultures* (4th edn, pp. 21–46). Thousand Oaks, CA: Sage.

Ruben, B. D. (1976). Assessing communication competency for intercultural adaptation. *Group and Organization Management, 1*(3), 334–54.

Ruben, B. D., & Kealey, D. J. (1979). Behavioral assessment of communication competency and the prediction of cross-cultural adaptation. *International Journal of Intercultural Relations, 3*(1), 15–47.

Seneca (1995). *Moral and political essays* (J. M. Cooper, Trans.). Cambridge: Cambridge University Press.

Spitzberg, B. H., & Changnon, G. (2009). In D. K. Deardorff (Ed.), *The Sage handbook of intercultural competence* (pp. 2–52). Thousand Oaks, CA: Sage.

Stepien K., & Baernstein A. (2006). *Educating for empathy: A review. Journal of General Internal Medicine 21(5)*, 524–30.

Thompson, E. (2001). Empathy and consciousness. *Journal of Consciousness Studies, 8*(5–7), 1–32.

Tichener, E. B. (1909). *A textbook of psychology.* Delmar, NY: Scholars' Facsimiles & Reprints.

Van der Zee, K. I., & Van Oudenhoven, J. P. (2000). The multicultural personality questionnaire: A multidimensional instrument for multicultural effectiveness. *European Journal of Personality, 14*(4), 291–309.

Vetlesen, A. J. (1994). *Perception, empathy, and judgment: An inquiry into the preconditions of moral performance.* University Park, PA: Pennsylvania State University.

Vico, G. (1968). *The new science of Giambattista Vico* (T. G. Bergin & M. H. Fisch, Trans.). Ithaca, NY: Cornell University Press.

Vischer, R. (1994). *Empathy, form and space: Progress in German aesthetics, 1873–1893.* Santa Monica, CA: Getty Center for History, Arts & Humanities, University of Chicago Press.

Weiner, P. P. (Ed.) (1974) *Dictionary of the history of ideas.* New York, NY: Charles Scribner's Sons.

Zhu, H. (2011). From intercultural awareness to intercultural empathy. *English Language Teaching, 4*(1), 116–19.

Chapter 4

Towards transformative reciprocity

Mapping the intersectionality of interdisciplinary intercultural competence

Daniel J. Paracka and Tom Pynn (Kennesaw State University)

Working for non-violent social change, where the means are implicit in the ends and where people work together to make decisions for the common planetary good, is critically important for establishing a sustainable future. Fully appreciating and understanding these process-oriented goals requires an integrative holistic worldview that moves far beyond immediate self-interests or specific group interests. In this regard, interdisciplinary intercultural competence takes on immense significance. This chapter presents a model for understanding cultural change and continuity that begins with developing the intercultural competence (Deardorff, 2006) necessary for establishing a greater sense of identity inclusivity (Kim, 2009) in order to engage more responsibly in relationships of transformative reciprocity. It posits that interdisciplinary intercultural competence is necessary for engaging responsibly as global citizens with the human family and living planet in order to maintain and strengthen the world's diversity (both cultural and ecological). It further proposes that interdisciplinary intercultural competence represents powerful praxes for generating collaborative capacity with the potential to transcend binaries such as self and other, modern and traditional, science and humanities, local and global.

Interdisciplinary intercultural competence

Interdisciplinary intercultural competence goes beyond obvious, largely superficial, and binary oppositions of similarity and difference in order to find underlying, deeper and more meaningful relationships.

One of the most important challenges that humanity faces today is how to work and live together in dignity across cultures. Interdisciplinary intercultural competence represents the type of critical pedagogy necessary for meaningful dialogue and reflection to occur in creative and caring multicultural contexts.

Cultural self-awareness

It can be difficult to appreciate one's own culture while one is immersed within it. Intercultural learning is about making the implicit explicit, the unconscious

conscious, and the unfamiliar familiar (Appiah, 1992). It requires mindfulness and intentionality that go beyond preconceptions, bias, and autopilot routines (Yeganeh & Kolb, 2009). The intercultural observer must make meaning from the ambiguity, uncertainty, and indirectness of unspoken and unwritten cultural norms. It is within this liminality of worldviews that reality is encountered, and it is only through negotiation that one can hope to approximate it. In other words, social reality in multicultural societies today is not owned by one cultural worldview but is co-created in shared intercultural contexts. The challenges of accomplishing this are different in each interpersonal encounter and situational context. Such sharing is made difficult by the inequalities and hierarchies that exist within and between cultures. The intersectionality or specific influence of different places, histories, religions, economic conditions, majority/minority demographics, etc., must be carefully weighed and considered.

Culture frames perception. It is an integrated system of learned behaviour and inscribed meaning that shapes and organises concepts and processes of identity formation. Culture designates what to pay attention to and what to ignore. It is complex, contextual, and ever-changing. Cultures are social constructs that demonstrate the interdependence of both what we know and who we are. At the same time, understanding that one's knowledge is incomplete can propel individuals and societies to reach beyond their own experiences to learn more.

Intercultural competence

As intercultural students begin appreciating the complexity of another culture and seeing how different aspects of that culture are interrelated, when the experience of another culture makes students more aware of how their own culture works, then they can be said to have developed intercultural competence. When awareness of others increases the students' self-awareness, one is ready not only to appreciate and understand the importance of cultural difference but also to develop skills necessary to engage others effectively and appropriately. Thus, intercultural competence can be conceptualised as (1) an awareness of one's own cultural perspective and an appreciation of the overall importance of culture; (2) empathy for others as fellow human beings, deserving of dignity and respect, from whom one has much to learn; and (3) the ability to adapt one's cultural preferences to such differences, expanding one's sense of identity and ability to communicate across cultures. Put simply, both awareness and empathy are necessary prerequisites for demonstrating respect, which in turn is essential for creating shared and inclusive contexts.

Interdisciplinary competence

Interdisciplinarity is a process of integrative reflection that goes beyond conventional forms of analysis and classification to reveal deeper connections among complex relationships, thereby uncovering issues and ideas hidden between fields of vision and recognising that all aspects of our respective cultures are sites for meaning and relationship-making. Juxtaposing two or more disciplines in new and unique ways thereby revealing greater depth of analysis and insight, interdisciplinarity expands both *what* we know and understand and *how* we know and understand (Latucca, 2001).

Understanding the world from multiple perspectives is aided by employing interdisciplinary analysis (Yershova, DaJaeghere, & Mestenhauser, 2000). Interdisciplinary competence works to deconstruct the privileging of traditional Western constructs of knowledge categories. It asks whose knowledge is privileged as it negotiates competing interpretations from multiple perspectives. Chief among these privileged, positivist concepts are the scientific and technological, or instrumental, use of reason that while improving some of the material conditions of existence, often does so at the cost of the psychological, environmental, and spiritual dimensions of human life. This is to say that conventional academic disciplines that matured through the nineteenth and into the twentieth centuries – the physical sciences and the social sciences most notably – that purport to use instrumental reason have been established as dominant and normative. Such disciplines privilege a view of human nature lording over the natural environment and raising the profit motive above both. Where this worldview becomes ethically and methodologically indefensible is when scientific and technological reason is claimed to be *the only* legitimate form of knowing, thereby reducing knowledge to empirical knowledge and then absolutising said knowledge to the exclusion of other ways of knowing. This either/or dichotomy and preference for grand narratives has the chilling effect of devaluing other ways of knowing, excluding the non-human from the sphere of moral concern, and devaluing cultures that do not conform to the above model of knowing.

Interdisciplinarity is similar to intercultural learning in that it facilitates the emergence of new ideas through engagement with different perspectives. Like culture, there is no pure field that is separate and distinct from other fields of inquiry; therefore, in the context of higher education, interdisciplinary intercultural perspectives provide a valuable and useful platform for studying everyday life.

Worldviews, cultural values, privilege, and power

The study of cultural values reveals the underlying rationale and import of different worldviews, and, in this way, the intercultural learner's attention shifts towards recognising best practices in preference to the identification of negative deficiencies. Worldviews, or cultural orientations, are not mutually exclusive (Kasulis, 2002). There are multiple ways of relating to others, the world, and ourselves; it depends on which way of relating is foregrounded in consciousness and which tends to be back-grounded in consciousness. Some Westerners, Kasulis explains, tend to see others and the world, in terms of *integrity*, as free, autonomous, self-interested individuals in a competitive society; whereas some non-Westerners tend to see others and the world in terms of *intimacy*, responsive, interrelated, and other-interested members of a fiduciary community. Most importantly, integrity and intimacy orientations are not mutually exclusive; both are needed and available. In the West, integrity tends to dominate people's ways of relating, but sometimes, such as with the loss of a loved one, an intimate mode of relating is emphasised. The spectrum of difference ranging from individualistic to collective is bridged by recognising affinities in the search for identity. Therefore, Kasulis concludes that we can and ought to become bi-orientational. Becoming bi-orientational means that we are conversant in another's way(s) of relating. Becoming bi-orientational does not demand that one give up one's own worldview for another but that individuals function effectively and appropriately in both contexts.

In general, then, an intimate worldview recognises strengths, emphasises complementarity rather than opposition, and develops a preference for both/and conceptualisation over an either/or perspective as it works to foster new and shared understanding. In framing relational worldview contexts, emphasis is placed on understanding processes over outcomes. While comparative studies tend to adjudicate differences in a hierarchical manner, relational studies emphasise learning about the mutual influences that different peoples and cultures exert on each other through appropriation, borrowing, adaptation, and integration. Noting that 'identities are always relational but seldom reciprocal', for de Sousa Santos (2002, p. 20) post-colonial hybridity and alterity rest along a continuum between Prospero and Caliban, between coloniser and colonised, as one is unthinkable without the other, and where learning occurs in relationship. De Sousa Santos (2002) continues this analysis, stating that 'hybridity opens spaces by discrediting hegemonic representations, thereby displacing antagonism in such a way that it stops sustaining the pure polarisations that made it up' (p. 14). Moving beyond stereotypes or superficial similarities and differences to reveal deeper connections among underlying values and across shared histories requires the ability to apply intercultural and interdisciplinary relational methods of analysis.

Peace studies, inclusive identity, and cosmopolitanism

Peace studies is an interdisciplinary and intercultural endeavour that works to connect the worlds of specialised knowledge and cultural dignity by advancing humanity's understanding of the world's many different and unequal glocal contexts within a context of non-violence. For Johann Galtung, sociologist and doyen of peace studies who coined the term 'positive peace' in 1959, 'peace studies makes peace visible, understandable, [and] obtainable' (Galtung, 2006, p. 17). One important link between the study of peace and interdisciplinary intercultural competence is developing the ability to imagine a future world without structural violence and warfare. Positive, holistic, organic, inclusive, and comprehensive conceptions and practices of peace all require justice, which requires understanding; it is not going to be achieved amidst debilitating poverty or injustice whether on the scale of structural violence, human-rights violations, or genocide

(Galtung, 1996; Reardon, 1992; Schirch 2004). Elise Boulding (1992), peace educator and peace historian, explains that the world imagined 'is a world they would like to work toward, and one they would like to live in' (p. 383).

It is in relationship with the other that we may find ourselves different from who we thought we were. The importance of relationship-building and how much one's worldview perceives the individual's well-being as tied to the well-being of other peoples and other life on the planet is a critical value orientation. Embedded in such understanding is the knowledge that all cultures are an amalgamation of constant cultural borrowing and adaptation over time. Global citizens are flexible, inclusive, and adaptive in orientation. They develop the cognitive, affective, and behavioural flexibility to shift frames of reference according to the specific and unique situational cultural context in which they find themselves.

As Young Yun Kim (2009) argues, 'the more inclusive an individual's identity orientation, the greater his or her capacity to engage in cooperative intercultural relationships' (p. 59). At the same time, demonstrating a strong sense of self and not being afraid to lose oneself in the process, Kim (2009) also claims that 'the more secure an individual's identity orientation, the greater his or her capacity to engage in cooperative relationships' (p. 59). In this way, there is no tension between identity security and identity inclusivity, between stability and change, between public and private selves, but rather mutual entailment, complementarity, as in the Daoist symbol of the alternating phases of yin/yang energy: *tai qi* (supreme ultimate). Each informs the other in co-creation; therefore, it is important to have a core sense of self as well as to be open to changing that self, which is to say that when we are bi-orientational the self is able to move fluidly between cultural orientations or worldviews depending on the context. If there is any tension within such a complementary conception of the self it is a creative tension and one that recognises ultimately that the self like everything else is in a state of flux. Without some form of cultural identity, spaces can be overwhelmed by globalisation; similarly, without some knowledge and experience at the global level, local communities are vulnerable to being taken advantage of. As Kasulis' heuristic demonstrates, cultural identity need not be static but dynamic.

Kwame Anthony Appiah's (2006) idea of rooted cosmopolitanism can be understood as both an alternative to the above dilemmas posed by ethnorelativism and as complementary to Kasulis' heuristic. Updating and expanding Diogenes' idea of cosmopolitan as one who is a citizen of the cosmos to living as a fellow citizen of the world, Appiah's (2006) intention is to show us how we can care 'more than we do'. In this way he is distinguishing between respecting difference versus respecting humans. Rooted cosmopolitanism resembles pluralism to the extent that one takes an active role in cultivating a wider interest in other people(s) and cultures. Instead of shying away from discussions about values and processes of valuation, one who is rooted in one's own tradition(s) and participates in a wider interconnected world with intelligence, curiosity, and engagement demonstrates a sincere interest in others through an ethic of care, engages without victimising or patronising, and recognises that the human family is in need of healing and reconciliation through relationship. A rooted cosmopolitan engages difference *and* insists on human dignity. A sense of interconnectedness in a world of relationships aids the ability to shift frames of reference.

An inclusive identity that encompasses a rooted cosmopolitanism and bi-orientationalism provides an important link between intercultural competence and global citizenship. It is a social and political concept, not just an individual orientation. It acknowledges the dignity of humankind by promoting empathy, cooperation, and respect (Kelly, 2014). The ability to learn about, adapt to, and build relationships across different cultural contexts along with a sincere commitment to peace, social justice, and environmental sustainability are the ingredients necessary to inspire responsible global citizens.

Transformative reciprocity

Finding the right time and place for difficult conversations, skilled interdisciplinary intercultural communicators work to bridge different systems of meaning, are aware of their own cultural limitations, and are prepared to share with and learn from others, thereby facilitating transformative reciprocity. Such sensitive and risk-taking engagement results in shared, inclusive understanding as well as integrative, innovative, and expanded worldviews. Transformative reciprocity occurs when different people come together to learn from each other in ways that improve the lives of everyone involved. It is an intentional process that includes consensus-building, meaning-making, and values creation. Valuing both the differences that make cultures unique and the commonalities across cultures that people share is important for developing intercultural competence and responsible global citizenship. Likewise, recognising the common core value of one human race bound inextricably together is essential to global citizenship but equally important is an understanding of the unique history and creative insights that each culture embodies and contributes to a dynamic world. Embracing as strengths the sometimes ambiguous both/and bi-orientationalism provides a basis for understanding different cultural traditions situated appropriately within shared contexts. Seen this way, local and global are not oppositional constructs but complementary cultural realities forming a vibrant community of dignity, respect, and trust in which emphasis is placed on people co-creating reality.

Good intentions alone are insufficient for building trusting relationships because intercultural contexts require translation (finding relatively equivalent meaning), negotiation (mutual adaptation towards shared meaning), and transformation (value creation). Asymmetries of power impact the degree to which these three types of interactions are shared and/or understood. While reciprocity implies complementarity, a win-win scenario, it is also much more than this: a willingness to change through the intentional process of engagement, to recognise that new and unique value is created. Transformative reciprocity goes beyond mutually shared benefits when it shares the burdens of stress and strain in relationship towards a shared future. In intercultural contexts, things are not always or even usually what they first appear to be; therefore, it is crucial that people patiently consider what may seem to be conflicting ideas. It is indicative of a higher stage of consciousness of our shared humanity that recognises how apparent contradictions need not be understood in reduced and absolutised terms.

Transformative reciprocity means developing empathetic relationships with respect and appreciation for our fellow human and non-human communities.

Situational contexts matter

Few critics of globalisation are as outspoken as Vandana Shiva. Since her earliest work, she has brought the field of international development into clearer focus through the broader critical discourse of eco-feminism. Shiva's arguments against neo-liberal globalisation, which she sees as a protracted war against the earth and its peoples, particularly women and the rural poor, focus on defence of 'the earth and people's rights to land and water, forests, seeds and biodiversity' (Shiva, 2013). She argues that 'a paradigm shift to earth-centered economics, politics and culture is our only chance of survival' (Shiva, 2013, p. 7).

Interdisciplinary intercultural competence is especially needed among community leaders to address modern conflicts arising at the intersections of identity and ecology. Scholars of ecology emphasise that 'cultural diversity is closely linked to biodiversity' and have, therefore, expressed serious concerns about the impact and costs that comparatively wealthy tourists and investors have on relatively poorer, remote, and marginalised traditional communities living in or near fragile ecosystems (Negi, 2010, p. 259). The specialised knowledge of the land held by traditional communities is often lost or ignored in favour of new paradigms brought in by wealthy outsiders. This issue becomes even more problematic when one considers that the power elite exercises enormous control over media and education, with unfettered access to the knowledge and technology needed to harness the power of information, sway public opinion, and gain access to land.

To cite just one example, Allen Isaacman and Barbara Isaacman (2013), marshalling evidence from a vast array of sources, painstakingly detail the failure to decolonise development at the Cahora Bassa Dam in Mozambique: 'fifty years after its completion, the Cahora Bassa Dam continues to impoverish the more than half a million residents of the lower Zambezi [river] valley and to devastate the region's local ecosystems and wildlife' despite repeated promises of improved livelihoods from the colonial Portuguese, the socialist Frelimo government, and today's more market-oriented government (p. 167). Rarely are poor communities, dependent on their relationship to the land (intimately and integrally), engaged in meaningful dialogue or active decision-making processes by power elites, even though it is widely recognised that maintaining both cultural diversity and ecological diversity is essential for creating sustainable communities capable of supporting all life (LaDuke, 2005).

Conclusion: the transformative reciprocity of interdisciplinary intercultural competence

Given the intensive and extensive forces of globalisation, forces that often seem to be out of our control and/or in the hands of the power elite, there is a great need for a much broader knowledge base in order to make informed, inclusive, responsive, and responsible decisions. Becoming a responsible global citizen, conscious of the great diversity of cultures, ideas, and life on the planet, requires flexible, collaborative, critical, and creative thinking. Such thinking is best advanced through engaging in mutually transformative relationship-building. Building reciprocal relationships depends upon developing interdisciplinary intercultural competence, not through negation of existing cultural or disciplinary frameworks but through their engagement and inclusion. As Epali Hau'ofa (1993) makes clear in his seminal essay on Oceania, colonialism and neo-colonialism promoted a worldview that divided, isolated, and separated humanity in belittling and demoralising ways rather than recognising a more empowering, holistic, and interconnected sense of community between peoples and their environments.

Interdisciplinary intercultural learning calls for bringing together different systems to recognise and co-create values, develop shared understanding, and expand worldviews. This process is about growing rather than discounting knowledge. It is about recognising and respecting the plurality of viewpoints in order to develop new perspectives. Thus, as both Kasulis and Appiah show, worldviews are not mutually exclusive but are mutually entailing and thereby when recognised and supported allow each to learn from another in complementary, creative, transformative, sustainable, and holistic ways. As Chimamanda Ngozi Adichie's 'Danger of a Single Story' illustrates so well, paradigms or metanarratives that try to be all-encompassing fail to take into account important, specific differences of context and circumstances, of various histories, peoples, environments, and economies. At the higher levels of intercultural consciousness, there exists an awareness of the debilitating effects of ethnocentricity and ethnorelativity at the personal, communal, and societal levels thereby enabling a sense of change and sustainability that is more inclusive and empowering. Such multi-perspectivalism is not bound by the 'tired dichotomy of relativism and universalism' (Kahn, 2015), but instead moves through the experience of complex ever-changing contexts to thoroughly examine processes and relationships.

The authors hope that this work contributes to the creation of transformative narratives and identification of peaceful processes demonstrating how humanity's destiny is interwoven together in mutual reciprocity with all life on the planet towards shared well-being. In this way, what we may call transformative justice creates a more respectful, inclusive, and caring world.

References

Appiah, K. (1992). *In my father's house.* Oxford: Oxford University Press.

—— (2006). *Cosmopolitanism: Ethics in a world of strangers.* New York, NY: W. W. Norton.

Bennett, M. J. (1993). Towards ethnorelativism: A developmental model of intercultural sensitivity. In M. Paige (Ed.), *Education for the intercultural experience* (pp. 21–71). Yarmouth, ME: Intercultural Press.

Boulding, E. (1992). Can peace be imagined? In J. J. Fahey & R. Armstrong (Eds.), *A peace reader: Essential readings on war, justice, non-violence and world order* (pp. 377–90). Mahwah, NJ: Paulist Press.

Deardorff, D. K. (2006). The identification and assessment of intercultural competence. *Journal of Studies in International Education, 10*(3), 241–66.

de Bary, W. (2004). *Nobility and civility: Asian ideals of leadership and the common good.* Cambridge, MA: Harvard University Press.

de Sousa Santos, B. (2002). Between Prospero and Caliban: Colonialism, postcolonialism, and inter-identity. *Lusa-Brazilian Review, 39*(2), 9–43.

Galtung, J. (1996). *Peace by peaceful means: Peace and conflict, development and civilization.* Thousand Oaks, CA: Sage.

—— (2006). Peace studies: A ten point primer. In Alan Hunter (Ed.), *Peace studies in the Chinese century: International perspectives* (pp. 15–20). Vermont, VT: Ashgate.

Hau'ofa, E. (1993). Our sea of islands. In E. Hau'ofa, V. Naidu, & E. Waddell (Eds.), *A new Oceania: Rediscovering our sea of islands* (pp. 2–16). Suva: University of the South Pacific in association with Beake House.

Hofstede, G. (2001). *Culture's consequences: Comparing values, behaviors, institutions, and organizations across cultures.* Thousand Oaks, CA: Sage.

Isaacman, A. F., & Isaacman, B. S. (2013) *Dams, displacement and the delusion of development: Cahora Bassa and its legacies in Mozambique, 1995–2007.* Athens, GA: Ohio University Press.

Kahn, H. (2015). Scales of global learning: Prisms, knots and a cup of coffee. *Diversity and Democracy, 18*(3), 4–7.

Kasulis, T. (2002). *Intimacy or integrity: Philosophy and cultural difference.* Honolulu, HI: University of Hawai'i Press.

Kelly, G. (Ed.) (2014). *Uncivil liberties: Deconstructing libertarianism.* Sonoma, CA: Praxis Peace Institute.

Kim, Y. Y. (2009) The identity factor in intercultural competence. In D. K. Deardorff (Ed.), *The Sage handbook of intercultural competence* (pp. 53–65). Thousand Oaks, CA: Sage.

LaDuke, W. (2005). Voices from White Earth. In C. Anderson & L. Runciman (Eds.), *Open questions: Readings for critical thinking and writing* (pp. 72–86). Boston, MA: Bedford/St. Martin's.

Latucca, L. (2001). *Creating interdisciplinarity: Interdisciplinary research and teaching among college and university faculty.* Nashville, TN: Vanderbilt University Press.

Mamdani, M. (2004). *Good Muslim, bad Muslim.* New York, NY: Pantheon Books.

Negi, C. S. (2010). Traditional culture and biodiversity conservation: Examples from Uttarakhand, Central Himalaya. *Mountain Research and Development, 30*(3), 259–65.

Paige, R. M. (1993). *Education for the intercultural experience.* Yarmouth, ME: Intercultural Press.

Reardon, B. (1992). Towards a paradigm of peace. In J. Fahey & R. Armstrong (Eds.), *A peace reader: Essential readings on war, justice, nonviolence and world order* (pp. 391–403). Mahwah, NJ: Paulist Press.

Repko, A. (2012). *Interdisciplinary research: Process and theory*. Thousand Oaks, CA: Sage.

Schirch, L. (2004). *The little book of strategic peacebuilding: A vision and framework for peace with justice*. Intercourse, PA: Good Books.

Shiva, V. (2013). *Making peace with the earth*. London: Pluto Press.

Spitzberg, B., & Changnon, G. (2009) Conceptualizing intercultural competence. In D. K. Deardorff (Ed.), *The Sage handbook of intercultural competence* (pp. 2–52). Thousand Oaks, CA: Sage.

Vande Berg, M., Paige, R. M., & Lou, K. (2012). Student learning abroad: Paradigms and assumptions. In M. Vande Berg, R. M. Paige, & K. Lou (Eds.), *Student learning abroad: What our students are learning, what they're not, and what we can do about it* (pp. 3–28). Sterling, VA: Stylus.

Yaganeh, B., & Kolb, D. (2009). Mindfulness and experiential learning. *OD Practitioner*, *41*(3), 13–18.

Yershova, Y., DaJaeghere, J., & Mestenhauser, J. (2000). Thinking not as usual. *Journal of Studies in International Education*, *4*(1), 39–78.

Chapter 5

The role of higher education institutions in developing intercultural competence in peace-building in the aftermath of violent conflict

Savo Heleta (Nelson Mandela Metropolitan University) and Darla K. Deardorff (Duke University)

> We must learn to live together as brothers or perish together as fools.
>
> Martin Luther King Jr. (1964)

Wartime destruction, displacement, and loss of life leave behind physical and psychological marks. Wars destroy infrastructure, economy, social fabric, and cohesion. In the aftermath of fighting, populations are often divided along ethnic, religious, or other lines while the government institutions are dysfunctional and lack capacity to provide even the most basic services to the citizens (Heleta, 2015).

Conflict disrupts all walks of life, including education. Higher education, in particular, is 'increasingly caught in the crossfire of violent conflict, with devastating consequences for the sector and for conflict-affected societies.' In most post-war societies, educational institutions lie in ruins once the relative peace and stability return. Universities suffer infrastructural damage, loss of academics, administrators, and students due to displacement, injury or death as well as the erosion of quality of teaching, learning, and research (Brookings Doha Center, 2015).

Many societies embroiled in violent conflict for an extended period of time develop a 'culture of conflict' that becomes ingrained in people's collective and individual memories and emotions (Bar-Tal & Rosen, 2009). In the aftermath of fighting, one of the priorities is to challenge and counter the 'selective, biased and distorted' narratives (Bar-Tal & Rosen, 2009, p. 557) that have led to and continue to maintain animosity, conflict, and violence between people. Education can assist in countering the narratives that can prevent the stability and peace from taking hold.

Intercultural competencies can assist in building trust and promoting peace and reconciliation among students, academics, and formerly separated communities. The way people engage with each other plays a major role in peace-building and reconciliation in the aftermath of violent conflict. Positive and constructive engagement can help overcome tensions and mistrust and bring people together. Learning to get along is crucial in reconciliation processes, and a key aspect of this is the development of intercultural competence in individuals. Higher education institutions have 'the potential to bring divided societies together, despite their varied ethnic and religious backgrounds, and to engage in critical inquiry on open and diverse campuses' (Barakat & Milton, 2015a). However, constructive engagement is unlikely to happen on its own; it has to be intentionally promoted to young people at universities.

This chapter discusses the context of peace-building and reconciliation after war, the importance of intercultural competence, and the role of universities in developing intercultural competencies as a way of building trust and promoting peace and reconciliation among (formerly) divided communities. The chapter also explores how higher education institutions can facilitate intercultural dialogue among diverse groups on campuses and in broader communities, in order to intentionally build intercultural competence among current and next generations.

Peace-building and reconciliation after war

Post-war recovery and peace-building aim to create a stable environment after war, prevent the return of conflict, and establish long-term peace (Paris, 2005; Barakat & Zyck, 2009). Peace-building programmes are intended to address 'underlining grievances and inequalities' that led to war and fighting (Hanlon, 2006, p. 32). According to Ali & Matthews (2004, p. 6), peace-building aims to 'revive a country's economy, to rebuild its society and to restore its polity'. This is a 'daunting task' that includes transition from war to peace, rebuilding of infrastructure, institutions, and economy, regeneration of service delivery to the population, and resettlement of refugees and displaced (Uvin, 1999, p. 10).

Peace-building is closely linked to the concept of conflict transformation, which aims to build long-term peace through a transformation of attitudes and relationships among groups and individuals. The key in this process is the move from destructive to constructive relationships and some form of understanding among former adversaries, and elimination of factors that had led to the conflict in the first place (Anstey, 2006). Peace-building is much more than the absence of armed conflict and violence, which Galtung (1975) calls 'negative peace'. Post-war societies need 'positive peace'; this includes reconstruction, development, reconciliation, justice, and other factors necessary for lasting peace and stability.

The 'culture of conflict', divisions, and animosity can be major obstacles to peace-building as they hinder processes that promote peace and reconciliation (Bar-Tal & Rosen, 2009). Murshed (2002) writes that the 'restoration of peace ... requires the reconstitution of the social contract' (pp. 387–92) among local communities, including formal and informal agreed-upon rules about peaceful coexistence, resolution of conflict, reduction of poverty, fair sharing of resources, and economic growth. A key aspect of peace-building is the repair of fractured relationships among communities which have been on the opposite sides during the conflict (MacGinty & Williams, 2009). Reconciliation processes are seen as key means that can help repair relationships among former adversaries. Bar-Tal

& Rosen (2009) explain that 'reconciliation consists of mutual recognition and acceptance, investing in the development of peaceful relations, mutual trust and positive attitudes, and fostering sensitivity and consideration of the other party's needs and interests' (p. 558).

Higher education in post-war settings

Annan (2015) stresses that 'education is one of the most effective forms of peace-building, a source of hope for each individual and the premise of development and progress in every society'. Higher education has the potential to contribute to the recovery, peace-building, better governance, and economic reconstruction and development in the aftermath of war (Buckland, 2006; Feuer, Hornidge, & Schetter, 2013; Barakat & Milton, 2015). However, despite the importance of higher education, rebuilding universities after war continues to be neglected by the international donors and local authorities (Heleta, 2015; Brookings Doha Center, 2015; Milton & Barakat, 2016).

The main reason for neglect of higher education is that post-war countries grapple with so many seemingly more pressing priorities such as stabilisation, peace-building, resettlement of displaced people, and livelihood improvements, to name only a few. International donors and organisations consider higher education as a 'luxury that war-torn societies can ill afford' (Barakat & Milton, 2015). They have failed to 'appreciate the strategic role of the [higher education] sector in stabilising and promoting the recovery of war-torn communities and states' (Barakat & Milton, 2015a, p. 1). The consequence of the neglect of higher education is that universities often lack capacity and quality to assist countries and communities recover, reconcile, and build peace.

The role of higher education in peace-building

In many countries, education has been/is 'actively used to reinforce political domination, the subordination of marginalized groups and ethnic segregation' (UNESCO, 2011, p. 17). This often leads to animosity and violence. In the aftermath of violent conflict, it is important to prevent the emergence of systems and structures that reproduce inequality and divisions and promote prejudice, segregation, or superiority of certain groups (Heleta, 2015). Universities need to promote tolerance on campuses and in the society. According to Bar-Tal & Rosen (2009), being tolerant means that one rejects the prejudice, bias, and stereotypes about 'the Other' and engages in considerate and meaningful dialogue about the past, present, and future with the people from different backgrounds.

School and university classrooms are major spaces of socialisation for young people. The role of educational institutions is to 'prepare [students] for a new normality of cooperation across groups, critical literacy and active challenge to injustice' (Davies, 2004). In any country, education 'provides the young generations with the ideology, ethos, values, goals, myths and beliefs that the society considers to be requisite for social functioning' (Bar-Tal & Rosen, 2009). Ensuring that education in post-war settings promotes peaceful coexistence, equality, and human rights is of utmost importance for social functioning and long-term peace and stability.

Milton & Barakat (2016) write that higher education can support conflict transformation and peace-building 'by fostering critical thinking skills that enable students to challenge established truths, decode and resist the messages of power-holders and violent ideologues, and creatively respond to conflict-induced challenges' (p. 413). Universities also have a responsibility to continuously promote dialogues on intercultural and interreligious encounters (Zaragoza, 2010). While this is relevant for any setting, the conflict-ridden societies are possibly in the greatest need of this.

Education can also have 'negative socialisation effects that work counter to reconciliation and conflict transformation' (Milton & Barakat, 2016, p. 414), especially if institutions allow divisions along ethnic, racial, or any other lines. Hawrylenko (2010) elaborates by noting that while education is one of the best ways to prevent conflict, it can also be used in negative ways such as for repression of minorities (by limiting access to education), discrimination, or manipulation by those in power through perpetuating the dominant narratives in textbooks. Thus, it is important to ensure that universities, especially in post-conflict societies, pay careful attention to treatment of minorities, equality of access, use of a balanced, multi-perspective curriculum, and development of non-discriminatory policies and structures.

Education can make a positive contribution to social cohesion and peace-building in post-war settings through a provision of equal educational opportunities for all; through a consensus on what to teach about difficult past; and through a provision of 'tolerant climate in the classroom environment' (Heyneman, 2000, p. 177). Higher education institutions need to be supported and enabled to 'promote the informed and peaceful confrontation of ideas, crucial to academic study and research, but also to deepening democratic governance and building peace' (Annan, 2015). Universities need to be one of the main conduits for addressing intercultural competence development among students as well as the society at large. This is crucial for the promotion of dialogue, peace, and reconciliation.

Understanding intercultural competence within higher education in conflict and post-conflict settings

On a macro level, it is important for policies and structures to be put in place that guard against a negative impact of education or that continue to exacerbate the conflict situation. Apart from the macro and leadership level, it is equally important to address competencies needed at the individual level to move society forward. Similar to the Truth and Reconciliation Commission in South Africa, the conflict must be dealt with at an individual level, given the devastating impact on so many individuals.

How will it be possible for those from warring sides to begin to live together again? How will all those impacted begin to humanise each other again? Policies and structures can play a role, but without other structures closer to the society and people's daily experiences, policies on their own are not sufficient. Educational institutions, including universities, play a key role in impacting the individual level – both among students and staff as well as within the broader community. This impact is implemented through an intentional focus on intercultural learning and specifically on the development of intercultural competence.

What is intercultural competence and how important is it in addressing post-conflict? There are many different definitions and frameworks, most coming from the Global North, and some of which can be contextualised to a post-conflict setting. Two frequently used frameworks are Byram's Intercultural Communicative Competence Model, which has been used quite a bit within a predominantly European context, and Deardorff's Intercultural Competence Framework (see Chapter 1). There are other emerging definitions and frameworks of intercultural competence including those from outside of Europe and North America (see Chapters 7 and 8). Ting-Toomey's Face Negotiation Theory (2004), for example, represents a more Eastern perspective and is one of the most well-known frameworks used in conflict management studies. Likewise, Oetzel's work (Oetzel, Arcos, Mabizel, Weinman, & Zhang, 2006) discusses conflict-management perspectives from outside of the Global North. From these different intercultural competence definitions and perspectives emerge some key considerations for universities, especially those in conflict and post-conflict situations:

1. Move beyond individual qualities to real-world engagement and relationship-building (including in the local community).
2. Move beyond knowledge to intentionally addressing skills and attitudes, including conflict-management skills and face negotiation skills.
3. Move beyond seeing individuals as one identity, especially if that identity is 'enemy'.
4. Move beyond results to process, given that peace-building in itself takes great time.
5. Contextualise intercultural competence within the history and realities of the society.

It is important to recognise that intercultural competence is particular to each context; this is especially essential within post-conflict settings. It is crucial to understand the historical, political, religious, economic, geographical, emotional, and societal dimensions of any context and the competencies needed to navigate successfully within the post-conflict setting.

In addition to intercultural competence, it is also important to recognise other needed competencies including conflict competence and reconciliation competence. Conflict competence, or the ability to navigate through conflict, requires the following: staying centred (and resisting polarisation of feelings, actions, or positions), staying creative, staying calm, staying positive (and resisting negativising), tolerating ambiguity, and focusing on the relationship through dialogue (and resisting isolation) (Augsburger, 1992). Intersections of conflict competence and intercultural competence include the following: listening, respect, openness, perspective-taking, self-awareness, and empathy (see Chapter 3). Higher education institutions need to examine ways in which these particular intersectional elements are embedded at every level of the institution, from the leadership to the classroom.

In addition to intercultural and conflict competencies, reconciliation competence (often addressed through peace education) becomes crucial to address. Reconciliation competence starts with forgiveness. Kaunda (1980) writes that forgiveness, while no substitute for justice, should be seen more as a gift that in the end is about establishing 'right' relationships between human beings regardless of what happened in the past.

Strategies for development of intercultural competencies in higher education settings

The way people engage with each other plays a major role in peace-building and reconciliation in the aftermath of violent conflict. Positive engagement can help overcome tensions and mistrust and bring people together. To that end, Allport's (1979) 'contact hypothesis' notes that certain criteria need to be present in order for positive contact and learning to occur, including equal status of the participants and working towards a common goal. For this to happen, it is important to engage and understand each other beyond the surface-level understanding and knowledge and reach the deep-level understanding about each other (Ting-Toomey & Chung, 2012).

Constructive engagement between people who until recently were on different sides in a violent conflict is unlikely to happen on its own. Leadership will be the key in implementing any of the strategies listed below. Such leadership needs to come from all sections of the university – from the university management, academic and administrative staff, and also from the students. Listening intently to the needs and concerns of all stakeholders (including parents) is an important step in providing the essential leadership needed in moving these efforts forward. Leaders and administrators can contribute positively through symbolic acts as well as formal statements and concrete actions, with the goal of creating a common future for the institution and all those connected to it. Where necessary, university leadership needs to address the invisible structural and cultural repression that may continue to pervade institutions (Galtung, 1990) and work actively to put policies, procedures, and structures in place that facilitate the creation of an equitable, stable, and peaceful climate within the institution and beyond.

A number of strategies can assist universities to intentionally foster positive engagement in building intercultural competence among individuals:

1. Ensure conducive policies and structures at all levels of the institution.
2. Secure leadership support, as well as stakeholder support.
3. Create a safe space for authentic dialogue.
4. Uphold key principles for interaction throughout the institution including:
   a. listening for understanding;
   b. speaking only for oneself;
   c. remember that we are on this journey *together*.
5. Focus on training for academics and administrators on intercultural, conflict, and reconciliation competencies.
6. Transform the curriculum to include multiple perspectives.
7. Utilise co-curricular and curricular opportunities for relationship-building (including story circles, debates, role plays, intramural sports, films, buddy/mentor programmes, study circles on contentious issues, and community volunteer projects).

Bringing divided groups and communities back together into university spaces will not be easy in any post-war setting (Feuer, Hornidge, & Schetter, 2013). University structures and academics must find ways to 'keep the peace' as individuals and communities begin to reconcile, rebuild trust, and build peace (Heleta, 2015). Educators, in particular, will need to be trained to manage the transition from war to peace in the classrooms and institutions. Providing educators with the knowledge and skills for dealing with disputes and conflicts in non-violent ways are crucial. Furthermore, as Smith (2010) points out, educators are the 'most important factor in mediating the curriculum and the values it conveys' (pp. 21–2). He adds that the educators require training that equips them with the skills for the development of intercultural competencies among their students (Ibid.). International intercultural experts and practitioners can help train local educators to meaningfully engage with the student body and develop their intercultural competencies. Moreover, teacher training at universities can greatly benefit from an intentional focus on intercultural development and conflict resolution skills as teachers work with students from different groups previously involved in conflict.

Some intercultural competence tools

Some intercultural competence tools can help educators work with students in post-conflict settings in processing divergent narratives and traumatic recent history. Below are a few examples (Deardorff, 2016):

1. 'How do you know what you know about … [fill in a 'category' of people]?' Posing this question can elicit many thought-provoking responses and help students interrogate sources of information, especially about former enemies, as well as to begin to examine different perspectives about a particular group of people and begin to recognise that there are commonalities, as well as a range of different identities even within one group of people.

2. 'If you were me...' Encouraging students to reflect on questions such as 'What would you feel if you were me? What would you do if you were me?' can help encourage the development of empathy, as students begin to listen to each other.
3. 'Is there more?' Asking this question encourages further exploration of the deeper contexts around a particular situation, including the emotions, memories, and truth-seeking that need to be acknowledged. Facilitator training can be crucial in delving further into individuals' stories. This tool encourages a focus on listening for understanding, a recognition that each person has only part of 'the truth' in every situation, and an affirmation that others will be ready to listen after and only after being heard and understood (Lederach, 2014).
4. 'What will you/I/we do next?' This question invites action from individuals and collectively in continuing to rebuild relationships and society.

Gill and Niens (2014) think that the dialogic pedagogy – which includes listening, asking probing questions (such as the ones listed above), and critically reflecting on one's own and others' knowledge and understanding of issues – is key for transformation from violence to stability and peace-building through education. They argue that in the post-war settings dialogic pedagogy can help 'raise students' consciousness about divergent narratives and oppressive social structures, criticise power imbalances, develop shared understandings of the past, present and future and expand the classroom practices in order to cultivate teachers' and students' capacity to act as agents of change' (Gill & Niens, 2014, p. 22). Critical examination of the difficult past can be quite sensitive as it might devolve into conflict discourse that had been so prevalent. Feuer, Hornidge, and Schetter (2013) write that 'confronting and reflecting on the past is admittedly a challenging task after a conflict, as there are still open wounds, sensitivities, and there are likely still perpetrators and victims coexisting' (p. 15). However, developing creative ways to help all students see the past and present from their own and others' perspectives can also be one of the first steps in moving towards genuine understanding.

The role of international partners

Rebuilding higher education in the aftermath of violent conflict 'is a major challenge that requires a collective effort between a range of national, regional and international educational actors' (Barakat & Milton, 2015). To develop intercultural competence in and beyond their institutions, universities in post-war settings will need constructive assistance from abroad. Higher education institutions, donors, experts, and practitioners from the developed and emerging world can assist universities in war-torn countries through sourcing of funding for projects and intercultural competence training, staff exchange, joint research, and curriculum development. However, it is very important that international partners do not impose their own ideas, models, ideological underpinnings, and worldviews onto the institutions and systems they are trying to assist; mutuality remains crucial. The rebuilding and reforming processes need to be locally driven and owned, meaning that choices, priorities, and strategies for the higher education systems and institutions must be locally decided (Heleta, 2017).

Conclusion

Education is critical for social transformation and promotion of peace and understanding among people who have been on different sides in a violent conflict (Gill & Niens, 2014). As such, rebuilding the education sector at all levels – from primary to higher education – needs to become a priority in post-war recovery planning. Within post-conflict societies, higher education institutions in particular can play a key role in not only developing much needed intercultural competence among students both in and out of the classroom but also in bringing different groups together in meaningful intercultural dialogue as well as in training teachers and others who will work within society. Leadership, both within and beyond the institutions, is critical in ensuring the success of such efforts, as is the support and assistance from the international community, including universities abroad. Policies and structures also need to be transformed to facilitate social transformation and promotion of peace. In the end, it is important to remember, 'We come to understand human relationships by encountering the other, by going beyond our own familiar ways of working through confusion, conflict and change to see new pathways, new patterns and perhaps new ways of creating peace' (Augsburger, 1992, p. 10). Universities need to be at the forefront of creation of platforms and initiatives where the people who experienced conflict, divisions, and animosity encounter each other to find new ways and pathways for a peaceful tomorrow.

References

Ali, T., & Matthews, R. (2004). Introduction. In T. Ali & R. Matthews (Eds.), *Durable peace: Challenges for peacebuilding in Africa* (pp. 3–15). Toronto: University of Toronto Press.

Allport, G. (1979). *The nature of prejudice*. Boston, MA: Addison-Wesley.

Annan, K. (2015). Higher education and Africa's social and political progress. *University World News*, 359, 20 March. Retrieved from www.universityworldnews.com/article.php?story=20150321104235 40

Anstey, M. (2006). *Managing change, negotiating conflict*. Cape Town: Juta & Co.

Augsburger, D. (1992). *Conflict mediation across cultures: Pathways and patterns*. London: Westminster John Knox Press.

Bar-Tal, D., & Rosen, Y. (2009). Peace education in societies involved in intractable conflicts: Direct and indirect models. *Review of Educational Research*, *79*(2), 557–75.

Barakat, S., & Milton, S. (2015a). *Houses of wisdom matter: The responsibility to protect and rebuild higher education in the Arab world*. Policy briefing. Doha: Brookings Doha Center.

—— (2015b). Higher education vital to post-conflict rebuilding. *University World News, 375*, 10 July. Retrieved from www.universityworldnews.com/article.php?story=20150710072233289

Barakat, S., & Zyck, S. (2009). The evolution of post-conflict recovery. *Third World Quarterly, 30*(6), 1069–86.

Brookings Doha Center (2015). *York Accord: The responsibility to protect and rebuild higher education during and after conflict*. Doha: Brookings Doha Center.

Byram, M. (1997). *Teaching and assessing intercultural communicative competence*. Bristol: Multilingual Matters.

Deardorff, D. K. (2006). The identification and assessment of intercultural competence as a student outcome of internationalization at institutions of higher education in the United States. *Journal of Studies in International Education*, 10(3), 241–66.

Deardorff, D. K. (2016). Invited talk at Global Education Think Tank, Harvard University, 29 May.

Davies, L. (2004). Building a civic culture post-conflict. *London Review of Education, 2*(3), 229–44.

Feuer, H., Hornidge, A., & Schetter, C. (2013). Rebuilding knowledge: Opportunities and risks for higher education in post-conflict regions. ZEF Working Paper Series. No. 121. Center for Development Research (ZEF), University of Bonn.

Galtung, J. (1975). Three approaches to peace: Peacekeeping, peace-making and peace-building. In *Peace, war and defence: Essays in peace research*, vol. II (pp. 282–304). Copenhagen: Christian Ejlers.

—— (1990). Cultural violence. *Journal of Peace Research, 27*(3), 291–305.

Gill, S., & Niens, U. (2014). Education as humanisation: A theoretical review on the role of dialogic pedagogy in peacebuilding education. *Compare: A Journal of Comparative and International Education, 44*(1), 10–31.

Hanlon, J. (2006). 200 wars and the humanitarian response. In H. Yanacopulos & J. Hanlon (Eds.), *Civil war, civil peace* (pp. 18–48). Milton Keynes: Open University Press.

Hawrylenko, J. (2010). Education in post-conflict societies. Unpublished master's treatise. Athabasca: Athabasca University.

Heleta, S. (2015). Higher education in post-conflict societies: Settings, challenges and priorities. *Handbook internationalisation of European higher education*, vol. I (pp. 1–20). Stuttgart: Raabe Verlag.

—— (2017). Higher education and its international dimensions in post-conflict settings. In H. de Wit, J. Gacel-Ávila, E. Jones, & N. Jooste, N. (Eds.), *The globalization of internationalization: Emerging voices and perspectives* (pp. 40–9). London and New York, NY: Routledge.

Heyneman, S. P. (2000). From the part/state to multiethnic democracy: Education and social cohesion in Europe and Central Asia. *Educational Evaluation and Policy Analysis, 22*(2), 173–91.

Kaunda, K. (1980). *The riddle of violence*. San Francisco, CA: Harper & Row.

Lederach, J. P. (2014). *Reconcile: Conflict transformation for ordinary Christians*. Harrisonburg, VA: Herald Press.

MacGinty, R., & Williams, A. (2009). *Conflict and development.* London and New York, NY: Routledge.

Milton, S., & Barakat, S. (2016). Higher education as the catalyst of recovery in conflict-affected societies. *Globalisation, Societies and Education, 14*(3), 403–21.

Murshed, M. (2002). Conflict, civil war and underdevelopment. *Journal of Peace Research, 39*(4), 387–93.

Oetzel, J., Arcos, B., Mabizel, P., Weinman, A. M., & Zhang, Q. (2006). Historical, political and spiritual factors of conflict: Understanding conflict perspectives and communication in the Muslim World, China, Colombia, and South Africa. In J. Oetzel & S. Ting-Toomey (Eds.), *The Sage handbook of conflict communication: Integrating theory, research and practice* (pp. 549–74). Thousand Oaks, CA: Sage.

Paris, R. (2005). Towards more effective peace-building. *Development in Practice, 15*(6), 767–77.

Smith, A. (2010). *The influence of education on conflict and peace-building.* Background paper prepared for the Education for All Global Monitoring Report 2011. Paris: UNESCO.

Ting-Toomey, S. (2004). Translating conflict face-negotiation theory into practice. In D. R. Landis, J. M. Bennett, & M. J. Bennett (Eds.), *Handbook of intercultural training* (pp. 217–48). Thousand Oaks, CA: Sage.

Ting-Toomey, S., & Chung, L. (2012). *Understanding intercultural communication.* Oxford: Oxford University Press.

UNESCO. (2011). *The hidden crisis: Armed conflict and education.* Paris: UNESCO.

Uvin, P. (1999). *The influence of aid in situations of violent conflict.* Paris: Organisation for Economic Cooperation and Development.

Zaragoza, F. M. (2010). The role of higher education in fostering a culture of peace and understanding. In S. Bergan & H. Van't Land (Eds.), *Speaking across borders: The role of higher education in furthering intercultural dialogue* (pp. 23–8). Strasbourg: Council of Europe.

Part II

Development and assessment of intercultural competence

Chapter 6

Intercultural competence development in higher education

Jeanine Gregersen-Hermans (Glasgow Caledonian University)

Our world and societies are changing because of continuous global political and economic transformations and the radical changes brought about by the emergence of virtual cultures. Increasingly this is expected to lead to more people living and working in and across multiple cultures and societies, both in physical and virtual realities. The changing global environment has also prompted the awareness in higher education institutions that they must respond to this arising societal need and deliver graduates who can function both as global professionals and responsible citizens. This chapter highlights key issues to consider in developing intercultural competence in higher education and concludes with implications for higher education institutions.

Introduction

Intercultural competence is perceived as an important and significant element of global readiness. This is reflected in the outcomes of the 4th Global Survey (Egron-Polak & Hudson, 2014) published by the International Association of Universities (IAU). Universities internationalise their campuses with a view to enhancing the intercultural awareness and understanding of their students and thereby their ability to function in this globalised world. The most salient strategies currently available to achieve this are student mobility, internationalisation at home, and internationalisation of the curriculum.

However, achieving this learning outcome of enhanced intercultural competence because of internationalisation is not an automatic given. Internationalisation has been critiqued because of its focus on outputs rather than outcomes. Enhancing student mobility or providing an internationalised university environment to offer students an intercultural experience as such does not necessarily lead to intercultural learning. Although students may have had a transformative experience because of these activities, this will not necessarily have been an intercultural one (Bennett, 2012).

In recent years, a call for evidence-based strategies for internationalisation has come strongly to the fore. The number of studies on the impact of internationalisation on the development of intercultural competence or related constructs has increased as a result. Reviewing this higher education discourse, it becomes evident there seems to be a great deal of conceptual diversity among both higher education leaders and among scholars in the field about what exactly is meant by the term 'a global-ready graduate' and the related assumed intercultural competence, which pedagogies are effective, and what this implies for competencies of academic staff. This conceptual diversity has hindered universities in putting effective strategies in place to successfully enhance intercultural competence development in students.

Although many universities identify intercultural competence as an essential learning outcome, their challenge is to further elaborate and implement this in their curriculum. The purpose of this chapter is to provide some insights on four of the key issues to consider that help transform international education experiences into meaningful intercultural learning and development.

These issues have been organised according to the following questions. How to create meaningful intercultural learning for all students? How to define intercultural competence as a learning outcome? How to facilitate and embed intercultural competence in the curriculum? What is the link between educating interculturally competent graduates and global citizens? What are the implications for the professional qualifications of staff?

How to create meaningful intercultural learning for *all* students?

Increasingly, universities are aware that intercultural competence should not just be a bonus for students who participate in education abroad programmes or for incoming international students. The first issue to consider is how to create intercultural learning opportunities that benefit all students. This is important because all graduates, whether they seek a career in their communities of origin or elsewhere, will have to be equipped to function in a globalised world as a professional and a global citizen. Issues they will be confronted with in their future lives and careers will have wider arching regional and international dimensions. Furthermore, their local communities will be impacted by developments globally and by the increasing diversity in their local communities.

The need to include all students (and staff and academics) is reflected in the literature on internationalisation of higher education. The outcomes of a recent study by de Wit & Hunter (2015) succinctly summarises this point. They propose a revised definition of internationalisation that builds on Knight's original working definition (2004). They suggest that internationalisation is '*the intentional* process of integrating an international, intercultural or global dimension into the purpose, functions and delivery of post-secondary education, *in order to enhance the quality of education and research* for *all students and staff* and *to make a meaningful contribution to society*' (p. 29, emphasis in original referring to the proposed revisions).

Even though education abroad is still viewed as an important component of international education, higher education institutions increasingly focus on internationalisation at home (IaH) (Beelen & Jones, 2015) and internationalisation of the curriculum (IoC) (Leask, 2015) since these efforts include all students. These learning and teaching strategies systematically and purposefully focus on developing intercultural competence in all students as well as staff and academics.

Internationalisation of the curriculum originates from Australia and is defined as 'the incorporation of international, intercultural, and/or global dimensions into the content of the curriculum as well as the learning outcomes, assessment tasks, teaching methods, and support services of a programme' (Leask, 2015, p. 9). It positions the development of intercultural competence into the core of the curriculum and the discipline and addresses mobile and non-mobile students. Internationalisation of the curriculum should be seen as a strategy to support students 'to become more aware of their own and other cultures' (Green & Whitsed, 2015, p. 9). Leask (2009) sees an internationalised curriculum as one that 'will engage students with internationally informed research and cultural and linguistic diversity and purposefully develop their international and intercultural perspectives as global professionals and citizens' (p. 209). In practice this means that intercultural competence is contextualised by the curriculum, the specific discipline, and the related professions. This enhances its transferability and perceived relevance.

In the context of IoC, Leask (2015) draws attention to the various forms of the curriculum. The formal curriculum refers to the syllabus and the learner activities that are formally assessed and credit-bearing. The informal curriculum consists of all the support services and student life activities and options that are usually not assessed but that contribute to student learning and development. The hidden curriculum consists of the 'unintended hidden messages to students' (Leask, 2015, p. 8). It informs students about the dominant values and beliefs, how and when to interact and with whom, and when not to, and reflects the social structure and the dominant culture of the university. It is important universities are aware of the hidden curriculum and its normative character as this refers to what students implicitly are learning and influences students' intercultural competence development.

In Europe, the use of IaH to target all higher education students has quickly gained ground (Beelen & Jones, 2015; Nilsson & Otten, 2003). In the United States, IaH often is referred to as campus internationalisation. Internationalisation at home aims to link the international and the intercultural (Teekens, 2007) and promotes 'broad mindedness and understanding and respect for other people and their cultures' (p. 5) within the daily reality of the international, multilingual, and multicultural classroom. Internationalisation at home can be viewed as a specific element of IoC in that IaH explicitly includes the diversity represented in the home student population and the diversity of the domestic learning environments in the process design of curriculum internationalisation (Gregersen-Hermans, 2016). De Wit & Hunter (2015) support this notion and assert that there is a need to focus on IaH in the context of IoC since it focuses on internationalising the formal curriculum and internationalised learning outcomes to enhance the quality of education and research.

In summary, to ensure that all students benefit from the opportunities internationalisation offers to develop their intercultural competence, integration into the core and content of the curriculum in its broadest sense is suggested. IoC provides a framework to help transform an international education experience which leads into intercultural competence for all students, mobile and non-mobile. Furthermore, connecting the curriculum with professional and societal needs contextualises intercultural competence development, gives it direction and meaning, and thereby enhances its transferability and relevance.

However, to successfully include intercultural competence as a learning outcome, the second issue to consider is what type of learning is expected of students.

How to develop learning outcomes for intercultural competence?

To establish learning outcomes and the accompanying rubrics, the challenge is to understand that intercultural competence is a complex construct that encapsulates various related concepts and behaviours rather than a single tangible entity. Because of its complexity, however, intercultural competence seems to have become a catch-all phrase. There is no consensus on which methods are most effective for its development. When including intercultural competence development as a learning outcome in the curriculum, the first step is to clarify what is expected of students in terms of knowledge, attitudes, skills, and behaviours. These expectations may vary per discipline or level of education (Green & Whitsed, 2015). This section offers a brief overview of intercultural competence (see also Chapter 1) to support the construction of learning outcomes and rubrics for students' development and assessment.

Defining intercultural competence

As stated above, a diversity of terms is used to delineate intercultural competence (Fantini, 2009). Most terms however 'allude only to limited aspects of a more complex phenomenon' (Fantini & Tirmizi, 2006, p. 11).

Deardorff's definition (2009) of intercultural competence, as the first research-based definition and framework for intercultural competence, can be used as a starting point as this definition refers to behavioural outcomes, highlights agreed-upon essential elements of intercultural competence, and captures some of the complexity of what constitutes intercultural competence. Her study defined intercultural competence as behaving and communicating effectively and appropriately in intercultural situations as well as delineating agreed-upon aspects of such competence, i.e. specific intercultural knowledge, skills, and attitudes, and combines these with relational/interactional aspects, i.e. the intention being to achieve one's goals to some degree and also allowing others to achieve their goals to some degree. The intercultural competence elements in this framework can be used to create more concrete learning outcomes within specific contexts (see Chapter 1).

There are other intercultural competence aspects to consider as well (see Chapters 2, 3, 7, and 8). Based on an extensive review of the literature, Spitzberg & Changnon (2009) categorised various models of intercultural competence development into five types. Their typology is based on the potential similarities they observed between the various models and theories. Table 6.1 synthesises their typology, the focus of these various models, and the related strengths and weaknesses. Some examples are given as well.

The list below summarises the key points that come forward from these definitions and models (Gregersen-Hermans, 2016):

- Intercultural competence builds on the awareness of the self as a cultural being, recognising that one is a member of various cultural collectives simultaneously.
- Intercultural competence consists of components in the domains of knowledge, skills, and motivation and attitude.
- Intercultural competence is associated with linguistic competence – a minimum level of linguistic competence is conditional for culturally competent behaviour.
- Motivational components and attitudes influence or drive the development of intercultural competence. At the same time, positive interactions with culturally different others enhance an individual's self-confidence and self-efficacy to engage in intercultural interactions.
- Intercultural competence includes processes of self-management, perception management, and relationship management.
- Intercultural competence is a process of balancing co-orientation towards a joint frame of reference and tolerance for ambiguity with the objective to stay in the relationship.
- Intercultural competence is a process of balancing adaptability (to the intercultural interaction and the culturally different others) with the negation of personal space and identity.
- Intercultural competence can be divided into developmental stages that are associated with different ways of constructing and perceiving daily reality. Developmental stages are progressive in nature, develop over time, and function as predictors of performance.
- Intercultural competence can be developed.

The list highlights key aspects that need to be considered when developing learning outcomes for intercultural competence. It also refers to levels or stages of competence and the developmental nature of intercultural competence over time. When establishing the specific rubrics that underpin intercultural

Table 6.1 Models of intercultural competence development: focus, strengths, and weaknesses. Based on Spitzberg & Changnon, 2009.

Types	*Focus*	*Strengths*	*Weaknesses*	*Examples*
Compositional models *Which are the elements that constitute intercultural competence?*	Components of intercultural competence in the knowledge, attitudes, and skills domains.	Provide the basic content for any theory of intercultural competence.	Do not specify the relationships between the components. Lack criteria for competence and progression.	The Facework Based Model for Intercultural Competence (Ting-Toomey & Kurogi, 1998) The Pyramid Model of Intercultural Competence (Deardorff, 2006) The Global Competencies Model (Hunter, 2006)
Co-orientational models *What happens in the intercultural encounter and how is success defined?*	Outcomes of interactional processes in terms of effectiveness, appropriateness, and satisfaction; Criteria for intercultural competence in terms of increasing correspondence of meaning between culturally different actors.	Attention for the need for clarity in an intercultural interaction and a minimum level of common reference; Include linguistic components.	Limited attention for management of ambiguity and dealing with uncertainty as key elements of intercultural competence.	Intercultural Interlocutor Competence (Fantini, 1995) Intercultural Communicative Competence Model (Byram 1997) Cohesion-Based Model for Intercultural Competence (Rathje, 2007)
Developmental models *How does intercultural competence develop and what are the levels of intercultural competence?*	Development and deepening of intercultural relationships over time to allow for co-orientation and intentional and reflective learning.	Systematically identify stages or levels of intercultural competence; Allow for rubrics and criteria of intercultural competence.	Lack components that facilitate the development of intercultural competence.	Intercultural Maturity Model (King & Baxter Magolda, 2005) The Developmental Model for Intercultural Sensitivity (Bennett, 1993; revised by Hammer, 2009) The U-Curve Model of Intercultural Adjustment (Gullahorn & Gullahorn, 1963)

Adaptational models *Which cognitive, attitudinal, and behavioural changes take shape to successfully engage in an intercultural encounter?*	Adaptation as a process and criterion for intercultural competence.	Adaptability as foundational for intercultural competence development.	Adaptability as a criterion has not been defined or validated.	Intercultural Communicative Competence Model (Kim, 2009) The Intercultural Communicative Accommodation Model (Gallois, Franklyn-Stokes, Giles, & Coupland, 1988) The Attitude Acculturation Model (Berry, Kim, Power, Young, & Bujaki, 1989)
Causal process models *Which factors lead to or influence the development of intercultural competence?*	Specify the relationships between the various components or variables in the development of intercultural competence.	Allow for the development of specific hypotheses for intercultural competence development.	Some of the models include too many feedback loops and two-way causal paths that limited rigorous testing.	Integrated Model of Intercultural Communication Competence (Arasaratnam, 2004) The Anxiety/Uncertainty Management Model of Intercultural Competence (Hammer, Wiseman, Rasmussen, & Bruschke, 1998) The Process Model of Intercultural Competence (Deardorff, 2006)

competence as a learning outcome, it is not only important to specify what an interculturally competent graduate looks like in terms of knowledge, attitudes, skills, and behaviours. To facilitate and evidence intercultural development, it is critical that this outcome is further deconstructed into outcomes per step or stage. (See Chapter 9.)

Delineating levels of intercultural competence

The third issue to consider is how to establish rubrics for the various levels of intercultural competence, that is, the specific behaviours attached to a certain level of competence and the developmental challenge that students must meet to progress to a more advanced level. As stated above, intercultural competence deepens over time: individually, in terms of an increasing ability to include diversity and the experience of diversity in the construction of daily reality; relationally, in terms of an increasing ability to make culturally appropriate attributions when engaging with culturally different others and to behave appropriately and effectively in a specific cultural context. See Chapter 9 for more detail on developing such rubrics.

Stuart (2012) differentiates between learning versus stepwise development. Learning refers to gaining new knowledge and skills on a gradual continuum in a more or less predictable timeframe. An example from Table 6.1 is the Intercultural Maturity Model (King & Baxter Magola, 2005), in which individuals progress from an initial development phase, through an intermediate level, to maturity. Characteristics are described for each of these phases at the cognitive, intrapersonal, and interpersonal level. The model's underlying assumption is that development is evolutionary over time and benefits from extended exposure and insider feedback.

Development, on the other hand, is transformative in nature and results in the radical rewiring of perspectives on how an individual perceives and interacts with his or her environment. Stuart (2012) describes this as follows: 'we are looking at the same world but suddenly seeing it differently' (p. 63). An example included in Table 6.1 is the Intercultural Development Continuum (IDC) (Hammer, 2009) based on the earlier model of Bennett (1993, 2004). The IDC assumes that intercultural competence development is revolutionary, with distinctly different worldviews and developmental conflicts underlying each stage. It describes five stages of intercultural awareness and competence, ranging from ethnocentric to global mindsets or worldviews. This makes the IDC useful for curriculum development and allows for detailed rubrics on intercultural learning activities and outcomes per level and their assessment (Gregersen-Hermans & Pusch, 2012, p. 33). They provide an example of a rubric for the stage-wise development of intercultural conflict management skills based on the IDC.

An example of a generic stage-wise rubric for intercultural competence development is the rubric for the US undergraduate students which has been developed by the Association of American Colleges and Universities (AAC&U) (n.d.)

based on Bennett's and Deardorff's frameworks of intercultural competence (Bennett, 2008; Deardorff, 2009). An example of an intercultural competence in a linguistic setting is Byram's rubric of learning outcomes based on his model for intercultural communication competence (1997). (See Chapter 1 for further detail on these frameworks.)

In conclusion, rubrics for intercultural competence that guide curriculum development and evidence the students' progress need to refer to specific learning outcomes for knowledge, attitudes, skills, and behaviour and formulate these outcomes for the various stages or levels of competence.

However, intercultural competence comes alive within the situation when people with diverse backgrounds interact with each other. To develop meaningful learning outcomes and their accompanying rubrics, intercultural competence needs to be further contextualised within disciplines and aligned to specific cultures and professional contexts in the process of IoC. The models and examples of rubrics described above therefore are best interpreted as helpful tools as they have been developed primarily in Euro-American contexts.

Facilitating and embedding intercultural competence development

Simple exposure to diversity does not ensure transformative intercultural development automatically occurs (Vande Berg, Paige, & Lou, 2012). So the fourth issue to consider is which effective pedagogical settings are most effective in enhancing intercultural competence development. The premise is that commonalities and differences in perspectives and understanding are seen as learning resources and as 'assets' (Ryan, 2012, p. 631) within a curriculum that is understood in its broadest sense. When constructing a curriculum that embeds intercultural competence development, three dimensions are relevant (Gregersen-Hermans, 2016):

1. The first dimension includes the personality structure of the student, his or her communication skills and motivation to engage in intercultural contact.
2. The second dimension includes the personal biography of the student, in particular living independently from the parents, previous experience abroad, and fluency in the language of instruction.
3. The third dimension refers to the quality of the contact with culturally different others.

These first two 'student' dimensions influence the current level of intercultural competence and hence the students' learning needs. It is important to explore these before or at the beginning of a programme as these will co-determine the pedagogical approach. Furthermore, diversity in learning needs among students within the same cohort should be taken into account. Different pedagogical interventions might be needed for the undergraduate and postgraduate level.

However, this should always be informed by an understanding of students' actual level of intercultural competence.

The focus here, however, is on the third dimension, which is the quality of the contact with culturally different others (Gregersen-Hermans, 2016). The contact dimension constitutes five elements: opportunities for engagement, the conditions under which this engagement takes place, the friendship potential, the specific pedagogical interventions, and the inclusiveness of the university environment. All five need to be considered when embedding intercultural competence development into the curriculum.

First, the curriculum needs to include ample opportunities for contact and engagement with a wide range of culturally different others. These can be present in the student population or in the domestic environment. Contact is expected to lead to increased familiarity, to reduced prejudice or ethnocentrism, and to constructive and positive contact (Pettigrew, Tropp, Wagner, & Christ, 2011). Second, this effect is stronger when students on equal footing have to cooperate with culturally different others to achieve common goals and when they are supported in this process by authority. Third, the social aspects of a curriculum are important. The contact needs to include sufficient opportunities and time to develop friendships (Pettigrew, 1998).

Fourth, to encourage the development of higher levels of intercultural competence, the curriculum has to include a series of pedagogical interventions that stimulate students to intentionally reflect on their and others' values and beliefs and the experience of engaging with culturally different others (Vande Berg, Paige, & Lou, 2012) and that help them develop a critical approach to attributing meaning to these experiences.

Furthermore, in order to develop contextually appropriate behavioural responses, students need to be motivated to also intentionally engage with culturally different others. This involves practising alternative unfamiliar behaviour which at first might feel counterintuitive. Intentional reflective engagement stimulates the development of appropriate and effective intercultural behaviour; it helps to build confidence and encourages increased involvement with culturally different others (Gregersen-Hermans, 2016). The aim is that students develop an understanding of the impact of their own behaviour on culturally different others and thereby deepen their empathic understanding of cultural differences and commonalities. A further series of even more advanced interventions could focus on the ability to reconcile cultural differences and mediate constructive solutions that function in a specific context and group, either between culturally different groups or within a diverse group.

The fifth element of the contact dimension is the inclusive university environment. It is in the university environment where the 'hidden curriculum' or 'how we do things here' can be observed. It is therefore important that intercultural competent behaviour is 'prevalent at all levels in the university, from senior management to hourly staff' (Moodian, 2008, p. 4). Highly visible intercultural competent role models can function as the university champions of more advanced levels of

Table 6.2 Elements constituting the quality of the contact.

Quality of the contact	
Opportunities for engagement	• wide spread of cultural diversity • in the student population • in the domestic environment
Conditions for the contact	• cooperation • equal status • common goals • authority support
Social aspects	• time/long term • friendships
Pedagogy	• intentional • reflective • practise new and unfamiliar behaviour • practise reconciliation and mediation
Inclusive environment	• high levels of intercultural competence the norm at all levels • visible and recognised interculturally competent role models

intercultural competent behaviour. Their presence and recognition is expected to facilitate the development of a culturally inclusive environment on campus and helps to promote intercultural competent behaviour as the norm on campus.

Table 6.2 summarises the elements for the quality of the contact that need to be considered when embedding intercultural competence development into the curriculum.

In conclusion, to facilitate students' intercultural competence development, the curriculum has to take into account the five elements that determine the quality of the intercultural contact in a meaningful interaction with the personality and the biography of the students as these latter two determine the current level of intercultural competence and hence the students' learning needs.

In our globalised world, graduates will be confronted with situations in which they have to make choices in conflicting intercultural situations or across cultures. Often these choices have to be made under pressure with limited opportunity to satisfy all involved.

Interculturally competent graduates as global citizens

As stated earlier in the chapter, not only does intercultural competence need to be contextualised by the academic disciplines and the professional needs of a global labour market, but universities also have to respond to the wider global societal needs. This means teaching students how to live productive and responsible lives in which global interdependence is not simply framed by economic benefits but also includes an understanding of their role in developing and maintaining a sustainable equitable society and world for humankind (see also Chapter 4). Such roles necessitate the ability to understand the intricacies and interdependencies of relationships within ever-evolving complex local, social, political, economic, and global contexts as well as how actions and decisions may directly or indirectly impact those within these contexts.

Furthermore, graduates need to be able to reconcile their 'situatedness in the world' (Rizvi, 2009, p. 264) and finesse interactions with culturally different others while retaining an ethical attitude towards global connectedness (Kwame, 2006). In practical terms, this means that graduates need to be able to conceptualise and behave inside and outside a local context simultaneously. They need to be able to make moral judgements and ethical choices that are based on a deep level of cultural awareness and understanding while engaging in culturally sensitive collaboration within the local environment. This ability is understood as an expression of advanced levels of intercultural competence.

It is also precisely at this point where the need for the connection between the content of the discipline and intercultural competence development becomes most evident. The pedagogical interventions to achieve this ability aim to connect high levels of professional competence with culturally sensitive mediation and reconciliation.

Connecting intercultural competence with the content of the discipline and positioning its development within the core of the curriculum has implications for what and how students are taught. It also has implications for the competencies of academic staff who teach the curriculum.

Implications for the academic discipline and staff development

Embedding intercultural competence development into the core of the curriculum and linking it to professional and societal needs involves changes in the structure and content of the curriculum, the teaching methodology, and the methods of assessment and evaluation. To transform traditional curricula to include intercultural and global perspectives requires time within the academic disciplines for critical interrogation and reflection on the tacit assumptions about the nature of the discipline and how it is taught (Whitsed & Green, 2015). Furthermore, to deliver a meaningful intercultural learning experience demands high levels of intercultural competence as well as specific pedagogic and didactical skills of an academic, which are not traditionally part of a university's definition of the academic profile. A university-wide, adequately resourced change programme with a specific focus on intercultural competence development seems to be needed in which a university actively engages with all its internal stakeholders. Table 6.3 offers an overview of possible measures to support staff and academics in achieving this transformation.

Examples of such approaches at the institutional level have been described for the Australian context by Leask (2009) and Jones and Killick (2013), by Killick (2011) for the UK and, by Childress (2010) for the United States. Childress

Table 6.3 Examples of possible measures to support staff and academics.

Area	*Possible measures that support development of staff and academics' competencies*
Leadership and governance *How can transformation be achieved?*	• lead by example • commit time and resources • create opportunities for sharing and joint learning within the institution • follow up on activities and celebrate success
Curriculum review *What type of graduates does our future society need?*	• reflect on the tacit assumptions on the nature of the discipline and how this 'should' be taught and assessed • use students as a resource • use diversity in the domestic environment as a resource • use employers and alumni as a resource • include intercultural and global perspectives in the content of the curriculum • reflect on international benchmarks and effective practice elsewhere • include intercultural competence development in annual student surveys
HR *How can staff be supported?*	• continuing professional development for teaching in an international classroom • opportunities to develop their own level of intercultural competence • international teaching mobility • include intercultural competence in job profiles • include intercultural competence development in annual staff appraisals

(2010) identified what she called the Five Is that support faculty engagement in internationalisation: intentionality, investments, infrastructure, institutional networks, and individual support. In the Netherlands, the University of Groningen has been engaging in a university-wide project since 2013 to fully integrate internationalisation throughout the organisation and policies and to link internationalisation with the quality of education and research (Van Gaalen, Hobbes, Roodenburg, & Gielesen, 2014). Notably, the Groningen project includes integrating the international classroom into the broader educational strategy of the university and developing support for staff (and students) for the development of intercultural competence, English language skills and pedagogical skills (Haines, Van de Hende, & Bos, 2015. See www.rug.nl/about-us/internationalization/international-classroom for more on this.)

Conclusion

Unless universities fully commit to a long-term and evidence-based systems-change approach in raising the level of their university's intercultural competence as a whole and embed the development of intercultural competence in the curriculum by closely aligning it to the disciplinary content, developing interculturally competent graduates may continue to be a challenge. Such commitment begins with a close examination and mapping of current efforts at all levels of the institution. Higher education institutions seeking to transform their efforts to better educate students in the twenty-first century will make this commitment.

References

Association of American Colleges and Universities (AACU). (n.d.). Intercultural knowledge and competence value rubrics. Retrieved from www.aacu.org/value/rubrics

Beelen, J., & Jones, E. (2015). Redefining internationalization at home. In A. Curaj, L. Matei, R. Pricopie, J. Salmi, & P. Scott (Eds.), *The European higher education area* (pp. 59–72). Springer International Publishing.

Bennett, M. (1993). Toward ethnorelativism: A developmental model of intercultural sensitivity. In R. Michael Paige (Ed.), *Education for the intercultural experience* (pp. 21–71). Yarmouth, ME: Intercultural Press.

Bennett, M. J. (2004). Becoming interculturally competent. In J. S. Wurzel (Ed.), *Toward multiculturalism: A reader in multicultural education* (pp. 62–77). Newton, MA: Intercultural Resource Corporation.

—— (2012). Paradigmatic assumptions and a developmental approach to intercultural learning. In M. Vande Berg, R. M. Paige, & K. H. Lou (Eds.), *Student learning abroad: What our students are learning, what they're not, and what we can do about it* (pp. 90–114). Sterling, VA: Stylus.

Byram, M. (1997). *Teaching and assessing intercultural communicative competence.* Clevedon: Multilingual Matters.

Childress, L. K. (2010). *The twenty-first century university: Developing faculty engagement in internationalization.* New York, NY: Peter Lang.

Deardorff, D. K. (2006). Identification and assessment of intercultural competence as a student outcome of internationalization. *Journal of Studies in International Education, 10*(3), 241–66.

—— (Ed.) (2009). *The Sage handbook of intercultural competence.* Thousand Oaks, CA: Sage.

de Wit, H., & Hunter, F. (Eds.) (2015). *Internationalisation of higher education: A study for the European Parliament.* Brussels: European Parliament Policy Department B: Structural and Cohesion Policies.

Egron-Polak, E., & Hudson, R. (2014). IAU 4th global survey. *Internationalization of Higher Education: Growing expectations, fundamental values, 4[a].* Paris: International Association of Universities.

Fantini, A. (2009). Assessing intercultural competence. In D. K. Deardorff (Ed.), *The Sage handbook of intercultural competence* (pp. 456–76). Thousand Oaks, CA: Sage.

Fantini, A., & Tirmizi, A. (2006). Exploring and assessing intercultural competence. *World Learning Publications.* Paper 1. Retrieved from http://digitalcollections.sit.edu/worldlearning_publications/1

Green, W., & Whitsed, C. (Eds.) (2015). *Critical perspectives on internationalising the curriculum in disciplines: Reflective narrative accounts from business, education and health.* Rotterdam: SensePublishers.

Gregersen-Hermans, J. (2016). The impact of an international university environment on students' intercultural competence development. Unpublished Ph.D. thesis. Centre for Higher Education Internationalisation, Università Cattolica del Sacro Cuore, Milan.

Gregersen-Hermans, J., & Pusch, P. (2012). How to design and assess an intercultural learning experience. In K. Berardo & D. K. Deardorff (Eds.), *Building intercultural competence: Innovative activities and models* (pp. 23–41). Sterling, VA: Stylus Publishing.

Haines, K. B., Van Den Hende, F. M., & Bos, N. A. (2015). From training initiative to fully-fledged innovative international programme. In W. Green & C. Whitsed (Eds.), *Critical perspectives on internationalising the curriculum in disciplines* (pp. 159–73). Rotterdam: SensePublishers.

Hammer, M. R. (2009). The intercultural development inventory. In M. A. Moodian (Ed.), *Contemporary leadership and intercultural competence* (pp. 203–18). Thousand Oaks, CA: Sage.

Jones, E., & Killick, D. (2013). Graduate attributes and the internationalised curriculum: Embedding a global outlook in disciplinary learning outcomes. *Journal of Studies in International Education*, *17*(2), 165–82.

Killick, D. (Ed.) (2011). Embedding a global outlook as a graduate attribute at Leeds Metropolitan University: Refocusing the undergraduate curriculum. Retrieved from www.leedsmet.ac.uk/staff/files/UG_Embedding_Global_Outlook.pdf

King, P. M., & Baxter Magolda, M. B. (2005). A developmental model of intercultural maturity. *Journal of College Student Development*, *46*(6), 571–92.

Knight, J. (2004). Internationalization remodeled: Definition, approaches, and rationales. *Journal of Studies in International Education*, *8*(1), 5–31.

Kwame, A. (2006). *Cosmopolitanism: Ethics in a world of strangers.* New York, NY: W. W. Norton.

Leask, B. (2009). Using formal and informal curricula to improve interactions between home and international students. *Journal of Studies in International Education*, *13*(2), 205–21.

—— (2015). *Internationalizing the curriculum.* London and New York, NY: Routledge.

Moodian, M. A. (Ed.) (2008). *Contemporary leadership and intercultural competence: Exploring the cross-cultural dynamics within organizations.* Thousand Oaks, CA: Sage.

Nilsson, B., & Otten, M. (Eds.) (2003). Internationalization at home [Special issue]. *Journal of Studies in International Education*, 7(1).

Pettigrew, T. F. (1998). Intergroup contact theory. *Annual Review of Psychology*, *49*(1), 65–85.

Pettigrew, T. F., Tropp, L. R., Wagner, U., & Christ, O. (2011). Recent advances in intergroup contact theory. *International Journal of Intercultural Relations*, *35*(3), 271–80.

Rizvi, F. (2005). International education and the production of cosmopolitan identities. Presentation at the Transnational Seminar Series, University of Illinois at Urbana-Champaign.

—— (2009). Towards cosmopolitan learning. *Discourse: Studies in the Cultural Politics of Education, 30*(3), 253–68.

Ryan, J. (2012). *Cross-cultural teaching and learning for home and international students: Internationalisation of pedagogy and curriculum in higher education*. London and New York, NY: Routledge.

Schein, E. H. (1992). *Organizational culture and leadership: A dynamic view*, 2nd edn. San Francisco, CA: Jossey-Bass.

Spitzberg, B. H., & Changnon, G. (2009). Conceptualizing intercultural competence. In D. K. Deardorff (Ed.), *The Sage handbook of intercultural competence* (pp. 2–52). Thousand Oaks, CA: Sage.

Stuart, D. K. (2012). Taking stage development theory seriously. In M. Vande Berg, R. M. Paige, & K. H. Lou (Eds.), *Student learning abroad: What our students are learning, what they're not, and what we can do about it* (pp. 61–89). Sterling, VA: Stylus.

Teekens, H. (2007). *Internationalization at home: Ideas and ideals*. Amsterdam: European Association for International Education.

Vande Berg, M. V., Paige, R. M., & Lou, K. H. (Eds.) (2012). *Student learning abroad: What our students are learning, what they're not, and what we can do about it*. Sterling, VA: Stylus.

Van Gaalen, A., Hobbes, H. J., Roodenburg, S., & Gielesen, R. (2014). *Managementsamenvatting Studenten Internationaliseren in eigen land: Deel I, Nederlands Instellingsbeleid* [*Executive Summary Internationalising Students in the Home Country – Part 1: Dutch Institutional Policy*]. The Hague: NUFFIC.

Chapter 7

New competencies for intercultural communication

Power, privilege, and the decolonisation of higher education in South Africa

Melissa Steyn and Finn Reygan (University of the Witwatersrand)

Introduction

Since 2015, student protests have disrupted universities across South Africa and challenged the ontological, epistemological, and pedagogical foundations of the South African academy. The demand for the decolonisation of higher education calls for a profound critique and reimagining of the sector. Sites of communicative possibility are urgently required as part of the project to create more just and equitable universities. This chapter argues that normative understandings of intercultural communication competence (ICC) may not be adequate to facilitate communication in a context of the enduring legacy of colonial and Apartheid privilege and oppression. A conception of ICC is needed that explicitly factors in the negotiation of power rather than assuming a stable centre and margins in the communication context. Within this context, this chapter discusses three tenets that need to inform a contextually appropriate understanding of ICC: (1) it needs to be situated within the critical tradition of communication theory; (2) it must factor in Eurocentrism; and (3) it must acknowledge South Africa's colonial legacy. The inclusion of Critical Diversity Literacy (CDL) is proposed to sharpen the conceptualisation of ICC for the situation facing higher education in South Africa.

Context

Since 2015, South African universities have been rocked by student uprisings that have made headlines around the world (*The Guardian*, 2015). The movement started at the University of Cape Town with the #RhodesMustFall protests. These memorably led to the removal from the campus of the imposing statue of Cecil Rhodes, the colonial-era British mining magnate and politician who was responsible for some of the worst abuses of colonised African people and whose bequests had provided the funding for establishing the university. This was followed by the #FeesMustFall protests that, at the time of writing, are still ongoing across the higher education sector. The protests have been led by students who are at two decades removed from the 1994 transition to democracy. Many have been to 'good' schools where they received an education that would enable them to be competitive anywhere in the Western world. Yet their protests speak not only to a sense of alienation from an education system that emphasises the assimilation of black students, remaining ideologically and pedagogically unchanged, but also to their outrage at the unchanged circumstances of their families and communities that struggle to provide the means for this education.

Higher education leaders and managers have met with only partial success to transform universities. The students have precipitated a challenge to enduring relations of domination and oppression where, despite black people being the numerical majority and the indigenous population of the continent, whiteness still retains the ideological hegemony and economic apparatus that makes it difficult to change how the colonially constructed populations are positioned relative to each other. The students are naming racist, sexist, and transphobic ideologies that continue to be perpetuated through and within curricula, exclusionary teaching practices, and the desperate obstacles faced by the African working class within higher education. This dislocation and alienation of blackness in higher education in South Africa is apparent in the large numbers of black students who continue to grapple with severe, and structurally perpetuated, resource constraints in relation to housing, food, and transport, among others. In initiating these challenges, the generation often referred to as the 'born frees' have reopened the space for collectively reimagining and envisioning more equitable and inclusive higher education in South Africa.

Any understanding of ICC in higher education in South Africa will have to be robust enough to deal with this fraught context. Given its history of struggle against British colonialism and Afrikaner nationalism, the diversity of the population, with its eleven official languages, and the progressive constitution that protects the rights of difference, the post-Apartheid nation is characterised by the contestation of plurality, multivocality, and diversity. At the same time, past and contemporary realities of violence, domination, exploitation, and marginalisation have created deep divisions. Widespread poverty, poor service delivery, high levels of unemployment – particularly among young black South Africans – economic crisis, and crime further hinder intercultural relations. In this context, what are often termed 'cultural' differences and 'intercultural relations' are more correctly understood as having to do with historical, economic, social, and political realities (Franchi, 2003; Steyn, 2009). Asante (1983) correctly reminds us that 'We cannot achieve intercultural communication which is mature and effective until we address the material conditions of the people' (p. 5).

Not only is there a need for ICC to do much more in the South African context than facilitate intercultural contact, but such contact must be equitable in a decolonised higher education system. Three tenets that should characterise any conceptualisation of ICC in South African higher education institutions:

1. ICC needs to be situated within the critical tradition of communication theory.
2. ICC needs to address Eurocentrism.
3. ICC needs to acknowledge the colonial legacy of South Africa.

A Critical Diversity Literacy framework may offer critical competencies for moving forward in rethinking intercultural communication in this South African context.

Intercultural Competence (ICC) in South African higher education needs to be situated within the critical tradition

Using terms such as 'understanding', 'relationship development', 'satisfaction', 'adjustment', 'assimilation', and 'adaptation to the host culture', Spitzberg and Changnon (2009) broadly define ICC in the North American setting as 'the appropriate and effective management of interaction between people who, to some degree or another, represent different or divergent affective, cognitive, and behavioral orientations to the world' (p. 7).

Such an understanding of ICC in the South African context would raise distrust. The 'appropriate and effective management' of difference in the colonial and Apartheid history of South Africa meant laws and an education philosophy geared to maintain spatial and educational segregation and oppression. Even the goals of achieving 'understanding' and 'relationship development', mentioned by Spitzberg and Changnon, can be employed as tools to reinforce a white-oriented hegemony in a context characterised by extreme inequality and ongoing racism. After all, the co-construction of a relationship of internalised dominance and internalised oppression could be regarded as the achievement of well-functioning mutual understanding. A conception of ICC is needed that explicitly factors in the negotiation of power rather than assuming a stable centre and margins in the communication context.

Rathje provides an overview of critiques that have been levelled against normative conceptualisations of ICC in noting that the goal of intercultural competence lies in problematic terms such as 'effectiveness', 'productivity', and 'optimal goal attainment' (2007, p. 256). She continues by observing that there is a lack of focus on differing power structures of those participating, thereby leaving the process of intercultural competence open to manipulation and further ignoring the 'situational objectives' of those involved. In addition, there is often an intent within Euro-American conceptualisations of some vague form of personal development with a lack of clarity around the scope of intercultural competence so that it can be either context-specific or generalised.

While cognisant of the critiques of the dominant articulations of ICC (Odağ, Wallin, & Kedzior, 2015), some form of intercultural competence is nevertheless essential for engaging with the current challenges in higher education. Intercultural competence has been defined as combating prejudice and bolstering systems with a limited historical capacity to embrace diversity as stated in a UNESCO document (2009):

> reflecting on diverse ways that societies have elaborated to mediate cultural difference, combat prejudice and strengthen social cohesion; socio-cultural fabric of our societies, combined with global interconnectedness, necessitate

> specific attitudes, behaviours, knowledge, skills and abilities to cope with the new cultural, media and emotional landscape when systems have shown limited capacity to embrace diversity.
>
> (p. 7)

UNESCO (2013) states that intercultural competence facilitates people's freedom from 'their own logic and cultural idioms' so as to listen more deeply, especially to those from cultural systems that 'are not valued or recognized in a given sociopolitical context' (p. 5). The de-culturing, de-historicising, and de-epistemologing of African subjectivities and knowledge production (Abdi, 2008; Mazrui, 2003) necessitate the revaluing of previously excluded communicative styles, knowledge forms, and ontological positions in higher education. This, then, becomes inclusive of philosophical diversity and makes these spaces more accessible and relevant for black students in particular. In such a case, intercultural competence may facilitate addressing structural barriers to tertiary education as well as the renegotiation of subjectivities in dialogue.

ICC in South African higher education needs to address Eurocentrism

UNESCO (2013) also indicates that possibilities for intercultural competence lie in facilitating a process whereby groups and individuals engage with 'cultural "others" with a view to bridging differences, defusing conflicts and setting the foundations of peaceful coexistence' (p. 6). In the post-Apartheid context there is a multivocality and plurality of voices that diverge from the previous monolithic voice of Apartheid-era oppression. Communicative strategies that allow for engagement across the multivocal student and academic bodies are necessary. Intercultural competencies offer some potential avenues for engagement. One UNESCO document speaks of the need for 'cultural literacy', which would be equivalent to other vital life skills such as reading or writing. This new cultural literary, according to this UNESCO document, would help address the clashes of ignorance that occur as well as be a key tool necessary for a lifelong competence in relating to others.

Yet, as Nwosu (2009) notes:

> models of intercultural competence ... are developed through a Western lens, by Western scholars, and for Western intercultural contexts (especially in the United States, Western Europe, and Australia). In contrast to the Western models, the non-Western models of intercultural competence appear to be focused on collectivistic aspects (community and social connectedness). For example, in Africa, seeking 'consensus and a common framework' and emphasizing 'community rather than the individual' are principles widely upheld to promote connection with friends and family.
>
> (p. 162)

The concept most often evoked to exemplify an African approach to communication is *Ubuntu*. There is a body of South African literature in fields such as communication studies, philosophy, theology, management studies, and development studies that makes reference to Ubuntu (see Gade, 2012; Louw, 2002; Mbigi & Maree, 2005; Mbiti, 1969; Nwosu, 2009; Khoza, 2012). Metz (2011) defines Ubuntu as a 'moral theory grounded in Southern African world views, one that suggests a promising new conception of human dignity' (p. 532). In Ubuntu, human dignity emerges through the value a person brings to their community. The concept has evident relevance to articulating regional intercultural competencies as it is embedded in a long history of South African communities and retains an ongoing relevance for many in building contemporary community. The concept of Ubuntu is, however, a contested one in the South African literature – sometimes cast as nativist, romanticised, and outdated by detractors or defended as unfairly trivialised by Eurocentrism. This has resulted in this concept having become compromised by escalating levels of violence and inequality in South Africa.

Numerous scholars have considered how Ubuntu informs South African communication competence and can enrich education practices. Letseka (2000), for example, argues that 'interpersonal skills have been shown to be an integral part of educating for Ubuntu' (p. 189) – displaying such ICC-related skills as reciprocity, fairness, and mutual dignity. Higgs (2003) maintains that Ubuntu in education, being a 'pluralistically sensitive philosophical framework', will assist in the liberation of South Africans:

> African philosophy respects diversity, acknowledges lived experience and challenges the hegemony of Western Eurocentric forms of universal knowledge … Educational discourse in South Africa certainly stands in need of this liberation from ideological hegemony which derives its power from the hegemony of Western Eurocentric forms of universal knowledge. People cannot be empowered if they are locked into ways of thinking that work to oppress them. Nor can people be empowered if they do not have access to those indigenous forms of knowledge which provide them with their identity as persons.
>
> (p. 17)

ICC in South African higher education needs to address the colonial legacy

While earlier efforts at transformation in South African universities have focused mostly on changing the demographic composition of educational settings and, to a (much) lesser extent, on the Africanisation of university, the new wave of protests focuses quite specifically on decolonisation.

Abdi (2007, following Nyerere, 1968) reminds us that colonialism was premised on denigrating African development and systems of education, on dismantling the conceptual and practical means of individual and collective livelihoods, and on destroying communities' deeply embedded and multilevel relationships, social and otherwise. Key in this process was alienation from language: '[Our] language, through images and symbols, gave us a [unique] view of the world ... Then I went to primary school and the bond was broken. The language of my education was no longer the language of my culture – it was a foreign language of domination, alienation and disenfranchisement' (Ngũgĩ, 1993, p. 13). Crucially, Ngũgĩ asserts that decolonisation is a struggle over what knowledge is to be taught. According to Ngũgĩ, liberatory teaching should recentre Africa and decentre the West from the core of Africa's cultural consciousness. A just response to the erasure of multiple epistemologies from education spaces entails the emergence of genuinely pluralistic forms of knowing, what Abdi (2007, following Stam & Shohat, 1994) refers to as radical equalisation across histories, life philosophies, and realities.

Moving forward

Abdi (2007) draws on Freire (2000) to argue for the recognition of a multiplicity of worldviews and ways of interrogating power relations. Noted scholar Achille Mbembe (n.d.) maintains that the process entails black students and staff inventing creative practices that make it impossible for them to go unrecognised, unseen, and unheard by university structures and processes. This will lead to a situation where black staff and students will be able to say, 'This is my home. I am not an outsider here. I do not have to beg or apologize to be here. I belong here' (Mbembe, n.d.). This process owes little to charity, tolerance, or assimilation into another culture so as to participate in the public life of the university. Instead, this process of reclamation and transformation reflects a strong sense of citizenship and engagement in a space that is a public, common good, including what Mbembe (n.d.) calls 'pedagogies of presence', requiring a 'politics of difference' rather than a 'politics of imitation and repetition' (p. 6).

Grosfoguel (2013) argues that epistemic racism and sexism are foundational to the knowledge superstructures of the Westernised university. He posits that the epistemic privilege of Westerners in these universities emerges from a series of genocides and epistemicides in the sixteenth century, such that the Cartesian 'I think therefore I am' is more aptly termed 'I conquer therefore I am' or, indeed, 'I exterminate therefore I am.' In this sense, Grosfoguel (2013) asks how the knowledge of Italy, France, Germany, the United Kingdom, and the United States came to be viewed as superior to all other sources of knowledge and how the knowledge from these five countries came to be considered as the authoritative knowledge of the world. Moreover, Mbembe (n.d.) argues that the process of decolonising education is a worldwide phenomenon and that it is 'an attempt at imaging what the alternative to this [Eurocentric] model could look like. This is where a lot remains to be done' (p. 18). So, how can ICC play a role in the decolonisation of higher education in South Africa?

Given the centrality of the colonial and Apartheid history of South Africa, ICC in the South African context needs a greater focus on issues of power, privilege, and oppression, and the renegotiation of such relations. In such highly politicised and contested contemporary spaces, the actualisation of envisioned futures requires communicative possibilities that grapple honestly with the flux of historical and contemporary realities of cultural domination, annihilation, and exclusion. Given that resources and new forms of cultural capital need to flow to the majority population, spaces and processes that perpetuate white hegemony require transformation. As a result, a form of critical cultural competence is necessary that allows for dialogic spaces to open up in which histories of power and privilege are engaged with, current social problems are rigorously critiqued, and where all university stakeholders continue the process of taking action for change.

Implications: incorporating Critical Diversity Literacy into ICC in South African higher education

The Africanisation of the curriculum, the democratisation of student/academic interaction, and generally the development of a safer and more welcoming space for the majority African student body are central concerns. In this regard, the tertiary sector's limited historical ability or desire to embrace diversity has come under forceful critique in very recent years. As a result, it can no longer be denied in some quarters that the entrenched whiteness of the system has functioned to perpetuate exclusion and prejudice, thereby holding back the process of strengthening social cohesion. For example, the process of transformation is occurring in a context where there are very low numbers of black academic staff and where only 14 per cent of professors are black (Africa Network expert panel, 2014).

In terms of curriculum, much greater attention is necessary in integrating not only African writing and knowledge forms but also for teaching through dialogue a form of critical consciousness that facilitates students' analysis and subversion of prevailing norms and dominant discourses. In terms of pedagogy, a more egalitarian and dialogic approach to teaching is urgently required (cf. Herwitz, 2015) that moves away from forms of banking education and the transmission of outmoded and oppressive knowledge structures to a more engaged and relational pedagogy that foregrounds students' own experiential knowledge.

Finally, while the ethical and social-justice imperatives in redressing and reversing the colonial legacy are clear, the ontological, epistemological, methodological, and pedagogical transformation of the academy is also closely tied to the radical strengthening of academic research in terms of both relevance and theoretical sophistication.

To facilitate the rethinking of ICC in the South African context, a 'critical intercultural competence' is needed that would integrate Steyn's (2015) Critical Diversity Literacy framework into the understanding of communication competence, so that ICC is alive to questions of historical injustice, ongoing inequality, and their dismantling.[1] Steyn (2015) presents a ten-criteria framework, CDL, for developing an 'analytical orientation' towards diversity that foregrounds the ongoing effects of power, privilege, and oppression:

1. an understanding of the role of power in constructing differences that make a difference;
2. recognition of the unequal symbolic and material value of different social locations (this includes acknowledging hegemonic positionalities and concomitant identities, such as whiteness, heterosexuality, masculinity, cisgender, ablebodiedness, middleclassness, etc., and how these dominant orders position those in non-hegemonic spaces);
3. analytic skill at unpacking how these systems of oppression intersect, interlock, co-construct, and constitute each other, and how they are reproduced, resisted, and reframed;
4. a definition of oppressive systems such as racism as current social problems and (not only) a historical legacy;
5. an understanding that social identities are learned and are an outcome of social practices;
6. the possession of a diversity grammar and a vocabulary that facilitates a discussion of privilege and oppression;
7. the ability to 'translate' (see through) and interpret coded hegemonic practices;
8. an analysis of the ways that diversity hierarchies and institutionalised oppressions are inflected through specific social contexts and material arrangements;
9. an understanding of the role of emotions, including our own emotional investments, in all of the above;
10. an engagement with issues of the transformation of these oppressive systems towards deepening social justice at all levels of social organisation.

Borrowing Steyn's (2015) criteria, critical cultural competence becomes a communicative tool that allows for participants to engage in a robust critique of historical forms of privilege and their ongoing perpetuation in the present. It also allows for the naming of 'differential power structures' and for the naming of each interlocutor's positioning thereby multiplying opportunities for relationality and connection. By incorporating these criteria into a revised understanding of competence, ICC becomes a dialogue that is robust and transformative.

Conclusion

Shor (1992) observed that:

> [We need] [h]abits of thought, reading, writing, and speaking which go beneath surface meaning, first impressions, dominant myths, official pronouncements, traditional clichés, received wisdom, and mere opinions, to understand the deep meaning, root causes, social context, ideology, and

> personal consequences of any action, event, object, process, organization, experience, text, subject matter, policy, mass media, or discourse.
>
> (p. 129)

In South Africa, there is a history of intercultural communication theory being deployed in service to the Apartheid regime (Steyn, 1997). In the post-Apartheid, post-colonial context, an understanding of intercultural competence in higher education in South Africa must be underpinned by cognisance of the need to redress often-traumatic economic and political processes that are both contemporary and historical and the moral imperative to engage in a renegotiation of personal subjectivities shaped within such relations. Communication constitutes much more than the sharing or exchange of messages and information but is rather inextricably bound up with power as well as the power to define meaning and in this context should not be used to reinforce established power relations as a means of maintaining the status quo (MacDonald & O'Regan, 2007). As a result, the project of developing conceptualisations of intercultural communication and competencies is also a moral project within the broader context of material inequality and unequal power relations. It is incumbent upon educators and those working with modalities of intercultural communication in higher education in South Africa to conceptualise and offer spaces of communicative possibility – possibilities that enable ways of knowing and being that work through, and ultimately transcend, historical divisions, and the wounds of epistemic violence.

Note

1 With due acknowledgement of indebtedness to Twine's concept of racial literacy (2004).

References

Abdi, A. A. (2007). Global multiculturalism: Africa and the recasting of the philosophical and epistemological plateaus. *Diaspora, Indigenous, and Minority Education*, *1*(4), 251–64.

—— (2008). Europe and African thought systems and philosophies of education. *Cultural Studies*, *22*(2), 309–27.

Africa Network expert panel (2014). Why are there so few black professors in South Africa? 6 October. Retrieved from www.theguardian.com/world/2014/oct/06/south-africa-race-black-professors

Asante, M. K. (1983). The ideological significance of Afrocentricity in intercultural communication. *Journal of Black Studies*, *14*(1), 3–19.

Banks, J. (1997). *Educating citizens in a multicultural society*. New York, NY: Columbia University Press.

Deardorff, D. K. (2006). Identification and assessment of intercultural competence as a student outcome of internationalization. *Journal of Studies in International Education*, *10*(3), 241–66.

Dei, G. (1998). Local knowledges and educational reforms in Ghana. *Canadian and International Education*, *29*(1), 37–51.
—— (2000). African development: The relevance and implications of indigenousness. In G. Dei, B. Hall, & D. Rosenberg (Eds.), *Indigenous knowledges in global contexts: Multiple readings of our world* (pp. 70–86). Toronto: University of Toronto Press.
England, A. (2015). South Africa: Barriers to entry. *Financial Times*, 25 October. Retrieved from www.ft.com/cms/s/0/671a0b68-77f2-11e5-933d-efcdc3c11c89.html#axzz3xmrPxt9x
Fairbanks, E. (2015). Why South African students have turned on their parents' generation. *The Guardian*, 18 November. Retrieved from www.theguardian.com/news/2015/nov/18/why-south-african-students-have-turned-on-their-parents-generation
Fantini, A., & Tirmizi, A (2006). Exploring and assessing intercultural competence. *World Learning Publications*. Paper 1. Retrieved from http://digitalcollections.sit.edu/worldlearning_publications/1
Franchi, V. (2003). Across or beyond the racialised divide? Current perspectives on 'race', racism and 'intercultural relations' in 'post-Apartheid' South Africa. *International Journal of Intercultural Relations*, *27*(2), 125–33.
Freire, P. (2000). *Pedagogy of the oppressed*. New York, NY: Continuum.
Gade, C. (2012). What is Ubuntu? Different interpretations among South Africans of African descent. *South African Journal of Philosophy*, *31*(3), 484–503.
Ghosh, R., & Abdi, A. A. (2004). *Education and the politics of difference: Canadian perspectives*. Toronto: Canadian Scholars' Press.
Grosfoguel, R. (2012). The dilemmas of ethnic studies in the United States: Between liberal multiculturalism, identity politics, disciplinary colonization, and decolonial epistemologies. *Human Architecture: Journal of the Sociology of Self-Knowledge*, *10*(1), 81–90.
—— (2013). The structure of knowledge in westernized universities. Epistemic racism/sexism and the four genocides/epistemicides of the long 16th century. *Human Architecture: Journal of the Sociology of Self-Knowledge*, *11*(1), 73–90.
Higgs, P. (2003). African philosophy and the transformation of educational discourse in South Africa. *Journal of Education*, *30*(1), 5–22.
Khoza, R. (2012). *Attuned leadership: African humanism as compass*. London: Penguin.
Letseka, M. (2000). African philosophy and educational discourse. In P. Higgs, N. C. G. Vikalisa, T. V. Mda, & N. T. Assie-Lumumba (Eds.), *African voices in education* (pp. 179–93). Lansdowne: Juta Academic.
Louw, D. (2002). *Ubuntu and the challenges of multiculturalism in post-Apartheid South Africa*. Sovenga: Expertisecentrum Zuidelijk Afrika.
MacDonald, M. N., & O'Regan, J. P. (2007). Cultural relativism and the discourse of intercultural communication: Aporias of praxis in the intercultural public sphere. *Language and Intercultural Communication*, *7*(4), 267–78.
Mazrui, A. A. (2003). Towards re-thinking African universities: Who killed intellectualism in the postcolonial era? *Alternatives: Turkish Journal of International Relations*, *2*(384), 135–63.
Mbembe, A. (2015). *Decolonizing knowledge and the question of the archive*. Retrieved from http://wiser.wits.ac.za/system/files/Achille%20Mbembe%20-%20Decolonizing%20Knowledge%20and%20the%20Question%20of%20the%20Archive.pdf

Mbigi, L., & Maree, J. (2005). *Ubuntu: The spirit of African transformation management*. Randburg: Knowres Publishing.
Mbiti, J. S. (1969). *African religions and philosophy*. London: Heinemann.
Metz, T. (2011). Ubuntu as moral theory and human rights in South Africa. *African Human Rights Law Journal, 11*, 532–59.
Mignolo, W. (2009). Epistemic disobedience, independent thought, and decolonial freedom. *Theory, Culture & Society, 26*(7–8), 159–81.
Ngũgĩ wa Thiong'o (1981). *Decolonizing the mind: The politics of language in African literature*. London: Heinemann.
—— (1993). *Moving the center: The struggle for cultural freedoms*. London: Curry.
Nwosu, P. O. (2009). Understanding Africans' conceptualizations of intercultural competence. In D. K. Deardorff (Ed.), *The Sage handbook of intercultural competence* (pp. 158–78). Thousand Oaks, CA: Sage.
Nyerere, J. (1968). *Freedom and socialism: A selection from writing and speeches, 1965–67*. Oxford: Oxford University Press.
Odağ, Ö., Wallin, H. R., & Kedzior, K. K. (2015). Definition of intercultural competence according to undergraduate students at an international university in Germany. *Journal of Studies in International Education, 20*(2), 118–39.
Opubor, A. (2004). What my grandmother taught me about communication: perspectives from African cultural values. *Africa Media Review, 12*(1), 43–57.
Rathje, S. (2007). Intercultural competence: The status and future of a controversial concept. *Language and Intercultural Communication, 7*(4), 254–66.
Shor, I. (1992). *Empowering education: Critical teaching for social change*. Chicago, IL: University of Chicago Press.
Spitzberg, B. H. (1989). Issues in the development of a theory of interpersonal competence in the intercultural context. *International Journal of Intercultural Relations, 13*(3), 241–68.
Spitzberg, B. H., & Changnon, G. (2009). Conceptualizing intercultural competence. In D. K. Deardorff (Ed.), *The Sage handbook of intercultural competence* (pp. 2–52). Thousand Oaks, CA: Sage.
Stam, R., & Shohat, E. (1994). Contested histories: Eurocentrism, multiculturalism and the media. In D. Goldberg (Ed.), *Multiculturalism: A critical reader* (pp. 296–324). Malden, MA: Blackwell.
Steyn, M. (2009). *Intercultural competencies in Southern Africa: The African philosophy of Ubuntu*. UNESCO, unpublished report.
—— (2015). Critical diversity literacy: Essentials for the twenty-first century. In S. Vertovec (Ed.), *Routledge international handbook of diversity studies* (pp. 379–89). London and New York, NY: Routledge.
—— (1997). African conceptions of competence: A proposal for new directions in research. *Communication, 23*(1), 66–72.
Twine, F. W. (2004). A white side of black Britain: The concept of racial literacy. *Ethnic and Racial Studies, 27*(6), 878–907.
UNESCO. (2009). *World Report No. 2: Investing in cultural diversity and intercultural dialogue*. Paris: UNESCO. Available from www.unesco.org/en/world-reports/cultural-diversity
—— (2013). *Intercultural competences: Conceptual and operational framework*. Paris: UNESCO.

University of the Witwatersrand (2016). Media briefing, 18 January. Retrieved from www.wits.ac.za/news/latest-news/generalnews/2016/feesmustfall2016/statements/gauteng-vcs-call-on-leaders-to-help-stabilise-higher education.html

Van Binsbergen, W. (2003). *Intercultural encounters: African and anthropological lessons towards a philosophy of interculturality*. Munster: Die Deutsche Bibliothek.

Chapter 8

Chinese perspectives on intercultural competence in international higher education

Yi'an Wang (Hangzhou Dianzi University), Darla K. Deardorff (Duke University), and Steve J. Kulich (Shanghai International Studies University)

Introduction

With ever-increasing globalisation of the twenty-first century, intercultural understanding and competence are increasingly featured in the core mission statements of governments or educational institutions to develop informed and well-equipped citizens for this new era. Intercultural competence is no longer a mere aspiration but a 'must have' skill for the young generations in their higher education.

For example, Carroll (2015) suggests that fostering and assessing intercultural competence is important for teaching in an educationally oriented world because 'after graduation, all students will live and work in an increasingly globalising and interconnected world, where cultural diversity is the norm and where interacting with people from various cultural backgrounds underpins effective citizenship' (p. 79). Killick (2015) proposes that internationalisation is a set of responses to the complexity of globalisation and therefore, 'the legitimate end – modeled primarily as a sense of *self-in-the-world* and secondarily as the capabilities to *act-in-the-world*' (p. 35). He also noted intercultural competence as the key competence which will 'help shape our flow among alterity, and through considerations of what general conditions might better support the development of the global student' (Killick, 2015, p. 36).

In China, with increasing Ministry of Education mandates for language and culture teaching and growing awareness and pressure to keep up with the pace of globalisation and international exchanges, the challenges and opportunities for understanding and applying intercultural competence have never been greater for scholars and practitioners. For example, business colleges and organisational training firms are also increasingly focusing on intercultural competence training in international work and management contexts. With such a rapidly growing market and acknowledged need, there is increased intercultural competence research and practice in China.

What are Chinese perspectives on intercultural communication, especially given that much of the research to date is predominantly Euro-American (Miyahara, 1992; Spitzberg & Changnon, 2009)? In China, most work on intercultural competence largely continues to borrow overseas conceptualisations and adapt them primarily to language learning or teaching contexts, seeking to prepare Chinese students and sojourners for interaction in international contexts. There is growing awareness of the need to explore and expand the dynamics of intercultural competence according to Chinese perceptions, given the increasing complexity of both Chinese and global contexts. This chapter provides an overview of the development of intercultural competence research in the higher education context in China and then examines key dimensions of and frameworks for intercultural competence from Chinese perspectives. Finally, the chapter outlines practical implications and suggestions for educators both in limited domestic 'home'-based situations in the higher education context in China as well as in Anglo-Western universities (Carroll, 2015), where the number of Chinese international students continues to increase significantly.

Overview of intercultural competence development in China

Since China's opening in the 1980s, intercultural communication in China has emerged as a field related to foreign-language education and developed rapidly with increasing awareness and pressure to keep up with the pace of globalisation. Meanwhile, intercultural competence has been a focus of the fields of not only foreign-language education but also intercultural communication studies in China. Progress in intercultural communication research and education has undergirded the trend of national efforts on integrating intercultural competence in foreign-language teaching (FLT) and TEFL programs.

Under the guidance of policy documents issued by China's Ministry of Education, foreign-language teaching was urged to include intercultural competence (cf. Xu, 2006) and is now attempting to do so at all levels. In 2000, the Chinese English Syllabus for English Majors (CESEM) emphasised cultivating English majors' intercultural competence for the first time. CESEM now requires that English majors should have intercultural awareness, tolerance, and flexibility in real intercultural contexts. In 2004, two more influential policy documents were launched. The Chinese College English Curriculum Requirements (CECR) gave intercultural competence the same important role as English knowledge and proficiencies for millions of college English students. In the same year, the Chinese High School English Curriculum Standard elaborated that English education in high schools should include cultural knowledge, awareness, and skills in intercultural communication. In 2015, the new version of CECR normally requires colleges and universities in China to include the course Intercultural Communication as one of the compulsory courses in English education with the aim to develop students' intercultural competence.

With these policy documents from the Chinese Ministry of Education, intercultural communication education and intercultural competence are gradually being integrated into English education across China. College English teachers nationwide, even high-school English teachers, now affirm the promotion of communicative competence but are still challenged with how to integrate intercultural competence effectively into their teaching of language. However, some scholars are addressing these issues by applying different intercultural practices in foreign-language classrooms. Fox example, Chang and Zhao (2012) carried out action research to investigate intercultural teaching in a college English integrated course showing the effectiveness of teaching towards 'cultural knowings' in raising students' intercultural awareness. Fu (2015) cultivated Chinese intercultural students through a three-round action research-based investigation model of intercultural competence.

Within this work from Chinese scholars, informed critiques on intercultural competence/education research and practices in China are growing. Zhang (2012) noted two weaknesses in intercultural teaching in foreign language education in China: (1) the affiliated role of intercultural communication teaching to foreign language education; and (2) unclear aims and less systematic content in intercultural communication teaching. Further, based on survey findings (N = 82, college teachers at seven universities), Wang (2012) noted the lack of (1) holistic design of intercultural teaching (e.g., curriculum, textbooks, evaluation); (2) intercultural training for the teaching staff; (3) both teachers and students' awareness of the importance of intercultural education, especially the deeper understanding of diversity and dynamics of cultures; and (4) theoretical preparations for Chinese applications of intercultural education. According to a review by Kong and Luan (2012), China's intercultural communication is not aligning with globalisation trends and is not yet providing substantial foundations for the nation's need of intercultural communication teaching and learning at the post-secondary levels. Some reasons for this are that intercultural pedagogy in China has traditionally focused on foreign-language teaching in which culture and society are superficially addressed. Due to increased pressure from updated curriculum requirements, language proficiency, and the continuing lack of qualified intercultural training, few educators have the energy, skills, or experience to design an in-depth intercultural course. Xu (2011) argued that intercultural competence in China is hindered by (1) Western traditions that have long dominated communication studies and (2) prevailing tendencies towards reductionism, fragmentation, pragmatism (a preoccupation with effectiveness), and non-cross-cultural orientations. Given the great need to upgrade the status of Chinese intercultural communication teaching and research, more explorative work and data-driven empirical studies are needed within the Chinese context.

Intercultural competence frameworks/dimensions in China

Conceptually, Chinese scholars have been grappling with appropriate ways to adapt intercultural competence to Chinese contexts. Chen and his colleagues are probably most active in this field, highlighting some Chinese philosophical concepts related to the qualities for a competent communicator or leader (Chen & An, 2009): *Harmony* (和谐) is the chief goal of human behaviour for most Chinese, and thus communication competence would ultimately result in harmony in relationships with others, in which mutuality, respect, and honesty are valued. Second, three components (i.e. *shi* 时 = temporal, *wei* 位 = spatial, and *ji* 机 = change), rooted in Chinese philosophy, are listed to achieve the ultimate goal of Great Harmony in human interactions. As the great Chinese military genius and philosopher Sun Zi specifies, the ability of knowing *shi*, *wei*, and *ji*, symbolising the affairs of humans, heaven, and earth, is a guarantee to overcome one's counterparts in different areas of human world (Li, Yang, & Tan, 1985, as cited in Chen & An, 2009). Third, *zhong dao* (中道), or the way of meaning, is introduced as 'the guidepost for the action to achieve the equilibrium state of communication or leadership competence' (Chen & An, 2009, p. 200). According to Chen and An (2009), '*Zhong dao* is the way of being appropriate, fitting one's communication to the situation. It provides a principle that leads interactants to recognise the trace of movement (*ji*) and to know the right time (*shi*) to behave appropriately to fit in with environments (*wei*)' (Chen & An, 2009, p. 200). Finally, *cheng* (诚, sincerity), as the axis of *zhong dao* (中道, nonlinear cyclic process favouring an intuitive, sensitive and indirect way of communicating), is sustained by three spokes: benevolence (*ren*, 仁), righteousness (*yi*, 义), and propriety (*li*, 礼).

Several other intercultural competence studies and proposed models have emerged in recent years including Gao (2002), Wen (2004), Yang and Zhuang (2007), Xu and Sun (2013), Yongchen Gao (2014), Wang and Kulich (2015), and Wang (2016) that provide Chinese perspectives of intercultural competence:

- Yihong Gao (2002) proposed two levels of intercultural competence: (1) *dao* (道, a going across), increasing target cultural proficiency, and (2) *qi* (器, a going beyond), gaining culture awareness and a reflective, tolerant attitude, suggesting that going beyond is the more important pedagogical objective for English language teaching in China.
- Wen (2004), based in EFL (English as a Foreign Language) teaching, proposed a two-component intercultural communication competence (ICC) model to measure students' second-language proficiency. Her two components focus on (1) communicative competence, which involves linguistic, pragmatic, and strategic competence; and (2) intercultural competence, which involves sensitivity to, tolerance of, and flexibility in dealing with cultural differences. She further suggested that: (1) all language-teaching programmes offer a course on intercultural communication that combines the daily teaching of cultural knowledge with promoting the students' intercultural competence, and that beyond language courses; and (2) intercultural competence should be part of general education to help students develop a competitive edge in a world where globalisation has become a reality.

- Yang and Zhuang's (2007) review of Chinese scholarship suggested a framework of intercultural communication competence that included global mentality, cultural adaptation, knowledge, and communicative management.
- Xu and Sun (2013) proposed a progressive-interactive model of intercultural competence development which incorporates motivation, knowledge, skills, contexts, and outcomes (similar to Spitzberg and Changnon's five concepts and factors of intercultural competence in 2009), with a goal of cultivating students' intercultural personality in a globalising context. This model sees intercultural competence as requiring interactants to engage in intercultural communication beyond any particular culture and maintain their own cultural identity at the same time.
- Yongchen Gao (2014), building on Yihong Gao's (2002) work, suggested a conceptual framework for assessing Chinese college students' intercultural competence based on the traditional Chinese philosophical principles of integration of theory and practice (*zhi xing he yi* 知行合一), which was proposed by the famous Chinese philosopher Yangming Wang in the Song Dynasty. There are two mutually interactive dimensions of ***knowing*** (*zhi*) and ***doing*** (*xing*) in Gao's framework, and each dimension has three subsections. The dimension of knowing includes knowledge, awareness, and critical thinking while the dimension of doing includes attitudes, skills, and strategies.
- Though most publications in China have been polemic, empirical research is starting. Yang (2009) designed a three-phase study including (1) pilot interviews; (2) a survey study to generate a framework; (3) the design of an intercultural competence test; and (4) administration of that instrument to 248 university students. Zhang and Yang (2012) reported data supporting the standard three variable framework (cultural awareness, cultural knowledge, and communicative practice, like Kluckhohn's reputed affective, cognitive, and behavioural proposal seen in Chen and Starosta's 1996 triangle model and many others).
- Wang and Kulich's (2015; Wang, 2016) studies were designed around a descriptive and reflective interview process in the domestic higher education context in China, which incorporated mixed-method quantitative and qualitative assessments of students' perspectives. Through enrolment in a specially designed intercultural communication college course, more than 100 students at two Chinese universities (Hangzhou Dianzi University, a middle-level science university, and Shanghai International Studies University, an upper-level language university) were guided through systematic training sessions to prepare them to conduct two multi-step cross-cultural interviews. The process of selecting and meeting with cultural others, making observations on those interactions, post-encounter reflections, and overall course/process evaluations were each recorded through written assignments aimed at cultivating their intercultural competence. The studies intentionally allowed students to identify 'cultural Others' not only from different races and countries but also from varied domestic cultural backgrounds

(ethnicities, regional, religious, age, gender, etc.) in China, which is important given the increased focus globally on the 'multicultural' classroom.

- Wu, Fan, and Peng (2013) collected data from Chinese college students at five universities (N = 447) and showed that, of six factors of intercultural competence, knowledge of others and intercultural communication skills were strongest. Knowledge of self and attitudes were mid-range. Intercultural cognitive skills were weak, and intercultural awareness the weakest. These highlight criticisms that the practices of intercultural teaching in China still mainly focus on knowledge and skill-oriented training.
- Shen and Gao (2015) constructed the Intercultural Communication Competence Inventory for Chinese College Students (ICCICCS) based on their concept framework of knowing-and-doing model developed in 2014, and then administered the ICCICCS to 500 college students from different academic backgrounds in China. They claimed that the inventory had good reliability and validity and therefore it had considerable potential utility in the research of assessing college students' intercultural communication competence in China.

A Chinese student perspective on intercultural competence

In Wang and Kulich's (2015) study, ten broader intercultural attributes emerged (see Table 8.1). Most of the extensive content collected fit under one or more of these categories, and the analysis of coded responses provided conclusive descriptive evidence of students' intercultural development, suggesting that these provide a reasonable exploratory thematic frame for this Chinese sample.

According to Table 8.1, the ten areas emerging from the qualitative analysis could be considered in one way to be a 'Chinese' list of attributes from a student perspective. While most of the items fit comfortably into established intercultural competence frameworks which often involve classic ABC (affective, behavioural, cognitive) classification, three distinctive Chinese characteristics emerged: (1) perception of *xintai* psychological/emotional intuitive attitudes; (2) greater 'collective (we/our)' approach to thoughtful attitudes, mutual sensitivity, own or other's face-related emotions and shared relationship-building; and (3) renewed awareness of Chinese traditional philosophical tenets for helping understand others or promote personal growth for a more indigenous understanding of competence. Given that these characteristics are considered distinct from non-Chinese intercultural competence frameworks, they are briefly highlighted here:

Transformation of xintai *(heart attitude) in intercultural communication*

Of all the concepts derived in this student-led interview exploration, the main indigenous item that emerged was that of *xintai* (heart attitude, intuitive

Table 8.1 Grouping the ten emerging competence areas with classic intercultural competence areas.

Cultural level/mode	*Emerging intercultural competence categories*
Cognitive (patterns, knowledge, awareness)	1. interacting with a diversity of cultural people and patterns 2. understanding the complexity of culture 3. relearning own culture with new awareness
Affective (psychological, attitudinal, sensitivity, motivation)	4. generating positive attitudes towards other cultures 5. overcoming stereotypes and prejudice (negative attitudes) 6. seeing from other perspectives/worldviews (empathy and ethnorelativism) 7. cultural humility (overcoming cultural superiority, power, privilege, pride) 8. transformation of *xintai* (intuitive emotion/attitudes) 9. obtaining confidence and motivation in intercultural communication
Behavioural (skills, responses, action)	10. obtaining communicative skills

affective responses/judgements). In Chinese, *xin tai* literally means 'heart' and 'attitude'. Because the Chinese believe emotions come from heart, *xintai* is a kind of psychological and emotional aspect of communication, a type of intuition, gut response, or impression management that subconsciously affects interaction. Many Chinese may appear sensitive to others' feelings in order to keep or gain good *guanxi* (relationship-building). These Chinese students' articulation of the Chinese term *xintai* captures some of the normally unperceived psychological and/or subconscious emotional elements that likely determine levels of satisfaction or success in intercultural communication. Many students considered the transformation from negative *xintai* such as anxiety and pressure to positive *xintai* such as peace and decency as their biggest step of progress as a result of the project. And several noted that some *xintai* barriers originate from within Chinese culture, e.g., being too sensitive to others' feelings for mutual relationship-building to keeping *guanxi*. Such ability to interpret emotional cues may contribute to Chinese students' abilities to monitor and reflect on their own and others' feelings (Holmes & O'Neill, 2012), while at the same time contribute to increased anxiety (Wang & Kulich, 2015).

Greater 'collective (we / our)' approach

Many Chinese believe that all the contractions of the universe, including human interactions, should be resolved through the process of the dynamic integration of *yin* and *yang*, symbolised by the Great Ultimate or Tai Chi 太极. According to Chen (2004), 'The holistic principle unfolds the developmental feature of the cyclic movement in which individual components are interdependent, and inter-determined in a network of relations', and 'The mutual dependency of relationship reflected in the part-whole interdetermination also indicates that all individual components are equally valid outcomes of *Tai Chi* or the dialectic interaction of *Yin* and *Yang*' (p. 10). This echoes some efforts made recently by some Chinese scholars to emphasise the group or one's interpersonal relationships in conceptualising and assessing intercultural competence. As Ting-Toomey indicated, people in more collectivist cultures 'think of themselves as individuals with interlocking connections with others' (2009, p. 108); the Chinese students in this study drew more attention to mutual respect, shared understanding, in-group/out-group tolerance, and sincerity of thoughts and actions for building or maintaining cross-cultural personal *guanxi* or relationships or networks, even if sometimes this relationship-building may lead to emotional anxiety or fact/status pressures.

Renewed awareness of Chinese traditional philosophical tenets

Linking intercultural competence development to traditional Chinese tenets may serve useful. The findings in the Wang and Kulich (2015; Wang, 2016) study showed that students tended to reflect on new understandings of Chinese traditional philosophy in their journal entries. Some students noted that many Chinese traditional ethic principles share similar meanings with these key components of intercultural competence, especially for these affective variables. For example, some students mentioned a big challenge in their intercultural interaction was dealing with the balance between keeping their own cultural identity and showing respect to other cultures, which reminded them of an old Chinese saying, *bu bei bu kang* (不卑不亢, no inferiority and superiority), to other cultures. It reflects how the Chinese 'Doctrine of the Mean' has influenced intercultural competence transformation. Some other examples include *tui ji ji ren* (推己及人, consider others as if in one's own place, similar in meaning to cultural empathy), *qiu tong cun yi* (求同存异, seek common ground while preserving differences, similar in meaning to tolerance), etc. The findings continue the line of a series of attempts to link Chinese philosophy to intercultural competence studies.

To sum up, Chinese scholarship on intercultural competence is yielding some different perspectives beyond those from Euro-American traditions; these perspectives, which are culturally rich, relational, and shared-emotion contextual perspectives are worth considering in assessing or updating other models.

Practical implications for international higher education

What do these Chinese perspectives on intercultural competence development mean for international higher education? There are some practical implications for intercultural education and suggestions for educators both in domestic 'home'-based situations in the higher education context in China and in Anglo-Western universities.

Focus on developing intercultural competence through an ongoing and interactive process

The models and studies discussed here support the process orientation in developing intercultural competence mentioned in previous intercultural competence literature (Deardorff, 2006; Holmes & O'Neill, 2012). The Chinese students in the various studies tend to develop their intercultural competence through their ongoing interaction and relationship-building with representatives of other cultures. For example, students' ten intercultural attributes all support the essential components of intercultural knowledge, attitude, and skills reflected in Deardorff's Process Model of Intercultural Competence (2006), which reflects a cyclical process through individual level factors (attitudes, knowledge, and skills) and interaction levels (internal and external outcomes), and movement from personal to interpersonal levels (intercultural interaction).

Therefore, if intercultural competence development is understood from a perspective of a transformation of intercultural interaction into culture itself and an ongoing relationship, we need to attach the importance of two essential elements which are usually missing in many training programmes and models: time (Spitzberg & Changnon, 2009) and patience, especially in the case of Chinese students, who probably require more time to transform the unperceived psychological and/or subconscious emotional elements such as *xintai* and build cross-cultural personal *guanxi* relationships or networks when these intercultural encounter happens.

Understand the noted gaps in the existing intercultural competence models

The focus on intercultural competence in Asian and African cultures is generally not the individual but rather the in-group or one's interpersonal relationship circle (Miyahara, 1992; Nwosu, 2009; Wang & Kulich, 2015). Chinese students tend to emphasise 'the collectivistic tendencies of Eastern perspectives' (Spitzberg & Changnon, 2009, p. 44) such as group-oriented attitudes, interpersonal sensitivity, shared emotions, and relationship-building rather than individual-oriented concepts or skill-driven aspects. Intercultural teachers and educators need to understand these noted gaps in the existing intercultural models when working with students from different cultural backgrounds and be more cautious in fostering and assessing intercultural competence accordingly.

For Chinese students, instead of making quick evaluative judgements, educators need to understand that emotional anxiety and pressure may originate from students' eagerness and sensitivity to maintain mutual relationship-building and therefore more patience, support, and resources are needed to help them initiate social interchanges, manage anxiety, and maintain peaceful *xintai* in intercultural communication. For example, in Wang and Kulich's study (2015; Wang, 2016), a series of measures were adopted to help Chinese students experience effective intercultural learning including carefully designed procedures for the course project, qualified training sessions organised to guide students to conduct their own projects, frequent interactions through an online platform among students and teachers, and a mixed-assessment approach to intercultural competence.

Consider ethnographic approaches to intercultural teaching and learning

The Wang and Kulich studies (2015; Wang, 2016) highlight the value of a descriptive and reflective intercultural ethnographic interview approach as an intervention and means of developing and assessing intercultural competence, particularly effective in the higher education context in China. In recent decades, more intercultural researchers and practitioners believe the use of ethnography has clear benefits on developing some core capacities related to intercultural competence such as empathy, sensitivities, awareness, and critical reflection (e.g., Roberts et al., 2001; Corbett, 2003; Du, 2008; Jackson, 2006, 2012; Wilkinson, 2012). Though there are some criticisms for time-limited curriculum to implement procedures that are adequately 'ethnographic', the training process in the course was designed carefully with the aim to cultivate 'ethnographic awareness' in order to facilitate the requisite engagement, analytical, and reflective processes needed to benefit this way from intercultural encounters. Corbett (2003) suggests that students should be encouraged to 'live the ethnographic life' (p. 116). Even for those students who are restricted to more limited access to native speakers and target cultural products, the basic materials for 'pragmatic ethnography' (someone to talk to and some events to observe) are available to some degree (i.e. via technology). The trainers can develop students' ethnography skills through 'decentring' activities that analyse the home culture, and make imaginative use of whatever cultural resources available (p. 116).

Remember the importance of cultural mentors within a well-designed training process

The Wang and Kulich study shows the importance of a cultural mentor in the learning intervention to enhance students' intercultural competence in the domestic context in China. One of the major findings from research in international education is that intercultural learning does not happen automatically abroad (Paige, Hegeman, & Jon, 2006; Deardorff, 2009b). Deardorff (2009b) notes that intercultural experience alone does not promote intercultural competence automatically which means intercultural educators or trainers must be 'intentional about students' intercultural competence' (p. xiii). She suggests that adequate preparation, substantive intercultural interactions, and authentic relationship-building can help to develop students' intercultural competence. Therefore, a systematic training programme for students and teachers can be quite helpful (Wang & Kulich, 2015). Moreover, cultural mentors may be even more important to those who have domestic intercultural education than international students, especially in initial stages of motivating and guiding them to engage in intercultural interactions due to the lack of an accessible multicultural environment.

Use online intercultural communication

The fact that the younger generations are more familiar with e-life suggests that online intercultural exchange should be explored more effectively and appropriately in intercultural education in the future (see Carroll, 2015). In addition, all of these suggest that intercultural understanding can happen not only in the obvious cross-cultural interactions abroad but also 'at home' through virtual online intercultural exchange (O'Dowd, 2007; Merryfield, 2007). Current Chinese work (including the first intercultural MOOC [Massive Online Open Course] in China, offered through Shanghai International Studies University) indicates that those who engage in online exchange ('epals', email, some online social network such QQ and Wechat) may see more intercultural growth than those in face-to-face interactions (Wang & Kulich, 2015; Wang, 2016).

Implement 'own-culture story' as a strategy for intercultural students

A very practical implication for the Wang and Kulich (2015) study is the use of 'own-culture story' as an important strategy for increasing students' intercultural sensitivity and awareness of their own identities and providing a benchmark before interaction with otherness. This implication concurs with other scholars' efforts on linking cultural self-study to intercultural competence (Weigel, 2009; Holliday, Hyde, & Kullman, 2010). As Killick (2015) points out, 'like the symbol of Yin-Yang there seems to be a complex relationship between self and other, somehow detached, but also formulating the frame for our development and understanding' (p. 35).

Use a mixed-methods assessment approach to intercultural competence

Studies in China (Wang & Kulich, 2015; Wang, 2016; Fu, 2015) indicate that a mix of qualitative and quantitative measures is effective in intercultural competence assessment, which supports similar studies (Deardorff, 2015). And, while self-report instruments can be used as acceptable tools to measure students' intercultural competence in China, they are insufficient in assessing the complexity of one's intercultural competence (Holmes & O'Neill, 2012). Utilising direct measures such as a reflective report throughout a course or intercultural experience provides a more contextualised and comprehensive way of understanding students' intercultural competence development.

Conclusion

This chapter has outlined intercultural competence research and definitions from a Chinese perspective to avoid the potential ethnocentricity of current models. With China's massive base of students, coupled with trends towards greater enrolment abroad, and the new national emphasis on intercultural competence within China, understanding the Chinese context is important both for theorising and for developing relevant and practical designs for cultivating intercultural competence within China and globally. Therefore, in an educationally mobile world, Chinese perspectives of intercultural competence help educators in higher education contexts around the world make better transitions between different educational values and beliefs in times of change.

References

Carroll, J. (2015). *Tools for teaching in an educationally mobile world*. London and New York, NY: Routledge.

Chang, X. M., & Zhao, Y. S. (2012). An action research on developing students' intercultural awareness in college English teaching. *Foreign Language World*, *2*, 27–34. (In Chinese.)

Chen, G.-M. (2004). Bian (*change*): A perceptual discourse of *I Ching*. Paper presented at the annual meeting of National Communication Association, Chicago, November.

Chen, G.-M., & An, R. (2009). A Chinese model of intercultural leadership competence. In D. K. Deardorff (Ed.), *The Sage handbook of intercultural competence* (pp. 196–208). Thousand Oaks, CA: Sage.

Chen, G. M., & Starosta, W. J. (1996). Intercultural communication competence: A synthesis. *Communication Yearbook*, *19*, 353–84.

—— (2005). *Foundations of intercultural communication* (2nd edn). Lanham, MD: University Press of America.

China's Ministry of Education. (2000). *English syllabus for English majors (ESEM)*. Beijing: Higher Education Press. (In Chinese.)

—— (2004a). *College English curriculum requirements*. Beijing: Foreign Language Teaching and Research Press. (In Chinese.)

—— (2004b). *High school English curriculum standard*. Beijing: People's Education Press. (In Chinese.)

Corbett, J. (2003). *An intercultural approach to English language teaching*. Clevedon: Multilingual Matters.

Deardorff, D. K. (2006). Identification and assessment of intercultural competence as a student outcome of internationalization. *Journal of Studies in Intercultural Education*, *10*(3), 241–66.

—— (2009a). Synthesizing conceptualizations of intercultural competence: A summary and emerging themes. In D. K. Deardorff (Ed.), *The Sage handbook of intercultural competence* (pp. 264–70). Thousand Oaks, CA: Sage.

—— (2009b). Preface. In D. K. Deardorff (Ed.), *The Sage handbook of intercultural competence* (pp. xi–xiv). Thousand Oaks, CA: Sage.

—— (2015) *Demystifying outcomes assessment for international educators: A practical approach*. Sterling, VA: Stylus.

Du, W. H. (2008). Integrating culture learning into foreign language curricula: An examination of the ethnographic interview approach in a Chinese as a foreign language classroom. Unpublished doctoral dissertation, University of Wisconsin, Milwaukee.

Fu, X. Q. (2015). Cultivating Chinese intercultural learners through an action research-based investigation model of intercultural communication competence. Unpublished doctoral dissertation. Shanghai International Studies University, Shanghai.

Gao, Y. C. (2014). Developing a conceptual framework for assessing Chinese college students' intercultural communication competence. *Foreign Language World*, *4*, 80–8. (In Chinese.)

Gao, Y. H. (2002). Cultivating intercultural communication: 'going across' and 'going beyond'. *Foreign Languages and Their Teaching*, *10*, 27–31. (In Chinese.)

Holliday, A., Hyde, M., & Kullman, J. (2010). *Intercultural communication: An advanced resource book for students*. London and New York, NY: Routledge.

Holmes, P., & O'Neill, G. (2012). Developing and evaluating intercultural competence: Ethnographies of intercultural encounters. *International Journal of Intercultural Relations*, *36*(5), 707–18.

Hymes, D. (1980). *Language in education: Ethnolinguistic essays*. Washington, DC: Center for Applied Linguistics.

Jackson, J. (2006). Ethnographic pedagogy and evaluation in short-term study abroad. In M. Byram & A. W. Feng (Eds.), *Living and studying abroad: Research and practice* (pp. 134–56). Clevedon: Multilingual Matters.

—— (2012). Education abroad. In J. Jackson (Ed.), *The Routledge handbook of language and intercultural communication* (pp. 449–63). London and New York, NY: Routledge.

Killick, D. (2015). *Developing the global student*. London and New York, NY: Routledge.

Kong, D. L., & Luan, S. W. (2012). Construction of modes for cross-cultural college English teaching. *Foreign Language World*, *2*, 17–26. (In Chinese.)

Li, S., Yang, X. J., and Tan, J. Z. (1985). *Sun Zi and management*. Hong Kong: San Lian.

Merryfield, M. M. (2007). The web and teachers' decision-making in global education. *Theory and Research in Social Education*, *35*(2), 256–75.

Miyahara, A. (1992). Cross-cultural views on interpersonal communication competence: A preliminary study proposal. *Human Communication Studies: Journal of the Communication Association of Japan*, *20*, 129–43.

Nwosu, P. O. (2009). Understanding Africans' conceptualizations of intercultural competence. In D. K. Deardorff (Ed.), *The Sage handbook of intercultural competence* (pp. 158–78). Thousand Oaks, CA: Sage.

O'Dowd, R. (2007). *Online intercultural exchange: An introduction for foreign language teachers*. Clevedon: Multilingual Matters.

Paige, R. M., Hegeman, R., & Jon. J.-E. (2006). Georgetown University research report. Unpublished manuscript. University of Minnesota, Minneapolis, MN.

Roberts, C., Byram, M., Barro, A., Jordan, S., & Street, B. (2001). *Language learners as ethnographers*. Clevedon: Multilingual Matters.

Shen, J. M., & Gao, Y. C. (2015). Construction of intercultural communication competence inventory for Chinese college students based on knowing-and-doing model. *Foreign Languages in China*, *12*(3), 14–21. (In Chinese.)

Spitzberg, B. H., & Changnon, G. (2009). Conceptualizing intercultural competence. In D. K. Deardorff (Ed.), *The Sage handbook of intercultural competence* (pp. 2–52). Thousand Oaks, CA: Sage.

Sun, S. N., & Xu, L. S. (2014). Computer-autonomous intercultural competence development in college English teaching. *Foreign Language World*, *4*, 89–95. (In Chinese.)

Ting-Toomey, S. (2009). Intercultural conflict competence as a facet of intercultural competence development: Multiple conceptual approaches. In D. K. Deardorff (Ed.), *The Sage handbook of intercultural competence* (pp. 100–20). Thousand Oaks, CA: Sage.

Wang, Y. A. (2012). An analysis on intercultural teaching in college: Based on a survey from college English teachers' perspectives in Zhejiang Province. In X. Chen & J. D. Guo (Eds.), *The theoretical exploration and practical innovation of foreign languages teaching in universities and colleges* (pp. 40–9). Zhangjiang: Zhejiang University Press. (In Chinese.)

—— (2016). Exploring model-based approaches to cultivate and assess intercultural competence through a domestic interview-based course design in China. Unpublished doctoral dissertation. Shanghai International Studies University, Shanghai.

Wang Y. A., & Kulich, S. J. (2015). Does context count? Developing and assessing intercultural competence through an interview- and model-based domestic course design in China. *The International Journal of Intercultural Relations*, *48*, 1–136.

Weigel, R. C. (2009). Intercultural competence through cultural self-study: A strategy for adult learners. *International Journal of Intercultural Relations*, *33*, 346–60.

Wen, Q. F. (2004). Globalization and intercultural competence. In K.-K. Tam & T. Weiss (Eds.), *English and globalization: Perspectives from Hong Kong and Mainland China* (pp. 169–80). Hong Kong: The Chinese University Press.

Wilkinson, J. (2012). The intercultural speaker and the acquisition of intercultural/global competence. In J. Jackson (Ed.), *The Routledge handbook of language and intercultural communication* (pp.s 296–309). London and New York, NY: Routledge.

Wu, W. P., Fan, W. W., & Peng, R. Z. (2013). An analysis of the assessment tools for Chinese college students intercultural communicative competence. *Foreign Language Teaching and Research*, *45*(4), 581–92. (In Chinese.)

Xu, L. S. (2006). *Intercultural communication competence.* Paper presented at the 6th Chinese Symposium for Intercultural Communications sponsored by the China Association for Intercultural Communication, Nanjing Normal University, 20–2 May.

—— (2011). Intercultural competence revisited. *Journal of Zhejiang University (Humanities and Social Science Edition)*, *3*, 132–9. (In Chinese.)

Xu, L. S., & Sun, S. N. (2013). Towards the construction of a progressive-interactive model of intercultural competence development. *Journal of Zhejiang University (Humanities and Social Science Edition)*, *43*(4), 113–21. (In Chinese.)

Yang, Y. (2009). *The defining and assessment of intercultural communicative competence.* Unpublished Ph.D. dissertation, Beijing Language and Cultural University, Beijing.

Yang, Y., & Zhuang, E. P. (2007). The construction of intercultural communication competence framework for foreign language teaching. *Foreign Language World*, *4*, 13–21. (In Chinese.)

Zhang, H. L. (2012). Intercultural education-oriented foreign language teaching: History, status and future. *Foreign Language World*, *2*, 2–7. (In Chinese.)

Zhang, W. D., & Yang, L. (2012). Construction of intercultural communicative competence: An empirical study from the perspective of foreign language education in China. *Foreign Language World*, *2*, 8–16. (In Chinese.)

Chapter 9

Mapping intercultural competence

Aligning goals, outcomes, evidence, rubrics, and assessment

Scott G. Blair (The Education Abroad Network)

Introduction

After over five decades of scholarly work around intercultural competence, one of the research-based definitions of this concept emerged in 2006 (Deardorff), following a long tradition of scholarship in intercultural competence. The literature on this concept indicates that intercultural competence requires foundational attributes, such as individual knowledge, skills, and attitudes, which, for those involved in intercultural interactions, foster observable outcomes both internally and externally that, in turn, lead to effective and appropriate communication and behaviour. A corresponding model of intercultural competence illustrates how students acquire this competence through an ongoing cycle or process of lifelong learning, the Deardorff Process Model of Intercultural Competence (see Figure 9.1). Research on intercultural competence also provides a greater understanding of what mix of optimal instructional environments – such as George Kuh's (2008) high-impact practices and David Kolb's (1984) Experiential Learning Cycle – is most effective for students seeking to acquire higher levels of intercultural competence. Taken together, these are considerable intellectual achievements.

One of the important results of this research is the accumulating proof of just how complex the construct of intercultural competence is. This is perhaps most clearly borne out in the cautious advice offered for those setting out to assess intercultural competence – that educators need to use a multimethod, multiperspective, multilayered mix of direct/indirect, formative/summative, student/programmatic, and task-based/longitudinal approaches using experiential and developmental methods. This can seem daunting to practitioners wishing to assess intercultural competence. This chapter, then, takes the Deardorff Process Model of Intercultural Competence, along with input from other intercultural competence models such as the Developmental Model of Intercultural Sensitivity by Milton Bennett (1993), and seeks to map out a process for generating more behavioural specificity around learning objectives and corresponding evidence of achievement.

Specifically, this chapter presents a research-based methodology for outlining what might be called an 'atomised' or 'disaggregated' approach to articulating

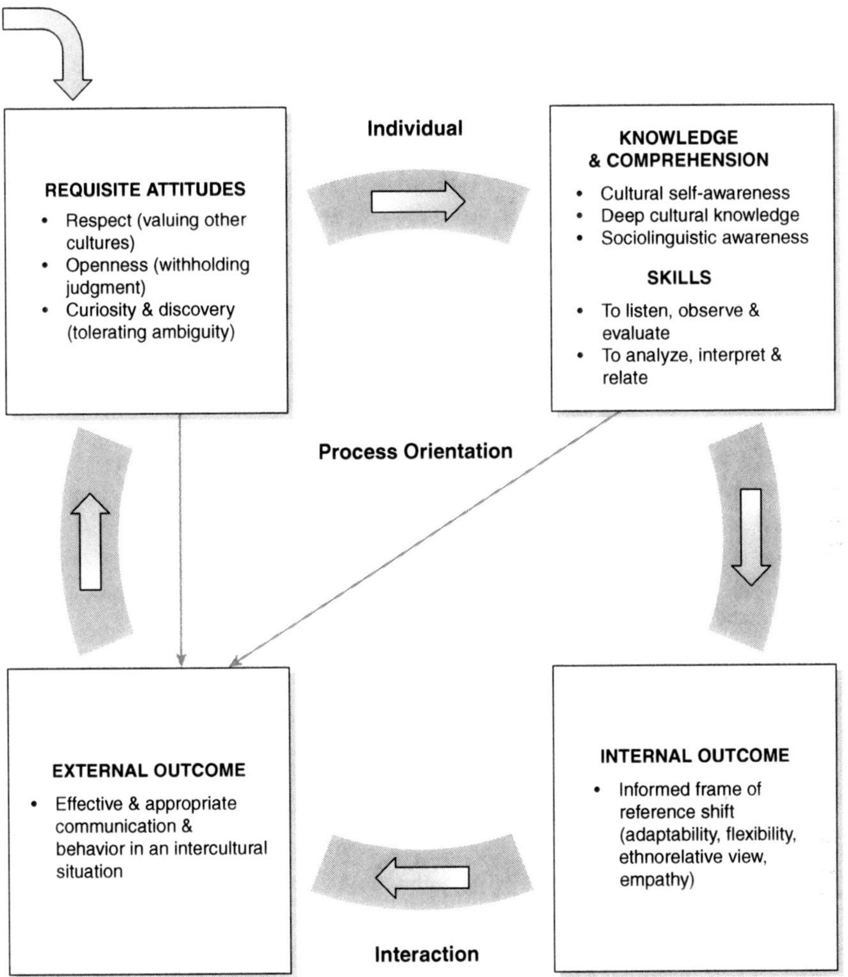

Figure 9.1 Deardorff Process Model of Intercultural Competence (2006).

and assessing intercultural competence. It describes why intercultural competence must be broken down and assessed piece by piece and why single methods or single inventories will always remain insufficient.

In terms of practical application, this chapter includes a selected set of detailed cognitive maps of the intercultural competence construct, complemented with the bank of recently developed Association of American Colleges & Universities (AAC&U) VALUE Rubrics which align to specific constituent elements of the intercultural competence construct. An example of the capstone intercultural competence map is included in this chapter along with several related maps for specific attributes of intercultural competence.

The underlying thesis of this chapter is both straightforward and oriented towards the practitioner: once educators take into account the standard recommendations for designing and implementing sound assessment processes, the teaching, learning, and assessing of intercultural competence can begin in earnest – but only after fully appreciating that the complexity of the construct requires that one do so selectively and methodically.

Mapping intercultural competence: Level 1 – the overview

To begin this endeavour in line with recent scholarship on the nature of this construct (Deardorff, 2015), intercultural competence can be viewed as the process of developing targeted knowledge, skills, and attitudes that lead to visible behaviour and communication that are both effective and appropriate in intercultural interactions (per Figure 9.1). While educators should adapt the wording of established definitions of intercultural competence to specific institutional settings, it is nevertheless prudent to retain several important ideas about intercultural competence.

First, intercultural competence is a lifelong *developmental process* or way of 'becoming' and 'being'; it is not a one-off act of achievement or acquisition. It can involve gains and losses in competence over both time and cultural space. Indeed, both the name of the schematic model of intercultural competence – called a *process* model – and its arrows indicating an ongoing cycle of learning and interaction convey its fundamentally developmental nature (Deardorff, 2006).

Second, the tripartite mix of knowledge, skills, and attitudes embedded in the definition, while a familiar typology to educators, must also articulate targeted outcomes that are *intentional* and specifically designed for intercultural learning within specific contexts. The broad categories of knowledge, skills, and attitudes need to be broken down into much more specific outcome statements that target discrete cultural learning.

Third, because intercultural competence is manifested only at the intersection of individual awareness and social/cultural interaction, it must be *behaviourally visible* and meaningful to all parties involved – and most certainly to third parties if there is to be any effort to assess it directly.

The schematic diagram of the Process Model of Intercultural Competence provides a useful starting point (see Figure 9.1). The diagram provides an overview of the constituent attributes of intercultural competence, organises them into appropriate categories, separates individual from interactional attributes, distinguishes between desired internal and external outcomes, relates each of the elements to one another within a cycle of developmental learning, and indicates where one should conceptually begin the process.

In order to begin building in the specificity and definitional detail that assessment of intercultural competence requires, we have disaggregated the Deardorff Process Model and transferred its contents to a separate analytic chart (see Table 9.1).

In this format, what the Process Model loses in its visual circular motion and process orientation it gains in definitional clarity and descriptive power. In addition, this analytic table introduces several additional insights, attributes, or language related to intercultural competence which have been drawn from the work of Alvino E. Fantini (2009) and the American Council on Education (2008).

The left side of Table 9.1 displays the foundational individual attributes of intercultural competence that Deardorff (2009, p. 479) isolated through the Delphi technique employed for achieving definitional consensus among experts in intercultural competence. These attributes are listed under the three categories Deardorff uses: 'attitudes', 'knowledge and comprehension', and 'skills'. Each category also includes the roughly corresponding and commonly used qualifier of 'affective', 'cognitive', or 'behavioural' for each domain respectively. In line with research in intercultural competence carried out by Fantini (1999; 2009, p. 459), the table also subordinates the attitude–skill–knowledge trinity to the concept of 'awareness'. For instructional purposes, it is important that students appreciate the special role 'awareness' plays in developing intercultural competence and for this reason it appears in the table.

In the domain of knowledge and comprehension, a fourth category has been added – grasp of global issues – in line with collaborative studies with Olson, Evans, and Schoenberg (2007) at the American Council on Education, along with AAC&U (2007), revealing the trends towards infusing global learning and knowledge into the content of intercultural learning outcomes. Finally, in the behavioural domain of skills, two learning objectives previously left implicit in recent research have been made more explicit: empathy and critical thinking.

Disaggregating the Deardorff Process Model of Intercultural Competence and presenting it as it appears in Table 9.1 provides a number of benefits to the process of assessment. As a complement to the schematic of the model, the table immediately provides the supplemental definitional clarity for a fuller understanding of the nature and interaction of the model's individual component parts. It also displays the remarkable complexity of intercultural competence which in turn explains why it is impossible to assess intercultural competence as a single construct or with any single instrument and at any single moment. Indeed, the table immediately conveys the necessity of determining which specific aspect of intercultural competence one wishes to focus on and, as such, the table makes it easier to prioritise the various aspects of intercultural competence, based upon one's overall mission, goals, and purposes of course, programme, or institution. As Deardorff (2015) affirms, 'Prioritization is not a onetime discussion, but rather an ongoing process' (p. 135). Finally, the table conveys how important it is to break down the intercultural competence construct into ever more specific and educationally manageable pieces. This, in turn, can only be achieved through the process of writing ever more specific and measurable learning-outcome statements for each subordinate attribute of the intercultural competence construct. In short, as both instructional tool and general guide, the analytic view in Table 9.1 makes the next step in the teaching, learning, and assessing of intercultural competence possible.

Table 9.1 **Deardorff Proces Model: Constituent Attributes of Intercultural Competence**

Definition of ***Intercultural Competence****: The process of developing targeted knowledge, skills, and attitudes that lead to visible behaviour and communication that are both effective and appropriate in intercultural interactions.*

Adapted from the Deardorff (2006) Process Model of Intercultural Competence.

		Foundational attributes (individual)			**Actionable/behavioural attributes** (interaction)	
		Learner objectives	**Learning outcome statements (examples)**		**Learner objectives**	**Learning outcome statements** (examples)
	Attitudes (motivation) (affective)	**Respect:** Valuing other cultures	• Value and appreciate cultural diversity • Recognise the attributes of host people, society and culture • Express disinterested comparisons of cultural habits • Show willingness to bridge cultural differences	**Internal outcome**	*Develop an informed frame of reference shift that includes:*	*Informed frame of reference shift revealed by the student's ability to:*
		Openness: Withholding judgement	• Show willingness to interact with culturally different others • Initiate and develop interaction with culturally different others • Suspend judgement in valuing cultural interactions • Reveal a disposition to being proven wrong		**Adaptability**	• Expand boundaries of one's comfort zones • Welcome and manage the unexpected • Align oneself to local habits or customs
		Curiosity: Interest in seeking out cultural interactions	• View one's cultural interaction as learning opportunities • Ask complex questions about other cultures and people • Articulate informed answers to complex questions • Value multiple perspectives when answering questions		**Flexibility**	• Show openness to the initiatives of others • Shift or redefines priorities • Avoid setting rigid expectations
		Discovery: Tolerating ambiguity	• View cultural ambiguity as a positive learning experience • Show distrustfulness of absolutes in cultural interactions • Welcome cultural discomfort as part of learning processes • Reflect deliberatively to eke out multiple meanings		**Ethnorelative view**	• Show awareness of one's own distinct culture • Show awareness of one's distinct personal history • Show acceptance of other's culture
...eness		**Cultural self-awareness**	• Articulate cultural forces within one's upbringing • Articulate insights into one's cultural rule and biases • Articulate how experience shapes one's worldview		**Empathy**	• Appreciate realities and struggles of others • Think deeply of living another's life

	Deep cultural knowledge	• Explain what culture is and how it affects people • Acquire basics of host history, politics and society • Identify links between people's beliefs, practices and history • Compare and contrast home and host cultures			
Knowledge/comprehension (cognitive)	**Sociolinguistic awareness**	• Acquire basic local language skills • Articulate differences in verbal/nonverbal communication • Articulate local direct/indirect and explicit/implicit styles • Use language awareness to negotiate shared relationships	**External outcome**	**Effective communication:** Within intercultural situations	• Adapt one's language to the desired objective • Use verbal and nonverbal communication skills to achieve one's objectives • Seek cooperation and involvement of cultural others • Minimise distortion and misunderstanding
	Grasp of global issues	• Explain meaning and significance of globalisation • Relate global forces to local issues and realities • Interrelate human, natural and global structures • Develop a global perspective for addressing current issues			
Skills (behavioural)	**Listening, observing, evaluating:** Using patience and perseverance	• Employ listening skills to unlock meaning • Employ observation skills to unlock meaning • Evaluate nature and dynamics of cultural difference • Show perseverance and patience within cultural interactions		**Appropriate communication:** Within intercultural situations	• Spark positive and ongoing engagement with interlocutors when using verbal and nonverbal communication skills to achieve one's objective • Receive positive assessment from others • Create cooperative rapport of reciprocity and mutuality
	Analysing, interpreting, relating: Comparatively and historically	• Analyse intercultural phenomena • Interpret intercultural phenomena • Relate home and host intercultural phenomena • Contextualise intercultural phenomena			
	Empathy: View world from other's perspectives	• Explain the meaning and significance of 'worldview' • Interpret intercultural experience from one's perspective • Interpret intercultural experience from other's perspective • Provide meaningful support to another cultural group		**Effective behaviour:** Within intercultural situations	• Adapt one's behaviour to the desired objective • Show behavioural ability to influence cultural others • Seek cooperation and engagement of cultural others
	Critical thinking	• Use principles of critical thinking • Recognise influence of context and assumptions • Describe problematic nature of evidence • Draw principled conclusions		**Appropriate behaviour:** Within intercultural situations	• Spark positive and ongoing engagement with interlocutors when using behavioural processes that advance one's objectives • Sustain and develop relationships • Receive positive assessment from others

Sources: Deardorff (2009, p. 28); Fantini (2009); American Council on Education (2008).

Table 9.2 **Foundational Individual Attributes**

Affective: Attitudes & Motivation

Affective Attitudes & Motivation *refers to a learner's emotional, psychological and experiential disposition towards cultural diversity generally and to one's intercultural engagement with diversity specifically. General attitudinal values such as awareness, respect, openness, curiosity, discovery, reciprocity, appreciation, and enthusiasm are requisites of intercultural competence.*

Adapted from the Deardorff (2006) Process Model of Intercultural Competence.

Learning objectives	***Learning outcome statements***	***Evidence*** *(examples)*	***Assessment***
Defined in terms of what success looks like when students are engaged in intercultural interactions.	***Defined in terms of concrete learning expectations and the means by which the larger goal is achieved. Objectives should be SMART: specific, measurable, action-oriented, realistic, and time-delineated.***	***Defined in terms of what general evidence can be gathered that shows progress towards the desired outcome.***	***Methods: direct and indirect***
Respect: Valuing other cultures The ability to engage and learn from perspectives and experiences different from one's own. This includes the curiosity to learn respectfully about the cultural diversity of other people and on an individual level to traverse cultural boundaries to bridge differences and collaboratively reach common goals. (AAC&U-VR-GL)	Value and appreciate cultural diversity	Writes and speaks positively about cultural differences	AAC&U-VR-GL
	Recognise the attributes of host people, society and culture	Collects positive data about habits and local customs	AAC&U-VR-GL
	Express disinterested comparisons of cultural habits	Writes and speaks non-defensively about differences	AAC&U-VR-GL
	Show willingness to bridge cultural differences	Builds ongoing engagement with cultural difference	AAC&U-VR-GL
Openness: Withholding judgement Willingness to initiate and develop interactions with culturally different others. Disposition to suspend judgement in valuing one's interactions with culturally different others. (AAC&U-VR-IKC)	Show willingness to interact with culturally different others	Expresses disinclination for automatic assessment	AAC&U-VR-IKC
	Initiate and develop interaction with culturally different others	Builds ongoing engagement with cultural difference	AAC&U-VR-IKC
	Suspend judgement in valuing cultural interactions	Employs non-judgemental verbal/ body language	AAC&U-VR-IKC
	Reveal a disposition to being proven wrong	Admits errors in one's thinking and actions	AAC&U-VR-IKC

Curiosity: Interest in seeking out cultural interactions The impulse to ask complex questions about other cultures, to seek out and articulate answers to these questions that reflect multiple cultural perspectives. (AAC&U-VR-IKC)	View one's cultural interaction as learning opportunities	Speaks and writes about learning moments seized	AAC&U-VR-IKC
	Ask complex questions about other cultures and people	Demonstrates an inquisitive and curious mind	AAC&U-VR-IKC
	Articulate informed answers to complex questions	Shows determination and methodology in getting answers	AAC&U-VR-IKC
	Value multiple perspectives when answering questions	Uses multiple sources when answering questions	AAC&U-VR-IKC
Discovery: Tolerating Ambiguity Suspends judgement in valuing their interactions with culturally different others: Postpones assessment or evaluation (positive or negative) of interactions with people culturally different from oneself. Disconnecting from the process of automatic judgment and taking time to reflect on possibly multiple meanings. (AAC&U-VR-IKC)	View cultural ambiguity as a positive learning experience	Conveys enthusiasm when discussing interactions	AAC&U-VR-IKC
	Show distrustfulness of absolutes in cultural interactions	Avoids absolutist, non-contextualised language/thought	AAC&U-VR-IKC
	Welcome cultural discomfort as part of learning processes	Expresses new and unsettling feelings positively	AAC&U-VR-IKC
	Reflect deliberatively to eke out multiple meanings	Employs a formal written method of reflection	AAC&U-VR-IKC

Mapping intercultural competence: Level 2 – general attributes

In line with the principles used to generate the overview of intercultural competence in Table 9.1, Table 9.2 presents a more complete and detailed exploration of the affective domain of attitudes appearing in Table 9.1.

On this second-level table, the definition of intercultural competence is retained while for the domain 'Affective attitudes and motivation', a fuller definition is provided, drawing upon the language of the Process Model itself. The four attributes of the Process Model related to the affective domain – respect, openness, curiosity, and discovery – still appear on the x-axis, retaining the title, order, and general descriptors that appeared in the original process-model schematic. On the y-axis appear columns for learning-outcome statements, evidence, and assessment, each with short corresponding definitional aides also drawn from research on the Process Model. However, mapping intercultural competence at this deeper level of detail requires that we define more specifically the meaning of these otherwise broad objectives. For this, we turn to AAC&U VALUE Rubrics.

In terms of establishing greater definitional clarity within intercultural competence, of articulating learning-outcome statements specifically tied to process-model domains, and of aligning assessment criteria to specific behavioural attributes of intercultural competence, the VALUE rubrics prove invaluable. Developed through the Association of American Colleges and Universities (AAC&U), the two VALUE rubrics, entitled Intercultural Knowledge and Competence (which are based on both Deardorff's Process Model as well as Bennett's Developmental Model) and Global Learning are particularly useful, and elements of others, such as civic engagement, ethical reasoning, and creative thinking, are equally helpful. Each rubric is introduced with a discussion of definition and framing language and includes a glossary.

There is insufficient space here to provide a detailed discussion of all four learning objectives on this table, much less address the two other domains, not to mention the internal/external outcomes. However, due to the centrality of respect to the process of developing intercultural competence, we can describe in some detail the method of articulating outcome statements, identifying corresponding evidence, and assessing outcomes related to this key attribute. For example, the definition provided here for 'Respect and valuing other cultures' draws from the glossary of the AAC&U VALUE Rubric on Global Learning, with specific language related to 'perspective taking' (i.e. 'The ability to engage and learn from perspectives and experiences different from one's own') and 'cultural diversity' (i.e. 'This includes the curiosity to learn respectfully about the cultural diversity of other people and on an individual level to traverse cultural boundaries to bridge differences and collaboratively reach common goals').

The value of Table 9.2, as with Table 9.1, is the important message it conveys vis-à-vis good practice in outcomes assessment. As such, the process of assessing intercultural competence requires the following actions:

- Disaggregate each of the construct's domain into its constituent parts.
- Clearly define the terms of each of these parts in line with established research (Hovland, 2014).
- Use these definitions to draw out the language of our learning-outcomes statements (Maki, 2010).
- Begin thinking about what sort of evidence each learning outcome might generate;
- Limit assessment ambitions to only a few selected attributes, two or three at most.
- Prioritise those attributes according to the importance they hold to our course, programme, or organisation.

In short, the effort to teach, learn, or assess intercultural competence comes with the same forewarning: it can only be done piece by piece and step by step.

Mapping intercultural competence: Level 3 – specific learning outcomes

Deardorff (2015) notes that, 'Writing specific outcomes statements (learning objectives) and developing indicators of the degree to which statements can be assessed remains an area in need of further research, especially within specific fields' (p. 136). By delving further into the next level of intercultural competence, by generating specific learning-outcome statements linked to evidence that can be gathered showing progress towards the desired outcome, and by indicating specific dimensions and scales of AAC&U VALUE Rubrics that are appropriate for assessing student performance, we strive to partially close this research gap. Table 9.3 shows the results of this effort.

In this final table – the most detailed – intercultural competence is fully atomised and disaggregated. As the title indicates, Table 9.3 applies to a unitary aspect of the Process Model, i.e. 'respect'. This single aspect is itself broken down into four related learning-outcome statements specifically related to respect, and each of these statements is accompanied by three examples of even more behaviourally concise evidence indicating achievement of the desired outcome, in this case of respect. Due to the large number of AAC&U rubrics as well as to the number of dimensions within each rubric, we use a simple coding system for easy navigation through the interconnected charts and rubrics. For example, in the 'Rubric' column, the codes GLVR-PT, GLVR-CD, and CEVR-CCS include references to both title of general rubrics and the specific domains included within rubrics. As such, these codes respectively refer to: Global Learning VALUE Rubric–Perspective Taking, Global Learning VALUE Rubric–Cultural Diversity, and Civic Engagement VALUE Rubric–Civic Contexts/Structures. When a single aspect of intercultural competence such as respect is defined and disaggregated as it is on Table 9.3, and when this important attitude is linked both to behavioural evidence demonstrating its presence and to a corresponding rubric where the

Table 9.3 **Foundational Individual Attributes**

Affective: Attitudes & Motivation

Respect

Respect: *The ability to value other cultures and to engage and learn from perspectives and experiences different from one's own. This includes the curiosity to learn respectfully about the cultural diversity of other people and on an individual level to traverse cultural boundaries to bridge differences and collaboratively reach common goals.* *(Source: AAC&U-VR-GL.)*

Adapted from the Deardorff (2006) Process Model of Intercultural Competence.

Learning outcome statements	**Evidence** (examples)	**Assessment methods and tools** (examples)		
Defined in terms of concrete learning expectations and the means by which the larger goal is achieved. Objectives should be SMART: specific, measurable, action-oriented, realistic, and time-delineated.	*Defined in terms of what evidence can be gathered that shows the achievement of the desired outcome.*	**Direct** writing, tests, portfolios, external observation	**Indirect** self-reports, pre-post surveys, interviews, focus groups	**Rubric** AAC&U
1. Value other cultures and the diversity they represent	Articulates cogent arguments on the value of cultural diversity	Review of journal, blog, portfolio, reflection assignments	Focus group work and interviews	• GLVR-PT • GLVR-CD
	Infuses cultural diversity into daily personal life	Monitoring of portfolio, oral presentations, social media	Interviews and focus group work	• GLVR-PT • GLVR-CD
	Advocates for cultural diversity within social/political settings	Monitoring of portfolio, oral presentations, social media	Interviews and focus group work	• GLVR-PT • GLVR-CD

attributes of host people, society, and culture	culture and people	of writing assignments and oral presentations	work and interviews	• GLVR-CD
	Partakes in local cultural, social, and political life	Review of journal, blog, reflection assignments	Interviews and focus group work	• GLVR-PT • GLVR-CD
	Conveys to cultural others that they are valued and respected	Review of journal, blog, reflection assignments	Interviews and focus group work	• GLVR-PT • GLVR-CD
3. Express disinterested comparisons of cultural habits	Practises ongoing monitoring of cultural phenomena	Observations, review of writing assignments and oral presentations	Focus group exercises	• GLVR-PT • GLVR-CD
	Employs observational language of 'different not better'	Review of journal, blog, reflection assignments	Interviews and focus group work	• GLVR-PT • GLVR-CD
	Seeks out 'inherent values' of customs over 'habitual values'	Observations, review of writing assignments, and oral presentations	Interviews and focus group work	• GLVR-PT • GLVR-CD
4. Show willingness to bridge cultural differences	Willingly engages with culturally different others	Review of writing assignments and oral presentations, observations	Focus group work and interviews	• GLVR-PT • GLVR-CD • CEVR-CCS
	Seeks to identify common goals among cultural different others	Review of journal, blog, reflection assignments, social media	Focus group work and interviews	• GLVR-PT • GLVR-CD • CEVR-CCS
	Uses problem-solving perspectives different from one's own	Monitoring of written and oral presentations, social media	Monitoring of interviews, focus group work	• GLVR-PT • GLVR-CD • CEVR-CCS

extent of its presence can be evaluated and scaled, the process of teaching and assessing intercultural competence becomes less daunting.

Conclusion

The process of mapping out the many distinct, specific, and subtle aspects of intercultural competence, as presented in this chapter, allows educators to initiate a manageable process of assessing this intricate construct. As these charts immediately reveal, this journey begins by first appreciating just how complex the construct of intercultural competence is. This is perhaps the most valuable lesson of this mapping exercise: understanding and accepting that assessing intercultural competence in the aggregate is impossible. There simply is no single instrument, method, or assessment moment that allows us to capture the complexity of the data. Because these charts articulate behaviourally specific learning outcomes appropriate to all intercultural settings and not just those found abroad, both instructors and student service administrators can draw from these charts when embedding desired intercultural learning outcomes into campus learning activities.

The method used here to disaggregate intercultural competence into its constituent elements generates some twenty-five separate analytic charts focused on the twenty specific learning objectives plus some eighty learning-outcome statements, and over 250 examples of corresponding performance evidence; the full complexity of intercultural competence becomes overwhelmingly apparent. The mapping exercise also reveals how important it is to think deeply about the language used when formulating learning-outcomes statements for intercultural competence (which should follow the SMART format: specific, measurable, action-oriented, realistic, and time-delineated). The principles of consensus, consistency, and alignment should guide educators in the creation and adaptation of such maps.

Of course, there are limitations to this approach. The models of intercultural competence presented here draw heavily from Western cultural traditions and can thus, at best, only *contribute* to assessment efforts to measure intercultural competence. Similarly, the approach to assessing intercultural competence presented here relies on pedagogical practices and a corresponding classroom culture more common in the anglophone world than perhaps elsewhere. As such, educators will want to adapt these charts and assessment processes to both cultural and institutional contexts.

Moreover, the integrative and complementary aspects of intercultural competence, global learning, civic engagement, and critical thinking – to mention but a few – that are embedded in these charts suggest that the deeper purpose of comprehensive internationalisation – 'making a meaningful contribution to society' in De Wit's words – should henceforth be understood as the achievement of as many of the learning outcomes of intercultural competence as possible across both campus and community. As such, these analytic maps inspired by the Deardorff Process Model of Intercultural Competence provide both a detailed teaching and learning agenda for the twenty-first century and a practical pathway to assessing instructional success in this endeavour.

References

Association of American Colleges & Universities (AAC&U) (2007). *College learning for the new global century.* Washington, DC: AAC&U.

—— *VALUE Rubrics.* Washington, DC: AAC&U. Retrieved from www.aacu.org/value/rubrics

American Council on Education. (2008). *Assessing international learning outcomes.* Washington, DC: American Council of Education.

Bennett, M. J. (1993). Towards ethno-relativism: A developmental model of intercultural sensitivity. In R. Paige (Ed.), *Educating for the intercultural experience*, 2nd edn (pp. 21–71). Yarmouth, ME: Intercultural Press.

Deardorff, D. K. (2006). The identification and assessment of intercultural competence as a student outcome of internationalization at institutions of higher education in the United States. *Journal of Studies in International Education, 10*(3), 241–66.

—— (Ed.) (2009). *The Sage handbook of intercultural competence.* Thousand Oaks, CA: Sage.

—— (2015). *Demystifying outcomes assessment for international educators.* Sterling, VA: Stylus.

De Wit, H. (2015). Remarks at INQAAHE (International Network for Quality Assurance Agencies in Higher Education). Chicago, IL, 30 March–3 April.

Fantini, A. E. (1999). *Foreign language standards: Linking research, theories, and practices* (J. K. Phillips, Ed.). Lincolnwood, IL: National Textbook Co.

—— (2000). *A central concern: Developing intercultural competence.* Brattleboro, VT. Retrieved from www.adam-europe.eu/prj/2935/prd/8/1/develop-I-com.pdf

—— (2009). Assessing intercultural competence: Issues and tools. In D. K. Deardorff (Ed.), *The Sage handbook of intercultural competence* (pp. 456–76). Thousand Oaks, CA: Sage.

Hovland, K. (2014). *Global learning: Defining, designing, demonstrating.* Washington, DC: AAC&U & NAFSA. Retrieved from www.aacu.org/globallearning

Kolb, D. A. (1984). *Experiential learning: Experience as the source of learning and development.* Englewood Cliffs, NJ: Prentice Hall.

Kuh, G. D. (2008). *High-impact educational practices: What they are, who has access to them, and why they matter.* Washington, DC: AAC&U.

Maki, P. L. (2010). *Assessing for learning*, 2nd edn. Sterling, VA: Stylus.

Olson, C., Evans, R., & Schoenberg, R. E. (2007). *At home in the world: Bridging the gap between internationalization and multicultural education.* Washington, DC: American Council on Education.

Chapter 10

The big picture of intercultural competence assessment

Darla K. Deardorff (Duke University)

Assessment of intercultural competence remains a crucial issue at higher education institutions around the world (Egron-Polak & Hudson, 2014). As illustrated in the twenty-nine case studies in this volume, there is no one 'right' approach or 'best' measurement tool for assessing this complex concept. This chapter begins by outlining key principles in intercultural competence assessment as well as student outcomes assessment, which are fundamental in ensuring that approaches to intercultural competence assessment follow good practice. This chapter also highlights some issues in intercultural competence assessment as well as exploring some key considerations to take into account and ends with a brief view to the changing paradigm of outcomes assessment in international education.

Principles of intercultural competence assessment

What are the underlying principles that are important in developing an assessment approach to intercultural competence? There are five key principles that are foundational to assessing intercultural competence, which can serve as first steps in developing an intercultural assessment protocol:

1. **Define.** Define intercultural competence within a programmatic or institutional context, based on the literature. In order to assess, we must first define what is being assessed. Too often, higher education institutions use generic words such as intercultural competence or global citizenship without defining them. How exactly is intercultural competence being defined in your context? According to whom? In some instances, it may be important to take into account different perspectives, as illustrated in chapters in this volume from Chinese and South African perspectives (see Chapters 7 and 8) or to draw on disciplinary perspectives such as those from health care (see Chapter 2). In defining intercultural competence, it may involve using more than one definition or framework, since many of these can be complementary, and by adapting a variety of definitions and frameworks, a more holistic definition of intercultural competence can be developed for a particular context. Many of the case studies here, for example, use more than one intercultural competence

framework or definition. In another example, the AAC&U Intercultural Knowledge and Competence rubric utilises both the Deardorff and Bennett definitions of intercultural competence to inform the development of the rubric. In the case of the South African case study in this book (CS3, p. 156), the definition was actually developed by the students themselves. This fits with other intercultural competence studies that have been done in developing institutional definitions specific to that institution, such as the work done at Macquarie University in Australia (Krajewski, 2011), at Jacobs University in Germany (Odağ, Wallin, & Kedzior, 2015), or at Shanghai International Studies University in China (Chapter 8).

2. **Prioritise.** Prioritise specific elements of intercultural competence within the learning context (i.e. course or programme). Intercultural competence is often a stated goal within international higher education courses and programmes, such as education abroad programmes. However, this goal is too broad and complex to assess as a whole as described in the previous chapter. Therefore, it is helpful to prioritise specific elements of intercultural competence by determining the key elements to emphasise in the particular course or programme based on what changes are desired in the learner (both from the learner-perspective as well as from the instructor perspective). Usually two to three elements are sufficient and manageable to assess. These elements can then be developed into specific, measurable learning outcomes statements indicating the desired change. (This process has been explained in depth in the previous chapter.)
3. **Align.** Align learning outcomes to the goals, learning activities/interventions with the learning outcomes, and assessment measures to the stated learning outcomes. Given that intercultural competence as a goal is too broad to assess, the prioritised elements of the concept become key and are aligned to the broader goal(s). In turn, specific learning activities/experiences can be mapped to learning outcomes to ensure that there is a close fit and that the outcomes are supported through intentional activities. Alignment also needs to occur through collecting evidence that fits the stated outcomes (see Principle No. 4 for further explanation). If it is determined that intercultural competence assessment measures are the most closely aligned way to collect the needed evidence (there are over 140 intercultural competence instruments; see Fantini 2009), it is crucial to understand exactly what the tool measures and how closely it aligns with the learning outcomes. If there is little to no alignment, then the evidence collected will be invalid, no matter how valid and reliable the tool is deemed to be.
4. **Identify evidence.** Identify both direct and indirect evidence of changes in the learner and that the stated learning outcomes are achieved to some degree. Instead of seeking particular assessment measures to use, it is more helpful to think first about what kinds of direct and indirect evidence can be collected to indicate that students are making progress towards achieving the stated learning outcomes in the course or programme. Direct evidence

is often defined as evidence of actual student learning collected during the learning experience. Examples of direct evidence can include course assignments (as in the presentations noted in the South African, Chinese, Serbian, Japanese, Spanish, New Zealander, and Australian case studies), reflections during the experience, projects (such as the community project at Duke in the United States or the project at University College Leuven-Limburg in Belgium), tests (as noted in the Hague University case study), observations of interactions (as in one of the Canadian case studies), peer assessments, and so on. Case studies in this book from Qatar, Spain, and the United States demonstrate use of peer assessment, for example. And numerous case studies utilise reflections collected during the learning experience as evidence of changes. Indirect evidence, on the other hand, involves perceptions of student learning, with evidence being collected often outside of the learning experience, such as through pre- and post-measures. Indirect evidence can also be collected through interviews and focus groups, as illustrated by several case studies including from Portugal, the United States, the UK, and Qatar.

With any evidence collected, it becomes important to analyse the information (ideally from more than one perspective since there can be different interpretations), identifying emerging common themes and issues. Evidence of intercultural development is collected through multiple means and should involve multiple perspectives (such as peer assessments and observations by others). Such a multi-measure, multi-perspective approach to intercultural assessment is essential in not only providing a more complete picture of the changes that occur but also in more adequately addressing the complexities of this concept itself. The case studies contained here provide examples of multi-measures and/or multi-perspectives in intercultural competence assessment.

5. **Use.** Use the collected information for learner improvement. Use of assessment information (data) is crucial and relates directly to the purpose of assessment. Why was the assessment undertaken? It is important to remember that learning outcomes assessment is different from programme evaluation, primarily due to the difference in purpose – learning outcomes assessment is for learner improvement whereas programme evaluation is for programme improvement. Questions to ask include: How will the collected information be used? Will this information be meaningful to the learner? How will this benefit the learner? In assessing intercultural competence, it becomes crucial to provide feedback to the learner in regard to further developing the learner's intercultural competence. For example, what are the areas of strength? Which areas are 'growth areas' and what are some ways to continue to grow in those areas? In the end, outcomes assessment can also be used for programme improvement too, by 'quantifying the qualitative'. This means that outcomes assessment can be viewed in the aggregate to report percentages of students who achieve specific learning outcomes. Mapping these percentages

can indicate areas in which programmes need to improve in terms of learning interventions (content and/or delivery), for example.

While the case studies may not necessarily follow all five of these principles, they can be analysed using them. As with any assessment, such efforts remain a work in progress as assessment continues to be reviewed and improved. This means that institutions do not have to 'do assessment' perfectly but will continue to learn from their own efforts.

Institutions can also learn and be informed by the vast amount of higher education assessment literature. When looking to the broader field of higher education assessment, a national organisation based in the United States (American Association of Higher Education) has developed nine principles of good practice for assessing student learning which provide further input into what makes for quality outcomes assessment in international higher education. The following principles can serve as a guide, or checklist, specifically for intercultural competence assessment:

1. The assessment of student learning begins with educational values.
2. Assessment is most effective when it reflects an understanding of learning as multidimensional, integrated, and revealed in performance over time.
3. Assessment works best when the programmes it seeks to improve have clear, explicitly stated purposes.
4. Assessment requires attention to outcomes but also and equally to the experiences that lead to those outcomes.
5. Assessment works best when it is ongoing, not episodic.
6. Assessment fosters wide improvement when representatives from across the educational community are involved.
7. Assessment makes a difference when it begins with issues of use and illuminates questions that people really care about.
8. Assessment is most likely to lead to improvement when it is part of a larger set of conditions that promote change.
9. Through assessment, educators meet responsibilities to students and to the public.

(Gardiner, Anderson, & Cambridge, 1997, pp. 11–12)

These classic assessment principles in learning outcomes assessment point to the importance of the learner within the assessment process. This may require a change of mindset in thinking about *assessment of learning* to *assessment for learning*, with assessment as being integral to the learning itself. Moreover, no longer is assessment viewed as something that is done *to* students but rather, assessment is done *with* students. While the case studies reflect both mindsets, there is a gradual change to a more learner-centred assessment approach within international higher education.

Issues in intercultural competence assessment

There are numerous issues that arise in the assessment of intercultural competence. Below are just a few:

- The conflation of programme evaluation and outcomes assessment, which are two different processes and serve different purposes.
- The necessary training in assessment for those engaged in these efforts. Too often in international education, staff and even academics have very little to no formal training in assessment, which can result in efforts that are not as robust or effective.
- The misalignment of assessment measures to the stated outcomes, resulting in invalid data (and a consequential waste of resources).
- The misuse or even non-use of collected assessment data/evidence. If data are not used (especially for student feedback), then there is no point in collecting them.
- The translatability of some assessment methods across cultures (for example, students trained in Socratic traditions of thinking will generally do better in assessment that requires critical thinking compared to students not trained in this tradition).
- Misinformation on intercultural assessment – even in conference presentations, workshops, and publications, which is then often connected to the lack of assessment training. Consumers of assessment materials need to be discerning in understanding what constitutes quality assessment efforts that adhere to principles of good practice (per the earlier discussion in this chapter).
- Resistance to assessment efforts or assessment fatigue. Given the outcomes-based assessment cultures at an increasing number of higher education institutions, resistance and fatigue become realities that are often encountered.

The considerations below address some of the issues listed here, and other assessment literature addresses much of what is outlined above. (See the list of references and resources at the end of this chapter.)

Considerations in intercultural competence assessment

In assessing intercultural competence, there are five considerations that can be utilised in designing the most effective process:

1. Consider a comprehensive approach, beyond numbers.
2. Map goals, outcomes, content, learning activities, evidence, and use.
3. Make it relevant to academics and to students.
4. Customise/personalise the feedback to students when possible.
5. Consider a more holistic approach to intercultural-competence assessment

Inputs --> Activities --> Outputs --> Outcomes --> Impact

Figure 10.1 Programme logic model.

Consider a comprehensive approach, beyond numbers

Often, higher education institutions focus on numbers: numbers of participants, test scores, international courses, and so on. Assessing intercultural competence focuses more on the meaning behind the numbers (not to say that numbers are not important). A comprehensive model to consider is the programme logic model, which takes into account not only the numbers but also the actual learning that occurs, as well as the learning activities that lead to the outcomes. See Figure 10.1 for the logic model, which can be used to not only ensure alignment (as discussed above) but also as a model of change in identifying gaps. There are five components to a logic model:

1. Inputs (including any human and physical resources such as experts within or beyond the institution, available technology, funding, staff, geographic location, physical buildings, and so on that make the programme/course possible);
2. Activities (any learning interventions including experiential activities, study abroad, service learning, and so on that help students achieve the stated outcomes);
3. Outputs (which involve numbers of participants, numbers of languages taught, etc.);
4. Outcomes (often focused on learning outcomes, these provide the meaning behind the numbers, looking at changes occurring in students in the short and medium term);
5. Impact (which involves looking at long-term change in broader policies, systems and structures), for example, how is an institution being changed as a result of international education programmes? The Agnes Scott case study demonstrates more of a longitudinal approach in looking further out at impact.

Map goals, outcomes, content, learning activities, evidence, and use

Similar to the logic model, it is often helpful to engage first in mapping goals, outcomes, content and delivery, learning activities, evidence of change in learning, and use of information collected. This mapping exercise can be quite revealing about existing gaps (for example, if multi-measures are being used) and misalignments and can be invaluable in improving the overall assessment efforts related to intercultural competence development within a course or programme.

Make it relevant to academics and to students

Too often there can be resistance to assessment efforts due in part to burnout and other priorities. It thus becomes important to understand what makes intercultural competence relevant to both faculty and to students and then adapt and adjust efforts accordingly. For students, it may be that intercultural competence is viewed as a key to better employability. For academics, intercultural competence may be required in accreditation standards. Regardless, adapting and integrating intercultural competence assessments into already existing efforts is key, instead of adding on 'more work'. How can current efforts be adapted to collect necessary evidence of student change? This could even be done by adding a question on an already existing form, asking students to articulate 'one significant change' that has occurred in their intercultural knowledge, skills, or attitudes. Relevance for students also means engaging in assessment in applied real-world, authentic settings through observations (moving beyond self-perspective), teamwork, relationship development, and so on, instead of the more traditional route of evidence collected through contrived instruments in forced, disconnected environments. Case studies in this book, for example, note simulations (Japanese study), workshops (Virginia Commonwealth), projects (Duke, Cardiff/Stenden, RMIT in Australia), and group work (Mount Royal) as examples of more authentic, relevant assessments.

Customise/personalise the feedback to students when possible

It is important to remember that students are at different places in their intercultural journeys (as are staff and academics). Thus, a one-size-fits-all approach to developing and assessing intercultural competence will unfortunately not be as effective or relevant to students. Instead, providing personalised feedback to students – either in writing or even recorded orally – can be instrumental in further developing each student's intercultural competence. One example of this being done in some of the case studies (Texas Christian University, University of British Columbia, The Hague University of Applied Sciences) is through the use of electronic portfolios where students can collect a wide variety of evidence (not only reflections and papers but also photos, videos, links, etc.) that illustrate growth and change, and then feedback can be provided in direct response to this evidence. The key to the use of e-portfolios is in the feedback given (usually using rubrics) as well as in the comprehensive reflection by students of their changes over time (found in the portfolio evidence) in regard to knowledge, skills, attitudes, and even ways of thinking.

Consider a more holistic approach to intercultural-competence assessment

Too often, intercultural-competence assessment is viewed as something separate from the other developmental, cognitive, emotional, and spiritual aspects of student learning. Instead, intercultural competence assessment needs to be integrated into a learner's overall development as a human being. To do this, it is often helpful to refer back to the initial mindset of whether assessment is something done *to* students or *with* students. In collaborating with students on their own learning and development through the capacity of self-authorship defined by Baxter Magolda as 'the internal capacity to define one's beliefs, identity, and social relations' (Evans, Forney, Guido, Patton, & Renn, 2010, p. 184). Self-authorship empowers students to engage actively and reflectively in their own holistic development as a person. The case studies in this book all illustrate how important it is to go beyond numbers or pre/post measures in regard to assessment. Many of them also indicate how valuable it is to use multiple measures in providing a more holistic picture of intercultural development in students.

The changing assessment paradigm

The considerations noted here are indicative of a changing paradigm of outcomes assessment in international higher education (see Table 10.1; for more detail, see Deardorff, 2015b). In this changing assessment paradigm, there is a shift from the traditional evidence collected through pre- and post-measures to more authentic evidence collected through actual teamwork and interactions beyond the context of a classroom (i.e. service learning). The focus becomes much more process-oriented rather than achieving intercultural competence, which, in the end, is a myth. Intercultural competence is a lifelong process for everyone and so is a continual 'work in process' that points to the importance of focusing more on developing 'intercultural thinking' (Bok, 2008; Deardorff, 2016) and in the role of critical reflection.

Looking to the big-picture view, other questions arise such as: How can we continue to make intercultural development more concrete within and beyond the classroom? What are the most effective ways to collect evidence of change in intercultural development? What is the impact of moving students around the world in regard to increased mutual understanding and intercultural dialogue?

Table 10.1 The changing paradigm of outcomes assessment in international education (adapted from Deardorff, 2015).

From...	*To...*
Programme/course centred	Learner-centred/engaged
Traditional evidence	Authentic evidence
Self-perspective	Multiple perspectives (including self)
Standardised	Tailored/customised
One approach	Multiple pathways
Separate	Holistic
Results	Process

Does educational exchange lead to a more peaceful world or does it serve to further widen the gap between the haves and the have nots? How can intercultural competence be developed within the local community? What is the role of higher education institutions in developing intercultural competence in post-conflict settings (as raised in Chapter 5)? These are just a few of the many questions that need further attention and exploration.

Conclusion

Outcomes assessment is here to stay in higher education, and, within international education, intercultural competence has become an emerging focus around the world (Deardorff & Jones, 2012). More programmes and courses are addressing intercultural competence as one of the goals, as illustrated by the case studies here. There is much that can be learned from past and current efforts in terms of how to further improve student learning and assessment in this area.

This chapter has outlined some key assessment principles, highlighted issues and considerations to take into account when assessing intercultural competence, in addition to introducing a changing assessment paradigm that can be applied to intercultural assessment efforts. In the end, the bigger picture of assessment is about focusing on the individual learner and in utilising assessment efforts as integral to the continued intercultural development of students in the twenty-first century.

References

Bok D. (2008). *Our underachieving colleges: A candid look at how much students learn and why they should be learning more.* Princeton, NJ: Princeton University Press.

Byram, M. (1997). *Developing and assessing intercultural communicative competence.* Clevedon: Multilingual Matters

Deardorff, D. K. (2015a). *Demystifying outcomes assessment for international educators: A practical approach.* Sterling, VA: Stylus.

—— (2015b). International education assessment: A changing paradigm. *IIENetworker*, Fall, 18–19.

—— (2016). Invited talk at Global Education Think Tank, Harvard University, 19 May.

Deardorff, D. K., & Jones, E. (2012). Intercultural competence: An emerging focus in international higher education. In D. K. Deardorff, H. de Wit, D. Heyl, & T. Adams (Eds.), *The Sage handbook of international higher education* (pp. 283–303).

Egron-Polak, E., & Hudson R. (2014). *Internationalization of higher education: Growing expectations, fundamental values.* Paris: International Association of Universities.

Evans, N., Forney, D., Guido, F., Patton, L., & Renn, K. (2010). *Student development in college: Theory, research and practice*, 2nd edn. San Francisco, CA: Jossey-Bass.

Fantini, A. (2009). Assessing intercultural competence: Issues and tools. In D. K. Deardorff (Ed.), *The Sage handbook of intercultural competence* (pp. 456–76). Thousand Oaks, CA: Sage.

Gardiner, L., Anderson, C., & Cambridge, B. (1997). *Learning through assessment: A resource guide for higher education*. Washington, DC: American Association for Higher Education.

Krajewski, S. (2011). *The next Buddha may be a community: Practising intercultural competence at Macquarie University, Sydney, Australia*. Newcastle-upon-Tyne: Cambridge Scholars Publishing.

Odağ, O., Wallin, H., & Kedzior, K. (2015). Definition of intercultural competence according to undergraduate students at an international university in Germany. *Journal of Studies in International Education*, *20*(2), 118–39.

Additional resources and readings

Banta, T. (2004). *Hallmarks of effective outcomes assessment*. San Francisco, CA: Jossey-Bass.

——(2007). *Assessing student learning in the disciplines*. San Francisco, CA: Jossey-Bass.

Banta, T., & Palomba, C. (2014). *Assessment essentials: Planning, implementing, and improving assessment in higher education*. San Francisco, CA: Jossey-Bass.

Bresciani, M. J. (2006). *Outcomes-based academic and co-curricular program review*. Sterling, VA: Stylus.

De Wit, H. (2009). *Measuring success in the internationalization of higher education*. Amsterdam: European Association of International Educators.

Driscoll, A., & Wood, S. (2007). *Developing outcomes-based assessment for learner-centered education: A faculty introduction*. Sterling, VA: Stylus.

Green, M. (2012). *Improving and assessing global learning*. Washington, DC: NAFSA.

Huba, M., & Freed, J. (2000). *Learner-centered assessment on college campuses: Shifting the focus from teaching to learning*. Boston, MA: Allyn & Bacon.

Musil, C. (2006). *Assessing global learning: Matching good intentions with good practice*. Washington, DC: AAC&U.

Suskie, L. (2009). *Assessing student learning: A common sense guide*. San Francisco, CA: Jossey-Bass.

Walvoord, B. E. (2004). *Assessment clear and simple: A practical guide for institutions, departments, and general education*. San Francisco, CA: Jossey-Bass.

Part III

Application of intercultural competence

Chapter 11

Introduction to case studies in developing and assessing intercultural competence

Twenty-nine case studies from around the world

Darla K. Deardorff (Duke University) and
Lily A. Arasaratnam-Smith (Alphacrusis College)

This brief introduction to the case studies describes more about the selection process, some caveats, as well as questions that can be used in discussions and/or analysis of the case studies presented here. In addition, some brief tips for using case studies are included here, followed by a table of the case studies.

As noted in the introduction to this book, the following twenty-nine case studies were selected from nearly 150 submitted from around the world (although regrettably, none was submitted from South America, Central America, and very few from Africa, which can actually be viewed as a learning opportunity – see 'Tips for Using Case Studies' here), nearly all of which were at the course or programme level. These case studies were selected based on the geographical representation, disciplines, context, and assessments utilised. While they are identified by university, these case studies are often an example of a microcosm within the university (such as a course or programme) and should not be indicative of institutional-wide assessment or common practice throughout the institution. References are included at the end of each case study to facilitate the ease of use in discussions and classroom activities.

It is necessary to note that these cases are not meant to represent best practice in intercultural competence development and assessment; rather, they are illustrative of current practice, and as such, are works in progress. This is highlighted by the thoughtful conclusions to each of the case studies of 'Lessons Learned' and then 'Ways to Improve', which models reflexivity on the process itself. There are many other examples, of course, of current practice, and the editors of this volume invite continued conversation and sharing of current practice on developing and assessing intercultural competence across geographic and institutional contexts. Join the conversation at ICC Global at www.iccglobal.org as well as at international education conferences such as at Asia Pacific Association of International Educators (APAIE), Association of International Education Administrators (AIEA), European Association of International Educators (EAIE), International

Education Association of South Africa (IEASA), and NAFSA: Association of International Educators, to name a few.

Discussing and analysing the case studies

These cases can be analysed and discussed based on a number of factors, including the articulation of intercultural competence development discussed in Chapter 6 and the assessment principles presented in Chapter 10. It is also important to read Chapter 1 in order to gain more of an understanding of the theoretical underpinnings mentioned in the case studies. In addition to the information provided in the chapters in this volume, the following questions can be specifically asked in analysing and discussing the cases here (as well as other current intercultural competence practices):

1. How is intercultural competence being defined in this context? Based on what? How well does this definition seem to fit within this particular context? How could other intercultural competence definitions (such as ones noted in Chapters 1, 2, 3, 7, and 8) from different disciplines and geographic/cultural contexts contribute to a more comprehensive understanding of intercultural competence? How can multiple intercultural competence definitions/models be used simultaneously and complementarily to provide a more holistic intercultural competence framework?
2. What are the specific goals and learning outcomes related to intercultural competence? How well do the learning outcomes align with the stated goals? How could the learning outcomes be made more explicit, particularly in regard to specific components of intercultural competence? How realistic are these outcomes within the parameters of the course or programme?
3. To what extent are the goals and outcomes aligned with the learning activities/interventions and assessments? How could the learning activities/interventions be adapted to better support realistic achievement of the stated learning outcomes? What might be some unintended outcomes of this particular course or programme?
4. How would you characterise the intercultural competence assessments being used in this particular context (i.e. direct, indirect, what kinds of evidence are being collected through the assessments, etc.)? How closely are the assessments aligned to the stated goals and outcomes? What kinds of evidence would best demonstrate achievement of the stated outcomes and what would be the best ways to collect such evidence? How is the collected assessment information being used to provide feedback to students?
5. Given the lessons learned and ways to improve, how would you redesign this particular course or programme so as to improve the development and assessment of intercultural competence in this context? Given this particular context, who else could be involved in this redesign? What role could the learner have in redesigning this particular course or programme? How

does your redesigned programme or course compare to the one in the case study in terms of strengths and weaknesses of each? What other ideas are stimulated for you by this case study in regard to developing and assessing intercultural competence in higher education?

Tips for using the case studies

Below are some tips and suggestions for making the most of the case studies as tools for further learning:

1. Use the above questions, as well as selected chapters in this volume (such as Chapters 6 and 10), for discussion and/or written analysis of the cases under study.
2. If time permits, discuss one of the cases together as a group before assigning individual or group work, modelling the type of analysis desired.
3. Make the case studies more interactive by assigning them as pair work or for group work. Be sure to have the students evaluate the process of working together, as well as what they achieved through the actual assignment. For example, what worked well in their discussions? What could be improved? What lessons did they learn from working together through this process?
4. Engage in meta-level questions that could go beyond a compare/contrast of the case studies, drawing out common themes and synthesising key points across several different case studies. What are the interconnections (at different levels) between some of the case studies, for example?
5. Assign accompanying readings to support the particular case studies assigned. These can be drawn from the references at the end of the case study and/or from the growing wealth of other publications on intercultural competence, international education, and assessment including from other books in this Routledge Internationalisation Series.
6. Stimulate further discussion by having students see how well and to what extent a certain case study would work in a different institutional or geographical context, exploring further information that may be needed, what would make it work, barriers to implementation in a different context, and potential ways to overcome such barriers.
7. Encourage pairs or groups to present their 'redesign' (as noted in Question 5 above) to the class and solicit broader group feedback on the 'redesign' presented (based on the chapters in Parts I and II of this volume).
8. Provide concrete feedback on responses to the questions and view the questions as a teaching tool to guide students in their thinking about intercultural competence so as to bridge the theory to praxis divide that is often present in much of the discourse on intercultural competence.
9. Encourage students to find or elicit other case studies on developing and assessing intercultural competence (particularly from geographic areas not

currently represented in this mix of case studies such as from South America), using the template of the case studies here.

10. Ask students to develop two or three research questions that could be drawn from the material presented in a particular case study. What are they curious about? What would they like to learn more about? What needs further investigation? How would they design a study based on those research questions?

These are tips for using case studies more effectively, particularly in formal learning situations. Regardless of the context, the emphasis should be placed on further exploration, discussion, and reflection in understanding concrete ways to effectively develop and assess intercultural competence in today's students.

Table 11.1 Intercultural competence in international higher education: case studies.

Below are the case studies in this section in alphabetical order by author last name. This serves as an at-a-glance reference and overview of the case studies.

	Author(s)	Discipline(s)	Institution(s)	Country	Target group	Assessments	Page No.
CS1	J. Almeida	Education	University of Aveiro	Portugal	Undergraduates and postgraduates	Questionnaires, focus groups, interviews, tests, worksheets, essays	p. 144
CS2	N. Binder	Social Sciences	Jacobs University Bremen	Germany	Undergraduates	Questionnaires, portfolio, reflective tasks	p. 151
CS3	H. Boshoff & A. Erasmus	International Partnerships and Global Citizenship	Stellenbosch University	South Africa	Undergraduates	Written reports, forums, presentations, intercultural mapping	p. 156
CS4	H. J. Cassil, T. Franson, A. Bennett Hill, & E. Kreydatus	Mathematics, Learning and Teaching, Global Education, Focused Enquiry	Virginia Commonwealth University	USA	Faculty and undergraduates	Self-assessment, collaborative papers, group workshops, reflections, peer assessment	p. 160
CS5	N. Chernyak	Medicine	Lomonosov Moscow State University	Russia	Medical students	Questionnaires, reflective journals, observation sheets	p. 164
CS6	L. Choi & S. L. Jakubec	Nursing and Midwifery	Mount Royal University	Canada	Undergraduate nursing students	Personal reflection, group work, cultural nursing assessment, essay	p. 169
CS7	D. Corder	Language and Culture	Auckland University of Technology	New Zealand	Undergraduates	Learning evaluations (blogs, wiki), presentations	p. 174
CS8	M. Elnashar, H. Abdelrahim, & Stella C. Major	Global Public Health, Medical Education	Weill Cornell Medicine-Qatar	Qatar	Medical students	Self-assessment, tutor assessment, peer assessment, focus group	p. 180
CS9	I. Golubeva	International Communication	University of Pannonia	Hungary	Undergraduates	Questionnaires, self-assessment, reflective writing	p. 186
CS10	C. T. Hightower	Institutional Effectiveness	Texas Christian University	USA	Undergraduates	Portfolio, self-reports, survey	p. 192

Table 11.1 (cont.)

	Author(s)	Discipline(s)	Institution(s)	Country	Target group	Assessments	Page No.
CS11	J. Jackson	English	The Chinese University of Hong Kong	Hong Kong SAR [Special Administrative Region], China	Undergraduates	Forums, fieldwork, essays, questionnaire	p. 197
CS12	A. Karseras	Business	Tokyo Metropolitan University	Japan	Undergraduates	Journal, simulation, presentation, self- and team evaluation	p. 202
CS13	C. Karsgaard & L. Sanford	International Programmes	University of British Columbia	Canada	Undergraduates and postgraduates	Observation, essays, reflection, portfolio	p. 209
CS14	N. Lazarević	English	University of Niš	Serbia	Undergraduates	Discussion, journal, lesson plan, presentation	p. 214
CS15	K. Mertens & J. Van Maele	Teacher Education and Engineering	UC Leuven-Limburg and KU Leuven	Belgium	Postgraduates	Project, portfolio	p. 219
CS16	S. Oguro	Arts and Sciences	University of Technology Sydney	Australia	Undergraduates	Reflection, report, presentation	p. 224
CS17	C. Peck, M. Brown, & F. Bouilheres	Learning and Teaching	Royal Melbourne Institute of Technology University	Australia/ Vietnam	Undergraduates	Critical incident narratives, critical inquiry project, critical reflection paper	p. 229
CS18	P. J. Pedersen	Psychology	University of Minnesota-Duluth	USA	Students, faculty, staff	Self-evaluation, online survey	p. 234
CS19	J. S. Peifer & E. Meyer-Lee	Psychology and Global Learning and Leadership Development	Agnes Scott College	USA	Undergraduates	Multi-method longitudinal assessment	p. 239
CS20	A. Ran	Multicultural Education	South China University of Technology	China	Undergraduates	Essay, presentation, attendance, discussion	p. 244

CS21	D. S. Reisinger	Romance Studies	Duke University	USA	Undergraduates	Self-assessment, community project, reflective writing	p. 249
CS22	C. B. Sánchez & E. de Louw	European Studies	The Hague University of Applied Sciences	The Netherlands	Undergraduates and postgraduates	Exams, presentations, essays, portfolio, reflections	p. 254
CS23	R. Santibáñez-Gruber, C. Maiztegui-Oñate, & M. Yarosh	Social Pedagogy and Diversity	University of Deusto	Spain	Undergraduates	Peer and facilitator feedback, oral presentation, portfolio	p. 260
CS24	P.-B. Smit, H. Radstake, G. Bertram-Troost, & S. Ramdas	Theology and Religious Studies	Vrije Universiteit Amsterdam	The Netherlands	Postgraduates	Written report, portfolio, reflections	p. 265
CS25	D. R. Togunde & R. Fall	Global Education	Spelman College	USA	Undergraduates	Reflective essays, evaluations, blogs	p. 269
CS26	E. Ujitani	Foreign Studies	Nagoya University of Foreign Studies	Japan/Vietnam	Undergraduates	Questionnaire, diaries, reflection, interview	p. 275
CS27	C. Whitelaw, S. Apedaile, & T. Odgers	Intercultural Education	NorQuest College	Canada	Community members	Questionnaire, reflection	p. 280
CS28	J. Williams & J. Hietbrink	Computing and Information Systems and Commerce	Cardiff Metropolitan University and Stenden University	UK/ The Netherlands	Undergraduates	Reflection, interviews, project	p. 285
CS29	T. Yakaboski & M. Birnbaum	Higher Education and Student Affairs	University of Northern Colorado and Universidad Intercultural Maya de Quintana Roo	USA/Mexico	Undergraduates	Self-assessment, self-reflection, questionnaire	p. 289

CS1

Intercultural seminars

An educational intervention with sojourners at a Portuguese university

Joana Almeida (University of Aveiro)

Context

The 'intercultural seminars' are an educational intervention designed as part of doctoral research to support and enhance the intercultural learning and development of thirty-one sojourners at a public university in Portugal.

The intervention was implemented by the researcher in two Portuguese foreign-language classrooms. One classroom was attended by nineteen incoming students of the European exchange programme Campus Europae (Case Study 1.1), and the other by three incoming Erasmus students and nine highly skilled immigrants (Case Study 1.2). Whereas Campus Europae and Erasmus students were still pursuing an undergraduate or master's degree and moved to Portugal to earn credits as recognition of their studies abroad, immigrant participants held a higher education degree and migrated for family reasons and/or professional added value. Naturally, participants represented diverse age groups, ranging from nineteen to fifty-six years of age, and came from nine countries: Austria, France, Latvia, Lithuania, Finland, Russia, Venezuela, Spain, and Poland.

Delivered as a sequence of eight two-hour modules over the second semester of the 2011–12 academic year, the seminars were conducted in Portuguese, using English as an auxiliary language of instruction.

Goals and outcomes

Each intervention module addressed a specific content area and learning goal. These goals were further broken down into teaching objectives and learning outcomes or indicators, as illustrated by Figure CS1.1.

The learning goals and outcomes for individual modules were crafted according to the areas of competency of the intercultural competence model at the heart of the intervention (see the next section). For the sake of conciseness, only the three most important learning outcomes (in range and relevance) are outlined in Table CS1.1.

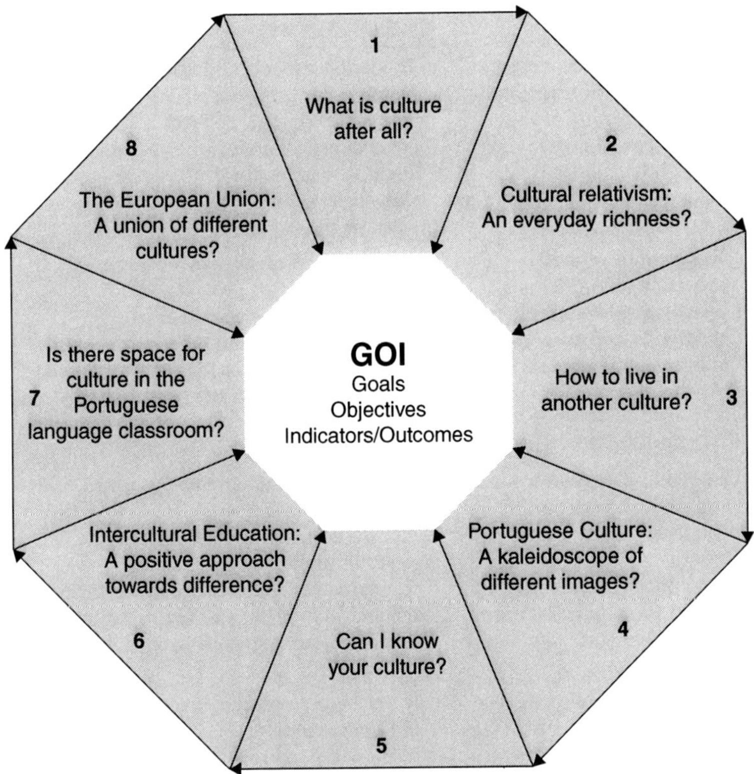

Figure CS1.1 Pedagogical and assessment frameworks.

Framework of intercultural competence

Conceptual foundations for the seminars were based on Fantini's model of intercultural communication competence (ICC), which depicts intercultural competence as a set of 'complex abilities needed to perform *effectively* and *appropriately* when interacting with others who are linguistically and culturally different from oneself' (2006, p. 1, italics in the original).

From among the components that constitute Fantini's model, the subset of four dimensions (cultural awareness, attitudes, skills, and knowledge) was selected as the basis for teaching and assessing the thirty-one sojourners at various stages of intercultural development and levels of host language proficiency (i.e. Portuguese). Intercultural communicative competence was, thus, operationalised as a cultural-linguistic construct embodying the necessary capacities to undertake the role of intercultural speaker and/or mediator as required by the context of interaction.

Table CS1.1 Goals and learning outcomes.

Modules	*Goals*	*Learning outcomes*
1	To raise understanding and critical reflection about the concept of culture while simulating self-awareness about how culture may influence individual identities	• To identify aspects and value of one's identity • To produce critical reflection about how culture may influence one's identity • To appreciate cultural differences, by showing openness, empathy, and tolerance towards the other
2	To promote critical reflection about culture relativism while enhancing abilities to compare values in home and host cultures	• To identify different manifestations of cultural relativism • To identify different sources of misunderstanding and mediate between conflicting interpretations of phenomena • To develop an explanatory system regarding culture values susceptible of application to students' own languages
3	To stimulate self-awareness and critical reflection about the challenges of living in another culture, and concepts like culture shock/stress, acculturation, stereotypes, and generalisations	• To discuss the human experience of migration • To differentiate between stereotypes, generalisations, and questioning • To explain the notions of culture shock and acculturation processes against the study aboard/sojourning experience
4	To promote understanding of host culture identity traits while enhancing abilities to relate and contrast home and host cultures	• To relate and contrast identity traits of host and home cultures • To display increased critical cultural awareness regarding one's self-representations of the host culture • To relate and contrast the socio-economic situation lived by Portuguese youth with the situation of the youth in the students' countries of origin
5	To stimulate understanding of cultures in the classroom while enhancing abilities to relate and contrast time value orientations of home and host culture	• To recognise one's culturally influenced values, behaviour, and ways of thinking • To relate and contrast time value orientations of home and host cultures • To value the different cultures represented in the classroom
6	To raise understanding and critical awareness about intercultural education, intercultural competencies, and interculturality in the Lusophone world	• To explain the intents of intercultural education as a positive approach towards difference • To discuss the role of intercultural competencies in sojourning • To display awareness of interculturality in the Lusophone world
7	To promote understanding of the language-culture nexus while empowering students with language-culture learning strategies	• To explain how language and culture relate • To discuss the role of culture in the Portuguese language classroom • To develop an explanatory system susceptible of application in situations of cultural misunderstanding/dysfunction

Modules	Goals	Learning outcomes
3	To reflect critically about the linguistic and cultural diversity of Europe and core concepts like European citizenship	• To articulate well-informed viewpoints about Europe's linguistic and cultural diversity • To relate and contrast national and supranational citizenry • To articulate sustained viewpoints about the role of the exchange student as an exemplary European citizen

Although only Fantini's model was explicitly adopted as the unit of analysis, another three models aided the understanding of sojourner intercultural development and learning. These models are Bennett's Developmental Model of Intercultural Sensitivity (1986, 1993), King and Baxter Magolda's Developmental Model of Intercultural Maturity (2005), and Byram's Model of Intercultural Communicative Competence (1997). Whereas the two developmental models offered insights into the psycho-social nuances of sojourner intercultural development, Byram's model clarified the formulation of teaching objectives and the notion of critical cultural awareness.

Developing intercultural communicative competence

The pedagogical framework of the 'intercultural seminars' was designed after Fantini's Model of Intercultural Communicative Competence (2006) and implemented through experiential activities sequenced into ascending levels of complexity. Using Kolb's Experiential Learning Cycle (1984), these activities utilised students' host country experience and cultural backgrounds as areas for learning.

Selection of contents builds on an extensive literature review and on a needs analysis of participants' stages of intercultural communicative competence development and their areas of interest for intercultural learning elicited by a pre-test questionnaire. This assessment was fundamental to designing a 'backwards curriculum design' wherein the intercultural curriculum was planned in reverse (Wiggins & McTighe, 2005). According to this approach to curriculum design, only after determining desired results and acceptable learning evidence is instruction planned. Thus, the intervention's instructional plan was designed upon 'diagnosing' participant intercultural learning needs and stages of development. This approach set the culture-specific intentions of the intervention, given the participant's wish to obtain a contextualised understanding of Portuguese culture reported in the pre-test. The host culture was, then, the leverage for developing student intercultural communicative competence across its areas of competence while exploring sojourning challenges and student identities.

Assessing intercultural communicative competence

Formative and summative assessments were used as part of a larger mixed methods evaluative inquiry involving the planned use and integration of quantitative and qualitative methods (Greene, 2005; Greene, Caracelli, & Graham, 1989) to produce a comprehensive evaluation regarding the *process* of implementing the intervention and its *learning outcomes* (i.e. enhanced intercultural communicative competencies of participants). Whereas summative assessment determines the effectiveness of the intervention in meeting its overarching mission, formative assessment focuses on defining, monitoring, and analysing how well student learning goals were achieved throughout and could be improved as a result.

1. *Summative assessment* undergirds the mixed methods evaluation and the programmatic component embodied by the intervention. Hence the plural adoption of research/ assessment methods to measure the value of the intervention, namely:

    - pre- and post-questionnaires administered to all thirty-one students;
    - focus groups conducted with Case Study 1.1 participants;
    - individual interviews conducted with the language teacher and five stakeholders with a legitimate interest in the intervention.

    Whereas the pre- and post-measures and focus groups ascertained the intrinsic value of the intervention to those 'inside' it (the students), individual interviews measured the extrinsic value to those 'outside' it (the stakeholders and the language teacher).

2. *Formative assessment* reports to the ongoing process of teaching and assessing student intercultural learning during the intervention. Specific assessment methods involved:

    - in-class activities/assignments: interpretation, listening comprehension and written exercises, gapping filling and matching exercises, oral presentations, guided discussions, dialogues, and quizzes;
    - formative tests, worksheets, and essays to measure student progress and content learning;
    - observation of student performance, attitudes, and abilities to reflect critically and suspend disbelief.

Lessons learned

Three major lessons can be drawn from the 'intercultural seminars' to develop and assess intercultural competencies. First, from an assessment perspective, an all-encompassing approach needs to be adopted to evaluate programme effectiveness and to assess student learning. Mixed-methods evaluations and the integration of quantitative and qualitative data can enhance the robustness of empirical findings. In this study, data integration addressed the intrinsic and extrinsic value of the intervention and was complemented by the formative assessment of student intercultural learning.

Second, from a developmental perspective, a holistic view of intercultural competence should attend to its behavioural, affective, cognitive, and developmental dimensions. Based on participant intercultural communicative competence development, four basic assumptions were made to form a framework for a holistic view of intercultural communicative competence:

1. Intercultural communicative competence is a complex and multidimensional competence with core dimensions being cultural awareness, attitudes, knowledge, and skills.
2. Intercultural communicative competence is a cultural-linguistic construct which can be culture-specific or culture-general.
3. Intercultural communicative competence is a higher-order developmental process of multidimensional growth in cognitive, intrapersonal, and interpersonal domains.
4. Intercultural communicative competence is a competence of qualitative growth whereby mature levels of performance may be related to abilities to de-centre oneself and reflect critically (Almeida, 2015).

Third, from a curriculum-based perspective, a proper understanding of design concepts and evaluation is fundamental to curriculum design and the shaping of realistic approaches to teaching and assessing intercultural competencies. To build deliberate intercultural educational support, careful attention needs to be paid to the procedural phases of ***designing***, ***implementing***, and ***evaluating*** an intercultural curriculum. These phases can be broken down into four steps: (1) mapping appropriate intercultural learning theories; (2) developing appropriate intercultural curricula and assessment approaches; (3) implementing/testing these curricula and assessment approaches; and (4) sharing results (Almeida, 2015). These steps inform an ongoing process wherein the sharing of results should have the potential to advance future efforts.

Ways to improve

Further improvement of the 'intercultural seminars' involves extending its duration and scope to the etic perspectives of hosts (other than the language teacher and stakeholders) in order to better capture the nuances of intercultural development within the local community. To this end, both formal and non-formal learning arenas should be taken into account (Almeida, Fantini, Simões, & Costa, in press) against a type of assessment that is not only multipurpose in terms of methods but also in the range of social actors involved.

References

Almeida, J. (2015). European student mobility and intercultural learning at a Portuguese university. *Doctoral thesis*, University of Aveiro.

Almeida, J., Fantini, A. E., Simões, A. R., & Costa, N. (in press). Enhancing the intercultural effectiveness of exchange programmes: Formal and non-formal educational interventions. *Intercultural Education.*

Bennett, M. J. (1986). A developmental approach to training for intercultural sensitivity. *International Journal of Intercultural Relations, 10*(2), 179–96.

—— (1993). *Towards ethnorelativism: A developmental model of intercultural sensitivity.* Yarmouth, ME: Intercultural Press.

Byram, M. (1997). *Teaching and assessing intercultural communication competence.* New York, NY: Multilingual Matters.

Fantini, A. E. (2006). *Exploring and assessing intercultural competence.* Brattleboro, VT: Federation of the Experiment in International Living.

Fantini, A., & Tirmizi, A. (2006). Exploring and assessing intercultural competence. *World Learning Publications.* Paper 1. Retrieved from http://digitalcollections.sit.edu/worldlearning_publications/1

Greene, J. C. (2005). Mixed-method evaluation. In S. Mathinson (Ed.), *Encyclopedia of evaluation* (pp. 255–6). Thousand Oaks, CA: Sage.

Greene, J. C., Caracelli, V. J., & Graham, W. F. (1989). Toward a conceptual framework for mixed-method evaluation designs. *Educational Evaluation and Policy Analysis, 11*(3), 255–74.

King, P. M., & Baxter Magolda, M. B. (2005). A developmental model of intercultural maturity. *Journal of College Student Development, 46*(6), 571–92.

Kolb, D. A. (1984). *Experience as the source of learning and development.* Englewood Cliffs, NJ: PTR Prentice Hall.

Wiggins, G. P., & McTighe, J. (2005). *Understanding by design* (2nd edn). Alexandria, VA: Association for Supervision and Curriculum Development.

CS2

Intercultural competence in practice

A peer-learning and reflection-based university course to develop intercultural competence

Nadine Binder (Bremen International Graduate School of Social Sciences/Jacobs University Bremen)

Context

I have designed the course 'Intercultural Competence in Practice' as part of my doctoral research on intercultural competence development of university students. In spring 2016, the course was first offered as an elective 2.5 ECTS (European Credit Transfer and Accumulation System) course for undergraduate first-year students of all majors at Jacobs University Bremen, a private international university in northern Germany. In total, thirty-four students were enrolled, representing eighteen different nationalities and various majors. With the aim of facilitating students' intercultural competence development, the course combined more traditional lectures instructed by faculty with experiential workshops facilitated by peer-trainers, who were third-year undergraduate students. Peer-trainers have completed an intercultural trainer education prior to their involvement in this course.[1] The course ran for fourteen weeks from February to May 2016 with alternating lectures (75 minutes with the whole group) and workshops (2.5 hours in two smaller groups). It was pass or fail, with students passing if they fulfilled the attendance requirement and completed their weekly written reflections.

Goals and outcomes

Upon successful completion of the course, students were expected to:

- have an in-depth understanding of how culture influences how we feel, think, and act;
- be able to relate this knowledge to their everyday experience in a multicultural environment;
- be familiar with the personal leadership methodology and critical moment dialogue (CMD) and able to apply it to their own experience to establish an intercultural practice.

Framework of intercultural competence

The course has been designed using Deardorff's (2006) Pyramid Model of Intercultural Competence. Essential attitudes such as openness and curiosity were taken as given to the extent that students selected this course out of interest. Concerning the knowledge dimension, lectures covered content to promote a deep understanding of culture by introducing students to basics of cross-cultural psychology, including the origins of culture, cultural influences on cognition and perception, as well as cultural differences in verbal and non-verbal behaviour. Cultural self-awareness was stimulated by reflective tasks in the assignments and workshops, e.g., by asking students to reflect upon their multiple identities and having them interview each other about their cultures. Relevant skills as well as internal outcomes such as adaptability and flexibility were practised in workshops, e.g., by using the DIE (describe, interpret, evaluate) activity, which forces students to clearly distinguish between their objective description of pictures or scenarios and their interpretations and evaluations of those, or exercises where students had to switch between direct and indirect communication.

This approach was complemented by the personal-leadership methodology by Schaetti, Ramsey, and Watanabe (2008, 2009), who conceptualise intercultural competence as consisting of culture-specific knowledge, culture-general knowledge, and an intercultural practice. Students were introduced to the personal-leadership methodology with its two principles (i.e. mindfulness, creativity) and six practices (i.e. attending to judgement, attending to emotion, attending to physical sensation, cultivating stillness, engaging ambiguity, aligning with vision) as well as its core process of the critical moment dialogue (CMD) which encourages reflection along the six practices. Through various activities such as drafting their vision as a student in a multicultural environment or a written CMD on a recently encountered intercultural challenge, students were encouraged to explore how personal leadership can serve them to transfer their learnings into an intercultural practice.

Developing intercultural competence

The course combined theoretical and experiential sessions to engage students with two major topics: (1) understanding culture and its influence on human cognition and behaviour and cultural self-awareness; and (2) the personal leadership methodology as a tool for developing an intercultural practice that transfers knowledge into practice. Lectures were based on mandatory readings, and the workshops used various activities such as individual reflection and group work to explore the lecture topics further. The topics included cultural identities (exploring one's own cultural identity and interviewing other students about their identity), culture and cognition (practising suspending judgement and enhancing cognitive flexibility), intercultural interaction (practising to switch communication styles), as well as personal leadership for intercultural practice (writing one's own vision, exploring personal leadership practices, and using the CMD).

Assessing intercultural competence

Students' intercultural competence development was assessed in a mixed methods, longitudinal design combining indirect and direct evidence (Deardorff, 2011). In the first and last session, all students completed a questionnaire including two self-report measures of intercultural competence (test to measure intercultural competence short form [TMIC-S] by Schnabel, Kelava, van de Vijver, & Seifert, 2015; short form cultural intelligence [SFCQ], by Thomas et al., 2015). This quantitative, indirect assessment was complemented by direct evidence from students' portfolios including twelve reflective tasks which students completed on a weekly basis as part of the coursework. While some questions were rather broad (e.g., 'What is your culture?'), others invited students to link theoretical concepts to their own experience ('Think back to how you grew up as a child and what you were taught at home and in school. Are you more used to an analytic or holistic thinking style? Provide examples to demonstrate why you think you are more used to the one or the other or both').

The indirect, quantitative self-report offered a more general assessment of students' intercultural competence development. A paired-samples t-test was conducted to compare intercultural competence measured by the TMIC-S and SFCQ in the beginning and end of the course. There was a significant difference in the TMIC-S scores in the pre-test ($M = 4.46$, $SD = 0.52$) and post-test ($M = 4.61$, $SD = 0.54$); $t(32) = -2.55$, $p = 0.016$. There was also a significant difference in the SFCQ scores in the pre-test ($M = 5.44$, $SD = 0.73$) and post-test ($M = 5.63$, $SD = 0.65$); $t(32) = -2.2$, $p = 0.035$. These results demonstrate that students achieved significantly higher scores on both intercultural competence measures at the end of the course (as compared to the beginning), suggesting that their intercultural competence increased. Students were also asked to visualise their own intercultural competence development which all of them drew as a rising learning curve. Furthermore, they were asked to rate various evaluative items on a 7-point Likert scale offering further evidence for students' perceived intercultural competence development.

Yet more direct evidence of students' learning comes from analysing their portfolios with special focus on the three specific learning objectives as outlined above. Students' assignments were checked not only for complying with length and content requirements but also for whether they provided evidence for either of the three learning goals. Such a simplified checklist to track learning over time offers a feasible approach to assess intercultural competence development of a group of students without having to rely on quantitative self-report only. All students' portfolios demonstrated progress over time, with strong evidence for gaining a deeper understanding of culture and its influence on how we feel, think, and act, specific examples showing how students related learnings to their everyday experience as well as their increasing familiarity with the personal-leadership methodology. In their final assignment, students were explicitly asked to reflect upon what they have learned about intercultural competence and how they can transfer these learnings to their student life at Jacobs University Bremen. The following quote represents some of the concluding remarks by students: 'Ultimately, I believe that the course has benefited me personally and rendered me more aware of the biases that we unintentionally develop … this awareness will now bring me a step towards controlling and managing such cultural and individual biases when interacting with other people.'

Lessons learned

First, having specific learning objectives and a clear theoretical framework of intercultural competence formed a solid foundation for the selection of content, didactic approaches, and assessment tools. Second, there is a strong need for combining direct and indirect evidence to get a comprehensive picture of students' intercultural competence development. Complementing quantitative self-reports with direct evidence from reflective papers provided a much more detailed assessment, allowing the course instructor to keep track of whether the learning objectives were met. Finally, one of the biggest challenges was to assess how students apply their learnings outside the classroom. Again, analysing portfolios as well as listening to students in the sessions offered evidence as many students discussed very specific examples of learning transfer; for example to multicultural group work or interactions with friends from other cultural backgrounds.

Ways to improve

The course was done as pass/fail, assuming that this reduces stress and thereby enables a more conducive learning environment. Next time, the course could use a transparent point scheme in which students can gain up to 100 points for active attendance, their reflective papers (including points for submission on time, fulfilling word count, and for content/progress towards learning goals), as well as a longer final assignment or project. Many students expressed a desire to have even more time to learn from each other, thus some of the individual assignments could be replaced with group projects. Finally, to support and track learning transfer beyond the course, one could encourage students to meet in their learning communities for one or two informal events in the upcoming semester, for example during an intercultural dinner or discussion round.

Note

1 The two-week Train-the-Trainer course has been offered as part of Jacobs University's Winter School since 2013 and allows students of intercultural majors to become certified intercultural trainers. More information is available on the programme's website (http://winteracademy-bremen.org/).

References

Deardorff, D. K. (2006). Identification and assessment of intercultural competence as a student outcome of internationalization. *Journal of Studies in International Education*, *10*(3), 241–66.

—— (2011). Assessing intercultural competence. *New Directions for Institutional Research*, *149*, 65–79.

Schaetti, B. F., Ramsey, S. J., & Watanabe, G. C. (2008). *Personal leadership: Making a world of difference – A methodology of two principles and six practices.* Seattle, WA: Flying Kite Publications.

—— (2009). From intercultural knowledge to intercultural competence: Developing an intercultural practice. In M. A. Moodian (Ed.), *Contemporary leadership and intercultural competence: Understanding and utilizing cultural diversity to build successful organizations* (pp. 125–38). Thousand Oaks, CA: Sage.

Schnabel, D. B. L., Kelava, A., van de Vijver, F. J. R., & Seifert, L. (2015). Examining psychometric properties, measurement invariance, and construct validity of a short version of the Test to Measure Intercultural competence (TMIC-S) in Germany and Brazil. *International Journal of Intercultural Relations*, *49*, 137–55.

Thomas, D. C., Liao, Y., Aycan, Z., Cerdin, J. L., Pekerti, A. A., Ravlin, E. C., Stahl, G. K., Lazarova, M. B., Fock, H., Arli, D., Moeller, M., Okimoto, T. G., & van de Vijver, F. (2015). Cultural intelligence: A theory-based, short form measure. *Journal of International Business Studies*, *46*(9), 1099–118.

CS3

Intercultural competence through global citizenship

Huba Boshoff and Alecia Erasmus (Stellenbosch University)

Context

The short course in global citizenship is an accredited co-curricular course with two distinct but interlinked phases. In each of these two phases there is a structured course component that has intercultural competence as a key outcome of the programme. The first (Phase 1 of the global citizenship programme) is an online collaboration with the University of Monterrey in Mexico in which students from both institutions do a set of assignments over a period of approximately four weeks. In each assignment they are divided into pairs (one from each geographical context) and complete three interwoven tasks that connect different aspects of intercultural competence. The second course that follows for a select group from the Phase I global citizenship course is a collaboration between five universities: University of Stuttgart (Germany), St. Xavier's College Mumbai (India), Saint Louis University (USA), Stellenbosch University (South Africa), and Peter the Great St. Petersburg Polytechnic University (Russia). This is a blended learning experience where students work together online, either in pairs or in groups, around a specific topic leading towards a culminating project week at one of the partners (for the past few years it has been Mumbai, India) where the students are divided into groups, predominately a geographical mix to ensure at least one student from each country in every group. The final task is a joint presentation on a subtheme of the annual theme. In both cases, students from Stellenbosch University do this co-curricular and do not earn credits towards their degrees whereas, in most cases, their partners in both projects need to do it for academic credit.

Goals and outcomes

For the interaction with the University of Monterrey specifically, the learning outcomes are as follows:

- Observe, exchange ideas, analyse and discuss the features to identify both the intercultural discourse, as the concepts of intercultural communication

through technological media (Edmodo, etc.) with the partners in Mexico/South Africa.
- Share thoughtful and reflexive assessments during the intercultural project with learning partner in Mexico/South Africa.

The outcomes of the Global Citizenship, Phase 2:

- It is expected that the project will enrich the learning of students and teachers involved on the activities.
- As a participating student you will benefit from the opportunity to develop intercultural communication skills through technology with students and residents of other countries.
- This project also expects you to acquire greater intercultural awareness which in turn can have a positive impact on your professional life.

Framework of intercultural competence

The premise of the intercultural competence interventions is entrenched in Martin Luther King's statement that 'we must learn to live together as brothers or perish together as fools'. This in turn fits with the premise of the Global Citizenship programme that is deeply rooted in Roosevelt's famous quote, 'We have learned to be citizens of the world, members of the human community.'

From a theoretical perspective, intercultural competence embodies a range of skills, knowledge, attitudes, and behaviours of which some are more assessable than others (Deardorff, 2006). In both cases, the application of the definition of intercultural competence is experienced rather than taught. Students discover the meaning of intercultural competence themselves through their engagements and reflections and are able to develop their own working definitions of the concept while still taking the latest writings on the topic into consideration.

Developing intercultural competence

This programme is designed to develop intercultural competencies by means of a set of assignments that students do in pairs. For the first activity, students write a letter to each other that includes a description of what they know or have heard about the other person's country, thoughts about their culture, and what they would like to learn about their culture during the project. They also attach two images which from their perspective are representative of the other culture or that represent the other country for the world. Each student then responds to the letter they have received, highlighting a lack of or dismissal of cultural, geographical or social facts. The outcomes of this activity include comprehension, understanding, and reflection and learning about the cultural perception that we have no prior knowledge.

The second activity entails an interview done via video chat. This activity focuses on specific topics such as student life, the position of women in the society, family relationships and values, as well as racism. The outcomes for this interview include a raised cultural self-awareness for the participants, gaining culture-specific knowledge from their partner, and reflecting and sharing in a way that spurs healthy curiosity and an open mindset.

The last activity entails a creative approach towards reflecting on the intercultural learning that the students have experienced. They design a visual depiction of the learning done in the previous activities, culminating in a cultural map that shows not only the journey they have embarked on but also the new dimensions of intercultural competencies that they have attained.

Phase 2 interaction is structured against the backdrop of an annual theme. The common goal and theme (the presentation at the end of the project week) enables the students to engage with, address, and cope with cultural differences in a way that ensures that they can work together successfully. The blended learning approach starts the collaborations and conversations online and makes it easier for the students to engage productively when they finally meet in person. The submersion of a diverse group of students into a host culture (with inherent cultural differences) accentuates the way in which personal learning is framed and enhanced through personal cultural lenses. The shared experience can create a type of 'common ground' to which they can relate and also by which they can identify similarities and differences between their own culture, the host culture, and the other cultures represented in the group.

Assessing intercultural competence

The following assessment measures were used to determine achievement of the stated objectives:

- Short written reports with a focus on personal reflection.
- Forum discussions around questions posed by programme directors.
- Informal engagements via social media such as a dedicated Facebook group and personal pages.
- Formal presentations in small (two to three people) and bigger (five to six) groups on a pre-identified theme, for example globalisation and identity. Through the formal presentations the components of intercultural competence (knowledge, skills, and attitudes) become visible through the structural learning as well as the engagements between group members.
- Intercultural mapping to visually depict the cultural differences and similarities with your global partner.

Lessons learned

- In an intercultural competence initiative where there is no mobility, it is particularly important that there is equal commitment between individual participants and programme directors.

- In an intercultural competence initiative where there is mobility, the same level of commitment and shared ownership of all aspects of the initiative is required and has a direct impact on the outcomes.
- Open-mindedness and willingness to share and learn are key components to the success of the intercultural competence intervention.
- The ability of programme directors to check their own cultural bias towards the host culture, their own culture, and that of student participants can be instrumental in enriching the experience.
- There is always room for a new cultural surprise, and intercultural competence is a lifelong learning experience.
- Simple but well-structured activities can have a big impact on developing intercultural competencies such as knowledge, skills, and attitudes.
- Intercultural competence is a mechanism to foster greater understanding of one's own culture. In a multicultural society such as South Africa, this will contribute to social cohesion and cultural tolerance.

Ways to improve

- Include a pre-intervention activity such as a self-evaluation of your own culture or perceptions/ knowledge. This will enable a participant to better reflect on his or her progress at the end of the intercultural competencies intervention provided that a post-intervention activity is also applied.
- With specific regard to the Global Citizenship Phase 2 programme, we aim to provide more resources on intercultural competence prior to the project week to equip the participants from a theoretical perspective.
- In a comparison between our two programmes/interventions discussed in this case study, we have surmised that the activities that take place online or electronically are a successful mechanism to instil the principles of intercultural competence but that the experiential learning that takes place in the Phase 2 project has a significantly higher impact on the sustained cultural sensitivity and awareness.
- As a further assessment in the Phase 2 programme we aim to include a personal reflection on cultural learning at the end of the project week.

References

Deardorff, D. K. (2006). The identification and assessment of intercultural competence as a student outcome of internationalization at institutions of higher education in the United States. *Journal of Studies in International Education*, *10*(3), 241–66.

CS4

The Virginia Commonwealth University Global Bridge

Closing academic and cultural spans in first-year courses

Hilary J. Cassil, Terry Franson, Amber Bennett Hill, and Beth Kreydatus (Virginia Commonwealth University)

Context

The Virginia Commonwealth University (VCU) Global Bridge included two concurrent programmes at VCU, one focused on the attitudes, knowledge, and skills of international and domestic students, the other on those of classroom faculty (academics), operating in tandem to bridge academic and cultural gaps faced by international students in their first undergraduate year. The programme brought together faculty teaching focused inquiry (VCU's 'freshman English'), algebra, and English as a second language in a series of seminars, workshops, and collaborative projects. Participants developed and put into pedagogical practice intercultural competence within their disciplinary contexts. Domestic and international students enrolled in participants' courses were taught and given opportunities to exercise appropriate competencies within each classroom relative to its content topics.

Focused inquiry is a two-semester sequence of core education seminar classes. This required first-year course teaches oral and written communication, ethical reasoning, critical thinking, research, and collaboration. In Global Bridge sections, between seven and ten international students were among twenty-two students taught by faculty working closely with language and international education specialists. In algebra, students apply mathematics in real-world settings through exploration in small groups with emphasis on direct student involvement, critical thinking, and communication to solve the problems presented. This course is a gateway for the majority of international business and engineering majors. Global Bridge sections had between five and ten international students among twenty-eight students in total.

Algebra, focused inquiry, and English Language Programme (ELP) instructors came together for an initial three-day academy to consider intercultural theory and pedagogy, culture and language acquisition, and the linguistic and academic challenges of international students. Participants collaboratively revised syllabi and assignments to include strategies and interventions of equal benefit to both international and domestic students. A series of meetings and workshops followed throughout the academic year.

Goals and outcomes

Both international students and native English speakers need support – scaffolding – in order to achieve acculturation into the university's learning environment, academic disciplines, and intercultural diversity. In the Global Bridge, native speakers and international students worked together towards this goal in an inclusive environment. Sharing a similar goal, instructors participated in a learning community that developed intercultural and disciplinary pedagogies and encouraged collegial support.

Focused-inquiry classes support students in achieving the goals of developing as writers, public speakers, critical thinkers, and participants in the university's culturally diverse community. VCU's algebra course exists to increase quantitative-reasoning and critical-thinking skills through problem exploration and, significantly, group discussion. Students engage with real-world data, moving from solution to interpretation within a team setting. Developing faculty awareness and skill in embedding intercultural skills within course content is imperative in students' development in target areas.

Both content knowledge and intercultural competence increased among students as faculty in both courses facilitated collaborative work in groups with diverse national backgrounds. Students described their successes and challenges in collaborating and communicating in groups. One major focused-inquiry assignment in paired international and American students is to interview each other and write an essay describing each other's personal history. To clarify expectations, detailed instructions for tasks were stated and written, and new concepts and processes were modelled and demonstrated. Cultural and linguistic scaffolds, such as clear expectations and modelling, were used early in the semester but were reduced as students achieved intercultural and linguistic proficiency and confidence.

Framework of intercultural competence

VCU's Global Bridge was designed to develop culturally competent teaching strategies in faculty, as described by Gopal (2011) as well as to enhance successful communication with those from other cultures, culturally competent pedagogical strategies on how to respond in culturally sensitive ways, and the ability to successfully communicate and work with students from other cultures. Like many such programmes, the Global Bridge takes as its foundation Deardorff's (2009) Intercultural Competence Model, with its focus on developing attitudes, knowledge and comprehension, and skills. The Global Bridge builds on this model through an intentional focus on academic content and a highly deliberate metamodernist discursive approach to pedagogy and assessment.

Developing intercultural competence

Two integrated programmes, one focused on the attitudes, knowledge, and skills of international and domestic students, the other on those of classroom faculty, sought to: (1) develop intercultural competence in core university constituencies; and (2) bridge the academic and cultural gaps faced by international students in their first undergraduate year. Explicit and implicit intercultural skills development by students were articulated learning outcomes of the content-based curricula of these courses, as were multiple opportunities for guided practice of these skills. Content knowledge growth and effective communication, external outcomes, were assessed, as were participants' ability to accommodate new communication demands and successfully find common ground with classroom peers, internal outcomes.

Assessing intercultural competence

Development over time among participants was assessed; domestic and international students were evaluated comparatively; and Bridge sections were compared to non-Bridge sections in the present and past. Qualitative and quantitative data were collected, including observed and self-reported data.

Faculty completed intercultural competence self-assessments before classes began and at the end of the fall term and were assessed using classroom observation by leaders and peers, evaluating use of scaffolding techniques, inclusion of students, and instruction of intercultural competence. Faculty were interviewed formally in a reflective format at the end of the fall and spring terms, considering intercultural skills and confidence in teaching internationals. Informal advising conversations during the fall term were used to coach faculty and to respond in real time to student and faculty needs.

Student assignments were designed to assess not only content knowledge but intercultural competence as well. Several key assignments in both courses, including collaborative papers, group workshops, and a semester-long project completed outside of the classroom, could not be successfully completed with demonstrating intercultural competence. Students' reflections, peer assessments, grades, and course evaluations revealed clearly that domestic and international students in targeted Global Bridge sections progressed further in intercultural proficiency and course content and had higher rates of satisfaction than courses, past and present, without articulated intercultural pedagogy and developmental outcomes. Students rated themselves as more confident in intercultural competence skills and their peers as more proficient, notably praising the effective collaboration within groups on long-term projects.

Lessons learned

The programme demonstrated conclusively that when intercultural competence learning interventions were used, classes ran smoother, students learned better, and faculty felt more confident facing the challenges of diverse and inclusive classrooms.

Based on initial experience, the programme now includes all undergraduates matriculating from the ELP and a significant number of faculty in both departments.

Equipped with theories and strategies of language acquisition and targeted instruction on scaffolding techniques, faculty felt better prepared to create inclusive environments beneficial to the development of intercultural competence in all students. Departmental programmes focused on inclusive pedagogical practices have been introduced, as have university-wide initiatives for faculty building on the results of the Global Bridge, most notably VCU's Global Zone training programme for faculty, advisers, and staff.

Students demonstrated initial reluctance to pursue intercultural communication, being initially much more comfortable working with students from the same linguistic and cultural backgrounds as their own. Shyness, habit, and cultural boundaries broke down more easily when the instructor created opportunities and established clear expectations for cross-cultural communication and rewarded students for building intercultural bridges.

Ways to improve

Intercultural competence is most likely to develop among faculty and students who explicitly strive to foster it. Early in the semester, intercultural competence was established as a central learning outcome, equal to content-based outcomes. This is being currently expanded upon by the incorporation of service learning and leadership opportunities in Global Bridge sections, where focused inquiry students will serve as cultural ambassadors to ELP students. Similarly, several international students who completed algebra in a Global Bridge section will serve as teaching assistants in upcoming sections of the course, and algebra students will play a central role in an initiative to deliver math content in advanced ELP courses.

Selective revision of content delivery was found helpful, including streamlining syllabi and instructions and providing videos before introducing a new concept so that students could take notes at their own pace. Building on these models, algebra will incorporate an online discussion, allowing students to prepare and review material at a comfortable pace. Algebra is also exploring a flipped classroom model to increase classroom participation.

The Global Bridge model has demonstrated that the successful development of intercultural competence and of content knowledge go hand in hand. The biggest challenges now are to expand its impact to more students, faculty, and disciplines, and to better assess its efficacy.

References

Deardorff, D. K. (2009). Implementing intercultural competence assessment. In D. K. Deardorff (Ed.), *The Sage handbook of intercultural competence* (pp. 477–91). Thousand Oaks, CA: Sage.

Gopal, A. (2011). Internationalization of higher education: Preparing faculty to teach cross-culturally. *International Journal of Teaching and Learning in Higher Education*, *23*(3), 373–81.

CS5

English for specific purposes course for Russian medical students

Focus on intercultural competence

Nadezda Chernyak (Lomonosov Moscow State University)

Context

This case study describes a language-for-specific-purposes course designed to develop the intercultural competence of medical students. The course was created in order to bridge the gap in medical students' instruction by the means available at Russian higher education institutions. Currently, intercultural communication, medical anthropology, or allied disciplines that examine health care in the cross-cultural perspective are not included in the compulsory part of Russian medical degree programmes. Incorporation of these disciplines in federal educational standards is a long and multilevel process. Conversely, by existing regulations, English is a required course for medical students across the country that could bring awareness of intercultural issues of the patient–doctor relationship.

This course was delivered simultaneously on campus at Lomonosov Moscow State University and online in spring 2015. Students (N = 39) from eight Russian medical schools took this elective course: (1) Evdokimov Moscow State University of Medicine and Dentistry, (2) Sechenov First Moscow State Medical University, (3) Samara State Medical University, (4) Volgograd State Medical University, (5) Pirogov Russian National Research Medical University, (6) Lomonosov Moscow State University, (7) Tver State Medical University, and (8) Russian Peoples' Friendship University.

Students' majors, as stated in the official list of programmes approved by the Russian ministry of education and science, included general medicine, paediatrics, preventive medicine, and dentistry. Each group consisted of five students.

The age of the students ranged from 18 to 27 years, with an average of 21.8 years. Most of the participants of the course were female (N = 29). Very few students (16 per cent) spent more than three months abroad. The students' native language was Russian. Students also knew English (upper intermediate level) and Latin. Some students (16 per cent) could speak another language like French, German, Armenian, or Tatar.

The same facilitator worked in online and on-campus groups. The teacher was female, aged 30, with an MA degree in linguistics and intercultural communication and an MA in bioethics/medical ethics. She had experience living abroad, working in culturally diverse healthcare organisations overseas, and teaching in higher education institutions.

Goals and outcomes

1. To increase cultural awareness level: students will become aware of their own attitudes and values and understand that they may differ from those of their colleagues and patients.
2. To develop empathy: students will be able to understand feelings and needs of patients from diverse cultural backgrounds.
3. To encourage self-reflection: students will demonstrate positive self-reflection on the past acts of intercultural communication in healthcare settings.

Framework of intercultural competence

The definition of intercultural competence offered in 1984 by Spitzberg and Cupach (1984) was used in this course. Intercultural competence is seen as learner ability to communicate effectively and appropriately with people of other cultures.

In search of a suitable intercultural competence model, sixty-six models created by scholars from thirteen countries were reviewed. Campinha-Bacote's model (Campinha-Bacote, Yahle, & Langenkamp, 1996) was found useful but not entirely appropriate for the course. Instead of referring to a particular model, three most common components of intercultural competence mentioned in relevant models were considered, namely, cognitive (cultural awareness), affective (empathy), and behavioural (self-reflection).

Developing intercultural competence

The course was delivered in two formats: online and on-campus. Apart from the different learning formats, other aspects of course instruction were similar. The course consisted of five units:

- Unit 0: Introduction;
- Unit 1: The Language Barrier Hurts Patients;
- Unit 2: Insiders' and Outsiders' Perspectives on Illness;
- Unit 3: What Culture Does Your Patient Hurt In?
- Unit 4: Between Medical Ethnocentrism and Cultural Relativism.

Every unit was developed in accordance with D. Kolb's (Kolb, Boyatzis, & Mainemelis, 2000) four-stage experiential learning cycle. Each stage of the experiential learning cycle included certain types of learning activities:

- Stage 1: Concrete experience. Students were given a case from clinical practice in which a doctor handled a conflict caused by cultural differences with a patient. Students proceeded with a text (maximum of 750 words) about the same issue. Reading comprehension exercises included alternative and open-ended questions.

- Stage 2: Reflective observation. Students were asked to write in reflective journals a short essay on the case from clinical practice and to do paraphrase and summary exercises.
- Stage 3: Abstract conceptualisation. Students worked with a short text (maximum of 250 words) that summarised theory of intercultural communication related to the clinical case discussed earlier. The learning activities included description of similarities and differences, argumentation for and against.
- Stage 4: Active experimentation. In role plays, students were given an opportunity to put into practice new knowledge and skills.

Assessing intercultural competence

Triangulation of the following methods was used in summative assessment before and after the course:

1. Quantitative analysis of questionnaires developed originally in Russian language: evaluation of similarities and differences among representatives of different nationalities by I. L. Pluzhnik for cultural awareness assessment; evaluation of empathic abilities level by V. V. Boyko for empathy assessment; evaluation of ontogenetic reflection level for self-reflection assessment.
2. Qualitative analysis of entries in reflective journals (aimed to explain quantitative analysis results).
3. Observation sheets with checklist of behavioural patterns (developed specifically for assessment during the role plays of the course).

The questionnaires were combined with the Crowne-Marlowe Social Desirability Scale (translated into Russian and validated) that helped to detect socially desirable responding and exclude corresponding results from the sample. The Mann–Whitney–Wilcoxon U test was applied to test for statistical significance of results.

Formative assessment included ongoing facilitator's feedback on learning activity results at every stage of the experiential learning cycle described above.

Lessons learned

Results showed minor differences in the development of intercultural competence components in online and on-campus learning. Understanding these differences can help design more effective online courses in future. At present, instructional designers share the view that it is not enough to copy course materials into an online learning environment to create a successful elearning experience. The following recommendations specify in what way online learning should differ from on-campus learning to ensure sustainable development of intercultural competence:

- The course had the largest effect on the cognitive component of intercultural competence, in our case cultural awareness, with 28 per cent increase in on-campus groups and 19 per cent increase in online groups. Course outcomes signify that texts as course materials were 30 per cent less effective in online learning than in on-campus learning. For that reason, it is not recommended to make texts the default medium of content transmission in online courses aimed at intercultural competence development. Instead, course materials should be available in different types of media (video, audio, animation, etc.). In the same manner, assessment could include video and audio recordings made by students, elements of gamification, etc.
- Empathy levels changed insignificantly, with 6 per cent increase in on-campus groups and 6 per cent decrease in online groups. It was found that it is remarkably difficult to develop the affective component of intercultural competence, especially via online learning. The literature review suggests that these difficulties are associated with a relatively small amount of contextual information that modern distance learning technologies can pass on. Our recommendation for course designers who specifically target affective component development would be to switch from an online learning format to a blended learning format that allows the combination of online with on-campus sessions.
- We found differences in self-reflection growth with 11 per cent in on-campus groups and 19 per cent in online groups. In our opinion, the reason lies in lack of continuous feedback provided to students by a facilitator and peers in the case of on-campus learning. In online learning, it is recommended to provide extra feedback with the help of automated notifications and reminders.

Ways to improve

When cases from clinical practice, which opened each unit, were followed by several variants of intercultural conflict resolution, students were prone to passively choose one of them. Less than 5 per cent opted for 'My own answer' and suggested a creative solution. This made discussion restricted and low-key. Giving the same cases without the variants could potentially result in improvement.

Acknowledgement

The author gratefully acknowledges the assistance of Dr Irina Kolesnik, without whom the present study could not have been completed.

References

Campinha-Bacote, J., Yahle, T., & Langenkamp, M. (1996). The challenge of cultural diversity for nurse educators. *The Journal of Continuing Education in Nursing*, *27*(2), 59–64.

Kolb, D. A., Boyatzis, R. E., & Mainemelis, C. (2000). Experiential learning theory: Previous research and new directions. In R. J. Sternberg & L. F. Zhang (Eds.), *Perspectives on cognitive, learning, and thinking styles* (pp. 227–47). Mahwah, NJ: Lawrence Erlbaum.

Spitzberg, B. H., & Cupach, W. R. (1984). *Interpersonal communication competence*. Beverly Hills, CA: Sage.

CS6

An online learning journey of diversity and bias

Liza Lai Shan Choi and Sonya L. Jakubec
(Mount Royal University)

Context

Nursing practice takes place at the most personal and intimate sites of people's lives. From cradle to grave, in homes and in hospices, nurses and nurse educators are responsible for ensuring that this practice is culturally congruent and culturally responsive to the beliefs of the individuals, families, and communities they serve. In Canada (the site of this case study), and globally, nurses provide care for increasingly diverse individuals, groups, and communities, with more practising nurses themselves coming from diverse groups.

NURS 4426, Diversity in Health, is a blended (part online, part in class) senior-level course at Mount Royal University (MRU), an undergraduate university in Calgary, Alberta. Based in a city of 1.4 million people, MRU's student population is rapidly becoming more culturally diverse with an expanding new immigrant population (predominantly South Asian, Chinese, Black, Filipino, Latin American, Arab and South-East Asian), people of diverse age groups, abilities as well as sexual identification and expressions (Statistics Canada, 2013).

In NURS 4426, students learn about bias, models of diversity, and intercultural competence. A nurse who is biased implements nursing care based on personal attitudes, cognitive errors, prejudices, and stereotypes. Bias, the negative evaluation of one group relative to another (Blair, Steiner, & Havranek, 2011), may be intentional or unconscious. In this elective (optional) course, taken in the fourth year of a Bachelor of Nursing programme, nursing students embark on a transformative journey that will aid them in gaining consciousness of personal bias and linking experiences at the local level with translocal policy and practice. In this chapter, we provide an overview of all objectives, assignments, lessons learned, and next steps.

Goals and outcomes

Goals and outcomes for the blended course are:

1. to explore personal biases, policy and practice exemplars as well as a variety of models of diversity and diversity assessment for health and nursing practice;

2. to explore how local attitudes about diversity are shaped translocally – and in turn shape intercultural competence for nursing students;
3. to examine the impact of intercultural competence on nursing practice and health assessment.

Framework of intercultural competence

The Diversity in Health course examines the key underpinnings of bias, diversity, intercultural competence, and cultural safety through a number of models and perspectives. Ranging from Leininger's (2006) cultural care and universality model to the model of intercultural competence acquisition (Campinha-Bacote, 2003), these models are further expanded to include postmodern nursing philosophical models and the application of critical social theory to nursing-care models for lesbian, gay, bisexual, or transgender clients (Dysart-Gale, 2010; Rodriguez & Kotarba, 2009). These critical approaches contribute to culturally safe practice, or practice that refers to gaining an understanding of others' health beliefs and practices so that healthcare actions work towards equity and avoid discrimination (Ramsden, 2002). Taken together, intercultural competence informed by these models is considered an ongoing process rather than an outcome.

Developing intercultural competence

In order to practise with intercultural competence, nurses must apply cultural knowledge and skills appropriate to client interactions without personal biases. NURS 4426 provides a strong foundation for intercultural competence and culturally safe nursing practice with diverse populations locally, nationally and globally. In this course, intercultural competence is explored on a personal level, first inviting students to explore their own bias. Development of intercultural competence is supported in the course through personal engagement in the study of a population of the students' choosing, a process that serves as a living case study. In the learning activities, presented though online learning modules, students are first introduced to various models of diversity through a series of exercises that explore diversity and bias on a personal level as well as in groups, using actual and fictional case studies. After the first module, students are introduced to a fictional society in which matriarchal and patriarchal archetypes are presented to them in an unorthodox manner. Another module instructs students in the performance of a cultural assessment using the Giger and Davidhizer (2012) model. The final module involves instruction in critical appraisal of a diversity programme under the auspices of the Canadian healthcare system. All of the learning activities are presented in online modules.

Assessing intercultural competence

Assessment is accomplished in a variety of ways, including: a personal reflection paper on views of diversity in light of dominant diversity models, online discussion surrounding the impact of matriarchal and patriarchal archetypes on personal bias, a cultural nursing assessment experience with a volunteer client, and a scholarly paper. The reflective paper is a foundational exercise where students examine a number of diversity models and discuss which model(s) best reflects their own views. Students are provided with various academic articles concerned with models of diversity. This exercise establishes a baseline of student views on diversity.

The next assignment is unorthodox and provocative in nature in so much as students are initially presented with a fictional society that is either overtly patriarchal or matriarchal in nature. Working in groups, students are then asked to comment on the aspects of diversity, intercultural competence, and cultural safety within the society. The fictional society is then presented in a manner that attends to respect for diversity, intercultural competence, and cultural safety. Students summarise their learning and integration from the exercise in an online discussion posting. Here students learn about intercultural competence by unearthing and reflecting upon any inherent self-bias. Assessment of intercultural competence in the exercise occurs with a rating of the depth and frequency of critical dialogue and online discussion, which is evaluated by the instructor.

In the practical patient assessment assignment, framed by the Giger–Davidhizer model, intercultural competence learning is enhanced by real-time practice with the cultural nursing assessment process in addition to careful reflection and self-appraisal. This assignment provides students with a useful tool for their future nursing practice with diverse clients, and an expanded self-awareness of their own strengths and areas for improvement in practice.

The final assignment is a scholarly paper in which students critique a health programme offered by a community health or social-services agency for an identified client group. In this assignment, intercultural competence is assessed by examining the application of course concepts in the critical appraisal of an actual health programme. This collection of assignments provides both peer and instructor feedback about student understanding of course concepts and the integration of intercultural competence into nursing practice.

Ways to improve

In course evaluations, many students expressed their preference for in-person interactions with fellow classmates and faculty. Students appreciated the opportunity to hear directly from fellow classmates and faculty with expertise in the area of diversity. The value of the online format must be considered in balance, however, as web learning and discussion board processes were also said to support student integration, allowing for reflection, open expression, and organisation of thoughts.

When asked to meet with clinical populations of interest, many students faced obstacles contacting agencies external to the university learning environment. Community health or social-services organisations' schedules did not always align with students' needs. It was essential that students locate these organisations early in the course, a step that might be useful to link to student evaluation.

Close examination of online discussion board postings revealed student biases; thus it will be important to assess the application of intercultural competence within online discussions as discussion moderators. A reflective paper that elaborates on the online discussion could expand student learning and enhance assessment of the integration of intercultural competence in routine behaviours and practices. Future research will involve the examination of this transformation journey through both qualitative (interviews) and quantitative (survey) methods to particularly understand the impact of this course on students' views of bias.

Lessons learned

Key lessons learned from implementation of the course include the following:

1. Personal connections matter in all aspects of diversity education – including pedagogical practices. While key course content was presented in an online context, students expressed that face-to-face interaction with the instructor at key junctures of the course was beneficial to linking theory and practice, and personal and political aspects of diversity.
2. Students are interested in learning about diversity, challenging their assumptions and biases, and critiquing dominant policy and practice. Students readily embraced the challenging exercises to learn about diversity and to practise assessment informed by intercultural competence.
3. More research and post-graduation follow-up are important. Anecdotally, students have reported that the learning experiences transformed their notion of bias. Future research will look specifically at this question of bias and the impact of this course on students' views of bias as they transition into their professional nursing careers.

The Diversity in Health course offers students a unique opportunity to learn about bias, diversity, and intercultural competence. It is a journey that begins with an exploration of self-bias and continues in the exposure of students to models of diversity, practical approaches to cultural assessments of clients in practice, political analysis, and critique of health programmes designed for diverse clients. Future studies will examine the experience of transformative learning for students and the impact of this course on the professional lives of students as they transition into professional nursing practice with diverse populations.

References

Blair, I., Steiner, J. L., & Havranek, E. L. (2011). Unconscious (implicit) bias and health disparities: Where do we go from here? *The Permanenete Journal*, *15*(2), 71–8.

Campinha-Bacote, J. (1999). A model and instrument for addressing cultural competence in health care. *Journal of Nursing Education*, *38*(5), 203–7.
Campinha-Bacote, J. (2003). Cultural desire: The key to unlocking cultural competence. *Journal of Nursing Education*, *42*(6), 239–40.
Dysart-Gale, D. (2010). Social justice and social determinants of health: Lesbian, gay, bisexual, transgendered, intersexed, and queer youth in Canada. *Journal of Child & Adolescent Psychiatric Nursing*, *23*(1), 23–8.
Giger, J. N., & Davidhizar, R. E. (2012). *Transcultural nursing: Assessment and intervention* (6th edn). St Louis, MO: Mosby Elsevier.
Leininger, M. M., & McFarland, M. R. (2006). *Culture care diversity and universality: A worldwide theory for nursing* (2nd edn). Sudbury, MA: Jones & Bartlett.
Ramsden, I. (2002). Cultural safety and nursing education in Aotearoa and Te Waipounamu. Doctor of philosophy thesis, Victoria University, Wellington.
Rodriguez, T., & Kotarba, J. A. (2009). Postmodern philosophies of science: Pathways to nursing reality. *Southern Online Journal of Nursing Research*, *9*(1).
Statistics Canada. (2013). 2011 National Household Survey. Retrieved from www12.statcan.gc.ca/nhs-enm/2011/dp-pd/prof/index.cfm?Lang=E

CS7

Intercultural competence for classes of mixed-discipline students in New Zealand

Deborah Corder (Auckland University of Technology)

Context

With the shift in language teaching from a focus on communicative competence to intercultural communicative competence, the School of Language and Culture, Auckland University of Technology, developed its intercultural competence course in 2007. It is a first-year, non-language-specific course to complement language majors and an elective for other majors and incoming-study abroad students. Intercultural competence is compulsory in the BA International Studies major, introduced in 2010, which has intercultural and transnational competence in the graduate profile. Intercultural Competence in a Global World (ICGW) was developed in 2010, to deepen understanding of theory and critical reflection. Both courses have three contact hours a week over twelve weeks, including one hour in a computer room to facilitate written reflection and group work.

There are always two lecturers, which ensures ongoing moderation of, and reflection on content, activities, and assessment. The lecturers have different ethnic backgrounds and specialise in language teaching and/or applied linguistics. Student ethnicities include European, Maori, Pacific Islands, Asian, Middle-Eastern, and North and South American.

Goals and outcomes

- To develop critical cultural awareness of self–other, in terms of one's own identity and worldview and the influence of values and beliefs on attitude, use of language and behaviour, including emotional responses to difference, uncertainty, and conflict.
- To understand the concept of individuals as cultural mediators, interact effectively, and establish and maintain relationships with others who have different language backgrounds, cultural orientations, and practices.

The specific learning outcomes for assessment are:

1. **knowledge:** values, norms, beliefs, socio-cultural/sociolinguistic and other relevant theories, concepts, and frameworks to interpret patterns of behaviour;
2. **skills and behaviour:** noticing, contrasting, interpreting, questioning differences in perspectives/communication styles, establishing and maintaining relationships;
3. **attitude:** curiosity, flexibility, respect for difference, willingness to interact and question values, beliefs, and presuppositions of own and others' cultures;
4. **critical cultural awareness:** reflection on self-other, identity, and worldview, assess changes in perspective and development.

There is some variation of focus (and hence wording in brackets) between the two courses. ICGW assessment criteria require deeper exploration of self–other, value judgements, and mediating conflicting interpretation.

Framework of intercultural competence

The theoretical framework and the learning outcomes for both courses, are based on the Byram (1997) and Deardorff (2006, 2011) models. Theoretical content includes concepts, models, and frameworks from a range of disciplines, e.g., value systems (Houghton, 2012; Schwartz et al, 1997), Bennett's Developmental Model of Intercultural Sensitivity (DMIS; Bennett, 1993), and Grice's Maxims (as cited in Bowe & Martin, 2007).

Developing intercultural competence

The learning and teaching approach is socio-constructivist (Byram, 2008; Deardorff, 2011; Kohonen, 2005; Witte, 2011), applying an adapted version of Kolb's Experiential Learning Model (1984), as shown in Figure CS7.1. This facilitates collaborative, dialogic experiential learning to explore and challenge values and beliefs.

Experiences/activities include video clips, readings, guest speakers, and immersion into the virtual world of Second Life (Corder & U-Mackey, 2015). Activities are followed by discussions, debriefs, and theory. ICGW activities include outside-the-classroom real-life immersive experiences in different socio-cultural contexts, e.g., the Deaf Education Center.

For the first five weeks, online blogs are used for student reflection on learning experiences. Reflection is guided and formative and includes Kohls' (1996) describe, interpret, and evaluate (DIE) structure. Students apply theory to interpret responses to triggers from class and immersive activities to understand their worldviews. In the final weeks, students also do collaborative projects in which they question their assumptions and practise interaction skills. Intercultural competence students work in groups to explore the influence of values and beliefs on their perspectives on a chosen social issue, with each member focusing on their own culture. ICGW

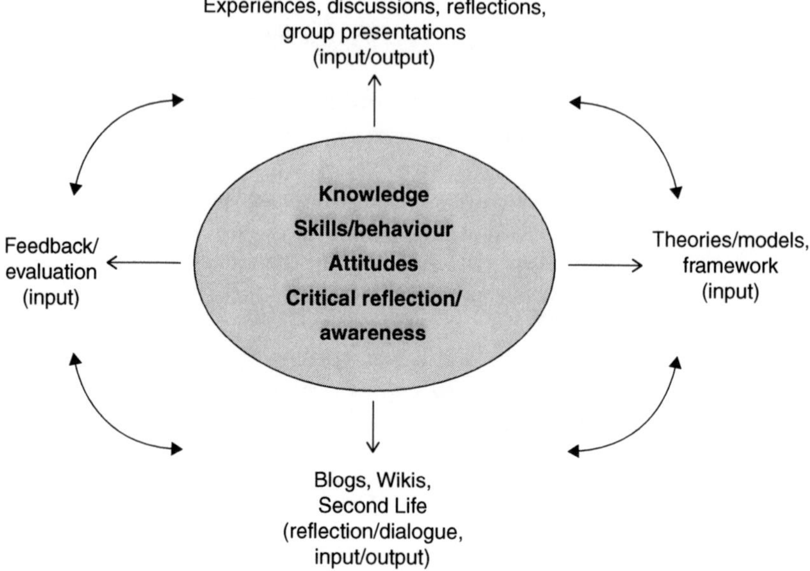

Figure CS7.1 Learning, teaching, and assessment model for ICC.

students undertake short ethnographic tasks in tandem pairs that include observations and interviewing each other. The groups and tandems are mixed ethnicities and genders. Wikis are used to record findings, discussion, peer feedback, and to reflect on triggers. Lecturer feedback is ongoing in the computer room and online.

With the collaborative learning approach, blogs and wikis are open for classmates to read and comment. This is found to be effective for students less comfortable in face-to-face discussions. The digital platform facilitates ongoing dialogue and engagement out of class and maximises learning opportunities from peer models and peer and lecturer feedback. Throughout the course, learning and development are captured, which is useful for assessment purposes, including student self-assessment.

Assessing intercultural competence

Summative assessments provide feedback at three points in time, with students and lecturers drawing on the formative blogs and wikis as evidence of learning and development for assessment purposes.

The tools for the first two assessments are the same as those used in the formative stages:

1. Preliminary evaluation of learning (Week 6). Using the DIE format, students assess their intercultural competence, providing examples from their

reflective blogs as evidence. The students' experiences are different, and selections vary based on individual development.

2. Final evaluation of learning (Week 11): using the DIE format, students critically evaluate examples of significant learning, using evidence from group work/tandem work recorded in wikis. They reflect on increased cultural knowledge, understanding of their interaction/communication skills (including conflict/misunderstanding), and strategies for ongoing development. While all students are required to show increased critical cultural awareness of self–other, the expectation is greater for ICGW students, with more discussion on the challenges they faced regarding assumptions and prejudice, and ways they believe they have become more effective as cultural mediators and in maintaining relationships.
3. Presentations (Week 13/14 or 15): students share their experiences with the class by presenting the significant learning from group work/tandem learning. The format allows for creative application of the DIE format to demonstrate interdependent, collaborative learning. ICGW students present in seminar style, which allows for peer participation with questions and discussion.

Each assessment is iterative, building on competencies developed, formative feedback, and, in the case of the second and third assessments, previous summative feedback. Guidelines are provided to scaffold the students, and they are expected to apply theoretical concepts in their analysis. Rubrics link task criteria (graded A, B, C, and D) to the learning outcomes and provide further guidelines for students. The criteria are used flexibly to capture the individual nature of intercultural learning. The assessments are not weighted. If students demonstrate achieving higher grades for each learning outcome in Assessments 2 and 3, previous lower grades are ignored, known as dynamic summative assessment, which gives students greater agency in the assessment process and provides a more reliable indication of student achievement by course end.

In the second week of group/tandem projects, students provide commendations/recommendations feedback on their peers' short presentations. At the end of the course, students complete confidential peer evaluations on themselves and their group/tandem partners. Criteria include level of contribution, collaboration and intercultural competence. The peer evaluations, assessments, and evidence from wikis provide triangulation for establishing a final grade for the course.

Lessons learned

- Using the rich resource of student perspectives facilitates engagement, reinforcing the value of individual identities and worldviews. It is a particularly effective way to give minority students with different worldviews, such as Maori and Pacific Island, a sense of empowerment in the co-construction of knowledge.

- Culture is often invisible to students if they believe that theirs is the norm or have never had their cultural identity challenged, for example European New Zealanders.
- Having a strong focus on values and beliefs in both courses has proved effective. This provides a basis for students to understand self–other, and develop theoretical understanding because values and beliefs are central in the theories/frameworks.
- Models of reflective writing have proved effective to scaffold students new to reflective writing. Models are provided at the beginning of the course, followed by models adapted from students' work after students have completed their weekly reflections.
- Regular constructive feedback on reflections is time-consuming but essential in the early weeks to maximise student engagement and reflective skills development.
- Students with different cultural orientations demonstrate intercultural development in different ways. Interpretation/application of assessment criteria needs to be flexible to allow for such differences. A holistic description of what might be an A student, a B student, and a C student is useful to guide determination of the final grade.
- It is important to have two lecturers involved in assessment or rigorous moderation to manage potential subjectivity.
- Lecturers' own intercultural competence and understanding of intercultural competence changes and develops through experience. This informs one's teaching but it can be challenging to create activities in order to apply new understandings in the classroom.

Ways to improve

Use pre- and post-course questionnaires for both courses as tools to stimulate self-assessment. Intercultural competence students could reflect on them to assess their intercultural development in their final presentations. ICGW students could use them to facilitate self- and peer assessment.

Find opportunities for full-day or overnight immersion experiences for ICGW students for ethnographic work/exposure to difference.

References

Bennett, M. J. (1993). Towards ethnorelativism: A developmental model of intercultural sensitivity. In R. M. Paige (Ed.), *Education for the intercultural experience* (pp. 21–7). Yarmouth, ME: Intercultural Press.

Bowe, H., & K. Martin (2007). *Communication across cultures: Mutual understanding in a global world*. Cambridge: Cambridge University Press.

Byram, M. (1997). *Teaching and assessing intercultural communicative competence*. Clevedon: Multilingual Matters.

—— (2008). *From foreign language education to education for intercultural citizenship: Essays and reflection*. Clevedon: Multilingual Matters.

Corder, D. M., & A. U-Mackey (2015). Encountering and dealing with difference: Second Life and intercultural competence. *Intercultural Education*, *16*(5), 409–24.

Deardorff, D. K. (2006). Identification and assessment of intercultural competence as a student outcome of internationalization. *Journal of Studies in Intercultural Education*, *10*(3), 241–66.

—— (2011). Intercultural competence in foreign language classrooms: A framework and implications for educators. In A. Witte & T. Harden, *Intercultural competence: Concepts, challenges evaluation* (pp. 37–54). Bern: Peter Lang.

Houghton, S. A. (2012). *Intercultural dialogue: Managing value judgement through foreign language education*. Bristol: Multilingual Matters.

Kohls, R. L. (1996). *Survival kit for living and working abroad*. Yarmouth, ME: Intercultural Press.

Kohonen, V. (2005). Experiential learning, intercultural learning and teacher development in foreign language education. In J. Smeds, K. Sarmavuori, E. Laakkonen, & R. de Cillia (Eds.), *Multicultural communities, multilingual practice* (pp. 123–35). Turku: Annales Universitatis Turkuensis B 285.

Kolb, D. A. (1984). *Experiential learning: Experience as the source of learning and development*. Englewood Cliffs, NJ: Prentice Hall.

Schwartz, S., Verkasalao, M., Antonovsky, A., & Sagiv, L. (1997). Value priorities and social desirability: Much substance, some style. *British Journal of Social Psychology*, *36*(1), 3–38.

Witte, A. (2011). On the teachability and learnability of intercultural competence: Developing facets of the 'Inter'. In A. Witte & T. Harden (Eds.), *Intercultural competence: Concepts, challenges, evaluations* (pp. 89–107). Bern: Peter Lang.

CS8

Weill Cornell Medicine-Qatar strives to instil cultural competence training in the medical education curriculum

Maha Elnashar, Huda Abdelrahim, and Stella C. Major (Weill Cornell Medicine-Qatar)

Context

Weill Cornell Medicine-Qatar (WCM-Q), a branch of Weill Cornell Medicine-New York, is the first American university to offer its MD degree overseas (Weill Cornell Medical College in Qatar, 2016); based in Qatar, an extremely high-density multicultural setting (Elnashar, Abdelrahim, & Fetters, 2012). Published data indicates that 28 per cent of Qatar's population are Arabs, 65 per cent South Asians, and 7 per cent from all over the world (Al Muhannadi, Al Kubaisi, Al Sheib, & Al Khayyat, n.d.). Clinical training takes place predominantly in Hamad Medical Corporation (HMC), Qatar's premier public hospital. When the first graduating class started their clinical clerkships, they experienced difficulty communicating. In collaboration with HMC, WCM-Q established a medical interpretation programme and appointed two professional medical interpreters (M. Elnashar and H. Abdelrahim) to run the programme. Despite a clear need for this service, it was underutilised. Leaders of WCM-Q clinical curriculum suggested conducting a pilot presentation for the students to gain insight into the role of language and cultural barriers impact on health care. Students' written evaluation recommended that they need such training before beginning their clinical rotations. The next step was to assess the scope of cultural competence training (CCT) within the curriculum. Tools for Assessing Cultural Competence Training (TACCT) (Association of American Medical Colleges, n.d.) of the Association of Americal Medical Colleges (AAMC) was administered to the clinical faculty. Results highlighted gaps in the curriculum that require tackling the local context (Elnashar, Abdelrahim, & Fetters, 2012).

Goals and objectives

The programme's main goal is to train medical students to be culturally mindful and proficient (i.e. to be able to practise medicine in any multicultural setting) (AAMC, n.d.; Ring, Nyquist, Mitchell, Flores, & Samaniego, 2008).

By the end of this module, students should be able to:

1. value diversity impact on health care with a special focus on Qatar;
2. define culture, cultural competence, race, ethnicity, bias and stereotype;
3. explain strategies to reduce physician's biases and stereotyping;
4. describe how to work with medical interpreters;
5. explore complementary/traditional models of common health systems, folk concepts and explanation of illness;
6. discuss the impact of patient's context (cultural heritage, gender, class, and spirituality) and family dynamics on clinical decision-making;
7. analyse the contributors to healthcare disparities and discuss challenges to eliminate them;
8. practise teaching cultural competence to colleagues and healthcare professionals;
9. establish a trusting and therapeutic relationship with culturally diverse patients;
10. be familiar with communication tools such BATHE (background, affect, trouble, handling, and empathy) to elicit cultural beliefs and practices.

(Ring et al., 2008; Stuart & Lieberman, 1993)

This training module is developed based on TACCT five domains (AAMC, n.d.) and guided by Ring's book *Curriculum for Culturally Responsive Health Care: The Step-by-Step Guide for Cultural Competence Training* (Ring et al., 2008). The content is compiled through an extensive literature review and additional suggestions from healthcare practitioners in practice at the local context. Furthermore, published local data is incorporated into the content, e.g., demographic data, local case studies, cultural beliefs, social dynamics, and traditional healing practices.

There are various definitions of cultural competence. Our programme relies mainly on the definition of Cross, Benjamin, and Isaacs (1989). We define cultural competence as the knowledge, skills, and attitude that enable health professionals to be responsive and respectful to the health needs of diverse patients and to work effectively in culturally diversified communities.

Developing cultural competence training

Guided by the objectives, six sessions were taught in medical year one, followed by two sessions in medical year three when students were actively seeing patients. A variety of teaching methods are used including didactic lectures, group discussions, web-based exercises (e.g., 'Implicit Association Test' to learn about individual hidden bias [Project Implicit, 2011]), role play (students act cultural/clinical scenarios and discuss how to solve it), and learning by teaching (students prepare presentations to their peers explaining how to be culturally competent) (Expert Panel on Cultural Competence Education for Students in Medicine and Public Health, 2012). Third-year teaching activities are concluded by one Objective Structured Clinical Examination (OSCE) session. OSCE is a versatile

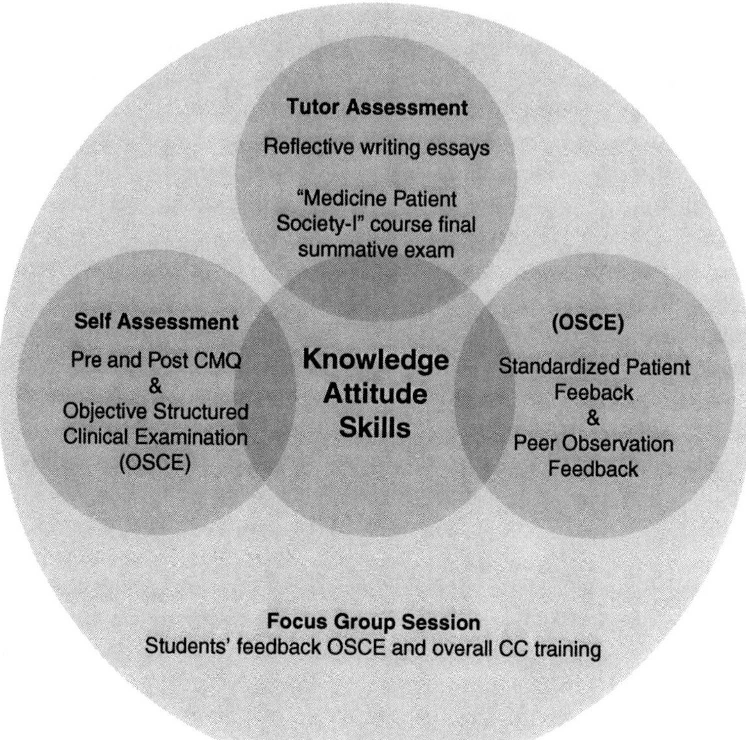

Figure CS8.1 Training module and assessment tools.

multipurpose tool, first described by Harden, Stevenson, Downie, and Wilson (1975), that can be used to evaluate healthcare professionals in a clinical setting. It is used here as a learning and evaluation tool. Students learn by practising and reflecting on their own and peers' performance during three-way feedback session with trained standardised patients.

Assessing cultural competence training

Students' knowledge, skills, and attitudes are measured through four assessment tools (see Figure CS8.1):

1. Pre-/post-self-assessment, modified from the Cultural Medicine Questionnaire (CMQ) (Ring et al., 2008), which includes the question, 'How knowledgeable are you about these topics: culture, ethnicity, race, healthcare disparities, biases and stereotypes?' Responses are collected through a 5-point Likert scale (from 'not at all' to 'very knowledgeable').

Outcome: There was an improvement in students' knowledge, skills, and attitude as per the pre-/post-CMQ.

2. Tutor assessment: students write reflective short essays on clinical scenarios that include cultural issues such as language barriers, health beliefs, family dynamics, or healthcare disparities. This assessment is included in the first-year Medicine, Patients, and Society I final exam. Outcome: Students successfully satisfied the requirements of writing reflective essays as part of the course summative exam.
3. OSCE (Harden et al., 1975). Students work in pairs, and each one conducts an interview with a standardised patient and observes a peer in another interview. The observer sits outside and watches through an audio-visual monitor. Each clinical interview has a distinct cultural scenario. To provide guided objective feedback, an evaluation checklist was developed that stated the goals in terms of cultural communication skills and attitudes within the interview. These were evaluated across a 5-point Likert scale (from 'strongly agree' to 'strongly disagree'). At the end of each encounter, the interviewing student, the peer, and the standardised patient complete the evaluation checklist independently then meet for fifteen minutes to have three-way face-to-face feedback. Outcome: Students rated themselves more poorly than their peers and standardised patients, in terms of their cross-cultural communication skills. Students were highly skilled in using BATHE to elicit cultural information.
4. Focus group: To further explore students' observations of OSCE and elicit their overall perspectives about cultural competence training, a voluntary one-hour focus group session is conducted at the end of the module. Outcome: Students provided valuable feedback about their OSCE experience. Students agreed that probing on cultural aspects helps the clinical diagnosis and cannot be neglected. They stated, 'This was a great starting point, that should be practised further and incorporated in other clinical encounters.'

Lessons learned

1. Implementation of CCT in medical schools in the Arab region is still in its early stages and needs intensive preparations, e.g., creating systematic approaches, allocating time, and finding suitable assessments.
2. Trained staff, committed faculty, and community resources are important factors in developing sustainable CCT.
3. Focus groups suggested earlier introduction of CCT modules and integration into the clinical curriculum.
4. The cultures of standardised patients play an important role in the learning and evaluation process during cultural competence OSCE.
5. There is a dire need for published research on CCT in the Arab region.

Ways to improve

1. Promote active engagement with regional and global medical networks to share resources and experiences.
2. Develop and utilise robust and validated tools that can be used for summative assessment and scholarly output.
3. Provide opportunities for faculty development in CCT for sustainability and to enhance commitment.
4. Introduce the cultural/clinical scenario discussions earlier and integrate them longitudinally across the clinical curriculum.
5. Recruit standardised patients from different cultures and diversify the OSCE scenarios to represent the diversity.
6. Maintain links with graduates to measure the long-term impact of CCT on their skills as physicians post-licensure and in practice. Compile, analyse, and publish these results to enrich literature and compare it internationally.

Acknowledgement

To Kelly Anne Nelson, Director of Student Affairs, for contributing to the first editing process, and to Ross MacDonald, Ph.D. MLIS, Information Services Librarian, for contributing to the references formatting.

References

Al Muhannadi, H. I., Al Kubaisi, M. A., Al Sheib, A. I., & Al Khayyat, H. E. (n.d.). Urban growth and internal migration. Retrieved from www.ppc.gov.qa/en/Publications/Pages/Studies.aspx

Association of American Medical Colleges. (n.d.). Tool for Assessing Cultural Competence Training (TACCT). Retrieved from www.aamc.org/initiatives/tacct

Cross, T. L., Benjamin, M. P., & Isaacs, M. R. (1989). *Towards a culturally competent system of care: A monograph on effective services for minority children who are severely emotionally disturbed*. Washington, DC: CASSP Technical Assistance Center, Georgetown University Child Development Center.

Elnashar, M., Abdelrahim, H., & Fetters, M. D. (2012). Cultural competence springs up in the desert: The story of the center for cultural competence in health care at Weill Cornell Medical College in Qatar. *Academic Medicine*, *87*(6), 759–66.

Expert Panel on Cultural Competence Education for Students in Medicine and Public Health. (2012). Cultural competence education for students in medicine and public health: Report of an expert panel. Retrieved from https://members.aamc.org/eweb/upload/Cultural%20Competence%20Education_revisedl.pdf

Harden, R. M., Stevenson, M., Downie, W. W., & Wilson, G. M. (1975). Assessment of clinical competence using objective structured examination. *British Medical Journal*, *1*(5955), 447–51.

Project Implicit. (2011). Implicit Associate Test. Retrieved from https://implicit.harvard.edu/implicit/takeatest.html

Ring, J. M., Nyquist, J. G., Mitchell, S., Flores, H., & Samaniego, L. (2008). *Curriculum for culturally responsive health care: The step-by-step guide for cultural competence training*. Oxford: Radcliffe Publishing.

Stuart, M. R., & Lieberman, J. A. (1993). *The fifteen minute hour: Applied psychotherapy for the primary care physician* (2nd edn). Westport, CT: Praeger.

Weill Cornell Medical College in Qatar. (2016). Overview. Retrieved from http://qatar-weill.cornell.edu/aboutUs/overview/cornell.html

CS9

Intercultural communication for international mobility

Irina Golubeva (University of Pannonia)

Context

In Hungary, following global tendencies, higher education institutions, including the University of Pannonia, view educational exchange (mobility) – both incoming and outgoing – as one of the main instruments of internationalisation. The proportion of foreign students at the University of Pannonia is not high (3.5 per cent in the academic year 2015–16), and some international students report having difficulties when socialising with locals. Only 1 per cent of University of Pannonia students studied abroad in the 2015–16 academic year due to economic, social, and cultural factors that negatively influence their decision to study abroad.

The international mobility office developed a plan to promote participation in mobility programmes and to facilitate cultural adjustment of foreign students. To support this initiative, I developed a course to prepare students for mobility. The idea of launching this course was influenced by the results of a needs analysis survey conducted by the IEREST project (Intercultural Educational Resources for Erasmus Students and their Teachers, a multilateral European project funded by the European Commission), which found that the majority of students study abroad without previous intercultural preparation (Beaven & Borghetti, 2014).

This case study introduces two variations of the course Intercultural Communication for International Mobility, which I designed and taught for students at University of Pannonia, Veszprém/Hungary:

1. Intercultural Communication for International Mobility (I): A course offered for outgoing Hungarian students in Hungarian before their education abroad in order to prepare them for study and professional life abroad and to motivate those who are considering to study abroad.
2. Intercultural Communication for International Mobility (II): A course for incoming international students (in the 'during abroad' stage) taught in English with the primary goal to prepare international students for successful studies at the University of Pannonia.

Table CS9.1 Learning goals and outcomes (from IEREST, 2015, p. 16).

Learning goals	Learning outcomes
Reflect on each person's uniqueness but also similarities.	Recognise and explain the variety and complexity that exist among individuals in social groups.
Understand that what people say about their culture may be interpreted as what they wish others to see about themselves, and which may not be applicable to others from that culture or group.	Interpret what people say about their culture as a personal observation, and possibly as evidence of what they wish others to see about themselves.
Understand how key concepts such as stereotyping, ethnocentrism, essentialising, and prejudice can lead to misunderstandings and misrepresentations of people from other horizons.	Recognise when misunderstandings may be the result of stereotyping, ethnocentrism, essentialising and prejudice.
Reflect on some of the myths about study abroad and interculturality (interaction, language learning, identity, culture, etc.) in order to (re)frame expectations about the mobility period.	Set realistic objectives in relation to intercultural encounters, including language and communication expectations, for their stay abroad.

Both courses were offered in the same format (twenty-eight contact hours/ semester; 3 credits).

At the moment of writing this case study, this initiative appeared to be unique and innovative in the Hungarian context. Most of the universities offer general courses on intercultural communication and/or short orientation trainings for international exchange students, but to my best knowledge, universities in Hungary do not offer specific preparation courses on Intercultural Communication for International Mobility.

Goals and outcomes

The learning goals and outcomes in Table CS9.1 were adapted from IEREST (2015, p. 16). The last objective is the most specific in the context of preparing students for education abroad.

Framework of intercultural competence

When designing the course, I applied Byram's (1997) definition of intercultural communicative competence, which defines it through five components, and tried to cover all components of Byram's model, with special attention to the fifth one:

1. attitudes;
2. knowledge;

3. skills of interpreting and relating;
4. skills of discovery and interaction;
5. critical cultural awareness/political education.

I adopted the non-essentialist approach of Holliday (2011) and Barnett's (1997) criticality to the development of intercultural competence.

The focus was on the elements described in Deardorff's (2006) Pyramid Model of Intercultural Competence as deep understanding of culture, cultural self-awareness, and an ethnorelative view.

Developing intercultural competence

Students were exposed to the basic concepts of intercultural communication with special emphasis on cultural differences and similarities, stereotypes and prejudices, and culture shock. We also discussed challenges and the importance of mobility in today's world (directly related to Objective 8 in Table CS9.1).

During the course students were invited to reflect on their experiences. The main topics of discussion were:

1. the emotional dimension of living abroad;
2. the academic experience of studying in a different higher education context;
3. communication and language problems in social contacts with locals.

In the case of the course offered for incoming students, one more topic provoked discussions:

4. the problem of sharing housing with other international students (e.g., disorderly conduct, noise, disregard of silent hours, untidy use of kitchen, selfish use of other facilities), which affects not only everyday life but academic progress as well.

Once, when the students reported feeling down and frustrated, I asked them to draw and present a poster for future generations of international exchange students, promoting study in Hungary. In the end, the students were pleasantly surprised about how many positive aspects about studying in Hungary they could collect in the allotted thirty minutes (e.g., low cost of living, security, safe public transport, excellent internet access, central position in Europe, etc.).

Several techniques were used to develop intercultural competence: total physical response, cultural incident, noticing, predicting, observing, comparing, reflecting, role playing, etc. According to students' responses regarding the methods used during the course, they preferred to listen to teachers' personal experiences of intercultural encounters (82 per cent) and to do interactive intercultural competence exercises (50 per cent). The least effective methods in their opinion were: lectures on intercultural communication theory (48 per cent), analysis of case studies (46 per cent), and short students' presentations (44 per cent).

Concerning the methodology, I applied an integrative approach, which consisted of (1) Kolb's experiential learning (1984), i.e. 'concrete experience-reflective observation-abstract conceptualization-active experimentation' circle; and (2) cognitive style approach, which puts emphasis on learning such cognitive strategies as generalisation, abstraction, hypothesis, analysis, synthesis, comparison, identification, classification, ranging, and mapping. Kolb's approach proved to be effective during piloting the IEREST activities (see, e.g., Beaven & Golubeva, 2016), while the cognitive style approach was applied to help students' cognitive readiness for intercultural encounters (see Soboleva & Obdalova, 2014).

Assessing intercultural competence

Three methods were used to assess students' performance and the development of their reflective thinking skills:

1. Students were asked to complete a questionnaire at the beginning and at the end of the course. Responses were compared. For example, before this course, 10 per cent of students did not consider studying intercultural communication to be important; after the course, all 100 per cent agreed that it is important.
2. Students had to identify their level of intercultural competence by using a self-assessment tool (adapted from the assessee version of INCA [International Review of Curriculum and Assessment] Framework; 2004). For example, they were invited to choose among three levels developed by the INCA project (INCA, 2004, p. 1). After the course, 46 per cent of students claimed that they have reached the highest level in comparison to only 8 per cent of students who described themselves as interculturally competent before the course.
3. Students were invited to submit a reflective writing assignment (autobiography of intercultural encounters; Byram et al., 2009). For example, students were asked to reflect critically on their intercultural experiences by choosing a specific encounter and analysing it, with special focus on adjustments in verbal and non-verbal communication (Byram et al., 2009, p. 14).

Lessons learned

Lessons learned based on my personal observations and insights from fifty students who responded to the questionnaire include:

1. Participation in intercultural preparation courses has a motivating effect on students who did not plan to go on international exchange before.

2. Most students tend to essentialise. According to the results of the questionnaire survey, especially for Hungarian students, many of them lack intercultural experience and seem to be culturally unaware. Therefore, university students and especially international exchange students should be provided with intercultural preparation courses in a systematic way, and this should become an institutionalised practice at universities in case of both groups of mobility students: incoming and outgoing.
3. University leadership support is essential for institutionalisation of such courses. Internationalisation needs to become an integral part of the university culture; the development of intercultural competence and an international mindset is a must for any modern higher education institution.
4. The main purpose of such intercultural courses should be the development of critical thinking and reflective skills.
5. More attention should be paid to teaching intercultural conflict resolution skills because it improves students' resilience given the challenges of international mobility.

Ways to improve

All participants of the first iteration of these courses would recommend the course to their peers. Eighty-six per cent of respondents mentioned that this course motivated them to study abroad. However, the analysis of students' responses ($\Sigma = 50$) showed that the intercultural preparation courses could be improved:

1. More interactive tasks should be included in the course.
2. The time spent on lecturing should be minimised.
3. The focus should be shifted from theory of intercultural communication to practice.
4. 'Mixing' the groups can enhance the exchange of insights from incoming and outgoing students.
5. More time should be allocated to reflections.
6. Online sources and especially social media should be better explored.
7. Developing 'knowledge and critical understanding of the world' (including politics, human rights, religions, history, etc.) should be more emphasised.
8. More should be learned *about* the students who decided to go to study abroad and those who do not dare to, i.e. their motivations, circumstances, attitudes, worldview, etc.
9. Formative assessment should be added, which would serve two functions: first, to help students identify their weaknesses and strengths in intercultural communication; second, to provide the teacher with immediate feedback, which would allow to 'fix' the emerged problems immediately.
10. Finally, longitudinal studies are needed to explore the impact of such preparation courses.

Acknowledgements

I would like to express my gratitude to my students for their enthusiasm and to Manuela Wagner for her valuable comments.

References

Barnett, R. (1997). *Higher education: A critical business*. Buckingham: SRHE/Open University Press.

Beaven, A., & Borghetti, C. (2014). *IEREST public progress report*. Retrieved from http://ierest-project.eu/sites/default/files/Progress_report.pdf

Beaven, A., & Golubeva, I. (2016). Intercultural preparation for future mobile students: A pedagogical experience, *Language and Intercultural Communication*, *16*(3), 491–501.

Byram, M. (1997). *Teaching and assessing intercultural communicative competence*. Clevedon: Multilingual Matters.

Byram, M., Barrett, M., Ipgrave, J., Jackson, R., & Méndez García, M. C. (2009). *Autobiography of intercultural encounters*. Strasbourg: Council of Europe Publishing. Retrieved from www.coe.int/t/dg4/autobiography/default_en.asp

Deardorff, D. K. (2006). The identification and assessment of intercultural competence. *Journal of Studies in International Education*, *10*(3), 241–66.

Holliday, A. (2011). *Intercultural communication and ideology*. London: Sage.

Intercultural Educational Resources for Erasmus Students and their Teachers (IEREST) (2015). *Intercultural education resources for Erasmus students and their Teachers*, Koper: Annales University Press.

International Review of Curriculum and Assessment (INCA) (2004). *Intercultural competence assessment*. INCA Framework (Assessee version). Retrieved from https://ec.europa.eu/migrant-integration/librarydoc/the-inca-project-intercultural-competence-assessment

Kolb, D. (1984). *Experiential learning: Experience as the source of learning and development*. Englewood Cliffs, NJ: Prentice Hall.

Soboleva, A. V., & Obdalova, O. A. (2014). The methodology of intercultural competence development on the basis of a cognitive style-inclusive approach. *Procedia: Social and Behavioral Sciences*, *154*, 155–61.

CS10

Intercultural competence at Texas Christian University

Christopher T. Hightower (Texas Christian University)

Context

Texas Christian University (TCU), a moderately sized, private university located in Fort Worth, Texas, conceptualised Discovering Global Citizenship (DGC) as a foundation for comprehensive internationalisation by infusing international and intercultural perspectives into existing curricular and co-curricular activities. The inspiration for the effort emerged from TCU's mission statement: 'To educate individuals to think and act as ethical leaders and responsible citizens in the global community.' The team designing the effort grounded the initiative in the philosophy that global citizenship is an institutional imperative and an individual student's responsibility.

Launched in the fall semester of 2013, DGC includes six initiatives and four student learning outcomes challenging students to rise to a higher level of global citizenship and to engage in the world both at home and abroad.

Goals and outcomes

TCU mission: To educate individuals to think and act as ethical leaders and responsible citizens in the global community.

TCU cardinal principle: Knowledge and ability to act as an ethical participant in the global community.

DGC mission: To engage TCU with the world by providing international and comparative experiences for students.

Goal(s): To provide a wide range of opportunities and experiences that encourage students to practise and develop skills, knowledge, and attitudes that help students achieve intercultural competence.

DGC objectives: DGC will impact all TCU undergraduate students in a variety of ways. Our goal is to see 80 per cent of students engaging with intentional international and comparative experiences beyond what is required in the TCU core curriculum. Therefore, this project will build a strong foundation in global citizenship for approximately 6,800 students, an increase from the approximately 2,550 students who currently participate in international experiences.

Outcomes

1. Students will identify global issues from perspectives of multiple disciplines and cultures.
2. Students will discuss critical questions about the impact of global issues on domestic and global communities.
3. Students will demonstrate cultural empathy and intercultural competence.
4. Students will develop responsible decision-making about global issues.

Framework of intercultural competence

DGC focused on global citizenship as expressed in our institutional mission statement and the culture of the institution. Morais and Ogden (2010) connected intercultural competence to global citizenship with a detailed description of global citizenship, which includes three general categories: social responsibility, global competence, and global civic engagement. These categories include various components from the intercultural competence literature such as interconnectedness, empathy, self-awareness, global knowledge, as well as many others (Deardorff, 2006). Knight (2012) also explained that the term 'global citizenship' is a generic term for internationalisation.

TCU draws from theoretical intercultural competence models across the five defined categories by Spitzberg and Changnon (2009). For example, the compositional model created by Deardorff (2006) highlights knowledge, skills, and attitudes within the components of the Pyramid Model of Intercultural Competence. Kim's adaptational approach (2001) encourages lifelong learning in global citizenship, which increases in complexity and adaptability. Another basic but powerful development model guiding our work comes from Sanford (1962), who explained the value of providing the right amount of challenge and support for our students to achieve higher levels of intercultural competence. Finally, Bennett's (1986) development model of intercultural sensitivity informed the development of student learning outcomes.

Developing intercultural competence

The six DGC initiatives promote student interaction with others in a variety of ways rather than through one single experience. These initiatives include an expansion of TCU Abroad, the study abroad programme. Global Academy engages students, faculty, and community leaders in a three-course transdisciplinary academic programme addressing a specific global issue faced by the region in which the course visits. Local–Global Leaders provides faculty and staff the opportunity to bring individuals or groups to campus to demonstrate the relationship between our global and local communities. Visiting Scholars allows faculty and staff to bring grass-roots leaders and experts from around the world who have demonstrated leadership and made a difference in addressing global issues to campus. Global Innovators offers faculty the ability to bring an international innovator from any discipline to campus for a longer term intensive curricular and co-curricular experience. The programme includes a $25,000 grant for sustained collaborative research. Using technology, Virtual Voyage provides entry to countries for which study abroad is not feasible.

Assessing intercultural competence

The DGC assessment team established a plan to collect data from multiple methods using both direct and indirect measures. When faculty and staff apply for funding and partnership with DGC, they are asked to select student learning outcomes, explain their assessment activities, and determine which measures will be used.

Direct measures demonstrate students' knowledge, skills, and attitudes through work products. The assessment team worked with collaborators across campus to establish an e-portfolio programme called FrogFolio. With assessment in mind, TCU specifically chose the provider Digication as the platform for our e-portfolio system because it allows the assessment team to assess intercultural competence across the campus. Assessment of e-portfolios may also be done on the course or individual level. TCU also adapted the AAC&U VALUE Rubrics based on our campus culture and our student learning outcomes. The adapted rubrics are used to assess portfolios, course assignments, papers, projects, presentations, video and photo documentaries, blog, and internet postings.

Indirect measures are self-reported perceptions of learning. TCU uses a psychometric instrument, the Intercultural Effectiveness Scale (IES), as a pre-/post-measure assessment. New students complete the IES after orientation, and seniors complete the instrument prior to graduation. The longitudinal data provides matched sets as well as cohort-to-cohort data for analysis. Other available data points include information gained from the Cooperative Institutional Research Program and National Survey of Student Engagement. TCU uses Qualtrics software, allowing staff and faculty to administer programme surveys for formative programme evaluation and student perceived learning.

Lessons learned

The design of the DGC intentionally decentralised the programmatic activities by placing the work in the hands of faculty and staff throughout the university. This design led to some assessment challenges, but we believe it is crucial to comprehensive internationalisation to maintain the design. Therefore, the assessment team decided to work more closely with individual staff and faculty members during early planning and development of programmatic activities and the corresponding assessment plans to facilitate consistency across the various programmes and assure smoother data collection.

Additionally, TCU students learned far more than expected from the international experiences. The assessment team named these outcomes *emergent learning* because they were not explicitly stated in our student learning outcomes. The assessment team has captured some of that data through anecdotal stories and written accounts. In addition, we have also found *collateral outcomes* among staff, faculty, and campus visitors, which was a desired but not stated objective of the programme. Like the emergent learning, we have captured various data points of the collateral outcomes to help inform future programming.

While our campus uses a portfolio provider that allows us to pull assessment data across all of the individual student portfolios, it only works if students respond to designated prompts about their intercultural or international experiences. For this to be truly effective, faculty must require students to respond to a specific prompt within an academic course because only a few students will reflect on their international or intercultural experiences if not required to do so. When students casually include international experiences, the depth of reflection has been lacking. Greater coordination and collaboration with FrogFolio and other units in both student and academic affairs could produce better artefacts from students to gather their reflective thoughts about their intercultural experiences.

Ways to improve

Some DGC programmes lack meaningful assessment data to measure student learning or to inform programming improvements. The assessment team attributes the lack of meaningful assessment to the decentralised design. Therefore, the team will reach out to the individual faculty or staff member responsible for the programme to ensure that assessment activities are prioritised rather than waiting for the programming faculty or staff member to contact them.

For those who comply, their assessment data are reviewed by the assessment team and the programme director. Occasionally, reports and analyses are shared with the DGC coordinating committee. More frequent reports would provide regular feedback, which would allow the supervising committee an opportunity to recommend improvements. Additionally, reporting assessment data and analysis to a wider institutional audience outside of the DGC committee would encourage more engagement with international education.

We have an abundance of quantitative data, but rich qualitative data would help us understand nuances and the individual impact of the programmatic activities. Because the nature of interviews is personal, the data gained would provide a descriptive narrative attempting to explain how or why students react to the programming. The interviews would include motives, personal perceptions, and variables that may influence their decisions. These data could be valuable in planning future learning opportunities. In cases where students have achieved higher-level learning, the interviews may illuminate a variable or factor not previously considered.

References

Bennett, M. J. (1986). A developmental approach to training for intercultural sensitivity. *International Journal of Intercultural Relations, 10*(2), 179–96.

Deardorff, D. K. (2006). Identification and assessment of intercultural competence as a student outcome of internationalization. *Journal of Studies in International Education, 10*(3), 241–66.

Kim, Y. Y. (2001). *Becoming intercultural: An integrative theory of communication and cross-cultural adaptation.* Thousand Oaks, CA: Sage Publications.

Knight, J. (2012). Concepts, rationales, and interpretive frameworks in the internationalization of higher education. In D. K. Deardorff, H. de Wit, & J. D. Heyl (Eds.), *The Sage handbook of international higher education* (pp. 27–42). Thousand Oaks, CA: Sage.

Morais, D. B., & Ogden, A. C. (2010). Initial development and validation of the global citizenship scale. *Journal of Studies in International Education, 15*(5), 445–66.

Sanford, N. (1962). Developmental status of the entering freshman. In N. Sanford (Ed.), *The American college: A psychological and social interpretation of the higher learning* (pp. 253–82). New York, NY: Wiley.

Spitzberg, B. H., & Changnon, G. (2009). Conceptualizing intercultural competence. In D. K. Deardorff (Ed.), *The Sage handbook of intercultural competence* (pp. 2–52). Thousand Oaks, CA: Sage.

CS11

Intercultural communication and engagement abroad

Jane Jackson (The Chinese University of Hong Kong)

Context

This case study centres on a fully online, credit-bearing, elective course that has been developed to bolster the intercultural learning and engagement of undergraduates from a Hong Kong university who are participating in an international exchange programme. Before developing Intercultural Communication and Engagement Abroad, I had offered an elective intercultural communication course for many years and, more recently, Intercultural Transitions: Making Sense of International Experience, an interactive course for students with recent or current international experience (Jackson, 2015a, 2015b). The lessons learned from these courses, insights from my study abroad research, and a review of the literature informed the design of the online course.

Goals and outcomes

To help the participants optimise their international exchange experience and make the most of the second-language environment, the course aims to ease their adjustment and propel them to a higher level of intercultural competence and engagement in the host environment. More specifically, the course strives to help them:

- identify and explain key concepts in intercultural communication;
- describe theories and models of transitions/adjustment, identity expansion, and intercultural competence, and test these ideas using their own and others' international/intercultural experiences;
- demonstrate more understanding and appreciation of diversity;
- interact more effectively and appropriately with people who have been socialised in a different linguistic and cultural environment;
- set realistic goals for further intercultural experience and the enhancement of their second language/intercultural competence.

Framework of intercultural competence

The online course draws on the Intercultural Development Continuum (IDC), post-structuralist notions of identity, and transformation theory. The IDC (Hammer, 2012) builds on Bennett's (1993) Developmental Model of Intercultural Sensitivity. Within the IDC, intercultural competence is defined as 'the capability to shift cultural perspective and appropriately adapt behaviour to cultural difference and commonalities' (Hammer, 2013, p. 26). Before the course starts, the Intercultural Development Inventory (IDI), a cross-culturally validated psychometric tool, is administered to provide a measure of intercultural competence; the IDI results and qualitative data (e.g., reflective essays, forum posts) are then reviewed to guide the process of critical reflection and meaning-making. IDI-guided development is a form of (inter)cultural mentoring, 'an intercultural pedagogy in which the mentor provides ongoing support for and facilitation of intercultural learning and development' (Paige, 2013, p. 6). By providing feedback appropriate to the participants' level of intercultural competence, this approach strives to help them 'achieve increased capability in shifting cultural perspective and adapting behavior across cultural differences' (Hammer, 2012, p. 116).

From a post-structuralist perspective, 'identity is generally pluralized as "identities"' and viewed as 'ongoing lifelong narratives in which individuals constantly attempt to maintain a sense of balance' (Block, 2008, p. 142). The course recognises that language and (inter)cultural development are affected by social, cognitive, and affective dimensions as students mediate the host environment in a second language and try to make sense of their evolving perceptions of themselves and individuals who have a different linguistic and cultural background. Through mentoring, the course aspires to help students develop an intercultural identity, that is, 'a negotiated investment in seeing the world through multiple cultural lenses' (Menard-Warwick, 2008, p. 622).

Mezirow's transformational learning theory (1994, 2000) posits that individuals who engage in critical self-analysis may experience significant change in response to major events in their lives, such as moving to an unfamiliar environment. In this adult learning theory, intercultural competence entails a continuous learning process with deep reflection leading to 'new or revised interpretations of the meaning of one's experience' (Mezirow, 1994, p. 222). Through intercultural mentoring, course participants may acquire the knowledge and skills that can help them to recognise and appreciate divergent ideas and experiences. Mezirow (1996) argues that this process can lead to the restructuring or broadening of one's sense of self.

Developing intercultural competence

Intercultural Communication and Engagement Abroad has been designed to propel international-exchange students towards higher levels of intercultural competence while they are in the host environment. At the heart of this initiative is guided critical reflection and meaning-making. As well as digesting readings, PowerPoint presentations, and related YouTube links, with the help of an eLearning platform, the participants exchange ideas online, carry out fieldwork tasks, and write reflective essays. The weekly, theme-based forum encourages them to examine their own (and others') international experience in relation to theories and models of adjustment, intercultural competence, and identity reconstruction. Mentoring prompts them to reflect more deeply on their language/intercultural attitudes and intercultural interactions. Fieldwork groups are arranged so that the feedback they receive is appropriate to their level of intercultural competence. Linked to the weekly theme (e.g., non-verbal communication, identity and Otherisation), the students carry out fieldwork that is designed to promote meaningful intercultural interactions and critical reflection. The reflective essays prompt the participants to take stock of their intercultural learning and set realistic goals for further enhancement of their language and (inter)cultural awareness.

In the first offering, a comparison of pre- and post-course IDI results found that the cohort as a whole made significant advances in intercultural competence, gaining 11.41 points, moving from the end of the 'Polarisation: Defence/Reversal' phase to the mid-point of 'Minimisation', the transitional phase (Jackson, 2016). With the help of NVivo, a software programme, a content analysis of the rich qualitative data (e.g., essays, online posts, interview transcripts, my field notes, IDI debriefing notes) also pointed to the benefits of this intervention to enhance intercultural competence and engagement.

Assessing intercultural competence

- To evaluate direct evidence of student learning and provide constructive feedback online, I designed a rubric for each course component (e.g., hypermedia forum, fieldwork, reflective essays). Each rubric included descriptions of achievement in categories linked to the course aims (e.g., cultural self-awareness, intercultural attitudes, engagement in our online community). As well as filling in each grid to indicate the performance level, I provided comments about the quality of their work and suggested areas for improvement.
- Pre- and post-course administrations of the IDI provided additional indirect measures of intercultural competence and the findings were shared with the participants in individual debriefing sessions.

Lessons learned

- Begin a course with a specific definition of intercultural competence in mind and build on this when developing materials/activities and assessing student learning.
- Be mindful of the participants' language proficiency and degree of intercultural competence when sequencing/devising material/fieldwork tasks, preparing instructions/prompts, and providing feedback.

- Develop reflective intercultural knowledge and competence rubrics to assist the assessment process and the provision of constructive feedback on all coursework, and post all rubrics on the eLearning platform.

Ways to improve

- In the pre-course workshop, provide more guidance for students who are new to critical reflection, intercultural fieldwork, hypermedia forums, and online learning (e.g., demonstrate what it means to be reflective and fully engaged in an online community, review rubrics for all course elements), and share this information in a micro module on the eLearning platform.
- Reduce the number of tasks to allow more time for reading, reflection, fieldwork, and online sharing.

References

Bennett, J. M. (2008). On becoming a global soul: A path to engagement during study abroad. In V. Savicki (Ed.), *Developing ICC and transformation: Theory, research, and application in international education* (pp. 13–31). Sterling, VA: Stylus.

Bennett, M. J. (1993). Towards ethnorelativism: A developmental model of intercultural sensitivity. In R. M. Paige (Ed.), *Education for the intercultural experience* (pp. 21–71). Yarmouth, ME: Intercultural Press.

Block, D. (2008). EFL narratives and English-mediated identities: Two ships passing in the night? In P. Kalaja, V. Menezes, & A. M. F. Barcelos (Eds.), *Narratives of learning and teaching EFL* (pp. 141–54). Basingstoke: Palgrave Macmillan.

Hammer, M. R. (2012). The intercultural development inventory: A new frontier in assessment and development of ICC. In M. Vande Berg, R. M. Paige, & K. H. Lou (Eds.), *Student learning abroad: What our students are learning, what they're not, and what we can do about it* (pp. 115–36). Sterling, VA: Stylus.

—— (2013). *A resource guide for effectively using the intercultural development inventory (IDI).* Berlin, MD: IDI, LLC.

Jackson, J. (2015a). 'Unpacking' international experience through blended intercultural praxis. In R. D. Williams & A. Lee (Eds.), *Internationalizing higher education: Critical collaborations across the curriculum* (pp. 231–52). Rotterdam: SENSE Publishers.

—— (2015b). Becoming interculturally competent: Theory to practice in international education. *International Journal of Intercultural Relations, 48*, 91–107.

—— (2016). Optimizing intercultural learning and engagement abroad through online mentoring. Plenary, Intercultural Learning through Study Abroad Colloquium, April, Bern.

Menard-Warwick, J. (2008). The cultural and intercultural identities of transnational English teachers: Two case studies from the Americas, *TESOL Quarterly, 42*(4): 617–40.

Mezirow, J. (1994). *Transformative dimensions of adult learning.* San Francisco, CA: Jossey-Bass.

—— (1996). Contemporary paradigms of learning. *Adult Education Quarterly*, *46*(3), 158–72.

—— (2000). *Learning as transformation: Critical perspectives on a theory in progress*. San Francisco, CA: Jossey-Bass.

Paige, R. M. (2013). Factors impacting intercultural development in study abroad. Paper presented at Elon University, 16 August.

CS12

GQ + CQ + SQ + EQ = Global Synergy

Annette Karseras (Keio University, Temple University Japan, Tokyo Metropolitan University, Tsuda College)

Context

Global Synergy is a modularised course designed for local Japanese and international exchange students at public and private Japanese universities. Learning is structured using a systems model that iterates through four scales from emotional to global intelligences (Figure CS12.1) and is taught through the simple systems formula: EQ + SQ + CQ + GQ = Global Synergy.

Global Synergy's four-scale competency framework is taught through an integrated systems formula that combines four intelligences: emotional, social, cultural, global. Developing students' competence *to integrate* these four intelligences increases capacity for human synergy through the next stage of globalisation and into the twenty-second century.

Goals and outcomes

1. **Emotional intelligence (EQ).** Raises self-awareness about how culture and personality combine to form students' personal core values and default communication style, psychological, and neurophysical aspects of culture shock in response to unfamiliar values/styles. Outcome: psychological resilience and an ability to moderate own emotional reactions using tools such as ODIS/O-DIVE (Observe–Describe–Interpret–Suspend evaluation, steps to click out of 'autopilot' and ensure ethnocentric assumptions do not go unchecked). Greater consciousness of personal beliefs/values creates self-confidence and a stronger foundation to communicate with others in intercultural situations.
2. **Social intelligence (SQ).** Extends students' range of interpersonal soft skills: facilitation, questioning, listening skills, etc. Outcome: greater behavioural flexibility to accommodate personality and/or cultural differences in pairs and with team members. Example: Switching between expressing tacit non-verbal agreement and verbalising cultural assumptions explicitly.
3. **Cultural Intelligence (CQ).** Develops awareness of cross-cultural differences and acculturation processes. Basic cultural dimensions are taught

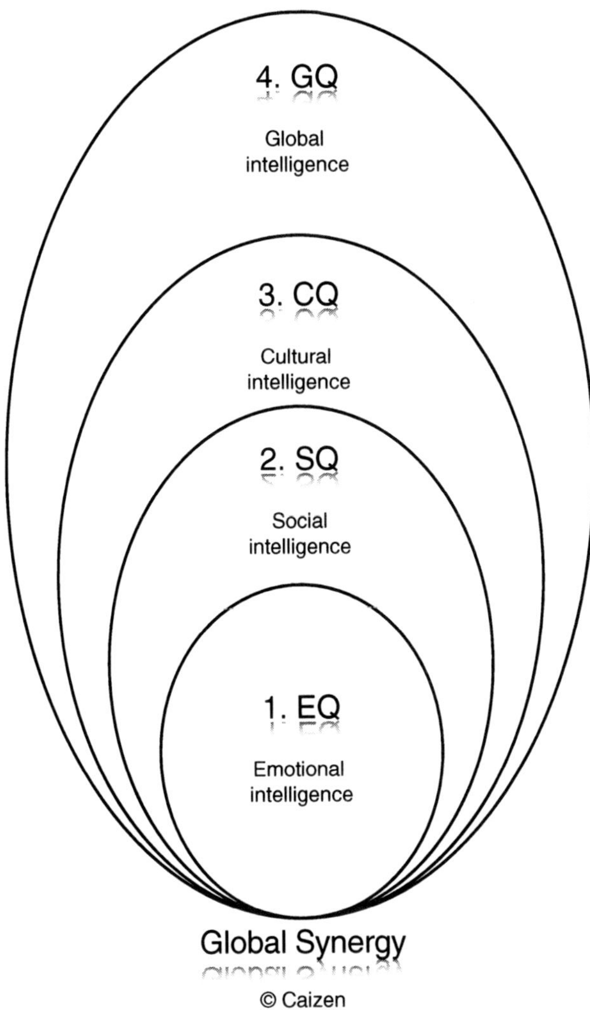

Figure CS12.1 EQ + SQ + CQ + GQ = Global Synergy.

using 'gap' and 'matrix' analysis using students' culture(s) of current residence and 'home' or 'partner' country/culture of students' own choice. Outcome: greater ability to use bridging strategies such as explaining individualistic/collectivistic cultural logic in neutral terms that validate both cultures; navigate decision-making pathways using a 'partnering' win-win mindset that respects people's acculturation expectations and core cultural values.

4. **Global intelligence (GQ).** Builds knowledge of current STEEP (social, technological, environmental, economic, political) challenges through

independent research mining global indexes and presenting data on between two and three countries in the global context. Outcome: greater ability to use platform/performance skills suitable for international audiences and to frame local and bilateral issues in a global context.

Framework of intercultural competence

The EQ-SQ-CQ-GQ intercultural competence framework draws on disciplines relevant *within and between* each of the four scales: neurophysiology, social psychology, sociology, comparative psychology, cultural anthropology, comparative epigenetics, organisational behaviour, management and business, critical theory, philosophy, etc. No single definition or framework is being used in the Global Synergy course.

1. **EQ.** Draws on the work of Goleman (1995), Gardner (2011), and Damasio (2003) infused with Eastern and Western contrasts, such as object and field perceptual differences extrapolated by Nisbett (2003). Jungian psychology is used to introduce personality types. The ability to reflect 'in action' and 'on action' in order to derive meta-learning from experiences in social settings (such as experiential activities and whole-class simulations) come from the classic work of Argyris and Schon (1983). An intercultural tool adapted from Ting-Toomey's (2004) ODIS helps students distinguish interpretation and value judgements from neutral description.
2. **SQ.** In the Japanese context, Masuda's work on relative attention to social cues (2008) has informed competency definitions. In global-Japanese business, Ikujiro Nonaka's SECI (Socialisation, Externalisation, Combination, Internalisation) model is used to introduce tacit-explicit knowledge conversion skills, and Glaser (2014) informs through-flow between neurochemistry and organisational anthropology. Rizzolatti's (2013) seminal work supports understanding of mirror neurons and empathy. Bohmian principles underlie pair and group dialogue (Bohm 2004).
3. **CQ:** Cross-cultural theory includes the Intercultural Development Inventory (2012), neurophysiological understandings of culture shock and acculturation in the context of Japanese society (Komisarof, 2014). Hall's (1959) classic work on high/low context is used to elaborate Nonaka's model. Intercultural conversion skills are developed through awareness of anthropological conceptions of Japanese 'emics' and cultural equivalence (Kuwayama, 2009). Rosinski's Cultural Orientation Framework (2003), which summarises dimensions defined by Hofstede (1994), is used together with the Global Synergy's 'mindset matrix' tool to train code-switching.
4. **GQ**: Online datasets from global surveys conducted by GLOBE (Global Leadership and Organizational Behavior Effectiveness), JETRO (Japan External Trade Organization), UNESCO (United Nations Education,

Scientific and Cultural Organization) Institute for Statistics, WHO (World Health Organisation), etc. define a range of STEEP issues. Global 'blue marble' consciousness is inspired by astronaut Chris Hadfield's outside-in perceptions from space (2016), Jungian intuition and Eastern mindfulness. *Caizen*, written with a soft-skills C, is a concept and practice developed throughout the course to underscore the need for a globalisation process that foregrounds continuous improvements in interpersonal communication and acculturation strategies.

Developing intercultural competence

Each Global Synergy module flows through the ASK (awareness, skills, knowledge) cycle, which combines Thomas and Inkson's definition of cultural intelligence (2009) with Thunderbird's (2015) three types of global mindset capital, Kolb's four learning cycles (abstract conceptualisation, concrete experience, reflective observation, and active experimentation; Joy & Kolb, 2009) and PDCA (Plan, Do, Check, Adjust).

Awareness

A core component of each Global Synergy module is a small-group or whole-class simulation. During simulations, students reflect in action. During practice briefings and debriefs, students preview and/or reflect on action in small groups (SQ). This enables them to understand the perspectives of others they interacted with and to 'check' their own socio-cultural assumptions and perceptions (SQ-CQ). Journaling enables individuals to consider why they anticipated something or reacted as they did and what other choices they might have in similar future intercultural encounters (EQ-CQ). This cultivates a mode of interacting that is increasingly purposeful, skillful and effective (*Caizen* and GQ).

Skills

Simulations create a safe learning environment where students can take risks, make mistakes, and adjust as they practise extending their intercultural communication style. Simulations involve navigating socio-cultural decision-making pathways in order to achieve a culturally intelligent and sometimes time-sensitive outcome (distributing a bonus between culturally diverse team members; building a tower through a cross-cultural partnership, inquiring about values/principles, etc.). During experiential activities, students actively practise communication skills (SQ), use cultural knowledge (CQ), and manage their own and others' emotional responses (EQ). During the final simulation each term, students vote for their global project dream team. Students also draw on all competencies to collaboratively research and deliver a presentation/performance that places local cross-cultural interactions in a global context.

Knowledge

Information input includes theoretical articles, online indexes, Ed.TED talks/quizzes, and mini-lectures pre- and/or post simulation. Being primed with theoretical concepts during the practice/brief for an experiential activity can help students become more mindful 'in the moment'. Information input also helps students gain clarity about the four competency scales (EQ, SQ, CQ, GQ) and an understanding of specific concepts, cultural dimensions, and theoretical models in a way that is abstracted from their direct experience. Abstracting understanding from their immediate experience is essential if students are to use what they learned to anticipate and collaborate on intercultural interventions in the future.

Lessons learned

1. Global Synergy classroom culture benefits from a design that consciously includes both Eastern and Western norms. This means encouraging objective, data-based research and quiz-style questioning as well as Bohmian dialogue, opinion, and inquiry; including individual as well as group assignments, goal- as well as process-oriented activities; elements of competition and cooperation in order to 'walk the talk' of Global Synergy by extending and leveraging a wide range of classroom norms.
2. Slight differences in briefing/debriefing simulations magnify differences in core and emergent learning outcomes. Because students bring their own past experiences and assumptions to bear on the simulation, open debrief questions such as 'What did you learn/notice...?' can trigger awareness of personal, emergent learning beyond the theory. Setting expectations to be open to this, as well as debriefing to raise awareness of core intercultural competence content ensures a greater element of reality and an opportunity to integrate the four intelligences, EQ, SQ, CQ, and GQ, within the dynamics of a specific class.
3. In integrating emotional, social, cultural, and global intelligences as a more holistic approach to intercultural competence development, it remains important to draw on the work of different disciplines in order to have a more comprehensive development approach.

Ways to improve

1. Define the intercultural course's design and classroom culture more explicitly in the next edition of the workbook.
2. Compile a glossary of terms for each module to support students' use of core concepts as a lens to 'reflection-on-action' in journal entries.
3. Tap/validate students' personal/emergent learning from simulations in addition to core learning evaluation.

Table CS12.1 Assessing intercultural competence.

Intercultural assignments, goals and competencies	**Design principles.** The *Caizen* approach encourages students to revise work both before submission and beyond the end of the course; to focus both on GPA (Grade Point Average) and personal growth. Assignments combine individualistic and collectivistic assessment methods, facilitator and peer evaluation, low context rubrics, and high context impression.
Journal entries EQ-CQ-GQ: awareness and knowledge	**Share journal entries 30 per cent (blog/notebook).** Students illustrate and write up independent research on their chosen countries and/or personal reflections on class simulations. Each blog/notebook entry comprises (1) visual, (2) text, and (3) questions for in-class perspective sharing and dialogue (see below). **Evaluated 1–2 times per semester.** Course facilitator writes *Caizen* comments and gives a numerical grade. Successive grades reflect mastery of ASK core concepts/theory and students' effort to take account of previous comments including personalised/emergent learning.
Journal dialogue and simulations EQ-SQ-CQ: awareness, skills, and knowledge	**Share journal dialogue, 10 per cent (peer evaluation).** Students share their journal entries in different pairs each week then grade each other's entry against the visual-paragraph-questions structure (5 points) and according to their engagement in the dialogue (5 points). Students write Johari-style adjectives/comments in their peers' journals to develop *Caizen* motivation. **Individual participation, 30 per cent.** Students participate during simulations by (1) proactively sharing their own opinions/feelings; (2) opening space for others to share opinions/feelings, especially those different from their own; and/or (3) answer multiple-choice and short-answer questions (depending on class size and/or theory/skills weighting). **Final simulation (peer evaluation).** Students vote for the three people they would most like to work with on a future intercultural project, their 'dream-team'. Votes received contribute to individual participation grade above.
Presentation/ performance EQ-SQ-CQ-GQ: awareness, skills, and knowledge	**Collaborative Presentation/performance, 30 per cent.** Students collaborate to research and co-deliver a presentation/performance concluding with a positive angle/opportunity for a STEEP global challenge. Students write each other *Caizen* feedback using the same core 'Keep-Caizen/Substance-Synergy' matrix analysis as the course facilitator. Slides/materials are submitted with *Caizen* analysis on their self- and team evaluation. (1) *EQ + SQ + CQ = Synergy 10 per cent.* Suitability of platform/ performance skills for international and Japanese audiences including delivery of emics/translation equivalence; co-presenter dynamics and audience engagement taken into consideration. (2) *CQ + GQ = Substance 10 per cent.* Comparing home and partner country in the global context of a STEEP issue/challenge. Culturally sensitive framing using like-with-like/matrix format that avoids polarisation. STEEP issue defined and interpreted using statistical data, case study/anecdotes and two or more dimensions from the cultural orientations framework. *Caizen*/opportunity focus in conclusion. All sources referenced. (3) *Caizen 10 per cent.* Ability to synthesise self- and peer feedback into constructive, practical steps for future improvement of (1) and (2) above.

4. Evaluate the practical validity of students' presentations by disciplinary experts.
5. Design methods to evaluate intercultural competence during experiential activities in classes with large student numbers.

References

Argyris, C., & Schon, D. (1983). *The reflective practitioner.* New York, NY: Basic.

Bohm, D. (2004). *On dialogue.* London: Routledge.

Damasio, D. (2003). *Looking for Spinoza: Joy, sorrow, and the feeling brain.* Orlando, FL: Harvest.

Gardner, H. (2011). *Frames of mind: The theory of multiple intelligences.* Philadelphia, PA: Basic.

Glaser, J. E. (2014). *Conversational intelligence: How great leaders build trust and get extraordinary results.* Brookline, MA: Bibliomotion.

Goleman, D. (1995). *Emotional intelligence.* New York, NY: Bantam.

Hadfield, C. (2016). *Lessons from an astronaut, Part 1/2* (Video file), 7 February. Retrieved from www.youtube.com/watch?v=t0Rn3e_czoE

Hall, E. T. (1959). *Silent language.* New York, NY: Anchor.

Hoftstede, G. (1994). *Cultures and organisations: Software of the mind.* London: HarperCollins.

Joy, S., & Kolb, D. A. (2009). Are there cultural differences in learning style? *International Journal of Intercultural Relations, 33*, 69–85.

Komisarof, A. (2014). Are Americans more successful at building intercultural relations than Japanese? A comparison and analysis of acculturation outcomes in Japan. *SpringerPlus, 3*(716).

Kuwayama, T. (2009). Japan's emic conceptions. In Y. Sugimoto (Ed.), *The Cambridge companion to modern Japanese culture* (pp. 38–55). Melbourne: Cambridge University Press.

Masuda, T., & Nisbett, R. A. (2001). Attending holistically versus analytically: Comparing the context sensitivity of Japanese and Americans. *Journal of Personality and Social Psychology, 81*(5), 922–34.

Nisbett, R. E. (2003). *Geography of thought: How Asians and Westerners think differently … and why.* New York, NY: The Free Press.

Nonaka, I., & Takeuchi, H. (1995) *The Knowledge-creating company: How Japanese companies create the dynamics of innovation.* Oxford: Oxford University Press.

Rizzolatti, G. (2013). *Empathie und die generation ich* (*Empathy and the generation I*) (Video file). 26 October. Retrieved from http://cultureofempathy.com/References/Experts/Giacomo-Rizzolatti.htm

Rosinski, P. (2003) *Coaching across cultures.* London: Nicholas Brealey.

Thomas, D. C., & Inkson, K. (2009). *Cultural intelligence.* San Francisco, CA: Berrett-Koehler.

Thunderbird Najafi Global Mindset Institute. (2015). *Global mindset's three capitals.* Retrieved from http://globalmindset.thunderbird.edu/home/global-mindset-inventory/three-capitals

Ting-Toomey, S., & Chung, L. C. (2004). *Understanding intercultural communication.* Los Angeles, CA: Roxbury.

CS13

Intercultural development programme

Carrie Karsgaard and Leah Sanford
(University of British Columbia)

Context

The University of British Columbia (UBC) aspires to cultivate intercultural fluency among the student body by engaging 'in reflection and action to build intercultural aptitudes, create a strong sense of inclusion, and enrich our intellectual and social life' (UBC, n.d.). UBC acknowledges with Pettigrew and Tropp (2006) that intercultural fluency will not arise simply through proximity to people who are different but it must be actively encouraged and taught. These efforts are particularly critical on UBC's Okanagan campus, which has grown and diversified very quickly since its inception in 2004; in 2015, there were 1,072 international students (12.7 per cent) and 403 aboriginal students (4.8 per cent).

Within this institutional context, the Intercultural Development Program (IDP) was developed as a pilot for the 2015–16 academic year through the international programmes and services unit, in consultation with campus partners and faculty members. To bridge diverse groups on campus, the IDP was actively promoted to students from all faculties, including both graduate and undergraduate students, domestic (including aboriginal) and international students, as well as students embarking on or returning from exchange.

Goals and outcomes

As a result of the programme, participants will be able to:

- identify and explore their own identities and relative power and privilege in relation to others;
- see themselves as part of a world community, where their actions have impacts beyond themselves and beyond the now;
- suspend judgement and notice personal bias when encountering others;
- become active agents for social change; develop effective strategies and increase willingness and confidence to intervene during every scenario of injustice or discrimination;

- develop intercultural fluency as a means to create more meaningful and sustainable social relationships;
- participate in and facilitate high-risk, sensitive, or courageous conversation;
- identify the value of learning with/from/alongside others rather than about others.

Framework of intercultural competence

The IDP infuses common intercultural frameworks (Deardorff, 2006; LeBaron, 2003; Shah, 2004) with critical approaches to global citizenship education (GCE) (Andreotti, 2006; Pike, 2008; Richardson, 2008; Schultz, 2007; Taylor, 2013). Taking the subject positions of students seriously, critical approaches involve a reflexive, learner-driven process that encourages students to engage with diverse perspectives in order to learn and transform their own views, identities, and relationships (Andreotti, 2006). The programme thus seeks to expose and address assumptions, biases, contexts, imbalances, injustices, relationships, and structures that maintain the privilege of some at the expense of others. Rather than promoting prescribed modes of behaviour, the goal of this approach is to encourage students to 'analyze and experiment with other forms of seeing/thinking and being/relating to one another' (Andreotti, 2006). Instead, critical GCE involves a 'pedagogy of transformation', whereby students are encouraged to challenge dominant ideologies and structures.

Developing intercultural competence

The objective of the programme is to provide the theory, reflection, and skills that enhance students' intercultural competencies through workshops, practical experience, and community.

Workshops

The core workshop, Fostering an Intercultural Campus Community, introduces students to the overlapping of culture, personality, structures/policies, language, and context. Following this workshop, students select five additional ninety-minute workshops or special lectures, including but not limited to topics such as power and privilege, designing programmes for diverse groups, media representations and culture, and intercultural communication.

Workshops leverage a number of pedagogical tools, including group discussions, personal reflections and inventories, think-pair-share, simulations, videos (and other cultural productions such as poems, articles, and images), scenarios, and handouts with helpful tools/summaries. Workshops encourage students to learn to assess their own biases, assumptions, and contexts in order to respond critically and imaginatively towards others rather than prescribing how to interact with diverse people.

Experiential learning

Students also complete a mandatory (inter)cultural experiential learning component. In this pilot year, students select any kind of involvement, from single-day events to ongoing commitments, either independently or in conjunction with the IDP adviser. Students then reflect on their practical involvement both through independent assessments and one-on-ones with the adviser. The goal of the pilot year is to determine the types and scope of involvement that students independently pursue before establishing more specific guidelines for this component.

Community of practice

Although it is not a requirement of the IDP, a community of practice has emerged as students share personal reflections, videos, articles, and involvement opportunities on a Facebook group and through student-directed discussions over communal meals.

Assessing intercultural competence

Assessment of the IDP is conducted at both the *workshop* and *programme* levels in order to develop and adapt curriculum content, programme structure, and pedagogy, as well as to justify the programme for budgetary and planning purposes. Rather than following an external measure of intercultural competence, assessments are tied directly to the student learning outcomes outlined above and include:

1. informal observation of student participation during workshops and reflection during advising sessions;
2. formal written surveys conducted at the
   (a) outset (asking students reasons for taking IDP);
   (b) mid-point (asking students for significant learnings and input into programme content, structure, and pedagogy); and
   (c) end of the programme (requesting significant feedback on programme content, pedagogy, community, and experiential learning components);
3. critical written reflections on how workshop content impacts approach to experiential learning;
4. assessment portfolio consisting of Facebook posts, community blog writings, and student initiatives log.

Lessons learned

First, while the IDP began with a flexible model to accommodate students' schedules, assessments indicate that a cohort-based model will be most successful for intercultural learning. As the IDP enrolled a diverse cohort of sixteen domestic and twenty international students from various geographical, ethnic, familial, and disciplinary backgrounds, participants identified the ongoing need to establish a consistent, community-oriented group in order to promote discussion of controversial topics, sharing of ideas outside of workshops, and working on projects as a collective.

Further, a diverse cohort requires careful work and reflection on behalf of the facilitator, who is required to negotiate between ranging and conflicting epistemologies. Student feedback and facilitator reflection indicate a need for even more diverse perspectives and pedagogies within workshop and online discussions, as well as interactive, relevant, and student-generated curricula.

This necessity is complicated by the neo-liberal university context where diverse students are seen as assets to a campus community, summarised in headcounts and valued for creating the image of a diverse university. In this context, it is difficult to find pre-existing programmes, materials, professional development opportunities, and journal articles that approach intercultural education from a more critical perspective. Furthermore, even when critical approaches are intended, we as facilitators find ourselves inadvertently reverting to a safe, politically correct environment where the real, material repercussions of our own and our students' assumptions remained unchallenged. Along these lines, student feedback at times referenced feelings of 'enlightenment' or 'fulfilment', perhaps indicating our tendencies as facilitators to quickly reassure students rather than having them face their culpability in perpetuating injustice. As a result, we recognise the need to continue to research and implement more critical pedagogies and engage in ongoing reflection as we explore a counterculture educational practice.

Ways to improve

As we continue to develop the critical approach of the IDP through research and pedagogical experimentation as outlined above, we as facilitators will work to ensure workshops are current and relevant, incorporate IDP graduates, consist of active-learning opportunities, include guest speakers, and comprise off-campus opportunities. Additionally, the IDP will offer more collaborative opportunities in the upcoming year such as group field trips, designated time for information-sharing in every workshop, specific workshops centred upon student projects (i.e. performances or interactive art displays), and the option to complete one collaborative experiential component per term. As we experiment with practical changes, we hope to engage in reflexive praxis to meet our IDP objectives.

References

Andreotti, V. (2006). Soft versus critical global citizenship education. *Policy and Practice: A Development Educational Review*, *3*, 40–51.

Deardorff, D. K. (2006). Identification and assessment of intercultural competence as a student outcome of internationalization. *Journal of Studies in International Education*, *10*(3), 241–66.

LeBaron, M. (2003). Communication tools for understanding cultural differences. Retrieved from www.beyondintractability.org/essay/communication-tools

Pettigrew, T., & Tropp, L. (2006). A meta-analytic test of intergroup contact theory. *Journal of Personality and Social Psychology, 90*(5), 751–83.

Pike, G. (2008). Reconstructing the legend: Educating for global citizenship. In A. Abdi & L. Schultz (Eds.), *Educating for human rights and global citizenship* (pp. 23–237). Albany, NY: University of New York Press.

Richardson, G. (2008). Conflicting imaginaries: Global citizenship in Canada as a site of contestation. In M. O'Sullivan & K. Pashby (Eds.), *Citizenship education in the era of globalization: Canadian perspectives* (pp. 53–70). Rotterdam: Sense.

Shah, S. (2004). The researcher/interviewer in intercultural context: A social intruder! *British Educational Research Journal, 30*(4), 549–75.

Shultz, L. (2007). Educating for global citizenship: Conflicting agendas and understandings. *Alberta Journal of Educational Research, 53*(3), 248–58.

Taylor, L. (2013). Against the tide: Working with and against the affective flows of resistance in social and global justice learning. *Critical Literacy: Theories and Practices, 7*(2), 58–68.

University of British Columbia (UBC). (n.d.). Place and promise: Intercultural understanding. Retrieved from http://strategicplan.ubc.ca/

CS14

Development of intercultural communicative competence

A course for pre-service EFL (English as a foreign language) teachers

Nina Lazarević (University of Niš)

Context

Developing Intercultural Communicative Competence is an elective, junior-year course offered to the students at the English department, Faculty of Philosophy, University of Niš, Serbia. Students taking the course are studying towards a BA in English, the language, literature, and language teaching. The student population is comprised of full-time students from south-east Serbia, who, though not exclusively, pursue a teaching career. The make-up of the student population is mostly monocultural and monolingual but does not reflect the actual make-up of the citizens in the area. The course has been redesigned twice since its introduction in 2008, mostly in terms of assessment.

Goals and outcomes

The most immediate aim of the course is for students to become familiar with different theoretical frameworks and models of culture, to recognise these elements, and to use them to analyse events and phenomena around them. Also, the course aims to:

- increase students' awareness about intercultural communication and factors that influence it and are reflected in popular culture, immediate surroundings, current events, their experience;
- enable students to study how culture is expressed in language and its influence on authentic communicative situations;
- help students become aware of and able to understand and explain how cultural dimensions and elements are expressed in a specific discourse;
- critically analyse actual communication contexts and examine intercultural interactions;
- develop intercultural communication skills and a sociolinguistic perspective of culture, as well as positive attitudes towards different cultures, including their own, empathy, and the ability to de-centre and see things from the perspective of 'the other' (be it in terms of gender, class, ethnicity, or culture);

- build up students' knowledge in order to plan English lesson classes where intercultural competence elements are included, thus providing chances for intercultural learning, reflection, and heightened awareness.

The work on these elements should result in students' improved intercultural competence and skills for intercultural communication and critical approach to the issues explored. It is hoped that this course would make students more aware of diversity that does exist in their society and better prepared to work with it in their future classrooms.

Framework of intercultural competence

In order to achieve these objectives, students are advised to always keep in mind the cognitive, behavioural, and affective domains as the basis for intercultural competence. That is why we believe that Antal and Friedman's (2008) definition of intercultural competence as 'the ability to *consciously* explore one's ways of thinking and acting so as to actively construct an appropriate strategy' (p. 365, our emphasis) might be valuable for students. Along the similar lines, Chen and Starosta (2008) believe that these three domains are interrelated, with the focus on intercultural sensitivity that 'enables individuals to be sensitive enough to acknowledge and respect cultural differences' and will lead to 'open-mindedness, nonjudgmental attitudes, and social relaxation' (p. 223).

Since our students are future language teachers, we believe that Byram's conceptualisation of a competent intercultural speaker provides a useful framework within which to work with students, to 'operate their linguistic competence and their sociolinguistic awareness ... in order to manage interaction across cultural boundaries, to anticipate misunderstandings caused by difference in values, meanings and beliefs, and... to cope with the affective as well as cognitive demands of engagement with others' (Byram, 1995, p. 25). Finally, the CEFR (Common European Framework of Reference) definition of intercultural competence, especially its behavioural segment, stresses the ability to explore both one's own and a new culture, 'cultural sensitivity and the ability to identify and use a variety of strategies for contact with those from other cultures; the capacity to fulfill the role of cultural intermediary between one's own culture and the foreign culture' (Council of Europe, 2001, p. 104).

Developing intercultural competence

The course gradually develops intercultural competence, first by giving students theoretical tools with which to approach phenomena and then by providing time and material to which these theoretical concerns might be applied. Students are constantly asked to reflect on the material in order to see the practical implications of the theory, while formative assessment on all their assignments gives them ample feedback. They have an opportunity to experience intercultural competence elements in simulations through Barnga or BaFá BaFá, as well as to bring their own experience into the classroom both as an illustration and a topic for discussions. Students explore certain concepts in their immediate surroundings and report on them through weekly assignments, for example, brief surveys in their neighbourhoods or commentary on the media coverage of current domestic and foreign events. For their teaching practice, students have to think about how to introduce intercultural competence elements in English language lessons: to provoke reflection and raise awareness of the related issues by adapting the material and going past surface culture with thought-provoking questions, discussions, and projects designed for their students. Therefore, students have a chance to explore culture not through literature or cultural studies but through intercultural frameworks that invite reflection and exploration of their own culture.

Assessing intercultural competence

The course is assessed continuously with several direct-evidence assessment tools based on embedded class assignments designed to ascertain students' intercultural competence development, and students can amass a maximum of 100 points with 70 needed to pass. Students are encouraged to actively participate in class discussions (5 points). In addition to the regular classroom hours, a discussion group convenes five times during the course, where attendance is not obligatory but is counted into the grade with 5 extra points. The discussion group meets for one hour and is moderated by a teaching assistant (during the past two school years, this was a Fulbright English teaching assistant).

Every two weeks students submit a journal entry through which they reflect on and apply the theoretical intercultural frameworks to topics that range from personal experience over the analyses of a TV series, film, or book in terms of a particular cultural model to interviewing people and exploring their beliefs or stereotypes. The journal entries are assessed for the form and intercultural content. They should be a short argumentative essay of around 500–750 words (30 points for six entries).

While other assessment tools assess students individually in regard to their intercultural development and course participation, a lesson-plan project is an applied group effort. The reasoning behind it is that students are just learning about the lesson-plan format in their obligatory methodology course, so, although they should be confident about lesson planning, it is still a learning process. Second, a lesson plan requires a lot of think-time and resource exploration so the workload is smaller in a group project where group members work as a team which is often another intercultural experience (30 points).

Finally, the last assessment tools are a draft of a presentation and the presentation itself. A draft is a blueprint of what students want to explore in more detail in their presentation. During a seminar session, students receive both peer and teacher feedback on their drafts (5 points). The presentation is done in groups of around ten students, with five minutes to present the problem, analysis based on the course material, and illustrations. A group discussion is expected after each presentation and can provide extra points for active and insightful participation, while presentations are marked for the content, organisation, and delivery (30 points).

Lessons learned

It has been proven over the years that when students start the course they are to a great extent unaware of their own biases and stereotypes. While this might be expected from a group of students who are not well travelled and are relatively young, it has also made us aware that students need more time to come to terms with the new concepts, their own understanding, and frame-shifting. This is why initial assignments can be redone and students are given continuous feedback.

Once the frame-shifting starts, it has transpired that students believe that the 'people are all equal' (Bennett, 1993) is the principle to go by and that it always takes a lot of reflection for students to see that if they are to become fully aware and non-judgemental, they have to move past this stage. We see this attitude resulting from their lack of experience but also as a stepping stone towards more ethnorelative stages, so we urge students to reflect on their work, watch films with intercultural competence content, and apply multiple perspectives while analysing them.

Another important realisation has been that despite a relative ease of access to information students prefer to stay within their comfort zone, with things they already know and can get on demand. While it might be easy for them to explore the current issues, living in 'here and now' (Tomlinson & Imbeau, 2010) leaves them without a wider picture which is needed when different cultures, beliefs, and values are brought together for an analysis. Their superficial knowledge of global and local events at times hindered discussions, and the instructors have realised that scaffolding debates and discussions (Liddicoat & Scarino, 2013), even at this level, gives better results.

Ways to improve

We hope to make more use of new technologies for connecting our students with lecturers and students from abroad and local communities with which students rarely interact to help them apply their skills and knowledge and develop their intercultural competence sensitivity which needs to be further assessed in multiple ways. Assessment remains an important aspect, and group projects might substitute individual presentations, with students exploring particular issues from multiple perspectives, thus bringing greater depth to the analysis through cooperative learning endeavours.

References

Antal, A. B., & Friedman, V. J. (2008). Learning to negotiate reality: A strategy for teaching intercultural competencies. *Journal of Management Education*, *32*(3), 363–86.

Bennett, M. J. (1993). Towards ethnorelativism: A developmental model of intercultural sensitivity. In R. M. Paige (Ed.), *Education for the intercultural experience* (pp. 21–71).Yarmouth, ME: Intercultural Press.

Byram, M. (1995). Intercultural competence and mobility in mulitinational context: A European view. In M. L. Tickoo (Ed.), *Language and culture in multilingual societies: Viewpoints and visions* (pp. 21–36). Singapore: SEAMEO Regional Language Centre.

Chen, G. M., & Starosta, W. J. (2008). Intercultural communication competence: A synthesis. In M. K. Asante, Y. Miike, & J. Yin (Eds.), *The global intercultural communication reader* (pp. 215–37). London and New York, NY: Routledge.

Council of Europe. (2001). *Common European framework of reference for languages: Learning, teaching, assessment.* Cambridge: Press Syndicate of the University of Cambridge.

Liddicoat, A. J., & Scarino, A. (2013). *Intercultural language teaching and learning.* Oxford: Wiley-Blackwell.

Tomlinson, C. A, & Imbeau, M. B. (2010). *Leading and managing a differentiated classroom.* Alexandria: ASCD.

CS15

Making cultural diversity work

Katrien Mertens (UC Leuven-Limburg)
and Jan Van Maele (KU Leuven)

Context

The course Making Cultural Diversity Work is part of a postgraduate programme on development studies at UC Leuven-Limburg, a university college made up of 170 nationalities located in Leuven, a small, historical college town. Since 2008, this programme has blended the theory and practice of capacity-building, development work, and education into one exploratory trajectory, and it attracts students seeking to contribute to the building of peace, sustainable development, and intercultural dialogue through education. The curriculum is inspired by and structured with UNESCO's five major programme areas, and its view on education known as the Four Pillars of Education (UNESCO, 1996). The course described here represents the UNESCO programme area of culture and focuses on making cultural diversity work through the effective application of intercultural competencies.

Typically, the student population is highly diverse in terms of academic background (such as education, law, business, and natural sciences), national background (a mix of mainly European, African, and Asian countries), and age bracket (early twenties to around fifty). Class size varies from fifteen to twenty-five students, with an even gender balance. The course has been developed and taught by Katrien Mertens and Jan Van Maele with the collaboration of various guest lecturers who represent different professional fields that face the challenge of making cultural diversity work.

Goals and outcomes

The course aims towards the following general learning goals:

- To develop awareness of the cultural diversity within each student and within the groups to which students belong.
- To hone students' intercultural competence by adopting requisite attitudes, by increasing knowledge, and by expanding their skills repertoire for communicating across cultures.

- To discover different ways of making cultural diversity work in personal projects and in professional pursuits.
- To learn about UNESCO policies and programmes on cultural diversity.

To facilitate the design and assessment of learning interventions, these general goals have been translated into specific learning outcomes. For instance, the general goal of 'expanding one's intercultural communication skills repertoire' is reflected in the specific expectation that students can apply the ODIS method (Observing, Describing, Interpreting, Suspending judgement; Ting-Toomey, 1999) during encounters with 'the other' in class and outside. Likewise, the general goal of 'discovering different ways of making cultural diversity work' translates into the specific challenge to mobilise the diversity of communication and collaboration styles within the student group for higher performance in time-pressed project work.

Framework of intercultural competence

The approach towards the intercultural that we adopt in our teaching stems from what is commonly referred to as a non-essentialist view of culture (Holliday, Hyde, & Kullman, 2010), which considers culturality as a process in which meaning is jointly constructed. For practical purposes, in this course we consider an encounter to be intercultural whenever one of the parties involved qualifies it as such, either at the moment of occurrence or in retrospect. Student narratives of such encounters are analysed for the views they contain of what constitutes intercultural competence. These often implicit student theories are subsequently related to frameworks of intercultural competence used in academic, professional, and policy contexts, such as Deardorff (2006), Global People (Spencer-Oatey & Stadler, 2009), TOPOI (Tongue, Order, Person, Organisation, Intention; Hoffman, 2014), and UNESCO (2013).

Developing intercultural competence

Our teaching approach integrates a variety of activity types centred around elicited prior student experiences as well as experiences that are created in the context of the course itself, for instance through icebreakers (e.g., *Go bananas!* in Pineda, 2012) or through more extended simulations (e.g., *Visit the Albatross culture*, 2008). As described elsewhere (Van Maele & Mertens, 2014), these activities comprise exercises in narrating, describing, interpreting, diagnosing, and advising as well as in underlying skills as observing, reframing, suspending judgement, and inventing options. These skills have been chosen because they are central to analysing intercultural situations and responding in effective and appropriate ways.

From a structural point of view, the approach is characterised by the integration of theory, practice, and reflection. At the onset of the course we explore the cultural diversity within the group itself through a wide range of hands-on experiences (including intercultural simulations, task-based group work, journal writing, and fireside storytelling) during an intensive residential two-day seminar. At the heart of the module, a number of experts are invited to enlighten students on making cultural diversity work in a range of professional fields, including inner-city social work, sustainable tourism, and mediation. Edwin Hoffman, who developed the TOPOI model for intercultural communication in the social sector, has delivered an annual workshop. A set of readings provides additional input so that students become more knowledgeable about the meaning and impact of intercultural competence in organisations like UNESCO. The latter stages of the module are devoted to the preparation, presentation, and evaluation of the team project deliverables (see below).

Assessing intercultural competence

At the outset, the student group is given an authentic project assignment which is to result in an end-of-course event on an intercultural theme in which students showcase their skills at making cultural diversity work. Examples have included the creation and inauguration of a 'cultural audio-tour' on the grounds of the seminar site and the preparation and facilitation of a ninety-minute activity on the theme of 'same and different' for primary-school children of two local schools during after-school care. The teachers assign a group score based on the performance during the event, taking into account the feedback of the external stakeholders who commissioned the project. This group score is mediated by peer assessment to account for individual contributions during the process.

Another format used is the assessment of individual portfolios in which students narrate personal intercultural experiences and make sense of them with reference to theoretical concepts from course readings such as multiple identities, otherising, or small cultures. In this way, they are encouraged to discuss personal encounters as intercultural vignettes, as with the international student who caught herself acting on ungrounded prejudices when a male student from another continent joined her and girlfriends without invitation, at the cafeteria.

Lessons learned

We have observed that the experience-based and interaction-oriented approach that we adopt in the course creates a conducive environment for the development of intercultural competence.

First, we have learned that the sustained emphasis on ODIS (Ting-Toomey, 1999) and other basic skills of perception, cognition, and communication functions as a powerful lever for intercultural competence in general.

Second, the combination of an internal orientation (What can we learn from the group dynamics within our group?) and external input (What can we learn from what people have done elsewhere in various fields?) provides complementary viewpoints that challenge students to shift perspectives and offer a starting point for theorising.

And, third, the integrated project assignment has been an effective way of taking the students out of the school environment into the local communities thanks to the involvement of external stakeholders, who function as commissioners and co-assessors of real-life tasks. It has also enabled us to return something of value to the sponsoring learning fund associated with the off-site retreat de Heerlijckyt, thanks to which all students, regardless of their financial resources, could participate in the activity.

Ways to improve

We found that the learning effect of an introductory off-site retreat which fully exploits the interaction as it unfolds within the group far outreaches that of teaching the same number of hours piecemeal over a longer time span. At the same time, it is also true that spreading the course over a longer term will provide students with the necessary time for transferring new insights into their day-to-day encounters. So far, we have tried to cope with this tension by experimenting with different combinations of pace and duration, but we have not discovered the optimal formula yet. Moreover, intercultural competence holds so many rooms that we have so far not succeeded to provide sufficient opportunities for practice, even for components that we hold dear, including empathy, coping with ambiguity, and an open awareness to notice where we are.

References

Deardorff, D. K. (2006). Identification and assessment of intercultural competence as a student outcome of internationalization. *Journal of Studies in Intercultural Education*, *10*(3), 241–66.

Hoffman, E. (2014). *Interculturele gespreksvoering: Theorie en praktijk van het Topoi-model.* Houten: Bohn Stafleu van Loghum.

Holliday, A., Hyde, M., & Kullman, J. (2010). *Intercultural education: An advanced resources book.* London and New York, NY: Routledge.

Pineda, K. (2012). Go bananas! In K. Berardo & D. K. Deardorff (Eds.), *Building cultural competence. Innovative activities and models* (pp. 69–71). Sterling, VA: Stylus.

Spencer-Oatey, H., & Stadler, S. (2009). *The global people competency framework: Competencies for effective intercultural interaction.* Warwick: Centre for Applied Linguistics, University of Warwick.

Ting-Toomey, S. (1999). *Communicating across cultures.* New York, NY: Guilford.

UNESCO. (1996). *Learning: The treasure within.* Paris: UNESCO.

—— (2013). *Intercultural competences. Conceptual and operational framework.* Paris: UNESCO. Retrieved from http://unesdoc.unesco.org/images/0021/002197/219768e.pdf

Van Maele, J., & Mertens, K. (2014). Towards an experience-driven approach to teaching intercultural communication. In P. Romanowski (Ed.), *Intercultural issues in the era of globalization* (pp. 122–9). Warsaw: IKSI Scientific Publishing House.

Visit the Albatross culture. (2008). Retrieved from www.salto-youth.net/tools/toolbox/tool/visiting-the-albatross-culture.417/

CS16

Facilitating intercultural competencies through international student internships

Making links to future professional selves after internships

Susan Oguro (University of Technology Sydney)

Context

This case study examines a course developed to facilitate the intercultural competencies of undergraduate students completing short-term international internships outside the regular teaching semesters. The elective course is available to students from a range of disciplinary areas including business, engineering, information technology, media studies, and science, all of whom are enrolled at a large urban Australian university: the University of Technology Sydney. Students choosing the course complete a two- to four-week programme in an international location with diverse international placement options including at the headquarters of a multinational corporation in Tokyo, a microfinance enterprise in Vietnam, a creative-arts enterprise in Cambodia, or a social-impact project in rural India. While students naturally gain discipline-specific skills and content knowledge through their internships at these diverse organisations, the focus of the course outlined here is to facilitate students' critical exploration of their internship experience in locations beyond Australia and in non-anglophone contexts in terms of intercultural competencies and to consider their application to their future professional selves.

Goals and outcomes

The international internship course sits within the overall framework of the university's model of learning, one feature of which specifically acknowledges that graduates will 'live and work in a culturally diverse and internationalized world ... [where] international and intercultural capabilities will be critical for their lives as professionals and citizens' (University of Technology Sydney, 2016). The international internship course specifies four learning outcomes relating to intercultural competence, namely that students:

- communicate effectively in intercultural contexts;
- reflect on the behaviours and values in the host and home cultures, thereby identifying and reflecting on cultural diversity;

- learn independently; and
- engage with the activities of the internship programme.

As the course is a 'for credit' subject, students' performance in the assigned tasks is graded against a set of assessment criteria. These relate to the following aspects of intercultural competence:

- depth of critical reflection on an aspect of the host society;
- awareness of own cultural assumptions;
- depth of reflection;
- communication of aspects of learned experiences.

Framework of intercultural competence

From the numerous definitions in the research literature, the approach to intercultural competence used in this course draws on the work of Deardorff (2009a) and Fantini (2009), highlighting the importance of encounters that allow students to compare cultural practices. Intercultural competence is also understood to develop through multiple experiences over time and through the process of reflection upon them (Deardorff, 2009b; Dervin, 2010). The process of developing intercultural competence is thus a highly dynamic one.

Developing intercultural competence

Formal learning interventions of workshop classes and assessment tasks are incorporated into this course to scaffold students' intercultural competencies. A growing body of research (e.g., Bathurst & La Brack, 2012; Giovanangeli & Oguro, 2016; Jackson, 2011; Oguro, 2016; Root & Ngampornchai, 2012; Vande Berg, 2007) has shown that universities need to prepare students comprehensively before departure and guide students' reflections upon their return 'home' to maximise the learning opportunity afforded by international opportunities.

The course therefore includes workshops both before and after students' international internship. The pre-departure workshops adopt a blended learning (Mason & Rennie, 2006) approach to learning that includes a combination of online materials (video and text) and also face-to-face interactive activities to explore notions of interculturality. Specifically, students are guided to articulate ideas of their own culture(s) and explore models of intercultural communication. This includes practice in critiquing and interpreting intercultural scenarios. Students also participate in an immersion 'foreign'-language activity requiring them to work in groups to complete tasks (listening and writing tasks) without any instructions in English. The post-internship workshops are opportunities for de-briefing and guided reflection and also for students to present orally one of their assessment tasks on possible applications of their learning to their future professional lives (see below).

Assessing intercultural competence

The course includes three tasks to assess students' intercultural competence, one of which is the satisfactory completion of the international internship itself. While this does not contribute to the students' grade for the subject, it is mandatory that students actively participate in all activities of the internship.

The second task is a report requiring students to explore a specific aspect of the culture(s) experienced and reflect on their understandings of their own cultural background(s). The first section is completed prior to departure and requires students to outline how they expect the cultural values and practices of their destination might be similar or different to their own. This requires independent research on the particular city, town, or village where students will be located as students are specifically instructed to avoid superficial statements about an imagined nation-state culture. The final report is completed after the students' return to Sydney. It contains a reflection on the student's initial expectations plus a description and reflection on an aspect experienced of the society/culture and what this has showed about their 'home' culture(s). Students are guided to focus on a particular encounter or experience and to reflect deeply on it rather than a series of superficial descriptions of experience.

The third task is a presentation on the intercultural understandings students have developed and how they might apply this knowledge to their profession. Students are therefore instructed to prepare for an imagined audience of a prospective employer. This focus encourages students to link the intercultural understandings gained to their future professional identities and practices. Student feedback on this has been extremely positive as the following two sample anonymous comments exemplify:

> 'The assessments were so helpful to not only process my experience overseas, but they also really equipped me to be able to articulate (in a professional context) how my time overseas developed me to be a more global citizen!'
>
> 'The form of presenting at the end was quite beneficial as it required a good amount of reflection regarding my experience and how this could be applied in the future.'

The students' comments underscore the importance of providing scaffolded opportunities for them to reflect on their intercultural experiences.

Lessons learned

The course as originally designed and delivered has been very popular with students and received positive feedback. However, upon evaluation by the academic staff the following lessons have emerged:

- Experience has shown the need for longer lead time in scheduling the predeparture workshops. In some cases, timetabling issues meant that some students participated in the workshops only in the week before their departure overseas. Compared with students who had a longer time for pre-readings and pre-departure reflections, the quality of the post-experience report and presentation generally suffered, and students themselves reported how they didn't make the most of the opportunity.

- While the range of disciplinary backgrounds of the students is an asset in this type of course, there is also great variation of students' previous experience and willingness to participate in reflective, interactive workshops requiring critical thinking and problem-solving activities.
- The assessment criteria for the intercultural report, as currently stated, are still reasonably vague, and some students find it hard to know what is expected of them. This is particularly the case for students from non-humanities disciplines.

Ways to improve

In response to some of the issues raised above, more consideration will be given in future to timetabling schedules and students' departure dates for their various international programmes. To address the issue of some students having less experience of programmes requiring reflective responses, more explicit explanation of the aims and value of reflection will be incorporated to ensure the opportunity for intercultural competence afforded by the international programme is maximised. In addition, a compilation of exemplars based on previous students' reflective reports will be made available to students taking this course in future. This is of course still problematic, given the desire to encourage the individual nature of intercultural reflection, and so will require a diverse range of reflections to demonstrate this individuality.

References

Bathurst, L., & La Brack, B. (2012). Intervening prior to and after student experiences abroad. In M. Vande Berg, M. Paige, & H. K. Lou (Eds.), *Student learning abroad: What our students are learning, what they're not, and what we can do about it* (pp. 261–83). Sterling: Stylus.

Deardorff, D. K. (2009a). Intercultural competence: A definition, model, and implications for education abroad. In V. Savicki (Ed.), *Developing intercultural competence and transformation: Theory, research, and application in international education* (pp. 32–52). Sterling, VA: Stylus.

—— (Ed.) (2009b). *The Sage handbook of intercultural competence.* Thousand Oaks, CA: Sage.

Dervin, F. (2010). Assessing intercultural competence in language learning and teaching: A critical review of current efforts. In F. Dervin & E. Suomela-Salmi (Eds.), *New approaches to assessment and (inter)cultural competences in higher education* (pp. 157–74). Bern: Peter Lang.

Fantini, A. E. (2009). Assessing intercultural competence. In D. K. Deardorff (Ed.), *The Sage handbook of intercultural competence* (pp. 456–76). Thousand Oaks, CA: Sage.

Giovanangeli, A., & Oguro, S. (2016). Cultural responsiveness: A framework for re-thinking students' interculturality through study abroad. *Intercultural Education, 27*(1), 70–84.

Jackson, J. (2011). Host language proficiency, intercultural sensitivity, and study abroad. *Frontiers: The Interdisciplinary Journal of Study Abroad, 21* (fall), 167–89.

Mason, R., & Rennie, F. (2006). *Elearning: The key concepts.* London and New York, NY: Routledge.

Oguro, S. (2016). Facilitating students' interaction and engagement with the local society during study abroad. In L. Bleichenbacher & B. Kürsteiner (Eds.), *Teacher education in the 21st century: A focus on convergence* (pp. 247–62). Cambridge: Cambridge Scholars Publishing.

Root, E., & Ngampornchai, A. (2012). 'I came back as a new human being': Student descriptions of intercultural competence acquired through education abroad experiences. *Journal of Studies in International Education, 17*(5), 513–32.

University of Technology Sydney. (2016). UTS model of learning: Global. Retrieved from www.uts.edu.au/research-and-teaching/teaching-and-learning/uts-model-learning/global

Vande Berg, M. (2007). Intervening in the learning of US students abroad. *Journal of Studies in International Education, 11*(3–4), 392–9.

CS17

Teaching intercultural competence to undergraduate international students in Vietnam

Catherine Peck, Melanie Brown, and Frederique Bouilheres (RMIT University Vietnam)

Context

At a transnational Australian university (English medium) with campus locations in the developing nation of Vietnam, a multidisciplinary 12-credit point course, Culture and Context in Vietnam, has been developed. The course serves undergraduate international students undertaking studies in various disciplines and is taken prior to commencement of programme-specific studies at the university. If enrolled to undertake a supervised international internship opportunity in Vietnamese industry rather than on-campus study, the course may be the only on-campus experience the students have. The course will be delivered in blended intensive mode, facilitated in the first iteration by academic staff from the Learning and Teaching Center, spanning no more than three weeks.

The course is intended to help students acculturate to the Vietnamese environment and to equip them with knowledge and skills that will help them navigate cultural differences and challenges encountered during their time in the country. This course is considered essential to the university's suite of supporting activities and services as the institution is seeing steady growth in international student numbers, many of whom are experiencing life in a developing country for the first time.

Goals and outcomes

An intercultural competence framework (Deardorff, 2006; Woods, 2007) was deemed appropriate to frame the purposes, outcomes, and delivery of the proposed course. The goal of intercultural competence development informs how students are presented with the broadly scoped course content (Vietnamese society and culture) and how they are asked to interact with and respond to that content.

This is represented in the course guide as follows:

Upon completion of the course, it is intended that you will have achieved the following Learning Outcomes:

- Be able to identify and discuss significant features of Vietnamese culture and society, including appropriate behaviours across a range of social settings.

- Developed your ability to interpret and relativise cultural behaviours, to adapt your own behaviour when appropriate and to interact appropriately in intercultural situations.
- Developed your inquiry skills, and capacity to discover through interaction, experience, and reflection.
- Developed your capacity to reflect critically on your own and other cultures.

Framework of intercultural competence

A widely agreed definition of intercultural competence by scholars in the field were reached in Deardorff's (2006) Delphi Study and is used as a primary reference point. These are the abilities to:

- communicate effectively and appropriately in intercultural situations based on one's intercultural knowledge, skills, and attitudes;
- shift frame of reference appropriately and adapt behaviour to cultural context, adaptability, expandability, and flexibility of one's frame of reference/filter;
- identify behaviours guided by culture and engage in new behaviours in other cultures even when behaviours are unfamiliar given a person's own socialisation.

(Deardorff, 2006, p. 249)

These are closely aligned to the conceptual framework of intercultural competence provided in Byram (1997). Byram's intercultural competence framework is related to the notion of learner competence and measurement and is organised conceptually around five *saviours*, which are considered to be integrated in function and can be summarised as attitudes, knowledge, skills of interpreting and relating, skills of discovery and interaction, and critical cultural awareness.

Developing intercultural competence

During the course, students learn about and experience at first hand aspects of Vietnamese culture and society, which provides the *context* element. They are then guided through analytical and reflective activities to explicitly develop their personal levels of intercultural competence, and in doing so engage directly with key concepts, frameworks and theories of the intercultural. This provides the *culture* emphasis, and together these two elements inform the course title, Culture and Context in Vietnam.

For all major topic areas, learning follows a three-part structure. Study begins in the online environment, commencing with a reflection on the student's own society or experience (fostering knowledge of self) before learning about the corresponding aspect of Vietnamese society (fostering knowledge of other). In the face-to-face environment, students transition to an interactive, inquiry-based and experiential learning mode. This variously entails field trips, interviews with Vietnamese peers, guest speakers, and other modes of exposure as appropriate (fostering abilities to discover, to interact, to acquire new knowledge). Finally, learning in each topic concludes with a structured reflection on the experience, the student's own performance in interactions and reactions/understandings (fostering abilities to interpret and relate and critical engagement).

To illustrate, when learning about the role of the family in Vietnamese society, students begin online with an introspective activity, defining their own understanding of the role of family in their own society. They then work through an online learning pathway (multimedia materials and short readings) on the topic. From this secondary exposure, students generate questions and are partnered with a volunteer Vietnamese student peer, with whom they discuss the role of family. Finally, they are guided through reflection on similarities and differences to their own experience, the implications of the role of family for Vietnamese society, and an evaluation of their own feelings or reactions to any prominent differences encountered.

The course includes five modules, the first of which, Representations of Vietnam, is completed online pre-departure. In this module, students explore iconic imagery, artefacts, and personal experiences that have shaped their preconceptions of Vietnam and how that may be different from the contemporary reality. Upon arrival in Vietnam, students complete the remaining four modules (Family and Work Life, Entrepreneurship, Popular Culture, and Creative Practice) in a blended intensive mode.

Assessing intercultural competence

Within the assessment structure, emphasis is placed on the process of developing intercultural competence and the analytical and reflective capabilities that are considered enablers. Students are largely assessed on their capacity to apply critical reflection and analysis to their experience (the process of learning). Assessment does not entail attempts to measure levels of intercultural competence through any psychometric inventories. There are three tasks:

1. Critical incident narratives (negotiated submission mode, individual): Within a critical incident framework, students reflect on a personal experience occurring within the first forty-eight hours of their arrival in Vietnam. Students step through a pattern of describing the experience, explaining its significance, describing their feelings at the time and afterwards, reflecting on their feelings or reactions and imagining those of others, and finally considering what has been learned and how this may help them in the future. Students are able to complete this task through a negotiated mode (text, video, audio file, images that accompany text, etc.).
2. Cultural inquiry project (presentation, group). Students collaboratively negotiate an investigation into an aspect of Vietnamese culture and reflect on

this process of discovery through an intercultural competence lens. Students are given the opportunity to present not only the outcomes of the inquiry but also an analysis of the process followed and reflection on lessons learned to the class, making reference to intercultural frameworks or concepts studied.

3. Critical reflection paper (written, individual). Students make direct connections between intercultural competence theory and their experiences in Vietnam in this paper and are encouraged to follow the critical incident narrative structure of the first assessment task and apply this in a critical analysis of personal experience, drawing upon intercultural competence concepts and frameworks in their reflection and discussion.

Assessments are supported by learning activities that introduce critical reflection and analysis strategies (including articulation of personal critical incidents) throughout the course, aimed at helping students to make sense of the Vietnamese context and their experiences within it.

Lessons learned

As a course development project with multiple stakeholders (academic programmes, marketing and recruitment, student services), lessons have been learned in negotiating diverse perspectives on the nature, purpose, and form of a course such as this.

Actively fostering the development of intercultural competence among undergraduate students immersed in a foreign culture entails eliciting personal responses to experiences that may be confronting for both the student and the teacher. While care in the design of learning activities can be taken, the potential vulnerability of students needs to be considered carefully. Staff should be appropriately trained to respond to students in this type of learning environment, and students must have easy access to counselling and support services during their acculturation and sojourn abroad period.

Delivery of a course of this nature requires substantial coordination. Facilitation of experience, a key element in the course design, requires planning not required in a 'traditional' course delivery. This is taken into account in course design, with some flexibility built into the delivery and assessment structure.

Ways to improve

As this course is interdisciplinary and intensive, limitations around developing a depth of knowledge in intercultural competence must be acknowledged. Given the immersive context of the course, priority can be given to developing students' capabilities to employ specific strategies for sense-making and coping with intercultural encounters. These can be contextualised within a theoretical framework, but the emphasis will remain on application of theory to experience rather than breadth of theoretical coverage.

Additionally, currency of the various elements of the course (e.g., first-hand experience and contextual content) needs to be ensured in a rapidly changing context. An annual review cycle needs to be complemented by a less formal interim review of content and learning activities each semester to ensure the course is optimising exposure to contemporary trends or events in Vietnamese society.

Finally, scalability of the content, in particular related to face-to-face debriefings, needs to be considered with potentially different formats used for larger groups. Requests to deliver the course offshore as a pre-departure preparation module have also been received, and these will necessitate a significant reframing of the experiential elements of the course.

References

Byram, M. (1997). *Teaching and assessing intercultural communicative competence*. Clevedon: Multilingual Matters.

Deardorff, D. K. (2006). Identification and assessment of intercultural competence as a student outcome of internationalization. *Journal of Studies in International Education*, *10*(3), 241–66.

Woods, C. (2007). Researching and developing interdisciplinary teaching: Towards a conceptual framework for classroom communication. *Higher Education*, *54*(6), 853–66.

CS18

Comprehensive and integrated intercultural development

A model for institutional change

Paula J. Pedersen (University of Minnesota-Duluth)

Context

The University of Minnesota-Duluth (UMD) is a regional comprehensive university in Minnesota. UMD is the second largest in the University of Minnesota system and in the state, enrolling approximately 11,000 students annually, employing over 2,400 faculty and staff.

To facilitate institution-wide increased intercultural competence, a faculty fellow for intercultural initiatives was hired in the chancellor's unit. In this role, I proposed a model (Fig. CS18.1) for institutional change that expanded upon the work of Adams and Love (2010). This expanded model aligns with UMD's strategic plan, Goal No. 2: 'Create a positive and inclusive campus climate for all by advancing equity, diversity and social justice.'

This case study outlines an institution-wide effort towards increased intercultural competence. This involves initiatives at each level of the model for institutional change.

Goals and outcomes

Adams and Love (2010) argue that we focus faculty development efforts on all four institutional quadrants. The adaptation for this institution-wide effort extended their model to encompass goals of comprehensive and integrated intercultural competence across all units: (1) *students* (extended to student cultural self-awareness and growth in curricular and co-curricular contexts); (2) *faculty* self-awareness (extended to faculty/staff and administration through professional development efforts); as well as comprehensive integrated curricular reform including: (3) *content* and (4) *process* around issues of intercultural competence, diversity, and social justice. Outcomes of the institution-wide effort include increased intercultural competence of individuals across campus, which, in turn, increases inclusion in policies and practices, pedagogy, and curriculum.

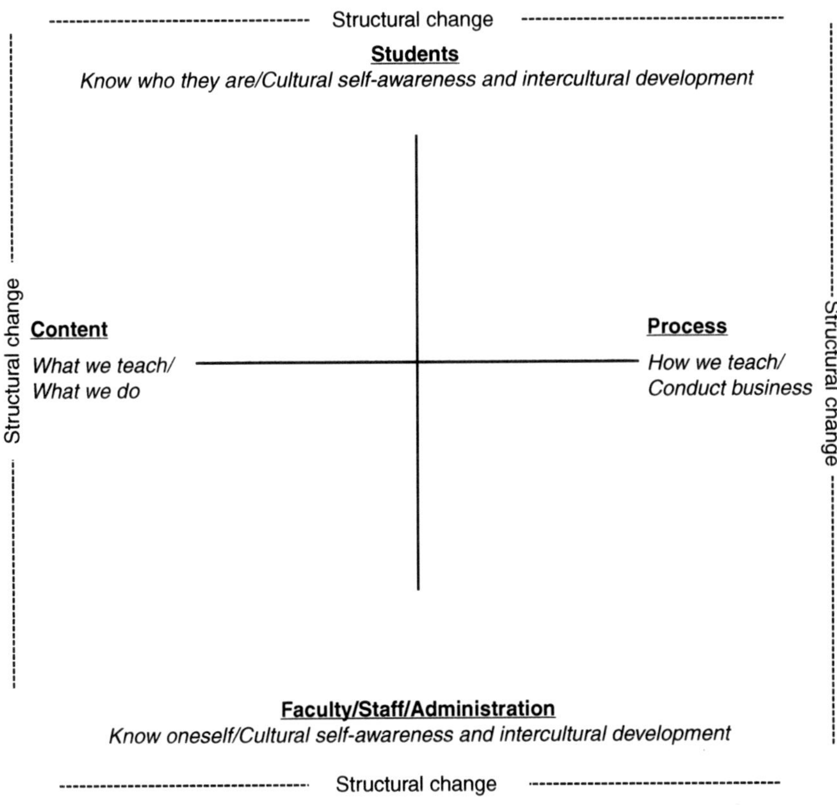

Figure C18.1 Adapted from Adams & Love (2010, p. 8); Four-Quadrant Analysis of Teaching and Learning. With permission by P. J. Pedersen.

Framework of intercultural competence

Student development efforts include all levels of the institution at UMD, from Welcome Week activities, to first-year experience, housing, student life, the classroom, and our degree programmes. Climate surveys and focus groups are conducted every three years to determine the level of inclusion/exclusion that underrepresented groups feel on campus. Other tracking takes place through the Campus Climate Initiative, where unit-level efforts that align with Goal 2 are reported. These are a less direct measure of our intercultural competence. The AAC&U Rubric on intercultural competence and knowledge based on Bennett's and Deardorff's theoretical work is used for course and programme efforts. The Intercultural Development Inventory and Intercultural Effectiveness Scale have been utilised (towards self-awareness/growth and as pre/post indicators) for some student efforts.

A focus on the *faculty*, staff, and administration self-development aspect is often neglected in higher education. The goal is to build internal capacity among all employees towards increased intercultural competence. Employee self-development is approached through a cohort-training model. Groups of eighteen take a 4.5-day off-campus experience to explore their cultural self-awareness, learn about 'the other', and various typologies of differences. This includes a variety of models/tools starting with the workplace DiSC profile to begin to learn about self/other and navigating differences. Other tools/models include the Intercultural Development Inventory, Intercultural Conflict Styles Inventory, Intercultural Intelligence Inventory (CQ), and an adapted version of the AAC&U VALUE Rubric (Intercultural Knowledge and Competence) as self-awareness/development tools.

At UMD, associated intervention efforts for *process* and *content* in the model include curriculum integration and inclusive pedagogy through instructional development and extend beyond the classroom context towards a more inclusive lens regarding *what* we do and *how* we do it, campus-wide. Curriculum reform is approached through an instructional development community of practice. Faculty meet throughout a semester to gain ideas, support, and resources towards inclusive pedagogy and curriculum infusion of diverse perspectives into their course(s). The community of practice begins with syllabus creation and class community-building and ends with assessment/evaluation.

Developing intercultural competence

The Developmental Model of Intercultural Sensitivity (DMIS; Bennett, 1986) is useful for differentiating the developmental worldviews for guiding intercultural growth and development. The DMIS looks at 'orientations toward cultural difference' as a progressive and developmental process. The focus is not on culture-specific information but rather on the development of a broader and more complex worldview when approaching difference. Our initiatives (described in the framework above) have focused on this more culture-general approach to difference with the intercultural competence goal of increasing overall range and possible lenses towards navigating difference.

Assessing intercultural competence

The Intercultural Development Inventory (Hammer, 2009) is used as a pre- and post-assessment and self-development intervention. The AAC&U VALUE Rubric on Intercultural Knowledge and Competence defines intercultural competence as 'a set of cognitive, affective, and behavioral skills and characteristics that support effective and appropriate interaction in a variety of cultural contexts' (Bennett, 2008). The rubric was also informed by Deardorff (2006) who organised attitudes, knowledge, skills, and internal and external outcomes into an intercultural competence model. The corresponding components of the

AAC&U Rubric knowledge (cultural self-awareness), skills (empathy, verbal and non-verbal communication), and attitudes (curiosity, openness) are used not only as intervention but also as assessment. An adapted version of the VALUE Rubric is administered as a retrospective pre- and post-tool for staff and faculty who have participated in personal intercultural competence development efforts.

Upon completion, employees enter an ongoing commitment to self-development and institutional change via regular continuing education, lunch-time conversations, and educational emails. Employees are also encouraged to participate in campus offerings from the office of cultural diversity and international programmes and continued intercultural competence offerings.

Annual ongoing assessment for staff and faculty development includes an online survey asking: (1) What have you done to facilitate your *own* journey towards the development of a more inclusive lens?; and (2) What have you done to bring that awareness, insight, and/or change to your own unit? Some units adapted these questions for annual performance evaluation purposes.

As this initiative ends its third year, interview data will be collected from staff and faculty to help determine more direct institutional impacts.

Lessons learned

The importance of administrative buy-in and strategic-level support was critical towards the success of this institution-wide effort. UMD is fortunate to have Goal 2 in our strategic plan such that the development of intercultural competence, institution-wide, is arguably a strategy towards this inclusive campus climate goal. All top administrators have completed the staff development component and encouraged their staff to attend. The additional support of resources for training, my position, as well as a seat on the chancellor's cabinet have all served to elevate this work to an important institution-wide effort.

Human Resources' interest in including Goal 2 as an item in performance evaluations has been a gift and curse. More staff are signing up for our programmes but don't always have the internal drives and motivations for them to be impactful. Due to contractual and union agreements, the same has not been the case for faculty, who argue that such efforts are not rewarded or valued in the promotion and tenure merit system.

Assessment is difficult: this work is slow and long term. It is difficult to measure personal impacts and even more difficult to determine institutional impact. This third year, I am working with our assessment coordinator to facilitate individual interviews with key constituents in an attempt to track and measure institutional impacts.

Ways to improve

Structural change was added to Adams and Love's (2010) model through efforts towards changes in policy and procedure that increase equity and inclusion.

Further structural shifts in the promotion and tenure merit system, where faculty cultural and intercultural competence is clearly articulated as a performance and evaluation indicator, would help greatly. Unless faculty have internal motivation towards their own intercultural growth and development, their participation is minimal. The argument of 'what counts' towards advancement and the culture of faculty content expertise as central will continue to hinder efforts to recruit faculty into the self-development and curricular reform aspects of this effort.

A more targeted and strategic approach, with broader buy-in and increased staff support, could have resulted in fewer roadblocks and greater involvement. We started with one person and position, building internal capacity for facilitation and training and scattered efforts that represent different aspects of the model. Ideally, faculty self-development would become the foundational intervention followed by curriculum integration efforts. After the faculty, content, and process aspects of the model have been addressed, a focus on classroom-based student intervention and intercultural competence development would likely follow.

References

Adams, M., & Love, B. (2010). A social justice education faculty development framework for a post-Grutter era. In K. Skubikowski, C. Wright, & R. Graf (Eds.), *Social justice education: Inviting faculty to transform their institutions* (pp. 3–25). Sterling, VA: Stylus.

Association of American Colleges & Universities. (n.d.). *Intercultural knowledge and competence VALUE rubric.* Retrieved from www.aacu.org/value/rubrics/intercultural-knowledge

Bennett, J. M. (2008). Transformative training: Designing programs for culture learning. In M. A. Moodian (Ed.), *Contemporary leadership and intercultural competence: Understanding and utilizing cultural diversity to build successful organizations* (pp. 95–110). Thousand Oaks, CA: Sage.

Bennett, M. J. (1986). A developmental approach to training for intercultural sensitivity. *International Journal of Intercultural Relations, 10*(2), 179–96.

Deardorff, D. K. (2006). Identification and assessment of intercultural competence as a student outcome of internationalization. *Journal of Studies in International Education, 10*(3), 241–66.

Hammer, M. R. (2009). The Intercultural Development Inventory (IDI): An approach for assessing and building intercultural competence. In M. A. Moodian (Ed.), *Contemporary leadership and intercultural competence: Understanding and utilizing cultural diversity to build successful organizations.* (pp. 203–17). Thousand Oaks, CA: Sage.

Pedersen, P. J. (2012). Comprehensive and integrated intercultural development: A model for institutional change. Retrieved from www.d.umn.edu/chancellor/climate/UMDModelforPoster.pdf

—— (2016). Toward intercultural development and a model for institutional change. In D. Gross, K. Abrams, & C. Z. Enns (Eds.), *Internationalizing the undergraduate psychology curriculum: Lessons learned at home and abroad.* Washington, DC: American Psychological Association Press.

CS19

Global learning at Agnes Scott College

Janelle S. Peifer and Elaine Meyer-Lee (Agnes Scott College)

Context

Agnes Scott College, a selective and remarkably diverse (racially, socio-economically, etc.) women's college in Decatur, Georgia, is reinventing a liberal-arts education for the twenty-first century through Summit. Summit is a unique initiative through which every student, regardless of major, is prepared to lead effectively in a global society through a curriculum and co-curriculum focused on global learning and leadership development. Students also create a digital portfolio that integrates their college experience and build a personal board of advisers who guide them throughout. Summit is Agnes Scott's strategic approach to enrolment growth that remains true to the college's identity and mission.

Since the fall of 2013, the faculty at Agnes Scott have driven the development of Summit, from discussions about the definition of 'global', to articulating learning outcomes, to designing all new general education requirements to address these outcomes, to developing the shared content and assignments for Journeys, the required 4-credit global-learning course. This foundation of the global-learning component of Summit for all first-year students includes a nine-day global cultural immersion in March.

This case study will focus on this Journeys course, which was piloted in 2014–15 and launched in 2015–16. It will offer transferable lessons learned relevant to launching innovative, comprehensive intercultural competence development initiatives on other campuses.

Goals and outcomes

As active participants in the Journeys course, students work towards the following intercultural competence-related learning outcomes, which are under the overarching Summit outcome of the capacity to 'Demonstrate knowledge and skills essential for global engagement':

1. Identify key global structures, systems, and processes.
2. Articulate evolving and competing views of globalisation and its benefits and challenges for human populations and natural systems.

3. Recognise diversity and inequalities within and among societies in a global context.
4. Critically analyse common motivations for travel to 'other' cultures.
5. Recognise varied perceptions and viewpoints of self and other cultures.
6. Identify the complexities of intercultural communication by articulating basic cultural norms and behaviours in travel destination.
7. Draw connections between travel destination/experiences and course concepts.

The concepts presented in class, embodied in the cultural immersion, and assessed through multimethod assessment techniques help first-year students develop basic intercultural knowledge, skills, and awareness that will be enhanced in subsequent college years.

Framework of intercultural competence

The working framework of the Summit Global Learning is informed by aspects of Braskamp, Braskamp, Merrill, and Engberg's (2008) model, Deardorff's (2006) Intercultural Competence Framework, and Bennett's (1993) Developmental Model of Intercultural Sensitivity. The framework incorporates intra- and inter-individual knowledge, skills, and attitudes related to intercultural competence as developed in a liberal-arts environment. The Journeys course focuses on the dynamic process of knowledge development, namely developing a deep understanding of one's home country and its historical and current role in the world (intrapersonal). It also encourages the development of sociolinguistic, culture-general, and culture-specific knowledge about others' countries (interpersonal). Some of the vital intercultural skills fostered include analysis, emotion regulation, and reflection (intrapersonal); and relating/engagement, observation, and listening (interpersonal). Regarding attitudes, the Journeys course focuses on self-knowledge, personal characteristics, and self-efficacy (intrapersonal); and respect, openness, and empathy (interpersonal). These intra- and interpersonal knowledge, skills, and attitudes are interpreted through the lens of liberal arts learning, in which intellectual, social, and personal development inform how students situate themselves within a wider context.

Developing intercultural competence

After completing a one-credit introductory course on global learning, all first-year students at Agnes Scott College enrol for the spring semester in a section of the common course: Journeys. Each section focuses on a different global destination (e.g., Jamaica, Panama, Puerto Rico, Martinique, Dominican Republic, Trinidad, Cuba, Bolivia, Nicaragua, Toronto, and New York City in 2016) and content topic (e.g., economics, public health, women's studies). The Journeys course focuses on building students' intellectual understanding, affective awareness, and intercultural skills.

Across all sections of the course, students focus on four key common global themes: (1) identity: self, culture, and Other; (2) ethics of travel; (3) globalisations; and (4) colonialism and imperialism. This content establishes a cognitive base for intercultural competence development with all students and addresses especially the first four learning outcomes through readings and discussion. The course then explores these themes through intentionally active, participatory pedagogical strategies including digital storytelling, community-based projects, and plenary panels and dialogues aimed at translating cognitive awareness into action. The embedded global cultural immersion enables all first-year students to apply and refine these more abstract skills in a lived, personalised way, especially intercultural competence Outcomes 3 and 4. For example, first-year students articulate in writing, class discussions, and pre-travel projects their motivations for wanting to travel outside of the United States and the implications of these motivations. Moreover, through on-site daily reflective practices (i.e. journaling, discussion-based debriefings) students connect wider concepts to a specific location and cultural context (Outcome 7), and grapple deeply with Outcomes 5 and 6. In particular, students are encouraged to explore their individual, intersectional cultural identities within the context of travel. In subsequent years, students will build on these classroom and immersion experiences to further specialise their intercultural knowledge, skills, and awareness.

Assessing intercultural competence

All students participate in a multimethod longitudinal assessment called the Global Perspectives Study (GPS). The GPS takes an intersectional approach to documenting the process of intercultural competence development and captures how different aspects of students' identity, behaviour, and experiences influence this trajectory. The GPS starts at baseline (before students arrive at the institution), includes a follow-up survey each year, and terminates with two long-term follow-up surveys given one and five years post-graduation. The instrument collects data on students':

1. basic demographics (e.g., age, gender, race/ethnicity, socio-economic status);
2. home community (e.g., region, racial/ethnic diversity of community and schools);
3. family variables (e.g., languages spoken at home, beliefs about travel and diversity, immigration status, education level); and
4. individual characteristics (self-efficacy, ethnic identity, national identity, cognitive empathy, big five personality traits, and anxiety/depression).

In addition, the instrument measures students' global competence, using the Global Perspectives Inventory (Braskamp et al., 2008) and tracks their travel and non-travel-based globally related academic, social, work-related, and co-curricular experiences. It also logs students' self-reported goals for their international travel experiences (e.g., to have a good time, greater understanding of different cultures). More broadly, our study will assess long- and short-term student outcomes (e.g., satisfaction, diversity of friendships, job placement) and institutional outcomes (e.g., alumni engagement, retention, admissions yield).

As part of the GPS, we also piloted an in-vivo travel observation and self-monitoring protocol of the time around the Journeys cultural immersion itself for one of the sections. Two weeks before the global study tour, students tracked their mood on a daily basis and reported their assumptions about (1) how they believed they would feel while travelling; and (2) how engaged they thought they would be with various aspects of the travel experience. While travelling, they continued tracking their mood and reporting their actual engagement on a daily basis. After returning, they also logged their mood for two weeks. Finally, all faculty completed a uniform rubric on each student assessing selected student learning outcomes related to the Summit objectives. For Outcomes 2, 3, 5, and 7 above, the rubric provided criteria to score students as advanced, competent, developing, or beginning. For example, for Outcome 2, the four criteria in order are:

1. Views are considered critically, stated clearly, and described comprehensively, providing all relevant information necessary for nuanced understanding.
2. Views are considered critically, described, and clarified so that understanding is not seriously impeded by omissions.
3. Views are stated but description leaves some terms undefined, ambiguities unexplored, boundaries undetermined, and/or backgrounds unknown.
4. Views are unstated or stated without clarification or description.

Lessons learned

1. Defining sharp, narrowly defined terms and learning outcomes at the outset is crucial, as faculty have many different views. Clear agreed-upon outcomes are also the bedrock of good assessment.
2. Full-time faculty must drive all curricular aspects, but broader-based buy-in across the staff, trustees, and even alumni is also key. Faculty/staff development and incentives are therefore imperative.
3. Required global study for a whole very diverse class at one time, while bold and exciting, creates many logistical challenges beyond the expected pedagogical ones. We are therefore now building some tasks (such as passport attainment) into the coursework and providing even more support for specific identity groups such as LGBT-identified students, students of colours, students with disabilities, and Muslim students, through both co-curricular workshops and an in-class guest lecture.

4. Assessing intercultural competence through one specific programme, such as Journeys, is difficult to parse from within a larger multidimensional initiative and requires some creativity. We are therefore experimenting with multiple qualitative methods to focus specifically on the Journeys experience, as described above.

Ways to improve

The first official iteration of the Journeys course proved remarkably successful pedagogically and logistically. In the future, Agnes Scott aims to build upon this success and

1. streamline student learning outcomes to ensure that each is tied to a clear, actionable, and measurable goal and aligned earning interventions, including team-based strategies and other approaches to encourage students as active collaborators;
2. integrate assessment (informed by the revised course outcomes) more naturally into the course for meaningful faculty and student participation, using data such as course artefacts, student interviews before and after travel, focus groups, and in-trip observational protocols completed by trip co-leaders;
3. support sustained multidisciplinary collaboration among faculty who design and lead the course through weekly informal lunch meetings to share highly effective activities and discuss approaches to tackling common content. We will also utilise online collaborative platforms to share and archive materials.

Overall, the Journeys course will continue to provide an academic and experiential foundation in global learning and intercultural competence for all Agnes Scott students to build from over the course of their college years.

References

Bennett, M. J. (1993). *Intercultural sensitivity: Principles of training and development.* Portland, OR: Portland State University.

Braskamp, L. A., Braskamp, D. C., Merrill, K. C., & Engberg, M. (2008). Global Perspective Inventory (GPI): Its purpose, construction, potential uses, and psychometric characteristics. Retrieved from www.gpi.hs.iastate.edu/documents/BraskampBraskampEngberg2014GPIPsychometrics.pdf

Deardorff, D. K. (2006). Identification and assessment of intercultural competence as a student outcome of internationalization. *Journal of Studies in International Education*, *10*(3), 241–66.

CS20

From intercultural adaptation experience to intercultural competence in a multicultural classroom

An Ran (South China University of Technology)

Context

This case study demonstrates the intercultural competence of mutual cultural adaptation in a Chinese multicultural classroom in which students come from more than fifteen different cultures, and how Chinese students as the host nationals improve their intercultural competence in the classroom. The case emphasises both the mutuality between international students and Chinese students and the adaptation of Chinese students.

The course integrates theory and practice of intercultural communication. It requires intercultural collaboration for students to succeed in this class. The teaching method reflects a Western learning model that emphasises interaction among participants. The teaching materials in this class include a textbook and other learning tools such as films, videos, research articles, stories, and student work.

The overall goal of the course is to develop student's understanding of their intercultural responses, by encouraging students to practise and test intercultural learning, to self-analyse, and finally to challenge students' (particularly Chinese students') cultural comfort in an unfamiliar language and classroom setting.

Goals and outcomes

Course goals:

- To promote intercultural interaction in the classroom.
- To increase students' cultural memory and shared individual experiences.
- To develop students' self-identity and intercultural identity.

These goals aim to help students cultivate intercultural competence in a multicultural classroom.

Course outcomes:

- To reach a better understanding of the concepts of intercultural adaptation and intercultural communication competence through the process of multicultural interaction and learning.
- To demonstrate the process of structuring the multicultural classroom to ensure that no one culture was dominant, that mutual adaptation occurred, and that individual intercultural communication competence improved.
- To canvas a variety of theoretical contexts from the observations of interactions within the intercultural classroom, and determine what further research might be undertaken to identify ways of enhancing the classroom experience for 'visitor' and 'host' participants at Chinese universities.

Framework of intercultural competence

The Yin Yang theory is employed to stipulate intercultural competence in a multicultural classroom. Chinese philosophy dictates that all universal phenomena are created by the dual cosmic forces called Yin and Yang. Yin represents feminine forces such as the moon, water, darkness, passivity, and femininity. Yang, on the other hand, represents masculine forces such as the sun, fire, light, activity, and masculinity. The image of Yin Yang suggests that there exists no absolute borderline between the dark (Yin) and the white (Yang) areas (see Figure CS20.1). The dark fish eye that exists in the white area and the white fish eye that exists in the dark area allows the two forces to interpenetrate and transform each other to form a dynamic unity. Figure CS20.1 illustrates the state of students as they choose to accept or refuse adaptation when the Yin Yang theory is applied to the multicultural classroom:

The theory of Yin Yang is used to explain the constant changes shown in a class. Changes occur when students decide to embrace intercultural contacts with classmates. In other words, students can decide whether 'I want to keep my own culture' or 'I want to change.' Moreover, the change is based on the degree to which students accept their counterparts' culture and retain their own. Choosing to change only certain aspects of one's culture in the process of acculturation often leads to feelings of dissonance. In order to establish inner harmony, it is

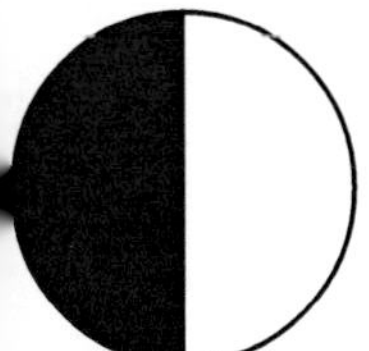

Figure CS20.1 The Yin Yang theory applied in the multicultural classroom.

necessary to keep a balance both in mind and action between the two options. Reaching this state of balance or harmony is a gradual cyclic transformation process for all involved.

Developing intercultural competence

Based on the learning goals and outcomes, the course aims to establish a new multicultural mode for interaction. In this specific environment, all students learn how to act, express themselves naturally, and ensure cooperative communication.

Figure CS20.2 shows that at the beginning of the course all students in the class will face cultural and linguistic problems, which will naturally lead to the experience of self-reflection. Negotiation, dialogue, and change should then follow until a state of balance has been reached. This process does not happen only once; instead, it is a cyclic process in which multiple revolutions present themselves throughout the course.

The context is important for the success of the class, specifically, a multicultural classroom in a Chinese higher education institution. In the class, Chinese students face the problems of language expression combined with an unfamiliar teaching and learning style. These students may experience frustration to the point of desiring withdrawal from the course. Intercultural communication theories are taught in the class, and students are assigned individual and group projects for the express purpose of creating situations to facilitate and observe progressive changes. In this special context, both the international and Chinese students are required to interact with each other through the process of negotiation and dialogue. This platform creates a safe space for students to develop skills in solving problems and managing conflicts to reach a state of harmonious balance.

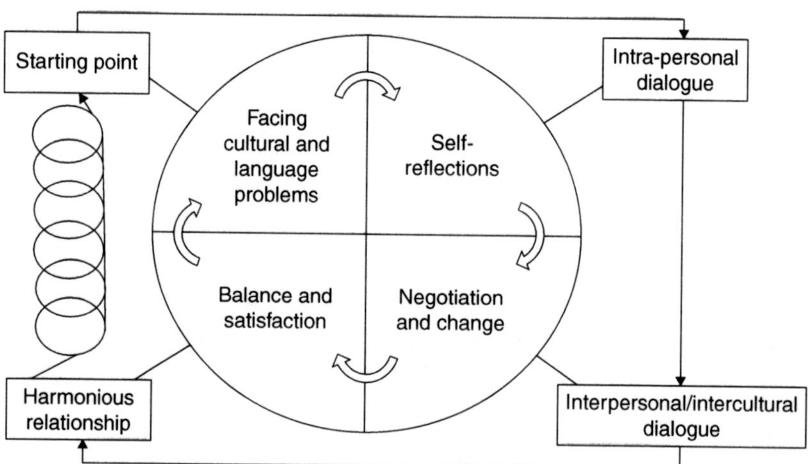

Figure CS20.2 A multicultural interaction model.

Assessing intercultural competence

Final grades will be cumulative and based on embedded course assignments designed to collect direct evidence of students' intercultural knowledge and development:

- essay 30 per cent
- presentation 20 per cent
- class attendance 20 per cent
- class discussion 20 per cent
- other assignments 10 per cent.

Students' class interactions were designed to see whether they can apply the intercultural theories that they learn into practice. For example, in the intercultural adaptation section, when the concept of the U-curve was first introduced, I used an academic article that challenged the U-curve. Students were also made familiar with Kim's dynamic model. This teaching aroused students' thinking to treat intercultural adaptation from one's personal experience and perspective not just in context of the dominant theory on the subject.

Students' daily journal assessments helped to evaluate their reflections through the whole course learning. This student excerpt will serve as an example:

> Jojo from the Philippines described his difficult situation when he got *herpes zoster*. The whole ordeal was very stressful for him because of the language barrier. He worried that not being able to effectively communicate might lead to a misdiagnosis. When I [as a Chinese person] heard this, I felt a foreigner's intercultural adaptation is even more difficult than mine. For me, adaptation is just limited to this classroom. Everyone describes his or her own intercultural experience uniquely. Mine is only one of those voices.

Drama is one method through which to show that students know different models of intercultural training. For the section of 'Models of Intercultural Training', students used drama to show the features of different training models. The other students, as the audience, then named the features they found in the drama. The instructor made a conclusion in the end. It was so informative that all the participants were fully engrossed in the process and responded that they had learned a lot from this lesson.

Video design is another way to display students' real life intercultural competence. Students were encouraged to make a video to reflect their own intercultural experience and to present their ideas and opinions for group discussion.

Team work is a strategy that serves to solve intercultural conflict. Again, a student excerpt will serve as an example:

> In the beginning, we (Chinese) were all afraid to speak to the international students, but we needed to finish our team assignments so we had to. We

had to make appointments with them about times and places for discussions. We arrived on time to the first two appointments but they didn't come. In order to change this situation, we had a meeting to discuss our attitude toward the assignment. After that, we came to an agreement that everyone should support the preparation of the assignment and should be actively engaged in it. Since then, when we have a problem, we address it, discuss it, and come to agreement.

Lessons learned

1. Introduce theory to students and help them relate these to personal experiences. This approach increases the degree of intercultural competence, which is demonstrated by the improvement of students' abilities in the aspects of intercultural awareness, intercultural sensitivity and intercultural adroitness.
2. 'Appropriateness' and 'effectiveness' are used as criteria for evaluating students' intercultural competence. All intercultural interaction in the class is expected to reflect the two criteria. That is, first, students should be trained to have the awareness that there are differences among different cultures but there is no right or wrong for these variations. Second, some social skills can be used to assess a better relationship within people from different cultural backgrounds. Third, language is very important in intercultural communication.
3. Use presentation or video design to assess student language usage, and whether they select appropriate words in intercultural interactions. Due to the richness of language, message content is easily distorted by individual decoders if the sender is not careful with word choice. For example, the colour 'red' is considered to be the equivalent of 'being dangerous' in some Western societies while it means 'being happy' for most of the Asian residents.

Ways to improve

1. In class, facilitators are fully occupied; however, outside of class, contact among those students needs more detailed observation.
2. An area for further investigation is exploring whether the close intercultural interaction which was developed in the multicultural classroom continued after the completion of the course.

References

Chen, G. M. (2001). Toward transcultural understanding: A harmony theory of Chinese communication. In V. H. Milhouse, M. K. Asante, & P. O. Nwosu (Eds.). *Transcultural realities: Interdisciplinary perspectives on cross-cultural relations* (pp 55–70). Thousand Oaks, CA: Sage.

Fang, T., & Faure, O. G. (2011). Chinese communication characteristics: A Yin Yang perspective. *International Journal of Intercultural Relations*, *35*(3), 320–33.

CS21

Issues in global displacement

Exploring community-based language learning

Deborah S. Reisinger (Duke University)

Context

Issues in Global Displacement is a discipline-based upper-level university course designed to develop learner intercultural competence through a community-based service-learning initiative. This course is taught at Duke University, a private institution in the south-eastern United States that enrols approximately 7,000 undergraduate students. The professor, Deb Reisinger, is a faculty member in the Department of Romance Studies and affiliate faculty in Global Health.

Issues in Global Displacement is taught on a yearly basis. It enrols approximately fifteen students each semester (the enrolment cap) and draws a mix of sophomores, juniors, and seniors. The course is based in the Romance Studies Department and is cross-listed with Global Health and the Certificate Program in Ethics. It is taught in French. The community-based learning component of this course provides students the opportunity to put into practice their study of global displacement. Students are paired with French-speaking refugee families in Durham, North Carolina, with whom they spend a minimum of twenty hours over the course of the semester. Each week, students spend one to two hours tutoring ESL (English as a Second Language), developing digital literacy skills, and fostering cultural understanding through shared experiences such as music, sports, and cooking.

Goals and outcomes

The course's learning outcomes state that by the end of the semester students should be able to:

- demonstrate *intercultural communicative competencies that include empathy, flexibility, and tolerance for other cultures*;
- articulate an understanding of the *complex interplay of individual and collective processes* related to refugee and community populations in host and home societies;

- appreciate the ways in which particular narratives of refugee experience *can both extend and/or diminish trauma*;
- critically analyse the histories of narrative and testimony and their *implications for recording refugee experience.*

Framework of intercultural competence

At the outset of the course, we share multiple models of intercultural competence but draw specifically on Deardorff's (2006) Process Model of Intercultural Competence and Bennett's (2008) definition of intercultural competence to frame our understanding of intercultural competence as a set of non-linear competencies that can be developed and honed, but not acquired. While bringing student awareness to cultural competence is important, we also believe that it is only through interaction with others that the skills of global competence can be demonstrated. Because our course takes place in another language, and because the students' interactions with their community partners are primarily in a second (or third language), we also use the ACTFL World-Readiness Standards (2015) as a way to frame and assess interculturality.

Developing intercultural competence

This course was intentionally designed according to Wiggins & McTighe's (2005) backward design model. Rather than first choosing readings, then creating assignments, and, finally, developing assessments, we began instead by identifying desired results for our students (What do we want them to be able to do?). Only then do we determine evidence for meeting those learning outcomes, and, afterwards, we develop the activities that will help foster student learning. In order to grasp both the scale of global migration and the challenges faced by an individual refugee, we determined that students need to develop intercultural competencies such as empathy, flexibility, and tolerance. The other course goals cannot be attained without this crucial element, so it is here that we focus our primary attention.

Assessing intercultural competence

With the goals of intercultural competence put into place, we then establish the kinds of acceptable evidence that will best demonstrate the development of intercultural competence, including its assessment. This evidence includes:

1. **Pre- and post-semester self-assessments.** In this exercise, students complete the AAC&U intercultural competence self-assessment rubric, at both the beginning and at the end of the semester. With each self-assessment, students write a reflective, analytic essay in which they explain their choices.

2. **Impactful community projects.** These projects include public-service announcements designed around a health or education issue, a campus community event (picnic, film showing, etc.), and a formal presentation or exhibit about refugee resettlement. Students curate these projects with their community partners, requiring them to create with, rather than just for, the community. In the museum exhibit, for instance, students interviewed refugees families, who selected photos and quotes that they thought would best represent their experience in the Durham community. In another project, students wrote a series of articles related to refugee resettlement that was published in a local newspaper. Community partners were part of the research project, contributing self-authored photography and interviews.
3. **Reflective writing assignments.** Weekly, guided reflections take the form of a blog (open only to class members) and a final reflective essay (submitted to their instructor). Since we did not want to set expectations for constant transformation around intercultural competence, we provided prompts to students, such as 'How does power manifest in your community partnership?' 'How does reading or listening to refugee testimony affect your understanding of migration?' and 'What is the role of language in cultural assimilation and integration?' The blog thus allowed students not only to reflect upon their partnerships but also to incorporate and synthesise analyses of course readings that included literature, law, witness testimony, and sociological theory. While intercultural competence cannot be staged, these kinds of questions can help lead students to reflect upon issues they might otherwise overlook. Finally, by using multiple methods to assess our objectives, both students and teachers can better gauge where they are at any given moment.

In the final stage of course planning using the backward design model, we create specific learning experiences that help foster the development of intercultural competence. First, we place students in partnership with local refugee families from the Democratic Republic of the Congo and the Central African Republic. Partnerships are assigned based on proximity to campus, preference for age group, shared interests, and particular skillsets. Home visits offer students a rare glimpse into the daily life of their community partners, but students can be overwhelmed and ill equipped to decode cultural differences or unpack the lived experiences they are witnessing. To help process these moments, we also invite to our class a series of expert guest speakers who have lived or worked with refugee communities both here and abroad. Class activities such as structured role plays help students recognise such moments of dissonance and give them the opportunity to work through feelings of discomfort, be they linguistic or psychological.

Next, we ask students to read refugee-authored narratives and testimonies. The goal of reading first-person stories is to develop empathy and understanding and both to support and to challenge their experiences (Kidd & Castano 2013; Djikic, Oatley, & Moldoveanu, 2013). Readings include accounts of internal displacement (Benou's *La Troupe de Bemba était tombée sous nos têtes*), testimonies by asylum seekers (Manson Vigou's *Journal d'un demandeur d'asile*), narratives of flight (ACAT's *Je n'avais plus le choix, il fallait fuir*), and first-person stories of host country integration (Laferrière's *Chronique de la dérive douce*, Kim Thuy's *Ru*). We also include poetry by survivors of the Rwandan genocide (Djedanoum, Rurangwa), a documentary film about refugee caseworkers in France (*Les Arrivants*, 2014), and a fictionalised account of economic refugees from Senegal (*La Pirogue*, 2010). (In addition to these first-person perspectives, we study the United Nations Declaration of Human Rights, United Nations High Commissioner for Refugees [UNHCR] policy, and US policies for refugee resettlement.)

Lessons learned

Through this course, we have learned that the development of intercultural competencies is neither sequential nor is it assured. We cannot 'make it happen' for our students. We can, however, foster learner growth throughout the semester by sharing historical and literary perspectives, by incorporating oral and written guided reflection, and by offering occasional mediation in challenging moments. These contiguous assessments and supported learning opportunities help students develop awareness of intercultural competence, and, by using multiple models of assessment, we can more accurately capture learner growth. Finally, it is valuable to make the process of intercultural competence transparent to students. Students come to community-based learning experiences with unconscious expectations that may need to be revisited and realigned to realities of their situations. By allowing students to self-assess their own learning, and also (re) adjust their attitudes, actions, and goals throughout the course, they can have a more positive experience.

Ways to improve

As we go forward with this project, we are actively seeking more deliberate ways to incorporate our community partners in our work. In the same ways and for the same reasons that we hope to increase the intercultural competence of our students, we can support our community partners. By being more explicit about these goals with our families, we may be able to accelerate their integration into US culture.

References

American Council on the Teaching of Foreign Languages. (2016). World-readiness standards for learning languages. Retrieved from www.actfl.org/publications/all/world-readiness-standards-learning-languages

Association of American Colleges and Universities (AAC&U). (2016). VALUE Rubric on intercultural knowledge and competence. Retrieved from www.aacu.org/value/rubrics/intercultural-knowledge

Bennett, M. (1993). Towards ethnorelativism: A developmental model of intercultural sensitivity. In R. Paige (Ed.), *Education for the intercultural experience* (pp. 22–71). Yarmouth, ME: Intercultural Press.

Deardorff, D. K. (2006). Identification and assessment of intercultural competence as a student outcome of internationalization. *Journal of Studies in International Education*, *10*(3), 241–66.

Djikic, M., Oatley, K., & Moldoveanu, M. (2013). Reading other minds: Effects of literature on empathy. *Scientific Study of Literature*, *3*(1), 28–47.

Kidd, D., & Castano, E. (2013). Reading literary fiction improves theory of mind. *Science*, *342*(6156), 377–80.

Wiggins, G., & McTighe, J. (2005). *Understanding by design*. Alexandria, VA: Association for Supervision and Curriculum Development.

CS22

'Intercultureality' at work

Claudia Bulnes Sánchez and Eveke de Louw
(The Hague University of Applied Sciences)

Context

European Studies is one of the most international English-medium programmes at The Hague University of Applied Sciences (THUAS), a medium-sized Dutch institution of higher education offering bachelor's and master's degree programmes to over 25,000 students of more than 143 different nationalities. Its primary goal is to deliver interculturally competent graduates for the international job market through a fully internationalised curriculum whereby students come to understand the global issues of the twenty-first-century world by experiencing them in the international classroom. Additionally, European Studies operates one of the largest exchange programmes in the Netherlands.

Goals and outcomes

The programme imparts twenty-first-century skills to international professionals. It combines the knowledge of business and public management with communication, critical thinking, and research skills allied to an international, intercultural, and multilingual approach that prepares students to meet the needs of employers in the public and private sectors worldwide. Its interdisciplinary nature, the strong presence of foreign languages, a semester-long exchange, and its geographic location are important pull factors. Typically, European Studies students are interested in other cultures, are open minded, and are eager to explore the world. The programme's strength is that the skills set conferred upon its alumni opens them up to multiple and diverse employability scenarios. In sum, European Studies graduates are multidisciplinary, mobile, flexible, and highly competent human resources, prepared for the new structures of employment in a constantly changing and challenging international socio-economic context. They are employed in all sectors in many different walks of life as they can apply employable skills, foreign languages, and divergent content knowledge in different cultural settings.

Framework of intercultural competence

The programme's philosophy is that intercultural competence can best be encouraged through a comprehensive approach and that it encompasses effective and appropriate communication with other cultures as well as discipline-specific dimensions of internationalisation. Inspired by definitions of Deardorff (2006) and Bennett (2008), among others, European Studies has formulated the following definition of intercultural competence: 'Intercultural competence is a lifelong intrinsic developmental process that transforms one's attitudes, knowledge and skills to communicate effectively and appropriately with people of different cultural backgrounds.' Given the prominent position of intercultural competence in the programme, intercultural competence development is placed at the core of the European Studies competency profile and is the main driver of internationalisation activities; hence the internationalisation goals are geared towards ensuring that the curriculum, its delivery, the learning environment, and its support are aligned and contribute to reaching the intercultural competence learning outcomes while at the same time actively involving students, lecturers, and other stakeholders.

Based on publications by the Association of American Colleges and Universities (2010), Deardorff (2006), Bennett (2008), Byram (1997), Byram and Risager (1999), the American Council on Education (2013), and INCA (European Commission, 2009), among others, a specification of intercultural competence as shown in Table CS22.1 was developed and included in the student learning outcomes.

The central position of intercultural competence in the curriculum and the strong presence of meaningful intercultural and international experiences at home and abroad (both in the formal and informal curriculum) are further supported in an intentional and comprehensive strategy set in an involved, interactive, and intercultural learning environment. European Studies refers to this learning environment as 'intercultureality' and has developed its own theoretical model, which is inspired by seminal works by Betty Leask (2012) and the American Council on Education (2013). The theoretical framework comprises five main pillars which complement each other: (1) the formal curriculum, (2) the informal curriculum, (3) pedagogy, (4) the student experience, and (5) organisational and strategic frameworks.

Development of intercultural competence

Intercultural competence development is embedded in the European Studies curriculum by means of a continuum supported by 'intercultureality'. In the formal curriculum, modules are defined in terms of international learning outcomes and delivered in an intercultural classroom that accommodates diverse cultural backgrounds, materials that include divergent perspectives and inclusive assessment methods. The student experience, which includes a compulsory study abroad

Table CS22.1 Intercultural competence in European Studies programme.

Knowledge	*Skills*	*Attitudes*
K1 Intercultural knowledge of subject area	**S1** Communicates and connects with people in other language communities in a range of settings for a variety of purposes	**A1** Respect for otherness: valuing cultural diversity
K2 Cultural self-awareness	**S2** Team work: • adapt one's own behaviour to different requirements and situations; • problem-solving skills; • negotiation skills.	**A2** Cultural sensitivity: appreciates different cultures and nuances of different cultural perspectives
K3 Culture-general knowledge and understanding: categorisation of cultures, role and impact of culture and others' worldviews	**S3** Relationship-building skills: • listens; • observes; • skills of discovery of otherness.	**A3** Openness: • suspends judgement; • openness to people from other cultures; • openness to international learning.
K4 Specific country and culture knowledge	**S4** Criticality: • analyses; • interprets; • relates; • uses alternate perspectives; • evaluates; • information-gathering skills.	**A4** Curiosity and discovery: initiates and develops interaction with culturally different others
K5 Understands the value of cultural diversity		**A5** Accept and engage ambiguity: • accepts lack of clarity and ambiguity and is able to deal with it constructively; • intuitively understands what other people think and how they feel in concrete situations.

Source: Bulnes & de Louw (2013).

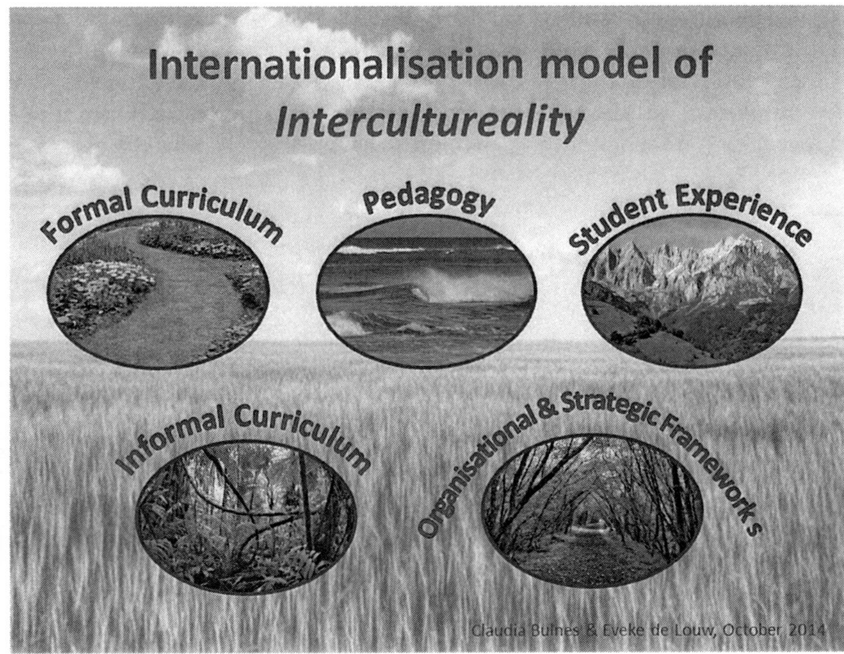

Figure CS22.1 Internationalisation model of intercultureality.

period and international internship, is intensified by group work in projects and other components of the curriculum. Moreover, the exchange period includes a guided trajectory of pre-departure, on-site, and re-entry training. The whole trajectory, called *i*Start, is supervised by specially trained mentors and is compulsory for all students going on exchange. 'Intercultureality' acknowledges the important role of the informal curriculum, and, as such, European Studies actively supports activities that provide students with a platform for informal interaction, envisaging that these ease the way to informal learning. To ensure robust 'intercultureality', the formal and informal curriculum, the pedagogy, and the student experience at European Studies are anchored in solid organisational structures such as a sound internationalisation policy, an internationalisation think tank (*i*Team), a country tutor team, study-abroad mentors, student and staff mobility frameworks, staff training, and investment in the resources required to endorse the internationalisation goals.

Assessment of intercultural competence

The knowledge, skills, and attitudinal components (KSAs) of intercultural competence in European Studies are assessed at different levels. At a modular level, international learning outcomes reflect the KSAs of intercultural competence defined by European Studies, and these are assessed in the different components of the programme (e.g., modules and projects). They include a diversity of assessment methods ranging from written examinations, oral exams, and presentations to comparative essays on contemporary European affairs, portfolios documenting student work in foreign languages, and simulation exercises where students are expected to assume different stakeholder roles in a variety of decision-making settings. This assessment is a direct demonstration of specific knowledge, skills and/or attitudes aided by assessment rubrics that include criteria such as the use of international perspectives and a comparative analysis of practices in different international contexts.

The programme also includes reflective assignments linked to key moments of intercultural competence development, such as *i*Start (aimed at helping students maximise their intercultural learning during their exchange programme) and *i*Reflect, a reflective essay as a condition for graduation. In *i*Reflect students are expected to look upon their intercultural competence development during the European Studies programme and to anticipate its relevance in their future professional careers. Moreover, European Studies considers the exchange and internship as assessment of intercultural competence by themselves. The exchange is not only an intervention to advance intercultural competence, it also constitutes a test of the academic achievement of students in an unfamiliar environment. Additionally, the performance of students during their internship at the end of the programme is evaluated by an in-company mentor, considering the perspective of the workplace while appraising the employability of European Studies graduates.

Lessons learned

The process of defining a transparent intercultural competence continuum in European Studies with its consequent assessment has led to numerous valuable insights. The most important lessons that can be drawn are the following:

- It is paramount that we provide students with the appropriate language tools to be able to express their own development. This will allow them to draw on their self-reflection and assessment, capitalising on their intercultural learning.
- Faculty buy-in is key and will sustain solid grounding of the internationalisation goals of a programme. Placing the discipline at the core of the learning experience and having a pertinent definition of international learning outcomes form the backbone of an international programme. On that account, academics must be given ownership and be aware of the vital contribution they make in the students' development.
- Intercultural competence holds a central position in the programme and needs to be facilitated as such with strategic policy. Investment in resources both at programme and institutional level is crucial to moving things forward.

Ways to improve

As a result of recent research on the development and assessment of the KSAs of intercultural competence in European Studies, the programme is in the process of drawing up a comprehensive assessment plan with a clearer link between key moments of intercultural competence development, which will lead to a more visible intercultural competence continuum, especially with the main stakeholders, our students. Communication and stronger alignment of course elements are vital in this process. An example of an immediate result of such a plan is the alignment of study abroad and internship, which were traditionally organised as separate entities at European Studies with their own processes and offices. This will further solidify the intercultural competence continuum and make the overall mobility organisation smoother. Moreover, more active and better structured involvement of internal and external stakeholders (such as the professional field of work) is sought so that 'intercultureality' remains what it sets out to be: an involved, interactive, and intercultural learning environment for all.

References

American Council on Education. (2013). CIGE model for comprehensive internationalization. Retrieved from www.acenet.edu/news-room/Pages/CIGE-Model-for-Comprehensive-Internationalization.aspx

Association of American Colleges and Universities (2010). Intercultural knowledge and competence VALUE rubric. Retrieved from www.aacu.org/value/rubrics/intercultural-knowledge

Bennett, J. M. (2008). Transformative training: Designing programs for culture learning. In M. A. Moodian (Ed.), *Contemporary leadership and intercultural competence: Understanding and utilizing cultural diversity to build successful organizations* (pp. 95–110). Thousand Oaks, CA: Sage.

Bulnes, C., & de Louw, E. (2013). *Intercultural competence in the European Studies programme*. The Hague: University of Applied Sciences.

Byram, M. (1997). *Teaching and assessing intercultural communicative competence*. Clevedon: Multilingual Matters

Byram, M., & Risager, K. (1999). *Language teachers, politics and cultures*. Clevedon: Multilingual Matters.

Deardorff, D. K. (2006). The identification and assessment of intercultural competence as a student outcome of internationalization at institutions of higher education in the United States. *Journal of Studies in International Education*, *10*(3), 241–6.

—— (Ed.) (2010). *The Sage handbook of intercultural competence*. Thousand Oaks, CA: Sage.

European Commission (2009). The INCA project: Intercultural competence assessment. Retrieved from https://ec.europa.eu/migrant-integration/librarydoc/the-inca-project-intercultural-competence-assessment

Hudzik, J. (2011). *Comprehensive internationalization: From concept to action*. Washington, DC: NAFSA.

Leask, B. (2012). *Internationalization of the curriculum in action: A guide*. University of South Australia.

CS23

Introducing intercultural awareness in a lifelong learning process

Reflections on a formal setting course

Rosa Santibáñez-Gruber, Concepción Maiztegui-Oñate, and Maria Yarosh (University of Deusto)

Context

The course entitled Globalization, Citizenship and Intercultural Competence: An Interdisciplinary Approach for a Cosmopolitan Citizenship reflects the commitment with social justice, core to the University of Deusto's mission and identity. It has been developed in the belief that dealing with difference, whatever its origin, is or will soon become indispensable in any professional activity and in life in general. Taught in a formal setting since 2010–11, this semester-long course is facilitated in English by two local instructors, both with experience of studying and researching abroad.

The course brings together local and international students of different backgrounds. First, second-year undergraduate Spanish students from any department can choose it as an elective. Second, it is open to all undergraduate international students who come to the University of Deusto.

Aimed at helping students become interculturally competent professionals and citizens, the course comprises three units: (1) globalisation; (2) migration and human rights; and (3) intercultural dialogue and intercultural competence. Unit 3 requires thirty-eight hours of work (twelve in class and twenty-six outside). Students are guided towards an awareness of the role cultures play in personal and professional relations and, subsequently, towards learning to look for means to establish effective and appropriate communication with people of different origins, beliefs, etc.

Goals and outcomes

Students who successfully complete this course will:

1. develop an initial but sound theoretical framework that accounts for key notions and associated ideas of intercultural competence;
2. be aware of their own and others' cultural conditioning and able to explain what makes each of us a cultural being;
3. reflect on their own intercultural competence development and incorporate it as a key section into their own CV;

4. be aware of implications of cultural diversity for their own social and future professional environment and, as an observable outcome, formulate recommendations to help a person in their personal and professional environment develop intercultural competence.

Framework of intercultural competence

Unit 3 focuses on intercultural competence as a competence to sensitively perceive, identify, and mediate conflicts grounded in cultural differences (Boecker & Ulama, 2008). Intercultural competence is understood as 'a form of social competence or life skills applied to environments or contexts characterized by cultural diversity' (Santibáñez, Eizaguirre, & Maiztegui, 2011, p. 103). It involves knowledge, attitudes, values, and skills. Intercultural competence is contextual, which means that the space, time, and sphere of application (private, professional, and/or institutional) are important. Finally, one of their main features of intercultural competence as understood here is that it is learned and may be taught.

The teaching and learning approach is based in part on the proposals of Deardorff (2009) and Boecker and Ulama (2008), which highlight the importance of the attitudinal component.

Developing intercultural competence

The emphasis is placed on cultural self-awareness (Berthoin & Friedman, 2003, p. 16; Weigl, 2009), with two major guiding principles: (1) analysing cultures through their values (Hofstede, 2009); and (2) understanding that we, as human and cultural beings, are in constant development (Bennett, 2011).

Cultural awareness comprises awareness of oneself and of oneself in relation to others. It requires critical awareness and capacity to question oneself as well as the other. Our main methodological principles are those of converting students into the protagonists of their own learning and of aiming at maximising exposure to difference while preserving the 'safe' environment of the university classroom.

The participatory methodology helps students become lifelong students. Strategies used include presentation of new contents through analysis of readings, personal reflection, and problem-solving. Students are guided towards seeing how every theoretical conception introduced relates to their life and how it can help them interpret differently their past experiences, current environments, and future interactions. An open class discussion is always followed by a private reflection stage to allow students to become conscious of the new insights.

The main activities are:

- intercultural awareness: our personal and social background;
- the way we cope with diversity: Bennett's stages of intercultural development;
- in contact with diversity: misunderstandings;
- analysing a film (e.g., *Crash*);

- my problem-solving style;
- describing ourselves as a community (Hofstede, 2009);
- summarising the learning and developing proposals for the future.

Every attempt is made to maximise exposure to different perspectives and include a wide range of voices and experiences. First, textual and audio-visual examples 'bring' different aspects of multiple cultures into the classroom while a number of 'guests' share their intercultural experiences. Second, students come from different regional, national, and disciplinary cultures and, therefore, interact with representatives of different cultures in the classroom, bring their own culturally different perspectives into the discussions, and work in culturally mixed groups on particular course tasks outside the classroom. Finally, the language of instruction is foreign to all local and most international students.

Assessing intercultural competence

Formative assessment in the form of peer and facilitator feedback as well as reflection on one's own learning is part of most of the learning activities. Summative assessment consists of an oral and a written part. First, each group orally presents their portfolio (see below) to instructors. Second, each student needs to answer, through a concept map, two general questions related to the contents and compulsory readings of the course. The portfolio for Unit 3 includes:

1. a general concept map integrating all the readings and specific concept maps of each compulsory reading (prepared in team);
2. comments on two questions: (a) What are the main implications of cultural diversity in your own professional field? (b) What could be a set of guidelines to properly deal with cultural diversity (prepared in team)?
3. individual intercultural competence curriculum (prepared individually).

Lessons learned

1. The tasks offered at each stage of the experiential learning cycle need to account for the cultural preferences of the students: e.g., different cultures feel differently about sharing and their representatives might not reflect deeply when afraid of having to share with the whole class afterwards. Therefore, students are informed from the start that they will not share their reflections if they do not feel comfortable with them, but they do need to reflect deeply; alternatively, students are given an opportunity to note down their reflections in writing and share a chosen part with facilitators.
2. If students feel that their peers will benefit from their cultural disclosure and feel that their role of cultural informants/representatives of their culture is valued by both peers and facilitators, they feel better, share more, and the resulting environment is even better for their own and others' intercultural

competence development. In other words, facilitated peer learning seems highly propitious for intercultural competence development.

3. If students have not previously developed awareness of themselves as cultural beings, conditioned by their own culture(s), they are much more likely to focus on superficial aspects of other cultures and are not likely to adopt a lifelong-learning approach to intercultural competence development.
4. Despite being crucial for intercultural competence development, critical reflection on one's own intercultural experience does not seem to come naturally. Learning about aspects of other cultures that are strikingly different from one's own attracts students more, since such knowledge is always listened to with interest and pleasure by peers. Most students, thus, need to be guided to get involved in critical reflection and to develop this habit.
5. Students are more likely to adopt non-superficial approaches to developing intercultural competence if more emphasis is put on formative than on summative assessment. First, students have time to act on feedback and see assessment as aimed at helping them learn better, which increases their motivation and involvement. Second, facilitators are perceived as valuing the process over (or at least as much as) the results, which helps students come to appreciate the process as well and eventually to become self-directed students (cf. assessment for and learning as related to promoting student learning and lifelong learning capacity) (Bloxham & Boyd, 2007).

Ways to improve

Two aspects could be further improved. First, it seems important to ensure that students are supported in their intercultural competence development in a coherent and consistent manner (see Boecker & Ulama, 2008). This means that ideally the university could offer not only a broad range of learning experiences (through separate courses or extra-curricular initiatives) but also a coordination of facilitators and the different activities that help increase students' intercultural competence in order to provide better development conditions.

Second, the effective combination of the 'learning environment' of the course and the methodology proposed to students depends largely on the student group composition. In other words, the transferability of the approach to other contexts might be uncertain. What we mean is that due to a high proportion of international students in the course, local students 'naturally' get involved in processes similar to those international students undergo during the semester abroad: self-analysis (of their values and beliefs) and negotiation with the surrounding environment. Such processes, supported by the tasks proposed, appear to be highly instrumental to intercultural competence development. Yet, since personal, social, and cultural backgrounds of the students are as important as pedagogical factors, the challenge is to discover how to create similar learning-rich environments with less culturally heterogeneous groups.

References

Bennett, M. J. (2011). A developmental model of intercultural sensitivity. Retrieved from www.idrinstitute.org/page.asp?menu1=15

Berthoin, A. A., & Friedman, V. (2003). *Negotiating reality as an approach to intercultural competence.* Berlin: Wissenschaftszentrum Berlin für Sozialforschung.

Bloxham, S., & Boyd, P. (2007). *Developing effective assessment in higher education: A practical guide.* Maidenhead: Open University Press.

Boecker, M. C., & Ulama, L. (2008). *Intercultural competence: The key competence in the 21st century?* Gütersloh: Bertelsmann Stifung & Fondazione Cariplo.

Deardorff, D. K. (Ed.) (2009). *The Sage handbook of intercultural competence.* Thousand Oaks, CA: Sage.

Hofstede, G. J. (2009). The moral circle in intercultural competence. In D. K. Deardorff (Ed.), *The Sage handbook of intercultural competence* (pp. 85–99). Thousand Oaks, CA: Sage.

Santibáñez, R., Eizaguirre, M., & Maiztegui, C. (2011). The importance of intercultural competence in the social intervention professions. In E. Domagala-Zysk & M. Nowak (Eds.). *European social work: Identity, international problems and interventions.* Lublin: Instytut Pedagogiki, Katolickiego Uniwersytelu Lubelskiego Jana Pawla II.

Weigl, R. C. (2009). Intercultural competence through cultural self-study: A strategy for adult learners. *International Journal of Intercultural Relations, 33*(4), 346–60.

CS24

Integrating diversity in academic teaching

Theology and Religious Studies

Peter-Ben Smit, Hester Radstake, Gerdien Bertram-Troost, and Siema Ramdas (Vrije Universiteit Amsterdam)

Context

The master's programme Exploring a Discipline offers a one-year curriculum in a sub-discipline within Theology and Religious Studies. This MA programme has been redeveloped with the aim to intentionally integrate attention for diversity in the teaching and learning processes. The programme's curriculum consists of three compulsory core modules: hermeneutics, research skills, and a master seminar. Besides these courses, students choose three master modules offered at the faculty of theology and write a thesis. A (research) internship is also part of the MA programme.

About fifteen students enrol annually, male and female students are equally represented. The student group shows a broad range considering age, professional backgrounds, prior training, and worldviews. Most students stem from the Western hemisphere, but African and Asian students also attend the programme.

The teachers involved in this programme reflect a broad range of expertise. Most of them are from a Western background and had a Western academic training. Most of them are Christian. Muslim, Buddhist, Hindu, etc., teachers constitute a minority. For the core modules, male and female lecturers are in balance.

Goals and outcomes

Besides stating goals and outcomes that offer possibilities to pay attention to the theme of diversity in teaching and learning, this MA programme also states goals and outcomes specifically related to diversity competencies. These are:

1. being aware of and be able to reflect on the connection between the students' own biography and personality and their academic involvement and interests;
2. being able to constructively participate in the community of students characterised by diversity;
3. being aware of the diversity of perspectives inherent within religious traditions and into factors that influence the way texts are interpreted;

4. being aware of the disciplinary and methodological diversity within the academic community and reflect on this diversity.

Framework of intercultural competence

The MA programme takes an intersectional view on diversity as a starting point. This means that the MA programme is designed upon the idea that somebody's worldview has to be understood as a result of interaction between different aspects of identity, such as age, gender, religion, nationality, ethnicity, and social class (Mackenzie & Stoljar, 2000; Muntinga, Krajenbrink, Peerdeman, Croiset, & Verdonk, 2015; Smit, 2014). This view on diversity is represented in the ultimate learning goal of the master's: students have to be able to integrate an academic perspective with their personal perspective. This implies that their own biography plays an important role in the process of teaching and learning, which requires a space for dialogue and reflection. Here we can see a link with the definition of Freeman et al. (2009) of intercultural competence: 'a dynamic, ongoing, interactive self-reflective learning process that transforms attitudes, skills and knowledge for effective communication and interaction across cultures and contexts' (p. 13). However, because the term 'intercultural competence' risks that diversity is too narrowly perceived from its cultural dimension, it is not used in the context of this MA programme. Instead, it is preferred to use the term 'diversity', in its broadest sense, thereby following the policy at faculty level.

Developing intercultural competence

The master's programme contains several specific learning interventions that intend to realise the diversity related goals as mentioned above. The number(s) behind each activity refer to the learning goals that are listed above.

- Intake interview. Before students enrol in this programme, they are invited for an intake interview. This interview is geared to students' own reflections on the connection between the students' biography and personality to their academic interests (Learning goal no. 1).
- Course hermeneutics. This module exposes students to a dialogical process of hermeneutics, thus initiating a process of interactive study of authoritative and sacred texts from a range of traditions and world views (Learning goals nos. 3, 4).
- Course research skills. This module uses the diversity in the group to stimulate further growth and to become aware of interdisciplinarity. By interacting and exchanging ideas about the research proposals of the students, the diversity within the group of students becomes visible and all research proposals are exposed to an interdisciplinary discussion and reflection (Learning goals nos. 2, 4).

- Master seminar. This module consists of joint and structured discussions about the learning process and problems of the students in relation to their internship. This takes place in an atmosphere of trust where elements of diversity (as gender, age, and worldview) are discussed and explored (Learning goals nos. 2, 3).
- The programme as a whole is characterised by the practice of dialogic learning, predicated on difference and diversity. The process is initiated by questions raised by students, related to their personality and inspiration for scholarship. As a result, new questions are asked to a text and the subject matter is made 'strange' again for the student who might feel so familiar with a religious text that it prevents her/his ability to appreciate its difference (e.g., stemming from a different time, written for a different audience and context, based on different cultural and religious assumptions, etc.) (Learning goals nos. 1, 2).

Assessing intercultural competence

Diversity learning goals are assessed in several ways. First, emphasis is placed on interreligious hermeneutics, in particular through an intense experience of 'Scriptural reasoning' (a method for the joint exploration of sacred texts). Students are evaluated based on their written reports of this experience, in relation to their own worldview and convictions. Second, during the course of the master seminar, students are to engage with each other concerning their fields of interest, motivation, their uniqueness, and 'otherness' in the processes of learning and researching. Students document their development during this course in a portfolio, in which diversity competencies play a significant role. Third, the (research) internship offers students the opportunity to navigate between the different 'cultures' of the world of the student (e.g., that of the academic researcher or of a societal organisation). Reflection on this process of negotiating different cultures is part of the supervisory process and of the final report of the student.

Lessons learned

First, the fact that diversity is integrated throughout the whole programme contributes to the insight that the perspective of diversity is not an 'add-on' but an integral part of academic dialogue and reflection in the field of Theology and Religious Studies. Second, the intentional use of diversity has proven to be heuristically helpful and a source of motivation for the students, leading to significant motivations for their studies and research and for the output they delivered. Third, it has also become clear that planning concerning diversity at the level of the entire programme is a requirement and that one should not rely on the enthusiasm and focus of individual lecturers. Consultation (for instance on how students are encouraged to use their own 'otherness') and coordination (e.g., what kind of diversity receives attention in which module) are of crucial importance here.

Ways to improve

Based on the experiences with teaching the master's this year, ideas for improvements arose. We propose to:

- use the master's seminar even more intensively as a catalyst for the dialogue that furthers the productive use of diversity;
- use 'peer-review assignments' more frequently in order to facilitate and foster dialogue between students;
- create thesis and internship subgroups based on shared interests.

Besides these ideas for improvement of the MA programme, we believe that in the communication about this MA programme a stronger emphasis can be put on the value that is given to diversity and to a more explicit formulation of learning goals related to diversity. This way, it will be clearer to students and staff that diversity is perceived as a resource and how this is put into practice in learning activities of the master's student. A more explicit communication also shows how the faculty's policy on diversity is implemented in this master's student. Besides, it will be important to continue the training and reflection on diversity of the teaching staff involved in the programme. This should also include the exchange of publications and papers on the subject of diversity. Finally, it will be powerful to create a platform for students where they can present their output (thesis, internship products) to each other and the teaching staff.

References

Freeman, M., Treleaven, L., Simpson, L., Ridings, S., Ramburuth, P., Leask, B., Caulfield, N., & Sykes, C. (2009). *Embedding the development of intercultural education in business education*. Sydney: Australian Learning and Teaching Council.

Mackenzie, C., & Stoljar, N. (2000). Introduction: Autonomy refigured. In C. Mackenzie & N. Stoljar (Eds.), *Relational autonomy: Feminist perspectives on autonomy, agency and the social self* (pp. 3–32). Oxford: Oxford University Press.

Muntinga, M. E., Krajenbrink, V. Q. E., Peerdeman, S. M., Croiset, G., & Verdonk, P. (2015). Toward diversity-responsive medical education: Taking an intersectionality-based approach to a curriculum evaluation. *Advances in Health Science Education, 21*(3), 541–59.

Smit, P.-B. (2014). Diversiteit in het onderwijs van het Nieuwe Testament: over het nut van biografische, levensbeschouwelijke en culturele diversiteit [Diversity in teaching of the New Testament: on the usefulness of biographic, life philosophy and cultural diversity]. *Nederlands Theologisch Tijdschrift, 68*(3), 277–96.

CS25

Developing intercultural competence through international travel experience at Spelman College

Dimeji R. Togunde and Rokhaya Fall (Spelman College)

Context

Spelman College is one of the Historically Black Colleges and Universities (HBCUs) in the United States. Comprising both public and private institutions, HBCUs were 'established before 1964 with a mission to educate black Americans although admission of all races has always been allowed' (Wikipedia, 2017). Established in 1881, Spelman enrols approximately 2,100 women undergraduates of African descent and offers a holistic education built on academic excellence in the liberal arts and sciences. Spelman is accredited by the Southern Association of Colleges and Schools, which requires all institutions in the southern region of the United States to develop a quality enhancement plan (QEP) that addresses a well-defined topic or issues related to enhancing student learning as part of the reaccreditation process. Subsequently, an impact report is required in the fifth year of the QEP's implementation.

Spelman's QEP, Developing Intercultural Competence, also known as Spelman Going Global!, was selected and developed through a broad-based process by campus stakeholders: faculty, senior administration, staff, students, and the board of trustees. It seeks to enhance student learning through global travel experiences connected to the college's liberal arts curriculum. The QEP initiative reaffirms the college's mission and commitment to engage students with 'the many cultures of the world'. It aims to provide students with the skills they will need to navigate the diverse global cultural landscapes, function effectively, and be successful global leaders. It is supported by a strategic plan (2010–17), whose goal is to provide opportunities for every student to have international travel experience before graduation. The implementation of the initiative began in 2011 with the establishment of the Gordon-Zeto Center for Global Education as an infrastructure to provide coherence and centralisation of all international initiatives. Established with a $17 million philanthropic endowment, the centre is led by the associate provost for global education to provide vision and strategic leadership and to lead the assessment of the students' global learning outcomes.

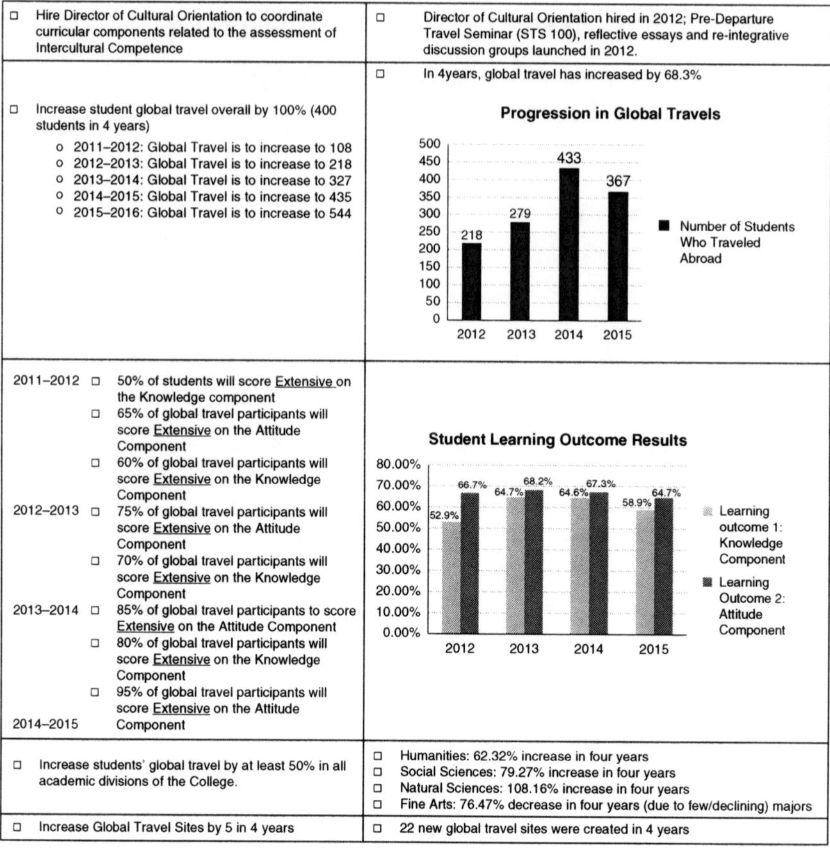

□ Hire Director of Cultural Orientation to coordinate curricular components related to the assessment of Intercultural Competence	□ Director of Cultural Orientation hired in 2012; Pre-Departure Travel Seminar (STS 100), reflective essays and re-integrative discussion groups launched in 2012.
□ Increase student global travel overall by 100% (400 students in 4 years) o 2011–2012: Global Travel is to increase to 108 o 2012–2013: Global Travel is to increase to 218 o 2013–2014: Global Travel is to increase to 327 o 2014–2015: Global Travel is to increase to 435 o 2015–2016: Global Travel is to increase to 544	□ In 4years, global travel has increased by 68.3% **Progression in Global Travels** 500 450 400 350 300 250 200 150 100 50 0 218 279 433 367 2012 2013 2014 2015 ■ Number of Students Who Traveled Abroad
2011–2012 □ 50% of students will score <u>Extensive</u> on the Knowledge component □ 65% of global travel participants will score <u>Extensive</u> on the Attitude Component □ 60% of global travel participants will score <u>Extensive</u> on the Knowledge Component 2012–2013 □ 75% of global travel participants will score <u>Extensive</u> on the Attitude Component □ 70% of global travel participants will score <u>Extensive</u> on the Knowledge Component 2013–2014 □ 85% of global travel participants to score <u>Extensive</u> on the Attitude Component □ 80% of global travel participants will score <u>Extensive</u> on the Knowledge Component □ 95% of global travel participants will score <u>Extensive</u> on the Attitude 2014–2015 Component	**Student Learning Outcome Results** 80.00% 70.00% 60.00% 50.00% 40.00% 30.00% 20.00% 10.00% 0.00% 2012: 52.9% 66.7% 2013: 64.7% 68.2% 2014: 64.6% 67.3% 2015: 58.9% 64.7% Learning outcome 1: Knowledge Component Learning Outcome 2: Attitude Component
□ Increase students' global travel by at least 50% in all academic divisions of the College.	□ Humanities: 62.32% increase in four years □ Social Sciences: 79.27% increase in four years □ Natural Sciences: 108.16% increase in four years □ Fine Arts: 76.47% decrease in four years (due to few/declining) majors
□ Increase Global Travel Sites by 5 in 4 years	□ 22 new global travel sites were created in 4 years

Figure CS25.1 Goals and outcomes.

Goals and outcomes

The goals and outcomes of this programme are outlined in Figure CS25.1.

Framework of intercultural competence

Spelman has defined intercultural competence as acquisition of knowledge about global issues and other cultures and the development of skills to interact and engage with different cultures. We were persuaded by the importance of helping students to explore their identities while abroad; to analyse issues from multiple perspectives; and to develop the learning skills necessary to function in an interconnected, increasingly complex, interdependent, and competitive global society (Hovland, 2005, 2006, 2009; Musil, 2006, 11). According to Deardorff and Hunter (2006), college graduates will now face national and international competition for jobs and will work with colleagues from different educational, cultural, and social backgrounds (p. 72). 'Students need to think and act in terms of living in a world in which they meet, work, and live with others with very different cultural backgrounds' (Braskamp, Braskamp, & Merrill, 2009, p. 101).

Developing intercultural competence

To demonstrate students' intercultural competence, Spelman has developed two learning outcomes across study-travel programmes:

1. **Knowledge component.** Identify differences and commonalities of two world societies based on political, economic, social and/or cultural values during each study-travel experience.
2. **Attitude component.** Develop a personal definition of cultural engagement that reflects openness to cultural difference.

These two learning outcomes were developed with the theoretical guidance provided by the Deardorff (2006) Process Model of Intercultural Competence. This model recognises that intercultural competence is based on attitudes, knowledge, and skills that the individual possesses and outcomes that are expressed in interactions. Simply put, the attitudes – respect, openness, and curiosity about other cultures – lead to the acquisition of knowledge about one's own culture and the development of skills – listening, observation, interpretation, and the ability to relate to difference. This model suggests that intercultural competence is an ongoing process that takes place at different intervals and different levels of intensity. Furthermore, we have drawn on a related article by Boecker and Ulama (2008), which offers a nuanced version of the Deardorff Process Model, using a spiral to denote the complexity and multidimensionality of intercultural competence acquisition. They both suggest that intercultural competence involves more than one component and that global knowledge or language acquisition alone does not guarantee intercultural competence. In recognition of this, Spelman has enhanced its curriculum internationalisation especially because students who have taken courses infused with international topics are more likely to demonstrate a higher level of intercultural competence.

To ensure achievement of these two student learning outcomes, we developed three curricular innovations connected to students' study-travel experience (see Figure CS25.2 for assessment):

1. **pre-departure**, a mandatory, one-credit study-travel seminar for all global travel programmes;
2. **while abroad**, weekly/monthly blogging and journaling;
3. **post-study abroad**, reintegrative round-table discussions for each destination (required as part of credit for study-travel experience).

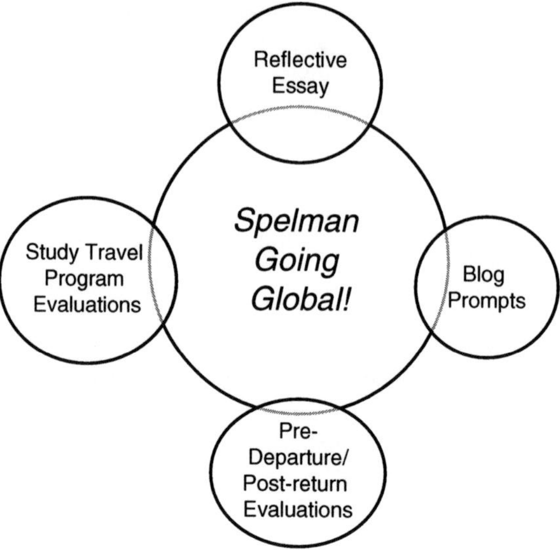

Figure CS25.2 Assessing intercultural competence.

4. **reflective essay**, required of students upon their post-global travel experience, a rubric was adapted from the ACE/FIPSE project rubrics and AAC&U Intercultural Knowledge and Competence VALUE Rubric (based on Deardorff and Bennett theories) to evaluate the essays;
5. **pre-departure/post-return evaluations**, employed to assess change and development in students' self-evaluation of their global knowledge and intercultural understanding;
6. **study-travel programme evaluations**, aimed at verifying the extent to which the pre-departure seminar and post-study abroad curricular innovations were useful;
7. **blog prompts**, included as a qualitative assessment tool to help in assessing students' knowledge about their destination country and to encourage acknowledgement and acceptance of cultural difference.

Lessons learned

- Our assessment results indicate that global travel experience adds a significant dimension to the intercultural learning process through acquisition of knowledge about other cultures, openness to new cultures and ideas, knowledge about the experiences of people of African descent in the diasporas, personal growth, self-discovery, and foreign language development.
- It appears that we had overestimated the percentage of students expected to demonstrate 'extensive knowledge' and 'extensive openness' of the two learning outcomes. Given the large number of students participating in

global travels, we found more viability in their ability to demonstrate intercultural competence.

- We probed deeper into how the two learning outcomes could vary with several other variables beside international travel and found that a semester abroad, living with a host family, taking a language course while abroad, being an honour student, and prior enrollment in an internationally focused course are associated with a higher level of intercultural competence.
- The QEP experience has also enabled us to explore the relationship between study abroad and students' graduation rate. We tracked graduation rate of students who did semester study abroad in their junior year from 2012 through 2014. We compared these rates with the college's highest historical graduation rate of 70 per cent in four years for the 2005 cohort. The result demonstrated an average of 24.3 per cent higher four-year graduation rate than the college's historical high. The result requires further investigation.

Ways to improve

- For a thorough reflection of students' travel experience, a five-page report will now be required rather than a three- to five-page limit.
- We will redesign the rubric for assessing students' reflective essays by changing the measurement scales to 3, where 1 = minimal; 2 = adequate and 3 = extensive. Currently, there are four scales: 1 = inadequate; 2 = minimal; 3 = moderate; and 4 = extensive. Faculty assessors do not see the difference between inadequate and minimal. They have also suggested that we replace 'moderate' with 'adequate' because of the perceived gap between 'extensive' and 'moderate'.
- The fourth indicator of the knowledge component of the learning outcome will be removed because it is not completely clear to faculty assessors and the students. Due to lack of clarity, students tend to score very low on this indicator.

References

Boecker, M., & Ulama, L. (2008). Intercultural competence: The key competence in the 21st century? Retrieved from www.ngobg.info/bg/documents/49/726bertelsmanninterculturalcompetences.pdf

Braskamp, L., Braskamp, D., & Merrill, K. (2009). Assessing progress in global learning and development of students with education abroad experiences. *Frontiers: The Interdisciplinary Journal of Study Abroad*, *18*, 101–18.

Deardorff, D. K. (2006). Identification and assessment of intercultural competence as a student outcome of internationalization. *Journal of Studies in International Education*, *10*(3), 241–66.

Deardorff, D. K., & Hunter, W. (2006). Education global-ready graduates. *International Educator*, *15*(3), 72–83.

Hovland, K. (2005). Shared futures: Global learning and social responsibility. *Diversity Digest*, *8*(3), 124.

—— (2006). *Shared futures: Global learning and liberal education*. Washington, DC: Association of American Colleges & Universities.
—— (2009). Global learning: What is it? Who is responsible for it? *Peer Review*, *11*(4), 4–7.
—— (2010). *Global learning: Aligning student learning outcomes with study abroad*. Washington, DC: NAFSA, Association of International Educators.
Musil, C. (2006). *Assessing learning: Matching good intentions with good practice*. Washington, DC: Association of American Colleges & Universities.
Wikipedia (2017) Historically black colleges and universities. Retrieved from https://en.wikipedia.org/wiki/Historically_black_colleges_and_universities

CS26

A collaborative volunteer project in Vietnam

Eiko Ujitani (Nagoya University of Foreign Studies)

Context

In order to improve Japanese students' intercultural competence, a two-week volunteer project involving collaborative activities with local Vietnamese students was organised in partnership with a Japanese NGO (NICE, Never-ending International Camps Exchange) and a local Vietnamese volunteer organisation (Volunteers for Peace Vietnam). Twelve Japanese students from my university and six Vietnamese volunteers recruited by VPV participated in this project from 1 February to 12 February 2015, in a rural village called An Lac Eco Community, about 150 kilometres north-east of Hanoi. Japanese students were divided into three groups and lived with a host family together with at least one Vietnamese student. During the daytime, both Japanese and Vietnamese students engaged in environmental work such as cleaning the forest park and the local community, helping with agricultural work in the field of one of the community members by weeding, and doing educational work such as teaching local elementary school children about not littering.

Every day after dinner, Japanese students had reflection meetings. In addition to volunteer work, this programme included a cultural exchange event at the end of the programme as well as two overnight trips, one to Ha Long Bay and one to Hanoi. In order to encourage bicultural collaboration between Japanese and Vietnamese students, an interview project was assigned by the accompanying supervisors. Japanese students interviewed their host family to learn more about their life in the rural community and then they presented their findings in the form of presentations at the final cultural exchange event with help from the Vietnamese students who acted as interpreters.

Goals and outcomes

A goal of this project was to improve Japanese students' intercultural attitudes, knowledge, and skills that support effective and appropriate interactions with host nationals. In order to improve their intercultural attitude and openness, they were expected to initiate and develop interactions with Vietnamese students.

In terms of knowledge, students were expected to gain deep cultural knowledge about life in a rural Vietnamese community and develop their cultural self-awareness. Expected areas of skill development included non-verbal communication skills and observation skills in order to communicate with people who do not share the same language and improving their adaptability skills by dealing with stressful feelings in a different cultural environment.

Framework of intercultural competence

Intercultural competence in this programme is defined as 'the ability to communicate effectively and appropriately in intercultural situations based on one's intercultural knowledge, skills and attitudes' (Deardorff, 2008, p. 33). Different programme features incorporated based on some intercultural theories may also contribute to the development of intercultural competence. For example, guided reflection, an integral component of experiential theory (Dewey, 1996; Kolb, 1984) is provided before, during, and after the programme. Since contact theory (Allport, 1954) states that increased contact with host nationals helps to promote intercultural competence, homestay, and collaborative volunteer activities are incorporated in this programme. This programme takes place in such a culturally challenging environment that stress contributes to cultural adaptation (Kim, 1995).

Developing intercultural competence

This programme included three crucial elements: cultural immersion, guided reflection, and contact reciprocity (Lough, 2011). These three elements are outlined below.

First, Japanese students in this programme were immersed in rural Vietnamese culture through living with a host family and working together with Vietnamese students. Intensive interaction with host country nationals could improve not only their language skills but also their communication skills of interacting with others in a cross-cultural setting while gaining deep self (and other) cultural knowledge.

Second, according to transformative learning theory (Mezirow, 1997), critical self-reflection enables individuals to accommodate different experiences. It further generates a frame of reference shift as an outcome. In a short-term project like ours, reflection is crucial since students tend to feel culture shock more often at the beginning of their stay. In order for students to regain equilibrium caused by the dilemma associated with new experiences and also not to lead to stereotypes or prejudice about the new culture, proper guidance was provided by the accompanying supervisors and local leaders in this programme.

Third, contact theory (Allport, 1954) suggests that increased intercultural contact helps to reduce intergroup prejudice and develop intercultural competence when the following four conditions are met:

1. Volunteers and community members perceive equal status.
2. They share common goals.
3. They experience no significant competition.
4. Authorities sanction the contact.

Both Vietnamese and Japanese participants in this programme perceived equal status since they were about the same age and worked in cooperative ways for the local community under the guidance of the local NGO leaders.

Assessing intercultural competence

Assessments consisted of quantitative and qualitative elements. Quantitative questionnaires included the Cross-Cultural Adaptability Inventory (CCAI; Kelly & Mayers, 1995) and Willingness to Communicate Scale (McCroskey & Richmond, 1987), and perceived English proficiency in five areas namely, speaking, listening, writing, and vocabulary before and after the project. The CCAI modified for this study measured three dimensions of cross-cultural adaptability: (1) emotional resilience, (2) flexibility and openness, and (3) perceptual acuity. For each dimension, questions were asked such as, for emotional resilience, 'I feel confident in my ability to cope with life, no matter where I am'; for flexibility and openness, 'When I meet people who are different from me, I am interested in learning more about them'; and for perceptual acuity, 'In talking with people from other cultures, I pay attention to body language.'

The Willingness to Communicate Scale assessed what degree students were willing to communicate or not in seven situations. The seven situations are a combination of four contexts (i.e. dyads, groups, meetings, and public presentations) with three types of receivers (i.e. strangers, acquaintances, and friends). For example, one item says, 'Talking with an acquaintance while standing in line.' An example of another item is, 'Giving a presentation in front of a group of thirty strangers.' Questions in the pre-questionnaire included students' age, gender, and previous overseas experiences.

Qualitative data collected during the sojourn included student diaries, transcriptions of several reflection meetings, and interviews with selected students. An interview about their learning and personal change in Vietnam was conducted one month after returning to Japan. Students were given several Post-it memo notes and asked to write about their discoveries and changes on these individual memo notes. Afterwards, they shared their notes by placing similar ideas together on a large piece of butcher paper which facilitated further group discussion and reflection.

Lessons learned

1. The importance of intercultural interaction: Intensive interactions with Vietnamese students enabled them to initiate and develop communication with them. It eventually assisted in the development of deep knowledge

about Vietnamese culture that led to awareness about their own country (e.g., differences and similarities in environment and family relationships).
2. The importance of having the same goals: Japanese students working together towards common goals with Vietnamese students helped them to acquire communication skills naturally.
3. The importance of guided reflection: If students only reflect by themselves, it might strengthen emerging stereotypes. It is crucial to listen to other students or a facilitator to improve their intercultural competence.
4. Implementing a programme that provides a chance to live in the same conditions as local people: Students felt stress about the challenging new environment (e.g., bathroom outside, cold shower) at the beginning, but their successful adaptation improved their self-efficacy, and it led to the acquisition of adaptability skills.

Ways to improve

In order to improve our programme, I would provide the following four suggestions.

1. Align real-life tasks with students' capabilities: The local partners chose work for students to do since partners are familiar with the local community. However, the agricultural work, for example, was too challenging for students who had never used agricultural tools such as hoes. During one reflection meeting, Japanese students wondered if their service was more disruptive rather than useful for the host community. It would be beneficial to assess participants' interests and skills before choosing what type of volunteer service since the value of service should outweigh the disruption to the host (Pusch & Merrill, 2008).
2. Assess reciprocal benefits: Like most previous studies, this study focused on the effect of an international volunteer project only on Japanese participants. As Lough (2011) states, assessing only volunteers without considering the host communities may provide a biased view of overall outcomes.
3. Use observable behavioural assessment: Many studies in the field of intercultural competence development still heavily depend on self-perspective measures (Deardorff, 2015), and this research is no exception. In order to measure willingness to communicate in particular, it would be helpful to include behavioural assessment, such as frequency of participation at reflection meetings, frequency of interactions with local students or the use of communication strategies as evidence of curiosity towards the host nationals
4. Longitudinal design: Since intercultural competence is a lifelong developmental process, long-term results concerning students' career choices and further civic engagement need to be explored (Deardorff & Edwards, 2013) Because it is difficult to trace students' change after the programme ends, it is important to assess their changes a year or more after the programme.

References

Allport, G. W. (1954). *The nature of prejudice.* Reading, MA: Addison-Wesley.

Deardorff, D. K. (2008). Intercultural competence: A definition, model, and implications for education abroad. In V. Savicki (Ed.), *Developing intercultural competence and transformation: Theory, research, and application in international education* (pp. 32–52). Sterling, VA: Stylus.

—— (2015). Intercultural competence: Mapping the future research agenda. *International Journal of Intercultural Relations, 48*, 3–5.

Deardorff, D. K., & Edwards, K. E. (2013). Framing and assessing students' intercultural competence in service learning. In P. H. Clayton, R. G. Bringle, & J. A. Hatcher (Eds.), *Research on service learning: Conceptual frameworks and assessment* (pp. 157–83). Sterling, VA: Stylus Publishing.

Dewey, J. (1996). Art as experience. In *The Later Works of John Dewey (1925–1953)*, ed. J. A. Boydston, vol. X. Carbondale, IL: Southern Illinois University Press.

Kelley, C., & Meyers, J. (1995). *CCAI Cross-Cultural Adaptability Inventory manual.* Minneapolis, MN: National Computer System, Inc.

Kim, Y. Y. (1995). Cross-cultural adaptation: An integrative theory. In R. L. Wiseman (Ed.), *Intercultural communication theory* (pp. 170–93). Thousand Oaks, CA: Sage.

Kolb, D. A. (1984). *Experiential learning: Experience as the source of learning and development.* Englewood Cliffs, NJ: Prentice-Hall.

Lough, B. J. (2011). International volunteers' perceptions of intercultural competence. *International Journal of Intercultural Relations, 35*(4), 452–64.

McCroskey, J. C., & Richmond, V. P. (1987). Willingness to communicate. In J. C. McCroskey & J. A. Daly (Eds.), *Personality and Interpersonal Communication* (pp. 129–59). Newbury Park, CA: Sage.

Mezirow, J. (1997). Transformative learning: Theory to practice. *New Directions for Adult and Continuing Education, 74*, 5–12.

Pusch, M. D., & Merrill, M. (2008). Reflection, reciprocity, responsibility, and committed relativism. In V. Savicki (Ed.), *Developing intercultural competence and transformation: Theory, research, and application in international education* (pp. 53–73). Sterling, VA: Stylus.

CS27

Inclusion through changing the conversation

A case study on the NorQuest community dialogue on inclusion

Cheryl Whitelaw, Sarah Apedaile, and Todd Odgers (Center for Intercultural Education, NorQuest College)

Context

The community dialogue on inclusion event is part of an ongoing initiative by the NorQuest Center for Intercultural Education (CIE) to increase inclusion outcomes through the development of intercultural competence. NorQuest is diverse. Of over 12,000 students, 57 per cent come from 134 countries with over seventy-two languages spoken. Over 500 students identify as Indigenous. Our team includes a principal, four faculty, and a research manager, all qualified Intercultural Development Inventory (IDI) administrators. With backgrounds in English instruction, intercultural communication/relations, internationalisation, applied research and Integral Coaching™, we bring our expertise to develop intercultural competence for the purpose of inclusion. The community dialogue on inclusion event is an expression of our inclusion = diversity + engagement framework (Whitelaw, 2016). We developed this framework to link theory to practise and to map inclusion at NorQuest College.

Goals and outcomes

The community dialogue on inclusion day began in our ceremonial room. Guided by our college elder, the facilitators prepared themselves to hold sacred space through smudging and setting positive intentions. Our elder opened the event with a prayer and invited participants to make an offering to an empty bowl by setting an intention on what to include of themselves for the day, and adding a small stone. At the close, participants took a stone to carry the spirit of the day. Participants were invited to attend talking circles, based on an Indigenous tradition of respectful story-sharing, co-creation of learning. This approach encouraged a sense of communion and interconnectedness. Participants were also invited to attend dialogue circles, based on the work of David Bohm (Bohm, Factor, & Garrett, n.d.) and Peter Senge (2006). This approach encouraged speaking from experiences, noticing, and suspending assumptions to emphasise learning and discovery. Two artists represented the day; a poet composed a poem to harvest his engagement experience, and an artist expressed her vision through a painting. Together, we created and practised inclusion.

The dialogue day was a guided intercultural experience to model holding space so each person is included, feels safe, and honoured for what they bring. The event modelled intercultural competence in action, creating safety to experience and practise skills for engaging differences. Based on IDI scores collected to date, NorQuest resides within a late minimisation orientation, meaning that most participants recognise their common humanity and are ready to explore differences. The event was calibrated to foster relationship-building, reduce the threat of polarities, and create the safety to explore important differences. The dialogue form enables practice of intercultural behaviours towards competence.

Developmental intercultural competence

CIE's approach is guided through the development model of intercultural sensitivity (DMIS) by Bennett (1993), using the IDI as an instrument to quantify intercultural competence (Hammer, 2009). We practise intercultural behaviours and cycles of reflection as a learning pathway towards intercultural competence, guided by Deardorff's (2006) Process Model. We calibrate for the developmental stage and practise the experiential component of our students, seeking evidence they can apply both learned and earned intercultural competence.

One definition of intercultural competence aligned with our practice is

> the appropriate and effective management of interaction between people, who ... represent different ... affective, cognitive, and behavioral orientations to the world. These orientations will most commonly be reflected in such normative categories as nationality, race, ethnicity, ... the extent to which individuals manifest aspects of, or are influenced by, their group or cultural affiliations ... is what makes an interaction an intercultural process.
>
> (Spitzberg & Changnon, 2009, p. 9)

A meta-framework was used to hold the institutional perspective of inclusion, the AQAL (All Quadrants All Levels) model by Ken Wilber (2000). The quadrant frame helps us to analyse inclusion on campus. Each quadrant describes dimensions of phenomena (e.g., individual experiential, behavioural dimensions and collective cultural, systemic dimensions). Looking at inclusion through this frame enabled us to map instances of capacities to support inclusion (e.g., inclusive culture outcomes) as well as ways to activate these capacities (e.g., the dialogue event). The quadrivia frame refers to these same four dimensions as perspectives of inclusion. Held lightly, the quadrivia frame opens up empathy. These four models are core ones applied to create the developmental inclusion = diversity + engagement framework.

Assessing intercultural competence

The dialogue event reinforced inclusion awareness and modelled intercultural competence. To understand its contribution, it is helpful to hold this event as a microcosm of our ongoing inclusion initiative. Two methods were used in the event to assess intercultural competence awareness. Participants completed an exit survey responding to questions on how beliefs or ideas on inclusion were challenged and how the format encouraged participation. Participants were also invited to complete reflections on questions related to new understandings of self and what is needed for inclusive physical/social spaces. For the dialogue event, we found participants responded from minimisation to acceptance orientations (as described by the DMIS); positive responses to the day emphasising shared humanity, connection, and appreciation of our diversity and feeling part of a community. The contribution of the dialogues to the overall college climate of inclusion is real, albeit not easily measured. In our initiative, programmatic interventions for students range from course modules to full courses to develop intercultural competence as part of programme outcomes. Assessment approaches vary according to the intervention. In addition to course-based assessments, CIE uses the IDI and the participant perception indicator (PPI) tool to show self-assessed gains in knowledge, experience, and confidence for intercultural competence behaviours (Berger, 2003). We use all of these approaches to gain a multi-point perspective of intercultural competence development.

The dialogue event is a highly visible promoter of intercultural competence awareness and an opportunity to practise skills to contribute to an inclusive campus culture. Building on the dialogue day, CIE also provides two training options for staff. Option 1 is a forty-five-hour intercultural practitioner's certificate including IDI assessment, IDI-guided facilitation, pre- and post-PPI, and course assessments. Option 2 is a fifteen-hour inclusive communication series workshop including class assessments and reflective questions.

CIE reports annually on inclusion performance indicators (e.g., 70 per cent of staff achieved satisfactory intercultural competence). To substantiate this metric, an inclusion engagement scale is used to define satisfactory/exemplary intercultural competence. The scale includes two conditions (see Table CS27.1): (1) participation in professional development; and (2) engagement in change related to individual behaviours affecting me, to practise changes affecting my immediate sphere of influence and to organisational changes capacities (e.g., processes) that introduce change to a wider sphere of influence.

Lessons learned

In an institutional context, it requires ongoing effort to connect separate intercultural competence-building events to an overall picture of intercultural

Table CS27.1 Inclusion engagement scale (excerpt).

Level	*Description*	*Measure (participation)*	*Measure (engagement)*
Exemplary	Participation in professional development related to inclusion. Activity that changes inclusion outcomes at NQ.	Complete 16–45 hours of professional development.	The individual demonstrates changes in individual and organisational capacity for inclusion.

competence at the institution. We have found it can be challenging to collect data that contributes to an overall approach and practice of building intercultural competence; it is much easier to focus on the work of planning and implementing events like the dialogue day in isolation. CIE has tried to work realistically with the contribution of activities to raise awareness, enable engagement, practise skills, and opportunities to apply knowledge to create changes in institutional processes and cultures. We hold each of these as part of ongoing cycles of intercultural competence development. Developmental work is challenging. Narrowing the orientation gap identified in the difference between perceived orientation and the developmental orientation on the IDI requires structured opportunities to practise intercultural competence behaviours as found in the dialogue day event. Developmentally, the benefit of the dialogue day was the combination of awareness raising, engagement, and skills practice in an event accessible to each person willing to participate from their own level of development (as described by the DMIS).

Ways to improve

1. We believe participation in the co-creation of the dialogue event contributes to developing intercultural competence on campus. The eighteen-person planning and hosting group is an informal core of a community of inclusive practice. To better document the contribution of participation of community practice, process evaluation, and documentation of changes in intercultural competence mind, heart, and skill sets would create greater transparency for the value of continuing to follow the principle of co-creative, co-ownership of inclusion (vs. top-down events).
2. We have engaged a living lab of inclusion, relying on opportunistic research design through attention to emergence. Using multiple assessment approaches enables us to better understand how intercultural competence relates to inclusion outcomes. We look to embed data collection into organisational processes to ensure we are continuing to inquire and learn from our

progress towards inclusion outcomes. We held this initiative as a developing proto-type, requiring us to:

- attend to the data from each engagement;
- listen to the conversations around us;
- look for emerging inclusion.

To move the needle on inclusion, we need more than a representative sample of IDI scores showing our collective intercultural competence. We need safe places to experience developmental edges when differences are difficult to include. We need assessment approaches for performance and for learning. Holding inclusion as an intercultural competence practice calls us to continue to try, learn, and reflect on how we are walking the talk of inclusion.

References

Bennett, M. J. (1993). Towards ethnorelativism: A developmental model of intercultural sensitivity. In R. M. Paige (Ed.), *Education for the intercultural experience* (pp. 21–71). Yarmouth, ME: Intercultural Press.

Berger, C. (2003). Participant perception indicator. Retrieved from www.merlot.org/merlot/viewMaterial.htm?id=80037

Bohm, D., Factor, D., & Garrett, P. (n.d.). Dialogue, a proposal. Retrieved from www.david-bohm.net/dialogue/dialogue_proposal.html

Deardorff, D. K. (2006). The identification and assessment of intercultural competence. *Journal of Studies in International Education*, *10*(3), 241–66.

Hammer, M. R. (2009). The intercultural development inventory. In M. A. Moodian (Ed.), *Contemporary leadership and intercultural competence* (pp. 203–18). Thousand Oaks, CA: Sage.

Senge, P. (2006). *The fifth discipline: The art and practice of the learning organization.* New York, NY: Random House.

Spitzberg, B. H., & Changnon, G. (2009). Conceptualizing intercultural competence. In D. K. Deardorff (Ed.), *The Sage handbook of intercultural competence* (pp. 2–52). Thousand Oaks, CA: Sage.

Whitelaw, C. (2016). Developing an inclusive perspective for a diverse college: Inclusion = diversity + engagement. *Integral Review*, *12*(1). Retrieved from http://integral-review.org/issues/vol_12_no_1_whitelaw_developing_an_inclusion_persp

Wilber, K. (2000). *Integral psychology, consciousness, spirit, psychology, therapy.* Boston, MA: Shambhala.

CS28

The Businet international weeks

Jason Williams (Cardiff Metropolitan University) and Joëlle Hietbrink (Stenden University)

Context

Students at Cardiff Metropolitan University (CMU) generally do not value the opportunity or recognise the benefits of exploring their subject area within an international context, and, further to this, computing students tend to be the least interested in the international workplace (Deardorff, 2011), even though their skills are transferable within any culture or country. They work within a sector that offers a wealth of opportunities for their particular skill set and knowledge, as these are required internationally. Concomitantly, this problem has been recognised by other institutions and discussed at length within the Businet organisation (www.businet.org.uk).

The main aim of Businet is to promote intercultural awareness along with student exchange, and this has resulted in the development of an International Businet week that each member hosts within their own institution aimed at achieving the competencies as identified by Deardorff (2006a). These projects are self-funded by students and part-funded by the host member, do not rely on Erasmus funding, and are not restricted with the paperwork that such funding entails. Each individual project covers a wide range of topics to study for the week, and students are offered a certificate of attendance after completion.

Goals and outcomes

The main goal of the international week on social media offered by CMU is primarily for students to develop a social-media presence through working in groups and then reflect on this as part of their assessment. In terms of outcomes, in addition to developing the social-media presence, the week is meant to introduce students to working as part of team with students from other countries, thus enhancing their cultural awareness and presenting them with opportunities for further exchanges and collaboration within an international context.

Students are placed into groups of four before they attend the week, ensuring that there are no students from the same country in any one group. Students are sent a project brief and are then asked to initiate the project through discussions prior to arriving at CMU via online tools such as Skype, Teamviewer, Messenger, Dropbox, or other similar tools, before they meet in person at the Businet week at the host institution. The International Businet week at CMU requires students to attend facilitated sessions throughout the week, where speakers from industry and academia give lectures and students then formulate a poster throughout the week, reflecting on what they learn and how they work together and present their ideas to fellow students along with a reflective report. Students then have the option of gaining 5 ECTS credits through submitting a 3,000-word reflective report on their experiences, and this is reviewed within the academic quality procedures at CMU before their grades are presented to them.

Framework of intercultural competence

Academically, the main aim of the module was to enable students to evaluate their skill and knowledge within the world of work, through which students will be able to develop their problem-solving, analytical skills, self-reflection, interpersonal, and communication skills by drawing on the experience of a virtual workplace setting. The module has been developed within the context of the Higher Education Academy's internationalisation framework with greater focus on the framework presented by Deardorff (2006), aiming to developing the knowledge, skills, and attitudes of the students.

Assessing intercultural competence

The assessment is part of a module, and the main aim of the module is to evaluate the students' skills and knowledge within the international world of work, where they develop their problem-solving, analytical, self-reflection, interpersonal, and communication skills by drawing on the experience of working as part of an intercultural team. This was achieved through students attaining the following learning outcomes: (1) reflect on their role within a project team and evaluate their own performance; (2) evaluate a given problem within a computing and international context and develop a solution as part of a team.

In reviewing the week, students were interviewed individually through semi-structured interviews and also as part of a group (N = 10). Some of the main findings were that students from CMU changed their attitude and were more open to the idea of studying and working in another country as the experience was a positive one. The week also gave them the confidence in working within an international context as they worked closely and socialised with students from different countries. They became more self-aware of their own culture along with identifying their personal strengths and weakness. Finally, they recognised the subtle cultural differences in working with students from other countries, thus enhancing their awareness of their own cultural identity.

The learning outcomes related to intercultural competence through presenting the students with the opportunity to work as part of an international team, which then introduced them to sharing cultures and values outside the norms of their home country. The reflective element of the assessment not only gave them the opportunity to engage with the assignment and project but also gave them the chance to reflect within an international context, giving them a deeper understanding of the challenges and opportunities of working with individuals from other countries. The knowledge aspect of the framework identified by Deardorff (2006) appeared to have the greatest effect through the international week as students became very aware of their own culture in addition to identifying the traits shown by their team members, which were specific to their own country and culture. Many of the students had not travelled a great deal before attending this week, therefore the impact of working within this environment awakened many of them to the possibility of working abroad and thinking more widely of working and travelling in other countries. The areas of skills and attitudes within the framework appeared to have been less affected as the students were only together for a week. However, with a longer time together there would be further scope to develop these competencies.

Lessons learned

In terms of identifying the lessons learned from running the international week, it was found that students needed clearer information with regards to what was expected of them before they arrived at the Businet International week and what was expected of them when attending. They had an understanding of what was expected, but they didn't really engage with the week until they physically arrived.

The students' understanding of the week when they arrived also gave some scope for improvement as they struggled to understand that the week was more about reflecting on their own learning and role within the team rather than producing a final artefact. The importance of reflection was lost on the students as they were unused to thinking and expressing their thoughts on what they had learned. This may be a cultural problem as students from the UK have been assessed through reflection in many subjects, both technical and non-technical. Finally, students wanted to have something more technical to complete as part of their international week, although the intention of the week was to try and stay away from this as it is difficult to teach students technical subjects within the given time period. This is a problem that many of the international weeks have had as it is difficult to identify projects that can be completed in a week as students with little or no prior knowledge of a technical area will work with students who may have far more interaction with the area of study.

Ways to improve

As a whole, the international week was considered a success by the department and university as it was with other partners within the Businet organisation as reported by CMU students who attended similar Businet international weeks. In terms of improving the areas identified there were a few areas that could be developed to enhance the student experience. Prior to the students arriving, students were given the brief of what they should be doing before attending the international week at Cardiff. However, there was very little discussion between students before they arrived, and this could have been addressed by asking students to present some work before they joined. This would also clarify what exactly they should be doing and remove any ambiguity and would also help in identifying any problems with teamwork and permit the facilitator to clarify any misunderstandings. The process of reflecting could also be highlighted at this point, and students could be directed to ways to improve their reflection. There will be a move towards developing the technical aspect of the international week at the next delivery. It is recognised that students appreciate being taught technical skills in addition to the theoretical knowledge they are given. The assessment will be carefully designed so that it is set at the correct technical level to include students with differing set of skills and previous knowledge. Finally, it is believed that the experience would be enhanced for students if the international week took place within a more diverse subject field, focusing on a multidisciplinary project which could be used as a vehicle for students to work together and offered to students on other programmes outside computing.

References

Deardorff, D. K. (2006). Identification and assessment of intercultural competence as a student outcome of internationalization. *Journal of Studies in International Education*, *10*(3), 241–66.

—— (2011). Assessing intercultural competence. *New Directions for Institutional Research*, *149*, 65–79.

CS29

(Dis)connecting Mayan and Mexican *interculturidad* with social justice in a US graduate preparation programme

Tamara Yakaboski and Matt Birnbaum (University of Northern Colorado, in partnership with Universidad Intercultural Maya de Quintana Roo)

Context

The University of Northern Colorado's Higher Education and Student Affairs Leadership (HESAL) is a graduate preparation programme that develops individuals to assume administrative and faculty positions at post-secondary institutions. The HESAL curriculum weaves social-justice issues throughout coursework and professional practice. Over the past two years, the faculty have implemented ways to further develop our students' social-justice and intercultural competence. This included developing a course using indigenous and neocolonial theories to explore (dis)connections between Mexican and Mayan *interculturidad* and US concepts of social justice while simultaneously prompting students to engage in their own development. The course required students to engage in understanding these theories through readings, discussions, and a week-long field experience at the Universidad Intercultural Maya de Quintana Roo (UIMQRoo) in the Yucatán, a new institution chartered to focus on indigenous higher education and the concept of *interculturidad*.

Goals and outcomes

The course curriculum blended (1) CAS Standards for Education Abroad student learning and development outcomes and (2) Deardorff's Model of Intercultural Competence (2006). The learning outcomes included:

- developing an understanding of local cultures and histories of Mexican and Mayan peoples from a higher education perspective;
- developing one's own professional identity and development plan including competencies and skill areas needed for best practice as intercultural student-affairs professionals;
- participating in a field-based educational experience to acquire first-hand knowledge of intercultural education and social inequities within Mayan communities;

- developing a commitment to social responsibility by acquiring knowledge, developing skills and desired attitude to operate effectively in a multicultural and intercultural context;
- reflecting on values and beliefs, describing these in the context of one's own national and cultural backgrounds while developing adaptability and empathy for others.

Framework of intercultural competence

We blended US conceptions of social justice and the Mexican and Mayan concept of *interculturidad* to develop the course framework. Definitions for social justice and inclusivity were developed from the American College Personnel Association (ACPA)/ National Association of Student Personnel Administrators (NASPA) professional competency areas for student-affairs practitioners matrix. We framed social justice as a component of interculturalism, with the understanding that intercultural competence requires the 'successful engagement or collaboration towards a single or shared set of goals between individuals or groups who do not share the same cultural origins or background' (Twombly, Salisbruy, Tumanut, & Klute, 2012, p. 69). Issues of imperialism, colonial histories, and indigenous theories were woven through the class's weekly readings.

UIMQRoo's *interculturidad* model stresses that students' embrace, celebrate, study, and understand their own identities and local community while successfully navigating different cultures, world visions, and ways of knowing and acting in the world. UIMQRoo defines *interculturidad* as the active integration between two or more cultures that lays the foundation for exchange, dialogue, and mutual enrichment between cultures, and seeks the exploration of new ways of thinking and alternative solutions to common and global challenges.

Developing intercultural competence

Three specific course elements supported students' intercultural competence development:

1. Readings critiqued study-abroad models through the lens of decolonisation because the 'pursuit of knowledge is deeply embedded in the multiple layers of imperial and colonial practices' (and both formal research and informal 'traveller's tales' can be colonising as it creates 'Otherness' [Tuhiwai Smith, 2012, p. 2]). The readings challenged students to embark with consciousness of their positionality and power.
2. Continuous self-assessment and reflection guided by activities and prompts related to intercultural competence. In addition to traditional approaches to reflection, students were required to develop presentations for staff and faculty at UIMQRoo and for the University of Northern Colorado that incorporated appropriate cultural considerations, knowledge, and

communication styles and required students to adapt and be flexible while reflecting simultaneously.

3. As language development is often included in intercultural assessment and development, students worked on Spanish language skills at the end of each class facilitated by another classmate who spoke Spanish to encourage more meaningful and authentic on-site interactions.

Assessing intercultural competence

Assessment of intercultural development included course assignments, formal assessment tools, in-class observations, and regular engagement during the week-long experience in Mexico. We used

1. activities from the *Building Cultural Competence: Innovative Intercultural Training Activities and Models* (Berardo & Deardorff, 2012) appropriate for graduate-level learning;
2. pre- and post-self-assessments through the intercultural competence model and Handout S1.1, Intercultural Competence Self-Reflection (Deardorff, 2012);
3. Wheels of Intercultural Skills by Berardo and Deardorff (2012) (Handout S9.1) combined with ACPA/NASPA professional competency areas for student affairs practitioners; social justice and inclusion area;
4. Intercultural Effectiveness Scale (IES), administered pre- and post-trip, by the Kozai Group, to measure changes across continuous learning, interpersonal engagement, and hardiness;
5. intercultural competence higher education and student-affairs practice reflection – we tweaked Handout S1.2 (Deardorff, 2012) from a focus on teaching to a broader focus on student-affairs professionals as transformative educators (Rhoads & Black, 1995), as most of our students will never teach in a traditional classroom but educate in the co-curriculum.

The professional fields of international education and higher education exist in parallel but rarely intersecting planes. As such, we needed to adapt and relate some of the international education language and activities to higher education and student affairs professionals and to help students think beyond the US context, which higher education and student affairs literature and theories are grounded in.

Lessons learned

1. Students, even experienced professionals, often do not think about social justice, multiculturalism, or diversity through intercultural or global perspectives. Our participants thought about multiculturalism or diversity in a US context, whereas UIMQRoo students function more seamlessly across

Mayan, Mexican, and international contexts, at times simultaneously. This made it challenging for students to see how powerful global forces are directly influencing the lives of individual Maya who have never travelled more than a few miles from their village but who may have more developed intercultural competence than these US students.

2. The use of self-reflective and external measurement tools reinforced the limitations with any assessment. Students often overrated intercultural competence and abilities around intercultural competence, and occasionally this divide was shown between variations in the self and external tools. However, consistent on the pre- and post-IES measure, 73 per cent reported they had high *self-awareness*, meaning they viewed themselves as capable of measuring their learning. On the S1.1 Handout where students self-assessed, only 47 per cent assigned a 3 (average), all other scoring were 4 (high) and 5 (very high), meaning most rated their abilities highly. As a result, students may complete the course believing they are competent to work in intercultural contexts when the instructors observed more foundational rather than advanced intercultural competence skills. Thus, instructor feedback is very important for students.
3. We designed the course and trip to focus on creating two-way learning relationships and partnerships rather than taking from an indigenous community to benefit self or instructing them how to practise higher education in a US manner. This showed up in the IES report where one of the main areas of notable change was in the *relationship interest* category. Prior to the trip, 65 per cent of the students had low to moderate interest in developing intercultural relationships, and this shifted to 33 per cent having moderate interest and 67 per cent having a high interest. As a programme with a foundation in social justice, this finding suggests a need for offering more intercultural competence opportunities on a regular basis. It also highlights the need for faculty and curriculum to incorporate 'internationalising at home' opportunities for those students who may not participate in outbound mobility class experiences.
4. There is privilege in promoting intercultural competence that requires careful reflection to avoid *othering* and viewing the US model of social justice as better. One student remarked that it was a privilege to assess herself as flexible during on-site social interactions but grasped after the trip that it was really the Mayan people in Mexico who demonstrated greater flexibility by managing her inability to speak the language and understand their culture. Whereas another student did not experience an *othering* because he spoke fairly fluent Spanish and shared a Mexican heritage identity but still reflected on the privilege of holding a US citizenship identity.

Ways to improve

It was beneficial to offer students pre- and post-trip assessments and multiple tools, which showed limited intercultural growth in most participants. In the future, we plan to add additional qualitative measures and post-trip interviews to better understand competency development. As coordinators of the first graduate-level faculty-led study-abroad course at our institution, we learned that our institution's infrastructure had not considered the unique elements this course presented when students hold multiple, non-traditional identities, such as graduate student, professional staff member, older, or with dependent children. The work required to develop the course curriculum paled in comparison to the campus logistics and bureaucracy we encountered. Professionally and organisationally, we believe there is an opportunity to develop better support and best practices for the development of study abroad and intercultural competence at the graduate level or within professional preparation degree.

References

ACPA/NASPA. (2015). ACPA/NASPA professional competency areas for student affairs practitioners. Retrieved from www.myacpa.org/professional-competency-areas-student-affairs-practitioners

Berardo, K., & Deardorff, D. K. (2012). *Building cultural competence: Innovative intercultural training activities and models.* Sterling, VA: Stylus.

Bondi, S. (2012). Students and institutions protecting Whiteness as property: A critical race theory analysis of student affairs preparation. *Journal of Student Affairs Research and Practice, 49*(4), 397–414.

Davis, T., & Harrison, L. M. (2013). *Advancing social justice: Tools, pedagogies, and strategies to transform your campus.* San Francisco, CA: Jossey-Bass.

Deardorff, D. K. (2006). The identification and assessment of intercultural competence as a student outcome of internationalization at institutions of higher education in the United States. *Journal of Studies in International Education, 10*(3), 241–66.

—— (2012). Framework: Intercultural competence model. In K. Berardo & D. K. Deardorff (Eds.), *Building Cultural Competence: Innovative Intercultural Training Activities and Models* (pp. 45–52). Sterling, VA: Stylus.

Deardorff, D. K., & Jones, E. (2012). Intercultural competence: An emerging focus in international higher education. In D. K. Deardorff, H. D. Wit, & J. D. Heyl (Eds.), *The Sage handbook of international higher education* (pp. 283–304). Thousand Oaks, CA: Sage.

Kozai Group. *Intercultural Effectiveness Scale* [Measurement instrument]. www.kozaigroup.com/intercultural-effectiveness-scale-ies/

Rhoads, R. A., & Black, M. A. (1995). Student affairs practitioners as transformative educators: Advancing a critical cultural perspective. In E. J. Whitt (Ed.), *ASHE Reader on College Student Affairs Administration* (pp. 407–15). Boston, MA: Pearson.

Tuhiwai Smith, L. (2012). *Decolonizing methodologies: Research and indigenous peoples.* London: Zed Books.

Twombly, S. B., Salisbury, M. H., Tumanut, S. D., & Klute, P. (2012). *Study abroad in a new global century.* San Francisco, CA: Jossey-Bass.

Chapter 12

Intercultural competence in international higher education

Emerging themes, issues, implications, and future directions

Darla K. Deardorff (Duke University) and
Lily A. Arasaratnam-Smith (Alphacrucis College)

Despite over sixty years of scholarly work on intercultural competence, this concept continues to be the focus of research and practice in many disciplines in higher education. The chapters in Part I in this volume are intended to expand traditional thinking on intercultural competence beyond one discipline, and particularly beyond international education contexts such as education abroad to those broader contexts of social justice and post-conflict reconstruction. The chapters in Part II engaged with developing and assessing intercultural competence, including cultural perspectives such as South African and Chinese. Together these chapters set the groundwork for the case studies that followed.

Increasingly, there are strong calls for concrete examples of what intercultural competence development and assessment look like in actual contexts. This book has sought to address this need by showcasing twenty-nine case studies of current intercultural competence practice at institutions of higher education around the world. Examining these case studies and the chapters as a whole, the following key themes and implications emerge:

The importance of intentionality

Intercultural competence does not just happen. Higher education is uniquely positioned to address intercultural competence development not only in students (undergraduates, postgraduates, domestic, and international) but also in academics and administrative staff. In an age that demands quick results and bullet-point solutions, international higher educators have a role to play in communicating that the development of intercultural competence is not only something that requires intentionality but also a process that cannot be reduced to a one-hour seminar or a booklet. It requires intentionality on the part of programme planners and administrators, as well as students. It also requires intentionality in terms of allocation of funds for such programmes and training of staff.

The relevance of context

While intercultural competence is a theoretical construct, the application of this construct in applied and practical ways within very specific contexts matters immensely. That context includes the target audience (i.e. undergraduates, postgraduates, staff, etc.), the discipline, the geographical context (not only country but also urban or rural settings), purpose of the course/programme, and institutional size, type, and mission, as well as the social, economic, historical, political, and cultural realities of the society. (See Chapters 5 and 7, this text, for example.) In other words, the intercultural competence required varies, depending on a complex context in which it is situated.

The centrality of the learner

As illustrated by the case studies, programmes and courses for developing intercultural competence focus on the learner. Empowerment of the learner can lead to more self-directed, relevant learning, and lifelong development of intercultural competence. This focus on the learner also necessitates contextualising intercultural competence within the social realities of the learner, including circumstances caused by power, privilege, and injustice. It must be noted, however, that we must further explore communal learning models as much as we have explored individual learning models, as communal learning is more relevant to parts of the world where individualism is not the dominant paradigm.

The indispensability of active engagement

From education abroad to community projects, the case studies in this volume highlight the value of active engagement. Pedagogy matters, and it needs to go beyond the traditional delivery mechanisms that involve more passive ways of learning. Moreover, engagement beyond the classroom is essential in terms of developing intercultural competence through real-world interactions. While active engagement may take different forms in different cultural and learning contexts, it is evident that it is an indispensable part of developing intercultural competence.

The limitation of knowledge

The case studies and chapters clearly propose that knowledge alone is not sufficient for developing intercultural competence. While knowledge is an important part of developing intercultural competence, variables such as cultural humility, empathy, curiosity, etc., are vital. This fact has already been established in decades of research in intercultural competence. However, especially in a discussion of intercultural competence in international higher education, it is appropriate to reiterate that knowledge alone does not develop intercultural competence.

The focus on process

As several of the case studies illustrated, there is more of a focus on process, particularly through reflection, rather than on results. Guided critical reflection is crucial for intercultural competence development but often does not come naturally. Such guided reflection needs to go beyond 'What did you learn?' to 'Why was that learning important?' and 'What will you do now as a result of that learning?' Individualised feedback to students also sends a message that process is valued over results, leading to more self-directed learning. Moreover, it is important to recognise that intercultural competence development is a lifelong process.

The significance of multiple perspectives

This book intentionally included chapters and case studies from a variety of disciplinary and cultural perspectives. There is a great need for interdisciplinary understandings of intercultural competence and continued impetus for understanding what intercultural competence 'looks like' from other perspectives around the world. While there is some research on perceptions of intercultural competence from multiple cultural perspectives, there is room for more. The study of intercultural competence inherently calls for multiplicity of perspectives, including those from within a society as well as culturally influenced perspectives from different parts of the world.

The variety of assessment

The case studies all use various assessment methods to measure intercultural competence development. Several of these indicate an increased focus on direct evidence/formative assessment with substantive feedback, which improves students' motivation and involvement. With the focus on direct evidence, there is a need for rubric development, informed by underlying theoretical constructs (such as the example of the AAC&U Intercultural rubric which is used/adapted in some of the case studies). In sum, intercultural competence assessment should include a variety of formative, summative, and progressive assessment using multiple methods and perspectives.

The need for customisation

Each context and institution are unique. Moreover, so are students at different places in their intercultural competence development (as are academics and staff). Therefore, as shown by the wide variety of courses and programmes described in the case studies, there is no 'one size fits all' in developing or assessing intercultural competence. It is necessary to customise the programme or course to the context and the needs of the students.

The impetus for developing intercultural competence in academics

Several of the case studies noted the pivotal role that academics have in developing and assessing intercultural competence in students. Focusing on academics and ensuring an interculturally competent faculty, through faculty development, is essential for sustaining intercultural competence efforts within an institution (Deardorff, 2012). Hence, programmes should focus on developing intercultural competence in academics and administrators as well as students.

Implications for higher education

Given these ten themes and numerous intercultural competence issues, what are some implications for higher education? Several implications were noted above; additionally, the following are worth highlighting:

- Internationalisation of the curriculum and graduate studies means the integration of intercultural competence throughout all courses (not just language courses) can play a key role in developing students' intercultural competence since the curriculum impacts all students. In integrating intercultural competence dimensions into the curriculum, it is important to go beyond intercultural knowledge to also include intercultural thinking skills and critical reflection.
- Delivery and pedagogy matter, beyond content. Higher education institutions need to examine and map how they are addressing intercultural competence – beyond static lectures, staid content detached from the real world, and traditional ways of teaching, to incorporate more active engagement and experiential learning.
- Focus on the core role of academics. This means there is a need to intentionally develop intercultural competence in academics through an ongoing approach that may include working groups, seminars, reading groups, and so on.
- Intercultural competence development occurs beyond the classroom. Higher education institutions need to focus more on what happens outside of the classroom, through the extra-curricular and co-curricular opportunities. This means intentionally bringing different groups together in meaningful ways, both within and beyond the campus community, with a focus on substantive interactions and relationship-building.
- Intercultural competence is not just for students, and especially not just for those engaged in educational exchanges. Given the diversity within an institution, intercultural competence is also needed in engaging with those across, within and beyond an institution.
- Institutions can utilise intercultural competence efforts in connecting to the local community, where diversity exists in terms of age, socio-economic differences as well as perhaps differences in religious and political beliefs,

cultural differences, and more. How is the institution engaging in the local community, especially around issues of power and privilege?

- There is much to investigate and research about intercultural competence (as indicated in the list of issues and questions below). Thus, institutions can play a crucial research role in continuing to expand understandings of this complex concept.

Considerations for further research

Research in intercultural competence has made great strides in the past few decades. There is, however, much room for further research. In a review of the past ten years of research in intercultural communication competence, Arasaratnam (2014) observes that there is little cross-disciplinary referencing in intercultural competence research. In other words, while intercultural competence research is being done in disciplines such as intercultural communication, medicine, nursing, cross-cultural psychology, and international higher education (to name a few), we are not reading one another's findings with sufficient regularity to build on the cumulative knowledge. This is something that needs consideration in future research. There are several other issues raised in this volume, as well as in other intercultural competence literature, some of these are worth reiterating:

First, within higher education, it is crucial that institutions address comprehensively the development of intercultural competence for all – not just in exchange students or those going abroad, but especially for students without the opportunity to engage in experiences abroad. Intentionally addressing intercultural competence for all students means that the curriculum plays a pivotal role, yet further research is needed in this area. Additionally, this means there is a need to study the most effective ways to address intercultural competence development intentionally for staff and academics who work with and guide students.

Second, there is need to further study the role of cognitive complexity in intercultural competence and the role of critical thinking in intercultural competence. While cognitive complexity has indeed been associated with intercultural competence in past research (e.g., Gudykunst & Kim, 2003), there is little empirical research in establishing a direct relationship between cognitive complexity and intercultural competence. There is, however, evidence to suggest a direct relationship between increased cognitive capacity (from learning a second or third language, for example) and intercultural competence (Arasaratnam-Smith, 2016). This is an area that is rich for future research, particularly in international higher education.

Third, higher education needs to prioritise teacher education and preparation related to intercultural competence development. How can institutions be most effective in preparing future teachers, especially beyond the provision of international experiences? What are the best ways to assess teachers' readiness to guide students' intercultural competence development?

Fourth, there needs to be further exploration between the relation of language to intercultural competence. As Fantini (2009) and others have noted, current models in intercultural competence do not sufficiently address the role of language competence in intercultural competence. Further, there needs to be more work on the integration of language teaching and intercultural competence development, including the most effective ways to integrate the two.

Fifth, it is necessary to engage with how intercultural competence is being studied at the individual level (one's own assessment), relational level (as negotiated between two or more communicators; reliant on the other's perception), and at the organisational level. For example, what does it mean for a higher education institution to be interculturally competent within and beyond the institution (in terms of policies, structures, leadership, outreach and service, and so on)? Or how can intercultural competence help transform the power-laden systemic structures within a university that privilege certain groups over others?

Sixth, what are explicit applications of intercultural competence in real-world contexts, including in peace-building efforts in post-conflict societies (see Chapter 5), so that intercultural competence moves beyond the abstract, as is often the case in higher education discourse? How can and will intercultural competence address the issues of power and privilege within conflicted societies? How can intercultural competence endeavours help bridge the widening gap between higher education institutions and local communities and the general populace?

Seventh, how can higher education institutions address the holistic development of intercultural competence in students, which includes attention to emotional intelligence, moral and ethical development, self-authorship (Baxter-Magolda & Creamer, 2010), cognitive processes, mindfulness, and more?

Eighth, it is important, particularly in quantitative research, to ensure that cultural and conceptual biases do not interfere with the data. Research in cross-cultural psychology has contributed significantly to identifying the types of biases of which an intercultural researcher must be aware (for more, see Matsumoto & van de Vijver, 2011; van de Vijver & Leung, 1997, 2009). How will new studies on intercultural competence help mitigate these biases?

Ninth, what are the implications of the changing paradigm of intercultural competence assessment (as discussed in Chapter 10; Deardorff, 2015)? What changes do education abroad programmes need to make, for example, in the ways they are currently assessing intercultural competence to expand beyond the insufficiencies of pre- and post-measures?

Finally, the importance and necessity of multiple perspectives on intercultural competence development and assessment (within and beyond a society) cannot be underestimated. Much more research and work are needed in this crucial area. The danger of continuing this conversation without listening to those perspectives is that we may develop an understanding of intercultural competence that is incomplete and heavily biased by the perspectives of English-speaking and economically affluent parts of the world. We must also be inclusive of multiple disciplinary perspectives. Though this volume is indeed a publication in English, we have included multiple global and disciplinary perspectives in our attempt to enrich this discussion of intercultural competence.

Other intercultural competence-related questions for further research and work in higher education include the following:

- What is the connection between primary/secondary education to post-secondary institutions in terms of intercultural competence development? How are the best ways to streamline this process so as not to reinvent but reinforce initial groundwork for intercultural competence development?
- Employing a systems thinking perspective (Mestenhauser, 2002), how can intercultural competence best be connected across disciplines and contexts and what are the implications of these interconnections?
- Given the increasing diversity within societies, how are the best ways to address intercultural competence development beyond academia?
- What is the role of ethics in intercultural competence?
- What are the intercultural competence linkages in furthering social justice and in rebuilding post-conflict societies (Lieberman & Gamst, 2015; Chapter 5)?
- What is the relation between identity and intercultural competence development, especially in navigating the complexity of identity in the twenty-first century?
- What are the intersections of intercultural competence in relation to domestic and global diversity?
- What role(s) does technology play in intercultural competence development and assessment?
- What are the most effective ways to ensure transferability of intercultural competence to different contexts?
- Despite the work on conceptualising intercultural competence over the years, questions still remain as to whether intercultural competence is a skill, a capacity, or social judgement, as Koester and Lustig (2015) suggest. Debates continue about the categorisations and conceptualisations of intercultural competence. How will conceptualisations of intercultural competence enhance the further understanding of intercultural competence development and assessment?
- How can cultural empathy be developed across and within disciplines (Chapter 3)?
- Given the role of adaptability in intercultural competence development, what specifically does adaptability look like in a wide variety of contexts and what are the best ways to develop and assess this?
- What does a focus on relational process mean in intercultural competence development and assessment?
- How are privilege and power being addressed in intercultural competence interventions?
- What are the connections between bias and intercultural competence development and assessment?

- What more can be done through research in connecting intercultural competence theory to practise in a variety of contexts?
- In the end, is it about intercultural competence or is it about how we approach others through cultural humility (see Chapter 2)?

There are numerous other research questions that could be explored in relation to intercultural competence development and assessment (see Deardorff, 2015), however; these are some of the ones that are particularly relevant within international higher education.

Conclusion

The conversation about better ways of understanding and measuring intercultural competence, equitable and inclusive training techniques and learning interventions, comprehensive theories, and interdisciplinary collaboration continues – as it must. This volume is one such contribution to this continuing conversation. We hope that, as the conversation progresses, it will be inclusive of perspectives from parts of the world that are currently underrepresented due to economic and language constraints, among others. We also hope the conversation continues, especially in higher education, on effective ways to develop and assess intercultural competence in the classroom and beyond. As a start, the case studies in this volume provide concrete examples of efforts in higher education in different parts of the world regarding how to engage in developing and assessing intercultural competence in today's students. Much more work remains to be done, though, as indicated by the questions and issues posed in this chapter. In continuing this conversation, the hope is that we continue to explore and learn together so as to fulfil the broader vision of intercultural competence, that of humans living together peaceably as we address the local and global challenges that confront our world.

References

Arasaratnam, L. A. (2014). Ten years of research in intercultural communication competence: A retrospective. *Journal of Intercultural Communication*, *35*. Retrieved from www.immi.se/intercultural/nr35/arasaratnam.html

Arasaratnam-Smith, L. A. (2016). An exploration of the relationship between intercultural communication competence and bilingualism. *Communication Research Reports*, *33*(3), 231–8.

Baxter-Magolda, M., & Creamer, E. (2010). *Development and assessment of self-authorship: Exploring the concept across cultures*. Sterling, VA: Stylus.

Deardorff, D. K. (2012). Building interculturally competent faculty. *IIE Networker*, spring, 39.

—— (2015a). Intercultural competence: Mapping the future research agenda. *International Journal of Intercultural Relations*, *48*, 3–5.

—— (2015b). *Outcomes assessment for international educators: A practical approach.* Sterling, VA: Stylus.

Fantini, A. (2009) Assessing intercultural competence: Issues and tools. In D. K. Deardorff (ed.), *The Sage Handbook of Intercultural Competence* (pp. 456–76). Thousand Oaks, CA: Sage.

Gudykunst, W. B., & Kim, Y. Y. (2003). *Communicating with strangers: An approach to intercultural communication.* New York, NY: McGraw Hill.

Koester, J., & Lustig, M. (2015). Intercultural communication competence: Theory, measurement, and application. *International Journal of Intercultural Relations, 48*, 20–1.

Lieberman, D., & Gamst, G. (2015). Intercultural communication competence revisited: Linking the intercultural and multicultural fields. *International Journal of Intercultural Relations, 48*, 17–19.

Matsumoto, D., & van de Vijver, F. J. R. (2011). *Cross-cultural research methods in psychology.* Cambridge: Cambridge University Press.

Mestenhauser, J. (2002). In search of a comprehensive approach to international education: A systems perspective. In W. Gruenzweig & N. Rinehart (Eds.), *Rockin' in red square: Critical approaches to international education in the age of cyberculture.* Münster: LIT Verlag.

van de Vijver, F., & Leung, K. (1997). *Methods and data analysis for cross-cultural research.* Thousand Oaks, CA: Sage.

—— (2009). Methodological issues in researching intercultural competence. In D. K. Deardorff (Ed.), *The Sage handbook of intercultural competence* (pp. 404–18). Thousand Oaks, CA: Sage.

Index

Abdi, A. A. 87–8
ACE/FIPSE project rubrics 272
ACTFL World-Readiness Standards 250
Adams, M. 234–5, 237–8
Adichie, C. N. 50
Africanisation 87, 89
age 20, 100, 241, 266–7
Almeida, J. 12
Ali, T. 54
All Quadrants All Levels model 281
Allen, M. 8
Allport, G. 58
American Association of Higher Education 127
American College Personnel Association 290
American Council on Education 113, 255
An, R. 98
Anand, R. 38
Anderson, C. 127
Andreotti, V. 210
Annan, K. 55
Antal, A. B. 215
anxiety 101, 103
Anxiety/Uncertainty Management Model 14–15, 73
Appiah, K. A. 47, 50
Arasaratnam-Smith, L. A. 1, 8–11, 35–6, 298; *see also* Integrated Model of Intercultural Communication Competence
Argyris, C. 204
Asante, M. K. 84
Asia Pacific Association of International Educators 137
assessment of intercultural competence 124–32, 148, 153–4, 158, 162, 166, 170–1, 174–7, 182–3, 189–90, 194, 199, 207, 211, 216–17, 221, 226, 231–2, 236–7, 241–2, 247–8, 250–2, 257–8, 262, 267, 272, 282, 286–7, 291–2, 299; *see also* self-assessment
Association of American Colleges and Universities 74–5, 111, 125, 250–2, 255, 296; VALUE Rubrics 111, 118–20, 194, 235–7, 272
Association of American Medical Colleges 180
Association of International Education Administrators 137
Attitude Acculturation Model 73
Aurelius, M. 36
Australia 125–6, 130, 224–7, 229
awareness 113, 219, 222, 260–1, 278; *see also* self-awareness

Banerjee, S. C. 35–6
Barakat, S. 56
Barnett, R. 188
Bar-Tal, D. 54–5
BATHE (background, affect, trouble, handling, and empathy) 181, 183
Baxter Magolda, M. B. 131, 147; *see also* Intercultural Maturity Model
Beisser, K. R. 8
Belgium 126, 219–22
Benjamin, M. P. 181
Bennett, J. M. 236, 255

Bennett, M. J. 13, 74–5, 110, 118, 125, 147, 175, 193, 198, 235, 240, 250, 261, 281; *see also* Developmental Model of Intercultural Sensitivity
Berardo, K. 291
Berman, S. H. 34
Berry, J. W. 73; *see also* Attitude Acculturation Model
biases 15, 22–3, 26, 44, 53, 55, 154, 159, 169–72, 181–2, 209–10, 217, 278, 299–300
bi-orientationism 46–8
Blair, S. G. 2
blended learning 156, 158, 167, 225
blogs 120–1, 141, 143, 175–7, 194, 207, 211, 251, 271–2
Boecker, M. C. 261, 271
Bohm, D. 204, 280
Boulding, E. 47
Bradford, L. 8
Braskamp, D. C. 240
Braskamp, L. A. 240
Bujaki, M. 73; *see also* Attitude Acculturation Model
Byram, M. 12–13, 57, 75, 147, 175, 187, 215, 230, 255; *see also* Intercultural Communicative Competence Model

Calloway-Thomas, C. 1
Cambodia 224
Cambridge, B. 127
Campinha-Bacote, J. 165; see also intercultural competence acquisition model
Canada 2, 126, 169–72, 209–12, 280–4
Carroll, J. 95
CAS Standards for Education Abroad 289
CEFR 215
Chang, X. M. 97
Changnon, G. 8–9, 71, 85, 193
Chen, G.-M. 97–8, 101–2, 215
Childress, L. K. 78–9
China 2, 22, 24, 124–6, 244–8, 294; perspectives on intercultural competence 2, 95–106
Chinese College English Curriculum Requirements 96
Chinese English Syllabus for English Majors 96
Chow, Y. 22
Cohesion-Based Model for Intercultural Competence 72
colonialism 22–3, 27, 49–50, 83–4, 87–9, 241; *see also* decolonisation
Common European Framework of Reference 215
common goals 39, 58, 76–7, 116, 118, 121, 158, 277–8
communication skills 13, 152, 162, 177, 205, 224, 246, 276–7, 286; *see also* intercultural communication
consensus-building 48
Consultation and Relational Empathy Measure 38
contact theory 276–7
Corbett, J. 104
Corder, D. 13
cosmopolitanism 46–8
Council of Europe 215
Coupland, N. 73; *see also* Intercultural Communication Accommodation Model
critical moment dialogue 151–3
Cross, T. L. 181
Cross-Cultural Adaptability Inventory 277
cross-cultural effectiveness 7–8; *see also* intercultural competence
Crowne-Marlowe Social Desirability Scale 166
cultural care and universality model 170
cultural competence 8–9, 19–21, 180–4; *see also* intercultural competence
Cultural Empathy Subscale of the Multicultural Personality Questionnaire 35
cultural humility 19–21, 25–7
cultural intelligence 202–8
cultural literacy 86
Cultural Medicine Questionnaire 182–3
Cultural Orientation Framework 204
Cupach, W. R. 8, 165

Damasio, D. 204
Davidhizer, R. E. 170–1
Davis, M. H. 38
de Sousa Santos, B. 46
de Wit, H. 68–70, 122
Deardorff, D. K. 1–2, 8–10, 22, 57, 75, 103, 112–17, 119–22, 132, 152, 161, 175, 188, 193, 220, 235–6, 240, 250, 261, 270–1, 281, 285–7, 289, 291; definition of intercultural competence 19, 70, 110, 125, 225, 230, 255; *see also* Process Model of Intercultural Competence, Pyramid Model of Intercultural Competence
decolonisation 83–91
dehumanisation 36
Dembek, K. 35–6
Depraz, N. 34–5
Dervin, F. 225
describe, interpret, and evaluate structure 152, 175–7
Developmental Model of Intercultural Maturity (Bennett) *see* Intercultural Maturity Model
Developmental Model of Intercultural Sensitivity 13–14, 72, 110, 118, 147, 175, 193, 198, 236, 240, 281
DIE structure *see* describe, interpret, and evaluate structure
dignity 36, 44, 48, 87
Diogenes 47
discrimination 22–3, 25, 56, 170, 209
Doerfel, M. L. 11
Downie, W. W. 182
DuBois, R. D. 7

eco-feminism 49
Einfuhlung 33; *see also* empathy
eLearning *see* online learning
emotional intelligence 202–8
Empathic Understanding Subscale of the Barrett–Lennard Relation Inventory 38
empathy 32–4, 39–40, 58, 60, 104, 165, 181, 204, 222, 237, 249–51, 300; barriers to developing 34; empathetic literacy 36–7; implications for higher education institutions 37–9; and intercultural competence 35–6; stages of 34–5
Empathy Construct Rating Scale 38
Engberg, M. 240
English as Second/Foreign Language *see* language (English, teaching)
environmental issues 48–9
e-portfolios 130, 194
Epstein, N. 38
Erasmus 285
ethics 78, 89, 241, 299
ethnicity 20, 53, 100, 181–2, 214, 241, 266
ethnocentrism 11–13, 21, 50, 74, 76, 106, 165, 187, 202
Eurocentrism 83–4, 86–8
European Association of International Educators 137
European Studies 254–9
Evans, R. 113
Experiential Learning Cycle 110, 147, 165–6, 175, 189, 262
experiential theory 276

Face Negotiation Theory 57
Facework Based Model 72
fairness 87
Fan, W. W. 100
Fang, T. 245–6
Fantini, A. E. 12, 113, 145, 147, 225, 299; *see also* Intercultural Communicative Competence Model; Intercultural Competencies Dimensions Model; Intercultural Interlocutor Competence
Faure, O. G. 245–6
Feuer, H. 60
focus groups 120–1, 126, 141, 148, 182–3, 235, 243
Fontaine, P. 33
forgiveness 58
Four Pillars of Education 219
France 88
Franklyn-Stokes, A. 73; *see also* Intercultural Communication Accommodation Model
Freeman, M. 266
Freire, P. 22, 39, 88

Friedman, V. J. 215
Fu, X. Q. 97
Fukuyama, F. 37

Gallois, C. 73; *see also* Intercultural Communication Accommodation Model
Galtung, J. 46–8, 54
Gao, Y. C. 98–100
Gao, Y. H. 98–9
Gardiner, L. 127
Gardner, H. 204
gender 100, 181, 214, 241, 266–7; *see also* sexism
genocide 19–20, 46–8, 88
Germany 33, 88, 125, 151–4, 156
Giger, J. N. 170–1
Giles, H. 73; *see also* Intercultural Communication Accommodation Model
Gill, S. 60
Glaser, J. E. 204
Global Bridge 160–3
global citizenship 19, 36, 43, 47–8, 50, 68, 77, 124, 141, 156–9, 192–3, 226
global citizenship education 210
Global Competencies Model 72
global intelligence 203–8
Global Leadership and Organizational Behavior Effectiveness 204
Global People 220
Global Synergy 202–8
globalisation 49–50, 77, 95–8, 239, 241, 260
Goleman, D. 204
Gopal, A. 161
Gregersen-Hermans, J. 2
Grice's Maxims 175
Grosfogiel, R. 88
Gudykunst, W. B. 14–15; *see also* Anxiety/Uncertainty Management Model
Gullahorn, J. T. and J. E. 72; *see also* U-Curve Model of Intercultural Adjustment

Hadfield, C. 205
Hall, E. T. 7, 204
Hammer, M. R. 72–3, 198; *see also* Developmental Model of Intercultural Sensitivity; Intercultural Development Continuum
Harden, R. M. 182–3
Hau'ofa, E. 50
Hawrylenko, J. 56
health-profession education 2, 19–28, 124, 164–7, 169–72, 180–4, 298; and empathy 37–8
Hegel, G. W. F. 33
Heleta, S. 2
Herder, J. G. 33
hidden curriculum 27, 69, 76
Higgs, P. 87
Hightower, C. 13
Hoffman, E. 221; see also TOPOI model
Hofstede, G. 204
Holliday, A. 188
Holzwarth, J. 33
Hong Kong 197–200
Hornidge, A. 60
human rights 46–8, 56, 190, 260
humility 24
Hungary 186–90
Hunter, F. 68–70
Hunter, W. 270–1; *see also* Global Competencies Model

ICC Global 137
IEREST 186–7, 189
immigration 22, 144, 169, 251, 260
imperialism 25, 241, 290
Implicit Association Test 181
INCA 189, 255
inclusive identity 46–8
income 23
India 22, 24, 156, 224
individualism 9
Inkson, K. 205
Integrated Model of Intercultural Communication Competence 9, 10, 73
integrity 45–6
intentionality 294

intercultural communication 8–10, 14, 16, 148, 164, 186–90, 214–18, 298; in China 95–106; in South Africa 2, 83–91
Intercultural Communication Accommodation Model 73
Intercultural Communication Competence for Chinese College Students 100
Intercultural Communicative Competence Model (Arasaratnam) 73
Intercultural Communicative Competence Model (Byram) 9, 13, 57, 72, 147, 187–8, 230
Intercultural Communicative Competence Model (Fantini) 145, 147
Intercultural Communicative Competence Model (Kim) 73
intercultural competence 1–3; in the aftermath of violent conflict 2, 53–61; assessment of *see* assessment of intercultural competence; Chinese perspectives on 2, 95–106; of the curriculum (IoC) 75; definition of intercultural competence 125; definitions of 8–9, 19, 70–4, 110, 138, 181, 187, 215, 225, 230, 250, 255, 270, 276; development in higher education 2, 67–80; and intercultural communication 2, 83–91; interdisciplinary 2, 43–50; mapping 2, 110–22, 158; models and frameworks 9–14, 72–3, *see also individual* models; overview of 7–16, 294–301; rethinking 1, 19–28; role of empathy in 35–6, *see also* empathy; through international travel 269–75
intercultural competence acquisition model 165, 170
Intercultural Competence Self-Reflection 291
Intercultural Competencies Dimensions Model 9, 11
Intercultural Conflict Styles Inventory 236
Intercultural Development Continuum 74, 198
Intercultural Development Inventory 198–200, 204, 235–6, 280–4
Intercultural Educational Resources for Erasmus Students and their Teachers *see* IEREST
Intercultural Effectiveness Scale 235, 291
Intercultural Intelligence Inventory 236
Intercultural Interlocutor Competence 72
Intercultural Maturity Model 72, 74
intercultural sensitivity *see* intercultural competence
interdisciplinary intercultural competence 2, 43–50
International Association of Universities 67
International Education Association of South Africa 137–8
International Journal of Intercultural Relations 8
International Review of Curriculum and Assessment *see* INCA
internationalisation 1, 67–8, 190, 192, 254–5, 257, 286, 297; of the curriculum (IoC) 69–70; at home (IaH) 69–70
internships 224–7, 229, 267
Interpersonal Reactivity Index 38
intimacy 45–6
Isaacman, A. F. 49
Isaacman, B. S. 49
Isaacs, M. R. 181
Italy 88

Jackson, J. 13
Japan 2, 22, 126, 130, 202–8, 224
Japan External Trade Organization 204
Jefferson Scale of Physician Empathy 38
Jon, J. 25
Jones, E. 78
Joseph, C. 23–4

Kant, I. 33
Kasulis, T. 45–7, 50
Kaunda, K. 58
Kealey, D. J. 35
Kelava, A. 153

Killick, D. 78, 95, 105
Kim, U. 73; *see also* Attitude Acculturation Model
Kim, Y. Y. 47, 193; *see also* Intercultural Communicative Competence Model
King, M. L. 20, 157
King, P. M. 147; *see also* Intercultural Maturity Model
Kitwood, T. 32
Knight, J. 68, 193
Koester, J. 300
Kohl, R. L. 175
Kolb, D. A. 110, 165, 175, 189; *see also* Experiential Learning Cycle
Kong, D. L. 97
Korea 25
Kuh, G. D. 110
Kulich, S. J. 2, 98–100, 102–5

Lahiri, I. 38
language 21, 88, 95–7, 118, 144, 160, 163–5, 174, 197–8, 214–18, 246, 249–53, 262, 271–2, 291–2, 299; English 15–16, 79, 161, 277, 299–300; English, teaching 25, 96, 98–9, 144, 160, 163–4, 214–18, 249
Lazarevic, N. 13
Leask, B. 69, 78, 255
LeBaron, M. 210
Leininger, M. M. 170
Letseka, M. 87
Liddicoat, A. J. 217
lifelong learning 22–3, 131, 260, 295
Lingle, D. W. 33
Lough, B. J. 278
Love, B. 234–5, 237–8
Luan, S. W. 97
Lustig, M. 300

Mann–Whitney–Wilcoxon U test 166
Masuda, T. 204
matriarchal archetypes 170–1
Matthews, R. 54
Mayson, S. 22
Mbembe, A. 88
McTique, J. 250
meaning-making 44–5, 48
media 23, 86, 216
medicine *see* health-profession education
Mehrabian, A. 38
Merrill, K. C. 240
Mertnes, K. 219
Mexico 2, 156–7, 289–93
Mezirow, J. 198
Milton, S. 56
mindfulness 14–15, 44, 152, 180, 199, 205–6, 299
mobility 186–90
Morais, D. B. 193
Mozambique 49
multicultural classrooms 244–8
Murdock, G. 37
Murray-García, J. 1, 21
Murshed, M. 54
mutuality 37, 39–40

NAFSA: Association of International Education 138
National Association of Student Personnel Administrators (NASPA) 290–1
neo-colonialism 50
Netherlands 79, 254–9, 265–8
New Zealand 22, 126, 174–8
Niens, U. 60
Nigeria 24
Nisbett, R. E. 204
Nonaka, I. 204; *see also* SECI model
non-paternalistic mutually beneficial relationships 26–7
nursing education 169–72, 298; *see also* health-profession education
Nwosu, P. O. 86

Objective Structured Clinical Exam 181–2
ODIS method 220–1
Oetzel, J. 57
Ogden, A. C. 193
Oguro, S. 12
Olson, C. 113
online learning 166–7, 169–72, 199–200
Other, the 22, 34, 36, 55, 99

Paige, R. M. 75–6, 104, 198
Paltridge, T. 22
Paracka, D. J. 2
paternalism 26–7
patient perspective 38
patriarchal archetypes 170–1
peace 46–8, 53–61; role of higher education in building 55–6
Peck, C. 13
Pedersen, P. J. 13
Peng, R. Z. 100
personal leadership methodology 151–3
Pettigrew, T. 209
pluralism 47, 84
portfolios 130, 153–4, 194, 258
Portugal 126, 144–9
post-structuralism 198
poverty 20, 46–8, 54, 84
power imbalances 23–7, 49–50, 60
Power, S. 73; *see also* Attitude Acculturation Model
prejudices 34, 55, 61, 76, 85, 89, 101, 169, 177, 187–8, 221, 276
privilege 24–5, 27–8, 45–6, 89, 209, 295, 300
Process Model of Intercultural Competence 9–10, 57, 73, 103, 110–22, 175, 240, 250, 271, 281, 289
Pynn, T. 2
Pyramid Model of Intercultural Competence 72, 152, 175, 188, 193

Qatar 2, 126, 180–4
quality enhancement plan 269, 273

race 20, 181–2, 241, 269; racism 21–3, 84–5, 88, 90; segregation 20–1, 55–6, 85
Ramsey, S. J. 152; *see also* personal leadership methodology
Rathje, S. 85; *see also* Cohesion-Based Model for Intercultural Competence
reconciliation processes 53–61
refugees 249–52
Reisinger, D. S. 249
relational studies 46
religion 2, 22, 53, 57, 100, 190, 242, 265–8
respect 36, 40, 44, 48, 58, 119; global 36, 40
Reygan, F. 2
Reynolds Empathy Scale 38
Rhodes, C. 83
Ridley, C. R. 33
Ring, J. M. 181
Risager, K. 255
Rizzolatti, G. 204
role modelling 26
Roosevelt, F. D. 157
Rosen, Y. 55
Rosinski, P. 204
Ruben, B. D. 33, 35
Russia 156, 164–7

Sanford, N. 193
scaffolding techniques 161–3, 217
Scarino, A. 217
Schaetti, B. F. 152; *see also* personal leadership methodology
Schapper, J. 22
Schematic Model of Intercultural Competence 112
Schetter, C. 60
Schnabel, D. B. L. 153
Schoenberg, R. E. 113
Schon, D. 204
SECI (Socialisation, Externalisation, Combination, Internalisation) model 204
Second Life 175
segregation 20–1, 55–6, 85
Seifert, L. 153
self-assessment 141, 143, 162, 176, 178, 182, 250, 252, 282, 290–2
self-authorship 131
self-awareness 43–4, 58, 152, 234–7, 276, 286
self-management 71
self-reflection 22–3, 27, 165, 167, 276, 292
seminars 144–9, 160, 217, 297
Seneca 40
Senge, P. 280
Serbia 126, 214–18

sexism 84, 88, 90
sexuality 170, 242
Shen, J. M. 100
Shiva, V. 49
Shor, I. 90–1
short form cultural intelligence (SFCQ) 153
Silent Language, The 7
skin-lightening industry 24
SMART format 122
Smith, A. 59
social intelligence 202–8
social justice 48
social media 120–1, 158, 190, 211, 285
South Africa 2, 124, 126, 156–7, 159, 294; decolonisation of higher education in 83–91; Truth and Reconciliation Councils 56
Spain 126, 260–3
Spencer-Oatey, H. 220
Spitzberg, B. H. 8–9, 71, 85, 165, 193
Stadler, S. 220
Starosta, W. J. 215
stereotypes 34, 36, 46, 55, 101, 146, 169–71, 181–2, 187–8, 216–17, 276, 278
Stevenson, M. 182
Steyn, M. 2, 89–90
Stuart, D. K. 74
student protests 83–4
Summit Global Learning 239–43
Sun, S. N. 98–9
Sun, Z. 98

Tervalon, M. 1, 21
test to measure intercultural competence short form (TMIC-S) 153
theology 2, 265–8
Thomas, D. C. 153, 205
Thompson, E. 34–5
Tichener, E. B. 33
Ting-Toomey, S. 57, 204; *see also* Face Negotiation Theory, Facework Based Model; ODIS method
Togo 24
Tools for Assessing Cultural Competence Training 180
TOPOI model 220–1
transformative learning theory 198, 276
transformative reciprocity 48–9
Triangle Model, 99
Tropp, L. 209
trust 37, 40, 48, 85, 267; building after conflict 53–5, 59
Twine, F. W. 91

Ubuntu 87
U-Curve Model of Intercultural Adjustment 72
Ulama, L. 261, 271
United Kingdom 78, 88, 126, 285–8
United Nations Declaration of Human Rights 36, 252
United Nations Education, Scientific and Cultural Organization 15, 85–6, 204–5, 219–21
United Nations High Commissioner for Refugees 251
United States 7, 16, 20, 23, 69, 74–5, 78, 88, 126–7, 156, 160–3, 192–6, 234–9, 249–53, 269–75, 289–93; medical education 19–28

value creation 48
van de Vijver, F. J. R. 153
Van Maele, J. 219
Vico, G. 33, 35
Vietnam 224, 229–35, 275–8
violence 2, 46, 53–61, 87, 91
Vischer, R. 32
volunteer work 26–7, 275–8

Wang, Y. 2
Wang, Y. A. 97–100, 102–5
Watanabe, G. C. 152; *see also* personal leadership methodology
Wen, Q. F. 98
Westernisation 15–16, 45, 88, 122; *see also* Eurocentrism
White, R. W. 7

Wiggins, G. 250
Wilber, K. 281
Willingness to Communicate Scale 277
Wilson, G. M. 182
workshops 2, 128, 130, 141, 151–2, 160–2, 200, 210–12, 221, 225–6, 242, 282
World Health Organization 205
worldviews 45–8, 50, 175, 177, 267
Wu, W. P. 100

xintai 100–1, 103
Xu, L. S. 97–9

Yang, Y. 98–9
Yin Yang theory 245–6
Young, M. 73; *see also* Attitude Acculturation Model

Zhang, H. L. 97
Zhao, Y. S. 97
Zhu, H. 34
Zhuang, E. P. 98–9